ALSO BY SUZANNE GOIN

Sunday Suppers at Lucques

the a.o.c. cookbook

the *A.O.C.* cookbook

suzanne goin

with wine notes by caroline styne

PHOTOGRAPHS BY SHIMON AND TAMMAR ROTHSTEIN

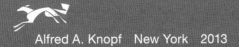

Alfred A. Knopf   New York   2013

THIS IS A BORZOI BOOK
PUBLISHED BY ALFRED A. KNOPF

Copyright © 2013 by Suzanne Goin
Photographs copyright © 2013 by Shimon and Tammar Photography, Inc.

www.aaknopf.com

Knopf, Borzoi Books, and the colophon are registered trademarks of Random House, Inc.

Library of Congress Cataloging-in-Publication Data
Goin, Suzanne, [date]
    The A.O.C. cookbook / by Suzanne Goin ; with wine notes by Caroline Styne ; photographs by Shimon and Tammar Rothstein.—First edition.
        pages cm
    "This is a Borzoi book"—Title page verso.
    Includes index.
    ISBN 978-0-307-95823-5 (alkaline paper)
        1. Cooking, American. 2. A.O.C. (Restaurant) 3. Appetizers.
    4. Food and wine pairing. I. Styne, Caroline. II. Title. III. Title: AOC cookbook.
    TX715.G61115   2013
    641.5973—dc23   2013005068

Jacket photography by Shimon and Tammar Photography, Inc.
Jacket design by Abby Weintraub
Case photography by Aaron Cook / AACKStudio

Manufactured in China
First Edition

This book is dedicated to my husband
DAVID LENTZ

and our little Lentz-ies:
ALEXANDRA STEWART LENTZ
JACK GOIN LENTZ
and
DAVID CHARLES LENTZ IV

Thank you for your patience with me,
for letting me do what I love,
and for loving me for (or in spite of) what I do.
I love the four of you more than infinity!

And, of course, to the family mascot Mr. Pug Lentz

contents

cheese

charcuterie

salads

SPRING

from the wood-burning oven

desserts

acknowledgments

It has taken me seven years to write my second book. In that time I have opened two more restaurants, had three children, moved homes, hired more people than I can count, and learned so very much.

How fun to get to share this amazing and sometimes torturous book experience with my restaurant partner in crime, Caroline Styne. I cannot imagine my life without you inside or outside of work.

I feel so lucky to have had the dream team of my agent Janis Donnaud, editors Christina Malach and Peter Gethers, photographers Shimon and Tammar Rothstein, and secret-weapon-sent-from-heaven Maria Zizka on my side to make creating this book even more pleasurable and rewarding than my firstborn, *Sunday Suppers at Lucques*.

Christina and I have spent way too many hours over a glass of rosé or two obsessing over vertical versus horizontal photographs, fonts and page colors, and the pros and cons of including the word *fresh* when listing herbs in the ingredients list. Her poor boyfriend, Ben, knows that if she says she's going to be with me for four hours it really means ten! Christina, this is very much your book, too, and I so appreciate the support you gave me, the confidence you had in me, and the bulldogish commitment to making this the book we both envisioned. You are a dream. Thank you, Janis and Peter, for setting this up so beautifully for us.

Thank you also to Abby Weintraub, Carol Devine Carson, Kathleen Fridella, Cassandra Pappas, Lisa Montebello, Sara Eagle, and everyone else at Knopf who helped make this book a reality.

Every couple of months, I get an e-mail from an eager culinary student or aspiring chef asking to come work for me for free or looking for clues to the best route to culinary success. But one day in the mail—I mean "snail mail" (you know, the one run by the U.S. Postal Service)—I received a letter from Bra, Italy, on the most gorgeous paper, typed in some fabulous font I had never seen before. It was from a young woman getting her master's in gastronomy who had interned at Chez Panisse, had run her own catering company, and was looking to come "apprentice" with me "in whatever capacity might be most helpful to you depending on your projects of the moment." Seriously? At that point I knew I must have done something decent in my previous life. So, of course, I stalled on writing her back. Buried the letter in my desk and promptly forgot about it. About a month later, when I really could not imagine how I was ever to finish this book, I opened my desk drawer looking for some way to procrastinate, and then I saw it, that beautiful letter, which thankfully *did* have an e-mail address on it. I wrote her a very hurried e-mail, all couched in "I'm not sure what you would be able to do to help" and "I can't guarantee your hours" and "I really don't even feel like I have time to schedule someone to help" and "I mean, I would have to meet you and interview you first" and on and on. I'm not quite sure why she kept being so lovely—well, actually now that I know her I know that it's just that she *is* that lovely.

Anyway, we set up a meeting when she got to L.A. to sort of see if something would work out. That Tuesday came and I was a mess: my kids had just started summer camp, we had a new nanny, and I couldn't find the keys to the SUV needed to pick the kids up at 3 p.m. Maria helped me search for about an hour until we frantically drove down to the camp in *her* car only to find the car keys in my son's lunch box! As I was stressing and swearing and apologizing, Maria just assured me everything was fine. "This is actually quite fun! What a great way to see L.A.," she said. "And so amazing to meet your kids! What a wonderful camp!" as she immediately started teaching my lovestruck five-year-old son Italian. "What's her deal?" my salty husband, David, asked later that night. "I don't know," I said. "I think she's just *really* nice!" You see, we jaded restaurant folks aren't really used to people like Maria.

Maria and I spent the summer working out of my house—me in my office writing away and she in my kitchen testing every single recipe. I honestly cannot imagine what I would do, Maria, if you had not sent that letter and been such a dream—not to mention so smart and such a great cook! Thank you.

And now for the people who really make A.O.C. happen, who worked so hard to help me develop these recipes for home and to test and retest them over and over. Our chef de cuisine Lauren Herman, executive sous-chef John Schlothauer, pastry genius Christina Olufson, sous-chef Don Dalao, and prep machine Ruben Garcia not only held down the fort at the restaurant (oh, did I mention we moved the actual restaurant in the middle of all this!) but were always there for me, despite the barrage of e-mails with the subject line "for the book" or "recipe test?" Thank you for all you give to me and to A.O.C.

After ten years a restaurant has so many employees who have come and gone, but I want to thank kitchen folks Brian Wolff, Stephanie Summers Bone,

Aliza Miner, Breanne Varela, and John Sadao for the lasting mark (there was that hole in the wall . . .) on the restaurant. Your spirits are still felt there and always will be.

In the front of the house, Julie Grimm Espinoza, Elisa Terrazas, Brett McDermott, Greg Weigel, Susanne Von-Euw, Amy Christine, Tom Hunter, Daryl Newmark, Susan Brink, and Monica Nauss could not have been more enthusiastic A.O.C. cheerleaders over all these years. I could not wish for a more dedicated soul and backbone for a restaurant than the veteran crew of Juan Carlos Larita, Alex Ascencio, David Diaz, Luis Cobain, Raul Varga, Manny Montana, and, most certainly not least, runner–driver–fix-it man extraordinaire Victor Rodriguez.

Julie Robles, Javier Espinoza, and Rodolfo Aguado help me hold together the madness more than they will ever know—they are all three amazing chefs in their own right and truly feel like family to me. Queen Bee Cynthia Longley somehow oversees everything that is front of house at all the restaurants, and our longstanding Lucques GM Matt Duggan always keeps a watchful eye on my baby when I'm distracted with other things, such as writing books. And thank you to my blessed, highly overeducated, and ever-perky assistant Christy Gersh. I love you guys!

When we moved A.O.C. in February 2013, we finally got a liquor license after ten years as a wine bar. Head barman Christiaan Rollich turned his seasoned, delicious, and spirited genius to A.O.C. (he was already running the cocktail programs at Lucques and Tavern) and really hit the ground running. Sometimes in the middle of an insane Saturday night it's the vision of his Fire and Smoke and Point Six cocktails that keeps me going! Thank you, Christiaan, for embracing my passion for the market and vision of how things should be, and turning them into potent and divine drinks. Special thanks to bartender Ignacio Murillo, who, from the moment he started as a busser, came to every wine and food tasting and took the time and effort to educate himself about everything A.O.C. The restaurant world needs more people like you!

Thank you to the farmers, ranchers, and fishermen who do all the real work in our business. Special thanks to Peter Schaner, the Colemans, Phil McGrath, Maryann Carpenter, James Birch, Jerry Rutiz, Alex Weiser, Barbara and Bill Spencer, Tamai Family Farm, Life's a Choke, Thao Farms, Laura Ramirez, Jaime Farms, Julee Harman, Steve Marks, and Willy Warner, who help us every day by bringing the beautiful and delicious ingredients to cook.

Just as chefs need great line cooks to be great chefs, cookbook authors need great recipe testers to be great cookbook authors, and I cannot imagine more enthusiastic, dedicated, and obsessive-compulsive recipe testers than Heather Platt and Michael Chessler.

There is getting the food to the plate, but then there is also trying to get the vision from inside my tightly wound head onto paper. Aaron Cook started as a server at Lucques, where he used to "help us out" with graphics for special menus and events. For the last few years he has basically been our in-house graphics guy—he designed our new A.O.C. logo when we moved and was my spiritual adviser on this book. Thank you, Aaron, for somehow magically knowing what I want without my knowing how to verbalize it.

Thank you to Jamie Rosenthal for lending me the gorgeous Irving Place Studio pottery as well as all the other jewels and treasures from Lost and Found for the photographs in this book.

Thanks to my mom Marcia Goin, my sister Jessica Goin, my brother-in-law Will Norton, and my in-laws Jean and David "Big Daddy" Lentz for being such a wonderful stable and loving family for David, me, and the kids in spite of all the weirdness of restaurant life.

To Sarah Roundtree and Christine Apa—the world's two most awesome nannies—thank you for "coparenting" with me, for putting up with my "idiosyncrasies," and for loving my kids.

Last—and while you may sometimes feel like you are the last ones on my mind, the opposite is true—to my beautiful family, especially my husband David Lentz, who always supports me and honors me and wants the best for me no matter what. David, Alex, Jack, and Charles—I love you.

the a.o.c. cookbook

introduction

Life was actually going along very well back in 2001. My first restaurant, Lucques, had opened a few years earlier to unexpected great success. I had finally gotten it up and running smoothly, hired a great staff, and established myself with our loyal clientele. Things were actually starting to normalize, so I did what any other not-so-sane chef would do—I started dreaming of the *next* restaurant.

The idea for A.O.C. grew out of the popularity of our tiny bar at Lucques. Though people reserved tables weeks in advance for the dining room, a more casual crowd would convene at the bar to taste the most recent wines-by-the-glass and nosh on an appetizer or snack from our small bar menu. The group of regulars grew, and the bar took on a culture of its own. They exchanged recommendations from the wine list and even shared food with one another. I loved the hustle and bustle of the bar, and I wanted to re-create that energy in this next fantasy restaurant.

I always say that A.O.C. is a full restaurant with the heart and soul of a wine bar. When I was conceiving the restaurant, I knew I wanted to explore my growing interest in Spanish, Portuguese, and North African flavors. And though I love the energy and tradition of European wine and tapas bars, I am a chef and I want to cook and serve more food than is usually offered at wine bars. How, I wondered, could I keep that bar feeling at a sit-down restaurant? I decided to offer a large menu of small dishes that were meant to be shared but that could, when eaten together, make a full meal.

The idea was to make everything small, so that guests could try more dishes. I wanted it to be informal and relaxed. There is something in the conversation about what to order, in the boisterous passing of plates, and in the sharing of food that truly adds to the diners' experience—guests are more aware, more engaged, and they tend to have a really good time! It's funny that once we opened, people tended to focus on the size of the plates—and they kept, to my chagrin, calling it "tapas." I love tapas, but the food at A.O.C. is not representative of that style. I was just trying to cook family-style for small groups.

Naming a restaurant is a very challenging proposition—actually harder than naming a child, I think. There are endless possibilities, and you are always trying to find that one word or phrase that will conjure up all the emotions and meanings of a restaurant's soul without being too obvious or too obscure. When we were working on opening Lucques, I remember going into a meeting with a graphic designer and trying to explain everything we wanted the restaurant to be—all the feelings and sensations we hoped it would evoke, all the hopes and dreams we had for it. The designer listened patiently to my blathering and then asked, "Well, that sounds good, so what's the name?" Upon hearing we didn't have one, he laughed. "Guess you need to come back when you have one." We were a month or so away from opening and we still hadn't named the place when my business partner, Caroline Styne, opened my notebook and saw the word LUCQUES written in a hundred different scripts in a hundred different variations. She looked at me and said, "Looks like we need to name the restaurant Lucques!"

With A.O.C. we were right back in that same place—lots of pretty good ideas but nothing that really felt right. It was down to the wire, as usual, when our insurance guy called and said if we didn't have a name by Monday at 9 a.m., the rates were going up. That weekend, Caroline and I racked our brains and scoured books for the right name. It was like a stream-of-consciousness therapy session. We knew we wanted the restaurant to be about tasting, about food and wine, about celebrating artisanal products and foods with tradition and stories behind them, about sharing and appreciating food. I kept thinking it should be the name of a wine or cheese, but I couldn't find just the right one. I was poring over a cheese glossary that Sunday night when, suddenly, I realized that the names I was most drawn to all had one thing in common—they were A.O.C. cheeses. Appellation d'Origine Contrôlée is the French government's system for regulating and designating wine, cheese, and other artisanal products. In short, it's the reason you can't call a sparkling wine from the Loire Valley "champagne." To be called "champagne," a sparkling wine must not just be from the region of Champagne, it must be made following strict regulations with regards to how densely the vines are planted, how the grapes are harvested (by hand only), and the method of fermentation in the bottle. I love the seriousness and dedication to the product and to greatness that these guidelines express. One of my favorite cheeses, Vacherin Mont D'Or, has some very particular A.O.C. regulations that I just love for existing—the cheese can only be made between August 15 and March 31, using the milk from two specific breeds of cows that must graze in a very particular area of the Alps, which must be 2,297 feet or more above sea level.

That's it, I thought—the one word (or abbreviation) that summed up the celebration of unique products and the joy of tasting and drinking them

that we were trying to evoke. I knew exactly what I wanted A.O.C. to be, and even though Caroline and I had eighteen painful months of escrow before we finally opened, it took me forever to get the concept of it, which was so clear in my head, onto paper. "Do you have a menu yet?" Caroline would timidly ask, knowing that under my seemingly calm exterior there could lurk a lot of fuming rage, most of which was aimed at servers with less-than-brilliant questions in the middle of a Saturday-night rush. "Almost," I would reply, asking myself why I couldn't seem to birth the actual piece of paper that would explain the restaurant more clearly to investors and others who couldn't wrap their heads around what we intended by "small plates meant to be shared."

It was getting close. Seriously, we were two months out and I still hadn't written a menu. Then, a week later, flying home from New York after cooking for a charity dinner, I opened my laptop right there in the window seat on United Flight 703, and it all came spewing out of me. In an attempt to organize my thoughts, I decided just to start thinking of categories of dishes and examples of what I might like to cook. A few hours later, I had a long list of dishes—under headlines such as "cheese," "charcuterie," "salads," "fish," "meat," "from the wood oven," "desserts," and the ever-eloquent "and," which really should have been called "vegetables and grains."

"OK, great!" I thought. "Now, how am I going to configure these categorized thoughts into an actual menu?" Looking down at my oddly organized list of small plates, I realized that I was done! I liked it like that. It totally made sense, and if that was the way I thought of the food, then that should be the way our guests ordered the food. To this day, I joke that I do my best work on an airplane. I love it: no interruptions, no dishwasher issues, no vegan substitutions, no phone, just me and my own spinning head.

The recipes in this book are arranged just like the menu at the restaurant, because I want you to feel free to pick and choose, mix and match the dishes as you like, to make a meal that appeals to you. At the restaurant, we encourage guests to order two or three dishes per person and then share among themselves. Realistically, I know that most home cooks don't want to prepare twelve dishes for a party of four! For that reason, **the recipes in this book serve six people as part of a traditional meal** unless otherwise noted.

It's funny that, though A.O.C. has such a reputation as a meat lover's paradise, it is also the perfect spot for vegetarians and vegans. Sometimes I feel a bit schizophrenic, because so much of my cooking is based on a love of seasonal and local produce and yet I love meat just as much.

As you look through the fish and meat chapters, you will see that the recipes are just as inspired by the fruits, vegetables, and grains they are paired with as they are by their inherent meaty selves. I am a true omnivore, giving equal attention and status to lettuces, tomatoes, halibut, and veal. My goal is to make it all delicious, whether it's the fresh and bright-tasting fruits and vegetables of summer, or the satisfying deep, earthy, and animal flavors of a winter stew. To help you navigate your way through this book, I have further divided the categories by season, so you will find spring salads, followed by summer salads, fall, and then winter.

It's fantastic to think of all the changes in the culinary landscape of our country just in the last fifteen years, since we opened Lucques. In 1998, getting all our produce from local farmers and farmers' markets was sort of wild and crazy, and now it's almost mainstream. The number of farmers' markets across the country has more than doubled since that time, and I know many people who buy all their produce for home at farmers' markets around L.A., driving to Santa Monica for certain items and waiting until the Sunday market in Hollywood for other specialties and favorite vendors.

The local farmers and the produce they are growing at any particular moment are the true inspiration for new dishes, and are why we do what we do at my restaurants. I literally could not do it without them. Now, working with farmers has its challenges. Though they are amazingly generous and lovely people, they are not always the most organized, and when something needs to be tended or changed in their fields, they just do it, without thinking about what is on our menu or a special party that booked a month ago for that Friday night. As chefs who purchase from farmers, we understand this and need to be flexible and willing to change our plan or our menu depending on what is truly available. I advise you to do the same. If nectarines are perfectly gorgeous, there is no reason to use mushy peaches! When the dandelion is wilted but arugula is bright and super-fresh, for goodness' sake, use the arugula. Let what you find at the market guide what you are cooking rather than the other way round. You will find a detailed seasonal market report in my first book, *Sunday Suppers at Lucques,* with plenty of tips on what is in season when, and how to chose particular fruits and vegetables.

People often tell me that they want to learn to cook and ask how they should go about it. Well, obviously, the first thing to do is to learn some knife skills and basic techniques, but after that, learning to cook really is just like learning another language. You have to do it rigorously, practice, and pay attention. Every time you cook, it is a chance to learn and take away a lesson; as with anything else, the more you put into it, in terms of thinking and analyzing, the more you get out of it. Wow, did I just suck all the love and life out of cooking? I hope I didn't, and I hope I am not deterring you, because I honestly love food and spending time in the kitchen more than just about anything. I am just saying that, to get conversational, never mind fluent, in the language of cooking, you need to watch the food and be very in tune with what is happening and why. And you must taste thoughtfully and critically.

While you are cooking, tasting, and eating, think about the balance of rich and refreshing; the brightness of acid and spice; the unexpected crunch of nuts or breadcrumbs; the silkiness of cream or yogurt; and the sharp saltiness added by a shaving of pecorino. Think about what you are tasting, and why certain flavors work or don't work, and what you could add (or what you need to take away) to make a dish sing. I hope these recipes will direct you and help in this learning process, and that as you are preparing them you think about the layers of flavor that are being developed, and why certain ingredients are added when they are, and what they bring to a dish.

One of the most important keys to a successful dish is the integration of flavors. I am constantly working to integrate and unite ingredients so that the sum of a dish is greater than its parts, so it's delicious not just because each item on the plate is delicious (this should be the case, too) but because there is something in the way all the components are brought together that intertwines them and creates something above and beyond what they were when they started.

Sometimes this integration means repeating or reinforcing flavors two or more times in one dish. You will see that I often do this in salads, for example, pounding juicy cherries into a vinaigrette for a spring salad of Arugula and

Cherries with Pickled Rhubarb and Fresh Ricotta (page 65), or adding dried mushrooms to the braising juices of Coq au Vin with Bacon, Potato Purée, Cipollini Onions, and Black Trumpets (page 206) to reiterate the mushroom on another level. Adding a splash of Pernod along with fresh fennel makes Fennel Purée (page 142) all that much more fennel-y. The diners probably won't consciously notice these layers of flavors specifically, but their palate will know the food is delicious and boldly flavored.

My business partner, Caroline Styne, is also our Wine Director, and she and I spend way too many hours tasting wine together every week. So you will find her wine notes with every dish in this book. We hope to demystify wine-and-food pairings and get you excited to taste and learn more about complementing flavors. Caroline is a great teacher, because she talks about why she feels these pairings work and what led her to her conclusions; it's more about the process than just the answers.

This is not the easiest cookbook you will ever use. I feel that part of the success of *Sunday Suppers at Lucques* was in not dumbing down the recipes or the concepts to meet what was perceived as "what the public wanted." In the era of thirty-minute meals, my recipes do take longer, but I hope you will be pleased with the results and also learn something along the way. The beauty is in the details, and those details do sometimes just take another step (or two). I have worked hard to double-check myself and make sure that if I am asking the reader to do something the "hard way" it really does make a difference. Personally, I know I have changed the way I cook at home since having children, and I now have a more realistic understanding of the need to get things done quickly on the home front. Before we had kids, I never kept canned garbanzos in the cabinets, or anything but ice cream and gin in the freezer, but I get it now, and I try to set myself up at home the same way I do at work. If you don't have the luxury of spending all day at the stove, or even if you do, getting your *mise en place,* or prepped items, ready to go will save you. Much of the preparation in this book can be done in advance. Even if you are making a salad, you can wash your greens and make the dressing in the morning to cut down on prep time later. Braises, stuffings, purées, and the like are fine, sometimes even better, done a day or even two (for braises) ahead of time. I do hope you will enjoy the process as well as the delicious results of your time in the kitchen. Happy cooking!

caroline styne's introduction

In opening A.O.C., Suzanne and I decided to create a restaurant where we were able to satisfy our mutual love of noncommittal eating. We wanted a place where people like us could share a wide range of items for dinner, nibbling on this and that while sampling wine and experiencing a whole spectrum of flavors. It's a fun way to dine, and a gratifying way to serve our clients. Each night, we front-of-the-house workers are challenged to find the perfect wine pairing for each of our guests. And since each table's combination of dishes from the menu is never the same, our pairing suggestions are constantly changing. Of course, we are lucky enough to have a pretty extensive and eclectic wine list to choose from, along with so many palates to please. But this challenge is a welcome one, and we absolutely adore being the diners' guides.

It may sound corny, but when food and wine meet in the right combination on the palate, something magical happens. The harsh becomes mellowed, the delicate becomes intense, the sweet becomes savory. The whole experience becomes more interesting. The hard part is figuring out exactly what that right combination is.

My goal from day one has been to make the wine aspect of the restaurant fun and approachable. I don't think that the process of wine pairing, and even the appreciation of wine itself, has to be esoteric, difficult, or exclusive. I've actually found that my most successful strategies with wine pairing have come from my desire to "marry" the food and wine, so I usually opt for wines that reflect the flavors and textures of the food and thereby create balance and synergy on the palate. There are definitely times for contrast, as with the need to pair high-acid wines with rich, fatty foods, but more often than not, the best option, in my opinion, is to pair like with like.

After each of Suzanne's recipes, I have given my two cents on wine pairings, explaining what the inspiration or thought process is behind my wine recommendation, and how the wine and food should work together on the palate. I have not mentioned specific wineries or vintages: the general world of winemaking is an ever-changing one, and I don't want to limit the pairing possibilities. These are meant to be suggestions, or guidelines, and to promote

adventurousness in one's experimentation with wine. Also, my recommendations differ from plate to plate, so, when putting recipes together for a menu, I say try them all, or find a common thread in my notes and choose two. Take each meal as an opportunity to taste different wines, learn about what makes the pairing work or not, and develop a new wine repertoire.

Of course, it's helpful to have some guidelines in the process. When working on a wine pairing, I look for various clues for inspiration and parameters, and I hope these will be helpful as you begin to experiment as well.

1. The Regional Element The beautiful thing about Old World wines—those from places where the winemaking tradition dates back hundreds of years—is that wines from these various regions were made to drink with the foods traditionally prepared there. The rosé wines from the southern coastal regions of France were made to drink with bouillabaisse and the fish dishes that are part of the area's traditional diet. The lean, high-acid red wines of the Piemonte region of northern Italy are made to drink with the area's refined, earthy cuisine. These examples go on and on. So, when I see a particular regional influence in a recipe, I immediately look to the wines of that area for ideas.

2. The Geographical Element Grapes, like many other agricultural products, often pick up qualities of the geographical areas in which they are grown, and thereby pass these qualities on to the wine. Wines made from vineyards located close to the sea will have notes on the palate that are reflective of the salty ocean air. The grapes for Chablis, in France's Burgundy appellation, are planted on limestone containing fossilized oyster shells, and this creates wines that have intense mineral elements reminiscent of salty seashells. The wines from the Barossa Valley in Australia, whose vineyards are surrounded by eucalyptus trees, display a definite and distinctive herbal, menthol aspect. I hope my notes on each suggested pairing will help educate you about some geographical elements to keep in mind in

the future, so you can experiment on your own. This geographical influence is particularly helpful when pairing wine with cheese.

3. `The Dominant Flavor` For each recipe, I look to the most dominant flavor in the preparation as my focus in wine pairing. Just knowing what the raw ingredients in each recipe taste like can be quite helpful. Oftentimes, though, it can be difficult to determine exactly what that element of the recipe is, if one has never tasted the finished dish; this is where my experience comes into play. I suggest forming one's own taste experience and getting to know the "palate" of each of the recipe's ingredients. Taste the element of each dish in its raw form (when safe) as well as after it has been cooked. Take note of how the flavors of the foods transform through cooking. Recognize how something becomes bolder and more expressive when sautéed, or earthier when roasted. Onions, for example, go from sharp and pungent when raw to rich and caramel-like when cooked. And with the completed recipe, pay attention to the ingredients that become the stars of the show and those that take more of a supporting role.

4. `The Arc of Flavor on the Palate` Suzanne's recipes all display a degree of intensity and drama that comes through as an arc of flavor on the palate. Though it is hard to describe, I often compare this to story development in drama and literature, wherein a story has a beginning, a dramatic climax, and a resolution. Her recipes display a degree of brightness, or spark, that takes the flavors on the palate from one level to another and back again. Wines tend to show a similar arc, with acidity and tannin taking on the main dramatic role. In wine pairing, I often try to combine recipes and wines that show similar arcs on the palate, so that the wine and food are in sync with each other.

I've been fortunate enough to taste a lot of different wines, and even more fortunate to taste each and every recipe on the A.O.C. menu, multiple times. The truth is, I've never had any kind of wine-pairing training at all. My experience comes from just this—tasting and tasting and tasting again. Everything I know has come from this continuous ritual, through trial and error, and experimentation. I do recognize that not everyone has the luxury of tasting wine and food every day at work, so I'm happy to do all of the heavy lifting, to bring my knowledge into play here, and be the wine guide.

cheese

C heese and wine are basically the heart and soul of A.O.C. In the early years at Lucques, I used to get so frustrated by our pathetic cheese sales. I would research and study, seeking out the best and most unusual cheeses I could find. I would do write-ups, give tastes to the staff, indoctrinate and convert the servers, but no matter what I did we would sell a measly two or three cheese plates a night. At that time, I used to get some of our cheeses from The Cheese Store of Beverly Hills, an amazing mecca for food lovers and cheese heads, and a virtual paradise for me. I used to have to hide the receipts from Caroline, like a wife who buys an expensive dress and cuts the price tag off before her husband can see it. I couldn't help it! I would get so carried away when Norbert, the Cheese Store owner, would hand me taste after taste of the most intriguing and beguiling cheeses that I couldn't stop buying them. Some people have shoes, some people have jewelry—me, I have cheese.

I started making little composed cheese plates at Lucques to show off whatever gorgeous piece of coagulated dairy product I had most recently fallen for. Being able to focus just on that one cheese and what would pair best with it was such a reprieve from focusing on a whole appetizer or main course. It was from this concept of tasting and being able to think small that the idea for A.O.C. was born.

To that end, I realized that I didn't want cheese to be relegated to the dessert page on the A.O.C. menu. Rather than thinking of cheese as a decadent option if you happen to have room at the end of your meal, I wanted cheese to be the focus, the main event, something to build your meal around rather than vice versa. And I wanted to have a lot of it, not just the lovely selection of five cheeses—goat, sheep, cow, mixed, and blue—that we had at Lucques. How limiting is that? One goat cheese? Is it soft or hard, mild or strong, French or Portuguese or American? I hated having to choose, and I wanted to let the diners have choices as well. I wanted goat-cheese lovers to have the opportunity to taste five completely different selections side by side. And I wanted to play around with pairings, to explore different honeys and mostardas, date and fig bars, walnut jams, sabas, and abbameles.

Cheese is very much like wine. It's just milk, which, based merely on where it came from and how it was treated, can taste an infinite number of ways. I find it fascinating that the *terroir* and the decisions a cheesemaker makes can so specifically define the end result when there really is just an ingredient or two. Another way in which cheese is like wine is that the only real way to learn about it, after you have read the books and seen the process, is by tasting, and tasting, and tasting.

There are so many great local cheese shops and places to order online now (that didn't really exist when we opened ten years ago), so it's easy to set up one of these tastings at home. Do your research first, because cheese is an expensive product and you want to know what you are dealing with. Plus, the stories are a big part of the joy of cheese (and wine) selecting. In the back of this book, I have included A.O.C. Cheese, a glossary that I started in 2002 to help our poor blessed servers keep track of all the cheeses on the list.

As you dive deeper into cheese, you will begin to seek out raw-milk cheeses and to follow particular *affineurs* (cheese agers) the way other people follow celebrities or fantasy football. I will never forget one summer years back, long before Lucques or A.O.C., when Peggy Smith (now the owner of Cowgirl Creamery but formerly one of my chefs at Chez Panisse) invited me to be part of something called Vinexpo in Bordeaux. Over the years at this biennial wine fair, the different regions of France had taken to doing basically pop-up restaurants to represent their region and entertain their clients. Robert Mondavi decided that California should also have its own one-week-long restaurant, too, and turned to Chez Panisse and Peggy to make it happen. Now, Peggy is just about the coolest person I know—someone I always say that I want to be if I ever grow up. She has gorgeous super-straight perfect salt-and-pepper hair (I think it was Reese Witherspoon in *Legally Blonde* who said, "The most important thing is my hair"), a wicked sharp wit, great taste in country music, an awesome cowgirl style, and an amazing palate and personality.

I couldn't believe Peggy invited me, along with many of the more experienced and seasoned Chez Panisse crew, to do this temporary restaurant with her. Well, it was brutal: nowhere to prep, no real purveyors, no real building, no containers for your prepped product, assuming you ever got it prepped. It was basically like one of those reality-TV "make a restaurant in one day" deals, except there were no cameras (thank God) and no prizes (except hanging out with Peggy and the gang day and night). My lowest moment was when Peg assigned me to grill about six hundred baby leeks on the charcoal grill we had set up outside. I had laid them out lovingly on sheet pans and seasoned them with olive oil, salt, and pepper. As I stood by my stack of twenty sheet pans, one of the more experienced and intimidating members of the team walked by and smirked, "Not sure you're *ever* gonna get all those done." I completely panicked, imagining how long it was going to take me to lay each leek on the grill, do a quarter-turn, turn again, flip, and finish cooking them. I took the whole sheet pan, olive-oil laden as it was, and dumped it upside down on the grill, thinking of all the time I would save if I could just get the leeks on the damned grill faster. Well, as you can imagine, when the oil hit the fire the whole thing basically blew up in my face, blackening my leeks and completely eradicating my eyebrows! The funny thing was, as a young cook, I was mostly just embarrassed and humiliated by my foolish decision, and not so concerned about my safety or the cosmetic failings of the moment.

Anyway, the upside of the whole trip was a visit to Jean d'Alos cheese shop in downtown Bordeaux, arranged by Peggy long before Cowgirl Creamery was a foodie household name. I will never forget walking five floors down the winding staircase of the fifteenth-century stone-walled former convent and seeing, firsthand, the art that is *affinage* (why does everything sound so much better in French?), or the aging of cheese. First, Monsieur d'Alos and his team travel all around France and Belgium, seeking out the best cheeses they can find. They purchase them young and bring them back to the natural cellars under the streets of Bordeaux to age them perfectly in separate rooms depending on the cheese, turning them and even bathing them in wine or liqueurs as they see fit. It's amazing what a difference this aging and fining can make. You know that if you are buying a Jean d'Alos cheese it will be perfectly chosen, perfectly aged, and outstandingly delicious.

To choose great cheese, I suggest developing a good relationship with your local cheesemonger, and following *affineurs* like Jean d'Alos—and purveyors like Cowgirl Creamery, Murray's Cheese in New York, and The Cheese Store of Beverly Hills (the last three have great online guides, including pairings and other suggestions). Steven Jenkins's wonderful book *Cheese Primer* is an indispensable road map for the aspiring and accomplished cheese head. And if you are serious about cheese, I would suggest writing down your thoughts as you taste. Sometimes, no matter how much you love something in the moment, it's easy to forget the details if you don't make notes at the time.

There are many different routes to take when putting together a cheese plate. The classic way is to choose three or five cheeses that express different levels of powerfulness and a variety of textures. You want a range of mildly flavored to strongly flavored and stinky, and of soft and buttery to semi-soft and harder cheese. But it's fun to think of a cheese plate as a sort of study, too. Try three sheep's milk cheeses, ranging from runny and stinky, to hard and dry. Or just a selection of goat cheeses all from different regions. Or three cheeses from the same region. There are as many themes and directions to guide your selections as there are cheeses. Isn't it actually interesting to taste three French triple crèmes side by side? I guess what I am saying is, don't worry so much about what is wrong and what is right. My husband, David, loves soft cheese, so, when I'm putting together a plate for us at home, I go heavy on the soft cheeses. As with anything in life, the more you know the more fun it is to play around and experiment; so trust your palate and eat more cheese! And check out A.O.C. Cheese, the glossary at the end of this book, for a list of every cheese we have ever served at the restaurant, with descriptions.

caroline styne on cheese

When pairing wines with cheese, I usually stick to a fairly straightforward and almost foolproof strategy. I opt for wines that come from the same region as the cheese itself. This scheme actually makes a great deal of sense intellectually as well as gastronomically. There is a strong correlation between what the dairy animal eats and the flavors that come through in its milk, and the same is true for grapevines. The animal grazes on grasses that come from the same soils that the grapevines are grown in, and from which they absorb their nutrients. As a result, the "flavors" of the soils, like salty mineral-rich limestone and chalky, earthy clay, come through in both the dairy milk and the wine of each region.

bacon-wrapped dates with parmesan

The funniest thing is that this iconic A.O.C. dish, the one that everyone says you "have to have" when you come to the restaurant, wasn't even on the menu until a week before we opened. We were in escrow for literally eighteen months on the space for A.O.C., and during that time some great friends of ours, who also happened to be investors, Anne Crawford and Dudley deZonia, got engaged. They were so excited about our impending new place that they asked us early on if they could hold their wedding reception at A.O.C. in December 2002. Assuming, like all overly optimistic restaurant owners, "Of course, we will definitely be open long before *then*," we booked it. Needless to say, December 10 rolled around and, in classic restaurant-business-renegade style, we pulled together a construction site, dimmed the lights, and put on a wedding.

Anne and Dudley were very cool through this whole ordeal, always knowing, even though we weren't so sure ourselves, that we would pull it off. Anne's one obsession about the wedding wasn't her dress or whether or not we would actually get open in time; it was that she desperately wanted to serve grilled pancetta-wrapped figs stuffed with Roquefort, which she had eaten at Lucques that summer. Of course, it was the dead of winter, with not a fig in sight, but I knew I had to think of something to please her—especially considering that her wedding location at that point looked like a very poorly maintained lumberyard. My mind racing, I asked myself, "What's like a fig?"—a question I ask myself surprisingly often when my mind is trying to catch up with my palate. Sometimes in cooking I know what ingredient would work in a particular dish but I can't use it because it is not in season. Kumquats, for example, are so perfect for the combination of tart flavor, chewy bitter skin, and burst of citrus juice they bring to a dish. When winter is long gone I find myself thinking: What is like a kumquat? What can give me those flavors and textures I'm looking for? Asking these questions can actually lead to great food discoveries once you break down what characteristics and flavors you are hoping to get from your desired but unobtainable ingredients.

But back to the question of "What's like a fig?" That winter the answer

24 deglet noor dates, pitted

¼ pound Parmigiano-Reggiano

Twenty-four 3-inch strips of very thinly sliced bacon

5 leaves flat-leaf parsley

was a date! I decided to stuff it with a little chunk of Parmesan and wrap it in bacon (sturdier than pancetta for a sturdier fruit). Instead of grilling them, I roasted them in our wood-burning oven, since I was newly obsessed with it. Warm brown-sugary dates with softened Parmigiano all wrapped in crispy bacon—they are truly the perfect union of sweet, salty, and umami (that elusive fifth sense associated with savoriness and meatiness). Anne was, I think, a little disappointed at first, because she had her mind set on the figs. But the wedding guests went crazy for them—I mean really crazy! By the end of the night, I looked at Caroline and said, "Well, I guess the dates are going on the menu."

Often described as "meat candy," they are pretty irresistible, and, fortunately, easy to make. One of our bartenders makes big batches at home, keeps them in the fridge, and cooks them late at night in a toaster oven more often than she would like to admit!

Preheat the oven to 400°F.

Using a small paring knife, cut a small slit across the length of each date.

Cut the cheese into approximately ½-inch-by-¼-inch rectangles (the cheese will not cut into perfect shapes, but that's OK).

Insert a piece of Parmigiano into each date.

Lay the strips of bacon out on a work space, next to each other. One by one, place each date at the end of a strip of bacon, and then carefully roll the date along the bacon strip, wrapping it tightly.

Place the bacon-wrapped dates on a roasting rack set in a baking sheet, and roast for 10 to 15 minutes, until golden brown and crispy on the outside.

Arrange the dates in a bowl with the parsley leaves.

Remember to warn your guests that the dates are hot!

I often try to be thematically or regionally pure when selecting wines for pairings. In this case, the intense punch of Parmesan in these flavor-filled nibbles takes me to Italy, more specifically to Lambrusco and the sparkling red wines produced in the regions around Parma. These wines are usually served slightly chilled and consumed with snacks as an apéritif. Though they are made in a variety of styles, I normally opt for one that is high in acid and vinified dry. As a result, the wine's touch of sweetness can mirror that of the dates without becoming cloying, while its acidity cuts through the fattiness of the bacon and cheese.

fried tetilla with quince paste and romesco

I remember that in the early days the less mature male members of our staff used to get a kick out of the name of this dish. *Tetilla* means "nipple" in Spanish (I can still hear the frat-house giggles in my head) and refers to the shape of this mild and buttery cow's milk cheese from Galicia. This dish is my play on *queso frito,* or fried cheese, popular in tapas bars. I originally tried frying the cheese directly in the pan, but I could never seem to get the crust I longed for. So I decided to sandwich that melty cheese between two super-thin slices of bread before frying it in olive oil. The tetilla is finished with little triangles of quince paste and a drizzle of romesco and its oil.

1 loaf good-quality country white or sourdough bread

3 ounces quince paste

8 ounces tetilla or other semi-firm melting cheese, such as Italian Fontina, a young Asiago, or an aged Jack

Approximately 6 tablespoons extra-virgin olive oil, as needed

2 tablespoons Romesco (recipe follows), thinned with olive oil to a drizzling consistency

¼ cup flat-leaf parsley leaves

Cut the crust off the bread, wrap the loaf, and place it in the freezer for 30 minutes before slicing it.

As the loaf starts to thaw, cut twelve very thin slices, about ⅛ inch thick. (At the restaurant, we use an electric slicer.) If one side of the bread becomes difficult to slice, work from the other end. If the bread becomes too soft, put it back in the freezer for a few minutes.

Slice the quince paste into ¼-inch-thick slabs, and then cut the slabs into thirty-six small triangles. Set aside.

Trim the thin, waxy rind from the cheese, and cut ¼-inch-thick slices. Make six cheese sandwiches with the bread and tetilla. The cheese should come just to the edges of the bread. Trim the cheese and rearrange as needed.

Heat a large sauté pan (ideally cast-iron) over high heat for 1 minute. Swirl in 2 tablespoons olive oil (per batch), turn down the heat to medium, and carefully place two sandwiches in the pan. (You will need to work in batches, or can use three pans if you like.)

Place a small pot or skillet on top of the sandwiches to weigh them down. Pan-fry the sandwiches until the bread is golden brown and the cheese is oozing, 3 to 4 minutes per side. Resist the temptation to move the sandwiches around the pan; instead, watch the edges to see when a crispy crust forms and the sandwiches are ready to be flipped. Transfer to a cutting board.

Wipe out the pan with paper towels after each batch, and repeat the process.

Cut each sandwich into three triangles, and transfer to a serving plate. Top each toasty bread triangle with two triangles of quince paste. Then drizzle on the romesco, and sprinkle the whole parsley leaves among the triangles.

romesco

5 ancho chiles

2 tablespoons raw almonds

2 tablespoons blanched hazelnuts

1¼ cups extra-virgin olive oil

1 slice country bread, about
    1 inch thick

⅓ cup canned tomatoes,
    San Marzano or Muir Glen

1 clove garlic, chopped

1 tablespoon chopped flat-leaf
    parsley

Juice of ½ lemon
    (about 1 tablespoon)

Kosher salt and freshly ground
    black pepper

Preheat the oven to 375°F.

Remove and discard the stems and seeds from the chiles, and then soak them in warm water for 15 minutes to soften. Strain the chiles, and pat dry with paper towels.

Meanwhile, spread the nuts on a baking sheet, and toast for 8 to 10 minutes, until they smell nutty and are golden brown.

Heat a large sauté pan over high heat for 2 minutes. Add 2 tablespoons olive oil, and wait a minute. Fry the slice of bread on both sides until golden brown. Remove the bread from the pan, and cool. Cut it into 1-inch cubes and set aside.

Return the pan to the stove over high heat. Add 2 tablespoons olive oil and the chiles, and sauté for a minute or two. Add the tomatoes. Season with ½ teaspoon salt, and cook 2 to 3 minutes, stirring often, until the tomato juices have evaporated and the tomato starts to color slightly. Turn off the heat, and leave the mixture in the pan.

In a food processor, pulse together the toasted nuts, garlic, and fried bread until the bread and nuts are coarsely ground. Add the chile-tomato mixture, and process for 1 minute more.

With the machine running, slowly pour in the remaining 1 cup olive oil, and process until you have a smooth purée. Don't worry: the romesco will "break," or separate into solids and oil; this is normal. Add the parsley, and season to taste with lemon juice, pepper, and more salt if you like.

This recipe is the Spanish answer to every craving in one, satisfying the need for both sweetness and saltiness, fruit and earth in each bite. The ideal wine pairing is one that does much the same. An example of this is Albariño, from the northern regions of Spain and Portugal. The beauty of this variety is that, when made well, it expresses beautiful aromatics of white flowers and honey alongside a seasidelike saltiness that makes the wine vibrant, fresh, and complex. This is a particularly interesting pairing, because the floral notes in the wine actually enhance the creaminess of the cheese, while the salt and mineral elements cut through and balance out the sweet ingredients in the dish.

young goat cheese with dried figs and saba

5 large shallots, peeled

3 tablespoons extra-virgin
olive oil

1 tablespoon unsalted butter

8-ounce log fresh goat cheese

1 large or 2 small heads radicchio

12 dried black Mission figs

½ cup flat-leaf parsley leaves

1 tablespoon plus 1 teaspoon
lemon juice

1½ tablespoons saba

¼ teaspoon cracked black pepper

Kosher salt and freshly ground
black pepper

This young-goat-cheese dish is pretty much what started the idea of A.O.C. for me in the first place. I had gotten some way-too-expensive but oh-so-delicious little young goat cheeses from The Cheese Store of Beverly Hills on a Saturday, and I ran a special off the side table in the Lucques kitchen while I worked the grill at the same time. Of course, I should have just shown the pantry cook how to do it, but I was so in love with the cheese that I just wanted to make each one myself. Bitter, sweet, salty, with a lovely crunch from the radicchio, and a burst of bright herb flavor from the parsley, this dish is a staple on the A.O.C. menu. The saba, a reduced grape must syrup, is one of my favorite condiments to drizzle over cheese, roasted vegetables, and grilled meats.

Cut the shallots in half lengthwise, and then cut each half into three wedges.

Heat a medium sauté pan over medium heat, then swirl in 1 tablespoon olive oil and the butter. When the butter foams, add the shallots, and toss to coat in the oil. Season with ½ teaspoon salt and a pinch of black pepper.

Turn the heat to medium-low, and cook the shallots for 15 minutes, stirring often. Reduce the heat to low, and cook for another 15 minutes, until completely caramelized and deep golden brown, stirring every 2 to 3 minutes. Transfer to a plate to cool.

Roll the goat cheese neatly in plastic wrap to create a uniform log shape. Twist the ends of the plastic wrap tight, and roll the log back and forth on a flat surface, such as a cutting board, a few times, so that the cheese takes on an even shape. Refrigerate at least 15 minutes, to make the cheese easier to slice.

Discard any wilted outer leaves of the radicchio, cut the head in half lengthwise, and cut out the core. Place the radicchio halves cut-side down on a cutting board, and slice them lengthwise into ⅓-inch-thick ribbons.

Remove the stems from the dried figs, and cut them lengthwise into five slices each.

Place the radicchio, caramelized shallots, dried figs, and parsley leaves in a large bowl, and toss the salad with the lemon juice, 1 tablespoon olive oil,

1 tablespoon saba, 1 teaspoon salt, and some freshly ground pepper. Taste for balance and seasoning, and arrange the salad on six plates.

Run a thin, sharp knife under hot water for a few seconds, and then wipe it dry. (This will help you slice the soft goat cheese more cleanly.) Remove and discard the plastic wrap, slice the cheese into twelve rounds (about ⅓ inch thick), season each round with a little cracked black pepper, and place the goat cheese at the center of each salad, with the slices overlapping slightly.

Make sure that some of the pretty parsley leaves and fig slices are peeking out from under the cheese. Drizzle the remaining ½ tablespoon saba and 1 tablespoon olive oil over the top of the goat cheese.

In France, goat cheese is produced in large quantity in the Loire Valley, the same region that grows some of the world's best Sauvignon Blanc. Interestingly, both Sauvignon Blanc and goat cheese have a bright forcefulness and a similar path, or arc, of flavor on the palate. They both read with an initial bright sweetness that becomes stronger and tangier, and finish with a pungent saltiness. For this particular dish, I would select a wine that has been aged in oak, giving it a deeper, richer flavor that will complement the dark fruitiness from the figs and saba.

seal bay triple cream with poached cherries and hazelnuts

½ cup blanched hazelnuts

1½ tablespoons hazelnut or extra-virgin olive oil

9 ounces Seal Bay Triple Cream or other buttery triple-crème cheese

2 tablespoons flat-leaf parsley leaves

2 tablespoons ½-inch-snipped chives

2 tablespoons tarragon leaves

Approximately ¾ cup Poached Cherries (recipe follows)

Kosher salt and freshly ground black pepper

Now, I love hard cheeses, and I would love to be that sophisticated person who chooses them over buttery, rich, creamy triple crèmes, but, sad to say, I am not. Give me the oozy, extra-creamy, 70-percent-butterfat-or-more triple crèmes any day! This Australian Seal Bay Triple Cream is really fabulous, because it also has a really ballsy and land-down-under rusticness to its flavor, which is a pleasant complement to the unctuous texture. I love the look of the extra-white cheese with cherries and their syrup, and a scattering of toasted hazelnuts.

Preheat the oven to 375°F.

Spread the hazelnuts on a baking sheet, and toast for 8 to 10 minutes, until they're slightly darkened and smell nutty. When they have cooled, crush the nuts slightly and toss them with 1 tablespoon oil, salt, and pepper.

Run the blade of a sharp knife under hot water, wipe it dry, and carefully cut six 1½-ounce slices of the cheese; place them on six salad plates. (You may need to run the knife under water a few times during the slicing to get nice clean pieces.)

In a small bowl, toss the herbs with the remaining ½ tablespoon oil and a pinch of salt and pepper. Arrange the herb salad next to the cheese, spoon a tablespoon or two of the cherry compote over and around each slice of cheese, and scatter the hazelnuts over the top and around the plate.

poached cherries

NOTE If the chiles de árbol are dry and brittle you can just crush or crumble them.

Make a sachet of thyme, bay leaves, chiles, star anise, cinnamon stick, and peppercorns in cheesecloth. Place the sugar and 1 cup water in a medium saucepan. Bring to a boil over medium-high heat, and then add the port, the orange juice, and the sachet. Turn down to a simmer, and add the cherries. Poach the cherries for 8 to 10 minutes, until just tender. (The cherries should retain their shape; if they've begun to look squashed, you have overcooked them.)

Strain the cherries over a bowl, and return the liquid to the saucepan. Cook the liquid over high heat for about 5 minutes, until it has reduced by two-thirds. It should be slightly thickened and have a glossy sheen. Strain the liquid, and cool. Stir in the cherries, and season to taste with salt and a pinch of pepper.

4 sprigs thyme

2 bay leaves, ideally fresh

2 chiles de árbol

3 star anise

1 cinnamon stick

1 teaspoon black peppercorns

¼ cup sugar

½ cup port

Juice of 2 oranges

1½ cups pitted cherries (from about ⅓ pound whole cherries)

Kosher salt and freshly ground black pepper

Seal Bay has to be one of the most luscious and enchanting of all cheeses. It has the texture of butter and a flavor just potent enough to make it a real people-pleaser. To pair with it, Australia produces some truly outstanding Rieslings that are quite different from those made in Germany and Austria. It's easy to assume that white wines from Australia would be as big and muscular as their reds. On the contrary, the Rieslings are very graceful and elegant, with bright citruslike tartness and vibrant acidity. They are not sweet, or off-dry, in any way, and are incredibly food-friendly, displaying a great deal of stone-fruit and mineral notes that cut through the fleshiness of this cheese and enhance its richness of flavor.

torta gorgonzola with walnuts in honey

1 cup walnut halves

1 cup medium-dark honey,
    such as avocado, buckwheat,
    or sage

2 tablespoons walnut oil

1 small sprig rosemary

6 ounces torta Gorgonzola,
    Saint Agur, or other creamy
    blue cheese

Cracked black pepper

Honey and blue cheese are pretty much a match made in heaven. The addition of the walnuts lends an earthy note and a nice crunchy texture. I first started thinking about this combination when I found a Spanish condiment made by one of the cheesemakers, called "walnuts in walnut honey." Ever self-reliant, I decided to try making my own, and fell in love with it spooned over blue cheese. In this recipe, the walnuts in honey are served over a torta Gorgonzola—mascarpone and Gorgonzola stacked together almost like a layer cake. The pungency of the Gorgonzola and the sweetness of the mascarpone are perfection with honey and nuts on top.

Preheat the oven to 375°F.

Spread the walnuts on a baking sheet, and toast for 8 to 10 minutes, until they're slightly darkened and smell nutty.

Meanwhile, gently warm the honey in a small pot over low heat until it is easily pourable.

Drizzle the hot nuts with the walnut oil, and immediately transfer them to a glass mason jar. Add the rosemary sprig, and pour the warm liquid honey over the top. When the honey cools, cover the jar, and let it sit overnight.

When you are ready to serve, run the blade of a sharp knife under hot water, wipe it dry, and carefully cut six 1-ounce slices of the cheese; place them on six salad plates. (You may need to run the knife under water a few times during the slicing to get nice clean pieces.)

Spoon the honey and walnuts over and around the cheese, and sprinkle the cracked black pepper on top.

Blue cheese has such an inherently intense quality about it, with its strong flavor and powerful acidity. It is not a passive visitor on the palate and really needs to be countered with a wine that has depth and concentration. For this reason, I almost always pair blues with red wines, particularly those that have the right combination of richness and acidity to allow the flavors in the pairing to blend without becoming too heavy or cloying. For this recipe and its creamy, decadent use of Gorgonzola and honey, I like Valpolicella, a dark and brooding wine from the Verona region in Italy. This wine is a bit like Amarone—fairly concentrated, with pronounced fig and dark-plum notes, though higher in acidity and a bit lighter in body. Wines like these, with their black-fruit profiles and weight, will mimic the seductive texture of the torta, while the acidity will keep the pairing vibrant.

charcuterie

Because our intention was to be sort of a modern-day American wine bar, the charcuterie aspect of A.O.C. was a big part of our opening agenda. I remember, all those years back, asking our good friend, pizza genius Chris Bianco of Pizzeria Bianco in Phoenix, if he would consider coming out to L.A. to see our new space and give us some guidance on the wood oven. That same trip, Chris and I spoke a lot about charcuterie, our goals, the size of the space, and the health-department requirements for refrigerated rooms and aging caves at the time. He said something very wise to me, which was also very much in keeping with the idea that A.O.C. was to be a celebration of artisanal and special handcrafted products: "Why not use the dried salumi that other craftspeople are already making? Celebrate and support people who have chosen *that* as their one craft." It really made sense to me, and we decided at that time to focus on fresh charcuterie rather than the aged, dried, and cured variety.

For the opening of A.O.C., back in 2002, Julie Robles was my culinary partner in crime. We have a very long history, going back to Campanile in the old, *old* days. Julie was an opening sous-chef at Lucques in 1998, and the opening chef at Tavern in 2009—let's just say she is a powerhouse of a cook and manager, and one of my favorite people on earth. With her dry and very quick wit, Julie really tells you how it is, and with all that goes on during the opening of a restaurant, let's just say "how it is" is not always that pretty.

Months and months before opening, Julie and I tested terrines, stirred up rillettes, and hung sausages as we awaited build-out and final approval of the restaurant. Randomly, one Tuesday during those pre-opening days, there was a knock on the back door at Lucques. I opened it, and there stood a cute but serious-looking young Frenchman in a suit who announced, "Ehhh, I am Steef-han and I am the son and grandson of a sha-coo-teeh-ay en France." I could not believe it, and I was smitten! It was like he was sent from the heavens to infuse our restaurant with his traditional and very French ways.

You see, I'm a tragic Francophile, and sometimes I am blinded by Frenchness. Now, Stephan had all those stereotypical French traits that I spent years trying to convince my friends were all a myth. Yes, he had some wonderful recipes and definitely knew his way around a pig, but pretty soon he had me searching for apartments for him and even finding him a *bicyclette* in the local paper—it was all worth it, I convinced myself, for the rillons, rillettes, and, *mon dieu,* the foie-gras terrine. Julie, on the other hand, was having none of it. "The guy is a fucking asshole—that's all there is to it," she'd say.

Well, it all came to a head one night a few months in, after Stephan had managed to sleep with all the waitresses, delegate most of his work to the prep cook, and wear that once-adorable but now cologne-and-sweat-stained checkered shirt just one too many times; let's just say the charm had worn off. I was working the cheese bar that night, as was my normal routine, when Julie came barreling out from the kitchen. "He has outdone himself this time, Suzanne. Seriously, he has a giant stockpot in the walk-in, and I swear to you, there is a rotten cow's head in it, and it stinks!" I was too busy to leave my post, so I called on Stephan to ask him what was going on—"Oh, Juh-lee, you know she is crah-zee, eh? She has some prob-leem with me, ehhh, *je ne sais pas, mais* . . . it is fine, I assure you, the head is for my terrine, it's fine, this is how we do it in France!" I told Julie that it was fine and that Stephan had seen it. Well, Julie nearly blew her top! "*What?* Is he out of his mind? You come back in here right now and look at what I have to show you." Urgh, I thought to myself, why am I always the babysitter? Why can't everyone just get along? What is Julie's issue with Stephan anyway?

And then I smelled it. It was like a steaming cauldron of death itself. I literally had to pull my apron over my head to try to stop the stench. It was beyond foul, like walking into an unrefrigerated morgue! That was pretty much the end for Stephan, and as I heard Julie screaming at him down the back alley—"This is America, Stephan! We don't serve food that will fucking *kill* people . . . so you can take your stockpot of rotten animal heads and you know where you can put it"—I thought to myself, I don't know why I ever doubted Julie. I may not like what she has to say, but she's pretty much always right!

That said, a few of our most beloved recipes were developed with Stephan—Pork Rillettes with Pickled Onions and Cornichons and the amazing and forbidden, at least in our great state of California for the moment, Foie Gras Terrine with Sweet-and-Sour Prunes. And, I have to say, the whole fiasco made for a great story, and one that comes up time and time again after a few drinks.

chicken liver crostini with pancetta

12 slices pancetta, ⅛ inch thick

1 baguette

½ cup extra-virgin olive oil

1½ cups Chicken Liver Pâté
(recipe follows)

6 ounces frisée

¼ cup chopped flat-leaf parsley

¼ cup thinly sliced scallions

½ cup flat-leaf parsley leaves

1½ teaspoons sherry vinegar

Kosher salt and freshly ground
black pepper

I first made this chicken-liver dish for a Hanukkah dinner at Campanile—yes, a Hanukkah dinner with chicken liver and pancetta. Blame the goy in me, but I wasn't really thinking about religion, or holidays, or even taboos; I was just trying to make the most delicious chicken-liver pâté I could. I still remember Nancy Silverton's face when I had her taste it. "Wow!" she said. "That is delicious. It almost tastes like there is pork in it!" That night, we obviously couldn't serve my creation, so I made a slightly less delicious pork-free version instead, but I remember Nancy and me sitting on the counter in the back of the kitchen late that night, after service, red wine in hand, devouring the illicit liver ourselves!

Preheat the oven to 350°F.

Place the pancetta slices on a baking sheet, between two pieces of parchment paper. Place a second baking sheet on top, and cook in oven about 30 minutes, until the pancetta is crisp.

Cut the baguette on a diagonal into twelve ¼-inch-thick slices (each slice should be 6 inches long). Brush both sides generously with olive oil (about ¼ cup in all). Arrange the slices on a baking sheet, and toast them in the oven for 10 to 12 minutes, until golden and crispy but still tender in the center.

When the crostini have cooled, spread each one with 2 tablespoons chicken-liver pâté. Arrange a piece of pancetta on top of each crostini.

Place the frisée, chopped parsley, scallions, and parsley leaves in a mixing bowl, and drizzle with the sherry vinegar, remaining ¼ cup olive oil, salt, and pepper. Toss well, and taste for balance and seasoning.

Arrange half the salad on six salad plates. Place a crostini on each salad, then arrange half the remaining salad over the plated crostini. Lean the rest of the crostini up against the plated ones, and top with the remaining salad.

chicken liver pâté

Season the chicken livers with 1 teaspoon salt and ¼ teaspoon pepper.

Heat a large sauté pan over high heat for 2 minutes. Swirl in 2 tablespoons olive oil, and carefully place half the chicken livers in the pan without crowding them (you will need to do this in two batches). Cook the livers for a minute or two, until they are nicely caramelized, then turn them over and cook another minute or so, until they are medium-rare. Transfer the livers to a platter or baking sheet. Repeat with 2 tablespoons olive oil and the remaining livers.

Wipe the pan clean with paper towels, and return it to the stove and heat over medium heat for 1 minute. Swirl in 1 tablespoon olive oil, add the pancetta, and cook for about 5 minutes, stirring frequently, until the pancetta is tender and lightly crisped. Add the onion and thyme, and continue cooking for another 5 to 7 minutes, until the onion is translucent and beginning to caramelize. Transfer to a platter.

Wipe the pan clean with paper towels again, and return it to the stove over medium heat. Pour in the balsamic vinegar and reduce it to 1 tablespoon. Using a rubber spatula, scrape the reduced vinegar into the bowl of a food processor fitted with the metal blade.

Place two-thirds of the livers and two-thirds of the pancetta-onion mixture in the food processor. Process until the liver is completely puréed. With the machine running, add the butter, a little at a time, until it is completely incorporated. Transfer to a large mixing bowl, and stir in the sherry vinegar.

Place the remaining one-third of the livers and one-third of the pancetta-onion mixture on a cutting board, and roughly chop them together. Add to the puréed liver mixture, and stir with a rubber spatula to combine. Taste for balance and seasoning.

1 pound chicken livers, cleaned

5 tablespoons extra-virgin olive oil

¼ pound pancetta, finely diced

¾ cup finely diced white onion

2 teaspoons thyme leaves

¼ cup balsamic vinegar

¼ pound (1 stick) unsalted butter, cut into small cubes and slightly softened

1 tablespoon sherry vinegar

Kosher salt and freshly ground black pepper

I love pairing these crostini with a glass of Prosecco, the sparkling wine of the Veneto region in Italy. These wines, made in a style that is slightly fruitier and lighter in body than champagne, are fresh, lively, and festive. Their delicate peachiness blends with the sweet meat aspect of the chicken liver, while their mineral component and acidity reflect the salty gaminess of the pancetta. The sparkle gives the whole union of flavors a bright lift.

duck sausage with candied kumquats

Because this super-simple duck-sausage recipe has no spices and very few ingredients, the gamy, rich flavor of the duck itself is really the star. I like to make a big batch of the candied kumquats and keep it in the fridge at home. They are delicious spooned over roasted pork, grilled duck breast, and even over nut tarts and ice cream.

MAKES 8 SAUSAGES

NOTE You will need six bamboo skewers, 6 inches long, soaked in water for this recipe.

In a large mixing bowl, combine the duck, pancetta, fatback, white wine, 1 tablespoon salt, and 2 teaspoons freshly ground black pepper. Mix well, cover, and chill at least 4 hours or overnight.

Light the grill 30 to 40 minutes before cooking.

Grind the meat through a medium die, and stuff it into the lamb casings using a sausage stuffer. (You could also ask a butcher to do this for you, or serve the duck sausage as patties.)

Portion the sausage into 5-ounce links, and roll each one into a coil. Skewer each coil with a bamboo skewer.

Toss the frisée, mizuna, and chopped parsley with 2 tablespoons olive oil, the lemon juice, salt, and pepper. Arrange the salads on eight plates.

When the coals are broken down, red, and glowing, brush the sausages with remaining 1 tablespoon olive oil. Place the sausages on the grill, and cook for about 2 minutes. Give the sausages a quarter-turn, and cook for another minute. When they are nicely seared, turn the sausages over and cook another minute or two, until they are just medium. Place the sausages on the salads.

Spoon the candied kumquats and some of the syrup over and around the sausages.

2 pounds boneless, skinless duck leg meat, cleaned, cut into 1-inch chunks

6 ounces pancetta, diced

2 ounces pork fatback, diced

3 tablespoons white wine

3 feet lamb casings, soaked in cold water (optional)

4 ounces (1 head) frisée, cleaned and dried

2 ounces (1 bunch) mizuna, cleaned and dried

2 tablespoons chopped flat-leaf parsley

3 tablespoons extra-virgin olive oil

2 teaspoons freshly squeezed lemon juice

Candied Kumquats (recipe follows)

Kosher salt and freshly ground black pepper

candied kumquats

½ pound kumquats

1 cup sugar

Thinly slice the kumquats, and discard the seeds.

Place the kumquats in a clean, nonreactive pot, and add 1¼ cups water. Cover, and let sit 24 hours at room temperature.

Bring to a boil over medium heat, add the sugar, and stir constantly until the sugar is dissolved. Reduce the heat to low, and simmer about 15 minutes, until an instant-read thermometer reads 220°F. You can also check doneness by spooning a small amount onto a plate and seeing if it gels.

The contrast of this dish's gamy, meaty flavors and sweet, intense citrus makes for an exciting experience on the palate. And whereas I often pair duck with Pinot Noir, the sausage aspect of this recipe leads me to Syrah. California's Central Coast has become a wonderful region for this grape since winemakers have become savvy about keeping alcohol levels relatively low and acidity high. These wines have an exotic, gamy quality about them and work really well with similarly smoky, earthy meats. They also show notes of pepper and concentrated blackberry and cassis that highlight the kumquat in the recipe, while also taming its tartness.

pork rillettes with pickled onions and cornichons

This very rustic, spreadable pâté is my husband David's very favorite thing to eat at A.O.C. In the early (read: before children) days, he used to come in late, sit at the bar with a plate of rillettes and a half-bottle of white wine, and wait for me to be done. Rillettes, like so many of the great foods we love now, was a result of necessity rather than the whim of a particular chef. Centuries ago, before refrigeration, the technique of salting meat, slow-cooking it in its own fat, shredding and combining it with some of the fat, and finally pouring another layer of fat over the mixture was a way to preserve meat, which was only butchered in spring and fall, for consumption throughout the year.

This recipe is interesting in that it has none of the spices that many rillettes recipes call for—cloves, allspice, and such. Instead, this one is all about the pork—fatback, shoulder, and belly—tons of onion and shallots, and a generous pour of white wine. Cooking the rillettes on the stove gives it some caramelization, which is a nice counterpoint to the soft and luscious confited meat and the pork fat. The rillettes keeps for at least a few weeks, and I love it spread on grilled toast with a little of the pickled red onion and cornichons on top.

MAKES 1 TERRINE, SERVING 12

½ recipe Pork Rillettes (recipe follows)

Approximately 1 teaspoon fleur de sel

Approximately ½ teaspoon cracked black pepper

6 slices country bread, about ¾ inch thick

9 tablespoons extra-virgin olive oil

4 ounces frisée, cleaned and dried

¼ cup flat-leaf parsley leaves

Juice of ½ lemon (about 1 tablespoon)

½ recipe Pickled Red Onions (recipe follows)

½ cup cornichons

Kosher salt and freshly ground black pepper

Cut six slices of rillettes (about ½ inch thick), season them with fleur de sel and cracked black pepper, and arrange them on six dinner plates. Brush both sides of the sliced bread, using 6 tablespoons olive oil total, and toast on a grill or under the broiler. Cut the toasts in half on the diagonal.

Toss the frisée and parsley leaves with remaining 3 tablespoons olive oil, the lemon juice, ¼ teaspoon salt, and several grinds of pepper. Arrange the salad, pickled onions, toasts, and cornichons around the rillettes.

pork rillettes

This is one of those recipes that is a bit of work so I prefer to make this larger batch and have leftovers rather than cooking a half batch.

SERVES 12

NOTE You will need a 1¼-quart terrine mold for this recipe. The pork needs to marinate for 2 days before cooking.

NOTE If you don't have a 14-inch-wide pot, divide the mixture and cook it in two smaller pots. If the pot is too small the meat will get too caramelized and dry out.

3 chopped dried bay leaves

1 tablespoon finely chopped thyme leaves

1¼ pounds pork fatback, cut into ¼-inch dice

2½ pounds pork shoulder, cut into 1½-inch dice

2½ pounds pork belly, cut into 1½-inch dice

3 cups finely diced onions

2 cups finely diced shallots

2 cups white wine

Kosher salt and freshly ground black pepper

In a large bowl, combine 1 tablespoon kosher salt, ½ teaspoon freshly ground black pepper, the bay leaves, and the thyme.

Add the fatback, shoulder, and belly, and toss well to combine. Cover, and refrigerate for 2 days.

Heat a 14-inch stainless steel pot, Dutch oven, or equivalent oven-safe pot over low heat. Add the seasoned shoulder, belly, and fat to the pot. Cook about 1 hour, stirring often, until most of the fat renders.

Preheat the oven to 350°F.

Add the onions and shallots to the pot, and cook about 10 minutes, until translucent. Use a spatula to scrape down the sides of the pot so that nothing burns. Add the wine, and simmer for 15 minutes. Then transfer to the oven and cook for 2 to 3 hours, stirring every 30 minutes to prevent the top from browning. When you can squeeze a piece of shoulder between your fingers and it falls apart, it is done.

Strain the meat, reserving the fat. When the meat has cooled enough to handle, shred it with your fingers, and place in a large mixing bowl. Using your hands to work the meat, make sure the different cuts of pork are well combined. Add enough reserved fat to achieve a spreadable consistency, approximately ½ cup of fat depending on the meat.

Taste for seasoning, adjust, and then tightly pack the meat into the terrine. Firmly tap the terrine a few times on a table, to remove any air bubbles. Cover, and chill overnight.

pickled red onions

2 large red onions

1 cup red-wine vinegar

⅔ cup sugar

1 star anise

1 cinnamon stick

½ teaspoon black peppercorns

½ teaspoon whole cloves

1 chile de árbol

1 bay leaf, preferably fresh

Peel the onions, slice them into ½-inch-thick rings, and place in a clean, dry bowl or container.

Combine the remaining ingredients with 2 cups water in a medium non-reactive saucepan, and bring to a boil. Pour the hot liquid over the onions. Place an upside-down saucer or plate on top of the onions to keep them submerged.

Cover, and refrigerate for several hours or overnight.

This pork-rillettes recipe is a slice of earthy, fatty heaven. It has a soft, meaty flavor and rich texture, and when eaten with the pickled onions, it is the perfect mix of low and high on the palate. This is one of those instances when the goal in selecting a wine is to find one with enough acidity to cut through the richness of the food on the plate without dominating it. I normally opt for a white wine from France, which seems appropriate, since the recipe's preparation has its roots there. Bright, high-acid wines from the Languedoc-Roussillon region work really well. Here white wines are made from grape varieties like Marsanne, Roussanne, and Clairette that tend to show notes of ripe stone fruit and baking spices that will bring out the exotic spice notes in the pickled onions and the sweetness of the rillettes.

foie gras terrine with sweet-and-sour prunes

If you read the Stephan story in the chapter introduction, I want you to understand that this was the recipe that made it all worthwhile. Foie gras is one of the most ethereal, decadent, luxurious, and delicious foods there is, and though I love it sautéed (if the California state government would allow me to make my own decision about whether to eat it or not), my true love is foie gras *en terrine.* If you can manage to confiscate some of the illicit product (you will probably drive by a medical-marijuana shop en route), you will not be disappointed by spending the time it takes to make this preparation. Actually, the work is pretty easy; it's more the time you will have to wait for the foie to marinate and age. You will probably have some extra foie "oil," which is insanely good for sautéing potatoes or brushing on brioche toasts.

Warm the prunes to room temperature.

Using a hot knife, cut ½-inch-thick slices of foie gras and place them on six large dinner plates. Season each slice with a little cracked black pepper. Toss the wild arugula and herbs with salt, pepper, and the olive oil. Toast the brioche or baguette.

Arrange small salads and toasts next to each slice of terrine. Spoon the prunes onto the plates next to the foie gras and drizzle a little of the syrup over the foie gras.

1 cup Sweet-and-Sour Prunes (recipe follows)

½ recipe Foie Gras Terrine (recipe follows)

½ teaspoon cracked black pepper

1½ cups wild arugula, small arugula, or mizuna

¼ cup tarragon leaves

¼ cup ½-inch-snipped chives

¼ cup flat-leaf parsley leaves

1 tablespoon extra-virgin olive oil

1 loaf brioche or baguette, cut into ¼-inch-thick slices

Kosher salt and freshly ground black pepper

foie gras terrine

3¼ pounds Grade A foie gras

1½ tablespoons kosher salt

½ teaspoon freshly ground
    white pepper

1 teaspoon sugar

½ teaspoon pink preserving salt

½ teaspoon ascorbic acid

1½ cups whole milk

This is one of those recipes that is a bit of work so I prefer to make a larger batch and have leftovers rather than cooking a half batch.

MAKES 1 TERRINE SERVING 12

NOTE You will need a 1¼-quart terrine mold for this recipe. The foie gras needs to marinate for 2 days and the terrine is best after it has had at least a day to age.

Remove the foie gras from the refrigerator at least 1½ hours before preparing so it will be more malleable. Use your fingers and a paring knife to carefully remove the veins and any bloody spots.

Place the foie gras in a shallow glass or other nonreactive baking dish. Season the foie gras with the salt, white pepper, sugar, pink preserving salt, and ascorbic acid. Pour the milk over the foie gras, and toss gently. Cover tightly with plastic wrap, pressing out all the air so the plastic wrap sits on the surface of the milk and the foie gras. Refrigerate for 2 to 3 days.

When you are ready to cook the foie gras, preheat the oven to 225°F.

Remove the foie gras from the refrigerator, and strain off all the liquid. Cut a piece of cheesecloth big enough to hang 6 inches over the sides of the terrine on all sides. Line the terrine mold with the cheesecloth, tightly pack the foie gras into the terrine, and fold the cloth over the foie. Place the terrine in a roasting pan, and pour warm water into the pan to come halfway up the sides of the terrine. Bake, uncovered, about 1 hour (at this point, keep checking often to make sure you don't miss the magic moment), until a meat thermometer inserted into the center reads 105°F.

Remove the terrine carefully from the roasting pan, discard the water, and place the terrine back in the roasting pan. Cut a piece of cardboard to fit exactly over the top of the terrine and wrap the cardboard in plastic.

After the terrine has cooled for 15 minutes, place the cardboard over the foie gras and weight it down with a few soup cans. Some fat and liquid will overflow into the roasting plan. Chill the terrine with the weights (in the roasting pan) in the refrigerator for at least 2 days.

sweet-and-sour prunes

This recipe is adapted from one of my biggest idols, Paula Wolfert, whose *The Cooking of Southwest France* and *Paula Wolfert's World of Food* are two of my all-time favorite cookbooks.

MAKES 2½ CUPS

¾ pound pitted prunes

4 cups Earl Grey tea

1⅓ cups sugar

2 cups white-wine vinegar

1 cinnamon stick

1 star anise

Place the prunes and the tea in a nonreactive medium saucepan, and bring to a boil over medium-high heat. Simmer for 5 minutes, and then remove from the heat, let cool, and refrigerate overnight.

Strain the prunes, and discard the tea.

Place the sugar and vinegar in a nonreactive saucepan, and bring to a boil over medium-high heat. Add the cinnamon and star anise, and let simmer for 10 minutes. Pour the hot liquid over the prunes, let cool, and refrigerate overnight. Bring to room temperature before serving.

Ask most wine experts and they will say that the classic wine to drink with foie gras is Sauternes, the syruplike, golden dessert wine from the Bordeaux region of France. And though it may seem crazy to pair a wine that is on the sweeter, fruity side of the flavor spectrum with something so rich and luscious, it somehow works beautifully. The problem for me is that Sauternes can be fairly pricey and not always appropriate to drink at the beginning of a meal. A lovely alternative, and one that can be enjoyed throughout a meal, is Chenin Blanc. It is vinified on the sweeter side, like demi-sec and Moelleux Vouvray from the Loire Valley in France. These wines have similar concentrated candied-peach-and-nectarine notes, while also possessing enough balancing acidity to give the pairing a lift on the palate.

speck with apples, apple balsamic, and arugula

Speck can be a confusing matter. This cured and cold-smoked pork product comes from the South Tyrol region, which has gone back and forth between Italy and Austria throughout history. Although it is now part of Italy, called Alto Adige, the majority of its citizens speak German. Italian speck is made from pork leg, just like prosciutto, the difference being that it is boned and cut into smaller pieces, then cured with salt, a heady amount of juniper, garlic, nutmeg, bay, and other spices. *Speck* in German simply means "pork fat" and is used similarly to *lardo* in Italian. We use an Italian speck from Alto Adige called Recla. La Quercia in Iowa also makes a delicious version.

This simple recipe is really just about arranging perfect ingredients on the plate in a beautiful manner and letting them speak for themselves. Speck is a really interesting change from the more expected prosciutto or jamón Serrano and, paired with the apples, arugula, and apple balsamic, yields a triumphant union of deliciousness. I love the way the crispy apples play off the juniper, which always just reminds me of gin!

3 apples, such as Pink Lady, Honeycrisp, or other firm, crisp, and juicy varieties

4 ounces arugula, cleaned

18 very thin slices speck

¼ cup very good extra-virgin olive oil

2 tablespoons apple-balsamic vinegar (see Sources)

Core and thinly slice the apples.

Scatter most of the arugula on six dinner plates, reserving about six to eight leaves. Arrange two-thirds of the apple slices among the arugula leaves.

Drape the speck over and around the arugula and apples in a "wavy" manner, leaving some of the arugula peeking through. Tuck in the remaining arugula and apples to create a natural look. Drizzle the olive oil and then the apple balsamic over the salad.

This almost saladlike mix of tart apple, tangy vinegar, and slightly salty meat is really bright and vibrant and works well with a wine that shows a good dose of fruitiness to balance out the inherent acidity in the recipe. This is actually one of the few opportunities to recommend drinking Gewürztraminer. This grape variety has a perfumed sweetness with white flower and lychee fruit notes and oily texture that will be the pairing's anchor and cut through the vinegar's acidity. Gewürztraminer also originated in the Alto Adige region of Italy, which produces speck, so the pairing makes regional sense.

salads

It's funny that, in the restaurant world, the pantry or salad station is considered the entry-level spot—the unimpressive rookie station from which young cooks with aspirations are constantly striving to move on. With visions of the glamorous grill station and the hot line, they count their days and look for every chance and reason to move "up."

Of course, it makes absolute sense that this is the station where you start. With salads and cold dishes, you can focus on the flavor and presentation, the handling and "personalities" of delicate greens and produce, and the ever-important balance of sweet, sour, salt, bitter, and umami, that hard-to-describe savory meatiness. All this without having to think about the heat of your pan, the timing of a sauté, the glazing of a braise, or the avoidance of burning your own flesh. Before all that there is pantry, and pantry, to me, is a little bit like paradise. It is, in fact, my favorite station in the restaurant, and I venture to say that salads are my favorite thing to eat as well. I have found, over time, that the cooks who shine in the pantry station and truly love it tend to be the best cooks when they do get to the hot line, because appreciating seasoning and balance, understanding ingredients, and making the food look beautiful on the plate are what makes a great cook.

Even though I love the pace and passion of the pantry station at A.O.C., when I am cooking at home, in a hurry and desperate to get dinner on the table, I must confess I rarely make a vinaigrette. I fill my salad bowl with greens and spoon over a little yogurt, drizzle in some olive oil, squeeze in a lemon or two, sprinkle with salt and some freshly ground pepper, toss well, and taste. Or sometimes it's really as simple as balsamic vinegar and olive oil (and, of course, salt and pepper). If I'm in the mood, I stir a little Dijon mustard together with some red-wine vinegar and pour that over the lettuces, again following with olive oil, salt, and pepper. The key, of course, is tasting and adjusting until it's perfect. How do you know when it's perfect? Try adding a pinch more salt and taste again. Ask yourself, "Is it flat? Does it need more acid? Is there enough of that glossy, silky mouthfeel that comes from olive oil? Would a little spice of black pepper increase or balance the flavor?" There is no school for this—the "secret" is in tasting thoughtfully, adjusting accordingly, tasting again and again, until you are happy. A great cook is rarely hungry by the time the meal is on the table!

Having just said that I don't make dressings at home, I must confess that I have trained Alex, my six-year-old daughter, to be the house salad-maker. She doesn't use a recipe, either, but I measured it just for fun, because one night she made salad for a new babysitter, who exclaimed it to be the best salad she had ever tasted. It's funny to me that people don't know how to make a basic vinaigrette. Christine, our babysitter, actually asked Alex for the recipe, which made her beam, ear to ear. Now her brothers love to request "Alex's Famous Salad Dressing," and I promised it would be in the book. So here it is. . . .

alex's famous salad dressing

MAKES ½ CUP

1 teaspoon Dijon mustard
1 tablespoon sherry vinegar
1 tablespoon balsamic vinegar
Juice of ½ lemon (about 1 tablespoon)
¼ cup extra-virgin olive oil
Kosher salt and freshly ground black pepper

Whisk together the mustard, vinegars, and lemon juice with a pinch of salt and pepper, and then whisk in the olive oil.

At the restaurant, however, I *am* in charge of the dressings, and I love making vinaigrettes. I always find myself pounding, crushing, and smashing ingredients into them to reiterate or emphasize the flavor of a dish. Ripe figs mashed into a dressing, cherries crushed into a vinaigrette, and peaches blended with sherry vinegar all help elevate greens with slices of fruit tossed with them to a new level, where the fruit is more deeply integrated into the salad itself. Suddenly the diner is tasting the fruit in two or more different ways—his palate might not even know what he's tasting and why he's loving it, but the effect of deliciousness is achieved.

Backing up a little, where does the idea for a particular salad come from? I divide the salad world into leafy salads and more substantial ones made up of vegetables, fruits, and grains. Let's start with the leafy salads. These usually start with one or two star ingredients that I want to highlight or show off. This inspiration comes, of course, from whatever is growing abundantly and locally and whatever is at its peak. When avocado genius Peter Schaner's Reed avocados are coming in by the crate-full, I can't resist puréeing some of them into a creamy green dressing and pairing thick wedges of avocado with crispy little gem lettuces (to counter and complement the soft, silky, lush texture of the avocado) and Cara Cara oranges (which add acidity and a juicy bite to the creamy, rich avocado dressing). When I taste this all together, I want something else, one more element to bring the whole dish together. Could it be something crunchy (yes—pepitas, maybe)? But it might be nice to leave this one nut-free—there is so much richness in the avocado, nuts might actually distract. I want something bright and green, and I think about avocados and ways I like to eat them, and I think about the dressing—creamy and spiked with lime, like guacamole—and then it comes to me: I realize that it's whole cilantro leaves that I want, or that the salad wants, actually. They add an extra note, a surprise bite. I love adding whole leaves of herbs to dishes for this exact reason—you get a big hit, almost a little shock of flavor, and then you don't get it again for a few more bites, until you almost forget . . . and then there it is again. I love that!

Heartier salads, composed of grains, fruits, and vegetables, generally need less complicated dressings. I usually choose a pretty straightforward lemon- or lime-based dressing in the spring and summer, and red-wine vinegar or sherry vinegar in the winter. The brightness of citrus seems more in keeping with spring and summer produce, whereas the richer flavors of fall and winter need that spark of acid that comes from a more traditional and full-flavored vinegar.

Nowhere else in cooking is the art of balance more important and easier to spot than in a salad. First, there is the balance of acid to oil. Without enough acid, a salad is flabby and bland; without enough oil, it lacks luscious mouth-feel and can have a matte texture that is not pleasing to the palate. Choosing which acid to use is a major part of the process. I take inspiration from the ingredients, but as you've learned from Caroline already, I also think of the region by which a particular salad is inspired. I love using a more subtle vinegar, like rice or champagne vinegar, to supplement the acidity of orange, tangerine, or grapefruit in a dressing. The earthy sweetness of tomatoes pairs beautifully with sweet balsamic vinegar but benefits, too, from the addition of a big strong and savory red-wine vinegar—so I use a mix of the two. Anything with Spanish influence cries out for sherry vinegar, which is maybe my favorite of all vinegars, for its deep, earthy, and subtle notes. Avocado, corn, and cilantro basically *tell* you they need lime! And in the springtime, it only makes sense that all those bright-green vegetables are dressed with the precious Meyer lemons with which they share their season.

The next step in balancing salads is thinking about what each element in the dish is contributing to the whole. Stone fruit, summer corn, and roasted root vegetables all bring sweetness. Citrus, tomatoes, and capers bring acidity. Mustard, Parmigiano-Reggiano, and slices of cured meats bring umami. Anchovies, toasted salted nuts, and olives bring saltiness. Radicchio, grapefruit, and escarole bring bitterness. In the perfect salad, we don't necessarily need all five of these—in fact, I think all five would probably be too much—but we need sour, salt, and/or bitter to counter sweet, umami to bring depth and layers of flavor, and enough contrast and complement for a dish to sing.

I love the small tweaks and surprises that make simple-seeming dishes fantastic. The crunch of the cumin seeds in the Peach and Arugula Salad with Burrata takes it to another level and dimension. The cumin plays on the exotic notes of the peach, which pairs nicely, and region-appropriately, with the almonds. A surprise bite of diced jalapeño in the dressing of the corn-and-avocado salad brightens the palate but also reminds us (without our thinking about it consciously) of the very Mexican pairing of corn and avocado. Salty, intense black olives change the mood and tone of sweet roasted carrots, while the dandelion, which might be too bitter on its own, cuts the carrots' sugar, and the carrots tame the dandelion's bitterness. Sherry vinegar works its magic in unifying the trio, and the salty, crumbly, and rich ricotta salata brings the whole dish together. It's important to think about texture, too. Crunchy toasted croutons are a happy treasure found in the leaves of Young Escarole with Anchovy Dressing. Toasted pecans, especially when tossed with olive oil and salt right out of the oven, add another savory flavor and textural dimension to Arugula and Autumn Grapes with Goat Cheese, Pecans, and Saba Vinaigrette.

Suddenly this "simple," "entry level" station is not seeming so simple anymore. It's a micro-example of great cooking itself. All these small, thoughtful choices, all the tasting and balancing, the artful plating of beautiful ingredients, is what food and cooking are really about. I encourage you, next time you make a salad, to think carefully about your choices and pairings, to push yourself a little to make that salad as delicious and interesting as it can possibly be. Plate it naturally, beautifully, and with respect. And most of all, taste, taste, taste.

grilled leeks and artichokes with burrata and salbitxada

I love traditions, especially bizarre food-related ones, so *salbitxada* is right up my alley. Every spring, in the Catalonia region of Spain, the masses gather for Calçotada, or "feast of local grilled spring onions." The revered onions, called *calçots,* are served up with bowlfuls of a delicious chunky tomato-almond-chile salsa called *salbitxada.* I have to love any culture that can get so worked up over the deliciousness of grilled spring onions that they actually create a festival around them—the family tree says otherwise, but surely I must have a Catalan gene in there somewhere. In this recipe, I substitute baby leeks and artichokes, which come to our southern-California markets early in the spring. Feel free to substitute scallions, spring onions, asparagus, or virtually any vegetable. It would be delicious in the summertime with grilled summer squash, peppers, and eggplant; or in fall or winter with roasted root vegetables and sweet winter squash.

18 baby artichokes

½ lemon (optional, for prepping artichokes in advance)

12 small or 6 large leeks

Approximately ½ cup extra-virgin olive oil

1 teaspoon thyme leaves

1 pound burrata cheese

4 ounces young dandelion greens, cleaned

1 recipe Salbitxada (recipe follows)

Kosher salt and freshly ground black pepper

Light the grill 30 to 40 minutes before you are ready to cook.

Cut off the top third of the artichokes, and remove the tough outer leaves until you reach the soft, pale-yellow-green leaves. Using a paring knife, trim the bottom of the stem, and cut any dark, bitter pieces away from where the stem meets the heart. Cut each artichoke in half, and remove the fuzzy choke if there is one. (If you do this step ahead of time, you can place the artichokes in a bowl of cold water for up to 4 hours with a squeeze of lemon juice to prevent browning. Make sure to dry the artichokes completely before cooking them.)

To clean the leeks, begin by removing any bruised outer layers. Trim the roots, leaving the root end intact so the leeks won't fall apart. Cut the leeks in half lengthwise, and submerge in a large bowl of cold water to clean them. Shake the leeks well to dislodge any dirt stuck inside. Soak the leeks for a few minutes, to allow any grit inside the layers to fall to the bottom of the bowl. Repeat the process until the water is clean. Place the leeks cut-side down on a towel, and pat dry completely.

Heat a large sauté pan over high heat for 2 minutes. Pour ¼ cup olive oil into the pan, and wait a minute. Add the artichokes cut-side down, and season with the thyme, 1 teaspoon salt, and a pinch of pepper. Reduce the heat to medium, and sauté for about 8 to 10 minutes, tossing often, until the artichokes are golden brown. (If the pan seems dry, add another tablespoon or two of olive oil.)

When the coals break down, turn red, and glow, brush the leeks with 3 to 4 tablespoons olive oil, and season on all sides with 1 teaspoon of salt and a few grindings of black pepper.

Place the leeks cut-side down on the grill, and cook for 3 to 4 minutes, rotating them once or twice, until they are nicely colored on the cut side. Carefully turn the leeks over, and move them to a cooler part of the grill. (If the tops start to burn, place them on a folded piece of aluminum foil.) Cook for a few more minutes, until the leeks are tender. If the leeks are particularly big, you can remove them to a baking sheet and finish cooking them in a 375°F oven.

Cut the burrata into twelve slices, and place two slices on each of six plates at the ten o'clock and three o'clock spots. Season the cheese with a few grinds of black pepper. Scatter several dandelion leaves around each plate, and nestle the leeks and artichokes in and around the burrata and greens. While lifting and twirling the leek tops, spoon about ¼ cup of the *salbitxada* over, under, and around the leeks, artichokes, and cheese.

salbitxada

Traditionally, *salbitxada* is made in a mortar with a pestle, but after trying it every which way, we at A.O.C. finally concluded that we prefer it hand-chopped. You can use a food processor if you like but the result is a little muddier and not as "clean." I love this recipe so much that I usually make a double batch so I can have some the next day. Try it spooned over grilled fish, roasted chicken, leg of lamb, or grilled steaks.

MAKES 1½ CUPS

1 pound ripe tomatoes, or 1 cup finely diced San Marzano canned tomatoes

2 cloves garlic, minced

1 jalapeño, finely diced

1 tablespoon red-wine vinegar

½ cup extra-virgin olive oil

1 tablespoon chopped flat-leaf parsley

3 tablespoons Marcona almonds, roughly chopped

Kosher salt and freshly ground black pepper

If you are using fresh tomatoes, make a shallow cross in the bottom of each one, and blanch them in boiling water for 30 seconds. Cool the tomatoes in a bowl of ice water for a few minutes, and then use your fingers to slip off their skins. Remove the cores, finely dice the tomatoes (if using canned, just drain and dice), and place them in a medium mixing bowl with the garlic, the diced jalapeño, ½ teaspoon salt, and a few grinds of black pepper.

Whisk in the vinegar, olive oil, and parsley. Stir the almonds in and taste for balance and seasoning.

I take my cue in pairing wine with this dish from *salbitxada*, the condiment's Catalan roots, and the fairly extensive array of wines made in the area. This Spanish accompaniment has a degree of heat and brightness that would make the perfect match for a firm yet light-bodied red. Wines made from Garnacha and Cariñena, from the region of Montsant, have a fruitiness that can highlight the sweetness and smoke in the grilled leeks, and enough tannin and structure to handle the *salbitxada*'s spicy kick.

sweet pea pancakes with dungeness crab and red onion crème fraîche

These green spring-flavored pancakes topped with crab and crème fraîche are the perfect starter for a spring meal. I love to serve them as passed appetizers or with cocktails and apéritifs as well. My son Jack, the family carb-monster, loves these pancakes so much that I have taken to making them for dinner, served with a big sauté of spring vegetables on top. They are good at room temperature or warmed.

NOTE You can make the pancake batter a few hours in advance and hold it in the refrigerator until you are ready to cook the pancakes.

Submerge the diced red onion in a small bowl of ice water for 5 minutes. Drain the onion, and dry well with paper towels. This will remove some of the harsh sting of the onion. In a small mixing bowl, combine the red onion, crème fraîche, 1 teaspoon Meyer lemon juice, ½ teaspoon salt, and a pinch of pepper. Taste for balance and seasoning. In a large bowl, toss the crab gently with 3 tablespoons of the red-onion-and-crème-fraîche mixture, the sugar snap peas, 1 tablespoon plus 1 teaspoon Meyer lemon juice, 1 tablespoon olive oil, and the parsley. Taste for balance and seasoning.

Arrange three pancakes on each of six salad plates, and top each one with a generous spoonful of crab. Scatter the watercress around the plate, and top each pancake with a dollop of the red-onion crème fraîche. Drizzle the remaining 1 tablespoon olive oil over and around the pancakes, and then squeeze a little Meyer lemon juice over the dish as well.

1 heaping tablespoon very finely diced red onion

¾ cup crème fraîche

2 tablespoons Meyer lemon juice (about 2 Meyer lemons)

½ pound picked-over steamed Dungeness crabmeat

½ cup thinly sliced sugar snap peas (1½ ounces total)

2 tablespoons extra-virgin olive oil

2 tablespoons finely chopped flat-leaf parsley

18 Sweet Pea Pancakes (recipe follows)

1 bunch watercress, cleaned

Kosher salt and freshly ground black pepper

sweet pea pancakes

1½ tablespoons unsalted butter, plus 2 teaspoons for each pancake pan

2 cups English peas (from about 1¼ pounds in pod)

1 extra-large egg

1 extra-large egg yolk

½ cup heavy cream

6 tablespoons all-purpose flour

Kosher salt and freshly ground black pepper

In a small sauté pan, cook 1½ tablespoons butter over medium heat 2 to 3 minutes, until it browns and smells nutty. Set aside to cool.

Blanch the peas in boiling water for 30 seconds. Cool the peas in a bowl of ice water for a few minutes, strain, dry well, and transfer them to the bowl of a food processor fitted with a metal blade. Purée the peas about 20 seconds, to a chunky consistency, and then add the egg, egg yolk, and cream. Purée to a not-quite-smooth texture, and transfer to a mixing bowl. Whisk in the flour, the reserved brown butter, 1 teaspoon salt, and some pepper. Taste for seasoning.

Heat a griddle or nonstick pan over high heat for 1 minute. (You may want to cook the pancakes in two or more pans.) Swirl 2 teaspoons butter into each pan, turn the heat down to medium, and when the butter foams, ladle tablespoonfuls of batter into each pan and cook about 4 minutes, until the pancakes are golden brown around the edges. Flip the pancakes, and cook another 3 minutes until set.

To pair wine with this dish, I look for one that mirrors the briny saltwater flavor inherent in the Dungeness crab, while also complementing the bright, sweet, and savory quality of the pea pancakes. I recently fell in love with the complex and aromatic wines from the island of Ischia, off the southern coast of Italy. These wines are made from indigenous Italian varieties, such as Biancolella, Forastera, San Lunardo, and Uva Rilla, and have delicate stone-fruit notes and lively acidity. These wines really convey the flavors and aromas of their vineyards' seaside locations, displaying a distinctive and clean saltiness akin to that in the crab.

spring vegetable salad with farro and meyer lemon

This recipe actually makes six main-course portions. You can easily cut it in half, but I'm always happy to have it in the fridge.

When we first opened, more than 10 years ago, we used to have to explain to every table, "Farro is an ancient grain popular in Roman times; it's similar to spelt or wheatberries." Now my favorite grain has been, for better or for worse, discovered, and it's not so hard to find anymore. No matter how many times I stray to quinoa, kasha, millet, or barley, I always come back to my true love—nutty, earthy, chewy farro. In this dish, I treat the farro like bulgur wheat in the classic tabbouleh preparation and toss it with a parsley-mint dressing that really soaks into the grains. For spring, the farro is topped with a salad of asparagus, peas, sugar snaps, and fennel, but really whatever vegetables you have in season work wonderfully. In summer, I would swap out basil for the mint and serve this with eggplant, tomatoes, and peppers; in fall or winter, roasted squash, chickpeas, radicchio, persimmons, and pomegranate would make us a hearty main-course dish as well.

6 tablespoons extra-virgin olive oil

½ cup diced onion

1 tablespoon thyme leaves

2 cups farro

½ cup English peas

½ cup sugar snap peas, sliced on the diagonal into ¼-inch-thick pieces

9 small or 3 medium carrots, peeled

1 bunch asparagus, trimmed and sliced on diagonal into 2-inch-long pieces

1 small bulb fennel

1 large Meyer lemon

Approximately 1 cup Parsley-Mint Dressing, as needed (recipe follows)

2 tablespoons lemon juice, plus more as needed

2 to 3 ounces tender pea shoots

¼ pound French feta, crumbled

Kosher salt and freshly ground black pepper

Heat a large saucepan over medium heat for 1 minute. Swirl in 2 tablespoons olive oil, the diced onion, and thyme. Cook, stirring often, 3 to 4 minutes, until the onion is translucent. Add the farro, stirring to coat it with the oil and toast it slightly. Add 10 cups of water and 2 teaspoons kosher salt, and bring to a boil. Turn the heat to low, and simmer for about 30 minutes, until the farro is tender and just cooked through. Strain the farro, and transfer it to a baking sheet to cool.

Blanch the English peas in salted boiling water for about 1 minute, until just tender. Shock them in ice water, drain, and dry on paper towels. Place the peas in a large bowl, with the sugar snap peas and the cooled farro.

Slice the carrots in half lengthwise, leaving the stems attached. If they are on the bigger side, cut each half in two, and then slice them lengthwise to resemble small carrots. Place the carrots in a large bowl and add the asparagus.

Trim the root end of the fennel, cut the stalks off where they meet the bulb, and peel off any outer layers that are brown or bruised. Cut the bulb in half lengthwise, leaving the core intact. Place the halves cut-side down on a cutting board, and slice the fennel thinly lengthwise. Add the fennel to the carrots and asparagus.

Slice the stem and blossom end from the Meyer lemon. Stand the lemon on one end, and cut it vertically into ⅛-inch slices. Stack the slices in small piles on a cutting board, and cut them lengthwise into ⅛-inch-thick matchsticks. Line up the matchsticks, and cut them into ⅛-inch cubes.

Add the chopped Meyer lemon to the bowl with the farro, sugar snap peas, and English peas. Pour about 1 cup parsley-mint dressing over the mixture, season with salt and pepper, and toss well to combine. Add more dressing, lemon juice, salt, and pepper to taste if needed. Spoon the farro onto six dinner plates.

Toss the fennel, carrots, and asparagus with 2 tablespoons lemon juice, the remaining ¼ cup olive oil, salt, and pepper. Toss in the pea shoots.

Arrange the vegetables on the farro, and crumble the feta over the top.

parsley-mint dressing

MAKES 1¼ CUPS

2 bunches flat-leaf parsley

1 cup mint leaves

1 clove garlic

¼ cup freshly squeezed lemon juice (from about 2 lemons)

½ cup extra-virgin olive oil

Kosher salt and freshly ground black pepper

Place the parsley, mint, garlic, lemon juice, 1 teaspoon salt, some black pepper, and half the oil in the blender. Turn on at low speed, and then quickly turn up to high, and pour in the rest of the oil. Taste for balance and seasoning.

There are certain ingredients in every recipe—various herbs, nuts, and vegetables—that really stand out for me and serve as the driving force in my wine-pairing decisions. In this recipe, my inspiration is the powerful punch of Meyer lemon, and its particularly deep, relatively rich flavor, for which I try to find a wine with equal vibrancy and depth. Sauvignon Blanc from New Zealand, and Sancerre from the Loire Valley in France both have a citrus-based intensity of flavor and power similar to that of the Meyer lemon. That, along with bright-green herbal notes of mint and parsley, allows the wine to complement the spring vegetables while standing up to the boldness of the vinaigrette.

arugula and cherries with pickled rhubarb
and fresh ricotta

Cherries are one of the last fruits with a truly short season—they always come on before I expect them, so I think, "Really? Cherries already?" Then, just when I figure out the perfect thing to do with them, they are gone! This salad was created by A.O.C. Chef de Cuisine Lauren Herman, and I think it's genius. I'm always looking for ways to use rhubarb, especially ways that avoid what can be a mushy consistency when it's cooked. Lauren really nailed it here—she cuts the rhubarb into small matchsticks, and then blanches it super-quickly in a well-seasoned pickling mixture. The rhubarb tastes almost raw and has a beautiful crunch and fresh, acidic, springy flavor. Both the cherries and rhubarb are pounded into the dressing—this girl knows how to integrate!—and then the cherries are tossed in while the rhubarb is scattered on top. If you have access to a good fresh ricotta (the supermarket stuff in the tubs will *not* work), use it. Otherwise, a fresh goat cheese or nice triple crème would also be divine.

2 tablespoons finely diced shallots, plus 2 small shallots, thinly sliced

1½ tablespoons sherry vinegar

1½ cups pitted cherries (about ⅓ pound unpitted)

½ cup Pickled Rhubarb (recipe follows)

½ cup extra-virgin olive oil

6 ounces arugula, cleaned and dried

6 ounces fresh ricotta or goat cheese

Kosher salt and freshly ground black pepper

Place the diced shallot, sherry vinegar, and ½ teaspoon salt in a bowl, and let sit 5 minutes. Using a mortar and pestle, pound ½ cup cherries to a coarse purée. Transfer to the shallot mixture, and repeat with 2 tablespoons pickled rhubarb. Whisk in the olive oil, and taste for balance and seasoning.

In a large salad bowl, toss the arugula, sliced shallots, and remaining cherries with the dressing, and season with salt, pepper, and a little of the rhubarb-pickling liquid if you like. Taste for balance and seasoning.

Arrange the salad on six plates, placing the cherries among the arugula leaves. Taste the cheese, and season it with salt and pepper as needed. Tuck little finger-fulls of the cheese into the leaves, and scatter the remaining pickled rhubarb around the salad.

pickled rhubarb

1 teaspoon juniper berries

1 teaspoon coriander seed

3 cloves

1 star anise

½ teaspoon black peppercorns

1 sprig thyme

1 chile de árbol

1 bay leaf, preferably fresh

1 cup sugar

1 cup champagne vinegar

½ pound rhubarb

The key here is not to overcook the rhubarb, so you keep that crunch and fresh fruit flavor. Try this pickled rhubarb with rillettes, terrines, and cured meats. It also makes a nice garnish for a light grilled fish dish served with a simple salad or green soubise (see page 114).

MAKES 2 CUPS

Place the juniper, coriander, cloves, star anise, black peppercorns, thyme, chile, and bay leaf in a cheesecloth sachet, tie with kitchen string, and place in a medium nonreactive pot with the sugar, vinegar, and 2 cups water.

Bring the mixture to a boil over high heat, turn down to a simmer, and reduce by a quarter.

Meanwhile, peel the rhubarb with a peeler, and cut it into 2-inch-by-¼-inch matchstick shapes. You should have 2 cups of prepared rhubarb. Add the rhubarb to the pot, turn off the heat, and wait 2 minutes. Strain the rhubarb immediately, reserving the liquid, and chill the rhubarb and the liquid separately.

When the rhubarb and the liquid are both completely cold, stir them together. Store in the refrigerator, ideally in a glass jar. The pickled rhubarb will last at least two weeks.

The minute I see cherries as an ingredient in a recipe, I immediately think of Pinot Noir. Cherries work so well with this grape variety because the essence of a cherry's taste, the high-toned red-fruit and dark-black juicy notes, is at the core of Pinot Noir's flavor profile. This is particularly true of the wines of California's Russian River Valley, where high-quality Pinot Noir is grown, and where the wines are known to have a distinctive cherry fruit quality. This region produces super-vibrant, seductive wines that, along with the distinct fruitiness, have great acidity, thanks to the region's proximity to the coast and the ocean's cooling influence. This bright quality works well with the salad's salty, pickled elements.

corn, summer squash, and avocado with chile-lime dressing

This salad is a pseudo-Mexican take on succotash. The chile-lime dressing gives it a nice punch of acid and spice, while the avocado and cilantro guide your palate blissfully toward Baja. You could add some grilled shrimp, crabmeat, or chopped chicken, and some more greens, to create a light summer supper. I find myself drizzling the chile-lime dressing over fish and tossing it with all kinds of summer vegetables this time of year. The vegetables can be prepped and sautéed way in advance, making this an easy dish to serve up quickly. I love vegetable salads—tossing cold roasted and grilled vegetables is a great way to turn last night's leftovers into a delicious and brightly flavored lunch or dinner.

¾ cup plus 1 tablespoon extra-virgin olive oil

3 cups fresh corn (from about 4 ears)

2 teaspoons thyme leaves

2 tablespoons finely diced shallots

2 to 3 tablespoons seeded, diced jalapeños

¼ cup freshly squeezed lime juice (about 2 limes)

½ pound summer squash

2 ripe avocados

¼ cup sliced spring onion

¼ cup chopped cilantro

1 bunch watercress, cleaned, tough stems removed

Kosher salt and freshly ground black pepper

Heat a large sauté pan over medium heat for 2 minutes. Add 3 tablespoons olive oil, the corn, the thyme, 1 teaspoon salt, and ¼ teaspoon pepper. Sauté quickly, tossing often, for about 2 minutes, until the corn is just tender. Remove to a platter or baking sheet to cool.

While the corn cools, make the vinaigrette. Combine the shallots, jalapeños, lime juice, and ½ teaspoon salt in a small bowl, and let sit 5 minutes. Whisk in remaining ½ cup olive oil. Taste for balance and seasoning.

Thinly slice the squash on the diagonal on a mandoline.

Cut the avocados in half lengthwise, remove the pits, and peel. Cut into ¼-inch-thick slices, and season with salt and freshly ground black pepper.

In a large bowl, toss the cooked corn, squash, spring onion, chopped cilantro, salt, and pepper with the chile-lime dressing. Gently toss in the watercress, and taste for seasoning.

Divide half the salad among six plates. Layer in the wedges of avocado, and then finish with the remaining corn salad.

I am not one to shy away from venturing to outlying or unusual wine regions to find a delicious wine for the list, or to achieve perfect pairing for one of Suzanne's dishes. This recipe is no exception. Its Southwestern influence immediately makes me think of the up-and-coming wineries in the state of New Mexico, where, surprisingly, some of the highest-altitude vineyards in the United States are planted and some really outstanding wines are being produced. Pinot Noir grown there shows bright red cherry fruit and spice notes, as well as fairly racy acidity, from the cold nights in those higher elevations. These wines tend to have a soft fruitiness to them—the result of hot summer growing temperatures—allowing them enough sweetness to complement the corn as well as body to handle the slight kick of heat from the combination of chile and lime. Of course, these wines can be fairly hard to find. So, when you are looking for other options, Pinot Noirs from California's Sonoma Coast, with their elegant fruitiness and high levels of acidity, will fit the bill.

fattoush salad with fried pita, cherry tomatoes, crumbled feta, and sumac

3 pita breads

¾ cup extra-virgin olive oil

1 clove garlic

¼ cup freshly squeezed lemon juice (about 2 lemons)

2 tablespoons heavy cream

2 large heads romaine lettuce

1 small red onion

3 Persian cucumbers, or 1 hothouse cucumber

1 pint cherry tomatoes

¼ cup chopped flat-leaf parsley, plus ½ cup whole flat-leaf parsley leaves

¼ pound feta cheese, crumbled

¼ cup mint leaves

1 tablespoon ground sumac

Kosher salt and freshly ground black pepper

Fattoush is the Arabic word for a traditional salad made in most Middle Eastern countries, originally as a vehicle to use up stale leftover pita bread. I think I must just be a leftover lover, because so many of my favorite foods—stuffings, daubes, terrines, meringues—all evolved from using up excess or old product so it wouldn't go to waste. Traditionally, the stale pita is torn into bigger-than-bite-sized pieces, fried, and then tossed with lettuces and seasonal vegetables.

I'm sure there are as many "recipes" for *fattoush* as there are cooks, but I credit the key to our delicious version to Brian Wolff—one of our A.O.C. chefs in the early days, who was determined to make a better *fattoush* than the one he ate every Sunday at the local Middle Eastern restaurant in his San Fernando Valley neighborhood. Besides, of course, the super-farm-fresh ripe and crispy ingredients, the secret behind this salad is the dressing—and it's the touch of cream in the dressing that really brings this *fattoush* to greatness.

For me there are two types of salads, the ones that need to be gently and carefully tossed, and the more rugged ones with bold-flavored dressings—like escarole with anchovies and Parmesan, the farro salad with spring vegetables, and this *fattoush,* which I like to toss *really* well, almost massaging the dressing into the greens and other components. The flavors and textures really need to be brought together and integrated to create one glorious whole. It's amazing to me that you can give the same ingredients, and even the same dressing, to two different cooks, and, between the seasoning and the way the salad is dressed and tossed, you can end up with two very different results. So remember to toss this salad well; get your hands in there, make sure every element is getting well coated, and taste. You actually want the tomatoes to break up a tiny bit, so their juices meld with the creamy lemon dressing and bring all the flavors of the salad together.

Preheat the oven to 400°F.

Tear the pita bread into rustic 1-inch pieces, and toss, using your hands, with ¼ cup olive oil until the pita is well coated and saturated. Spread on a baking sheet, and toast for about 20 minutes, tossing once or twice, until the pita squares are golden and crispy. (You can also deep-fry the pita if you like.)

Using a mortar and pestle (or the side of a knife on a cutting board), smash the garlic clove to a paste with a little salt, and then transfer it to a mixing bowl. Add the lemon juice and a heaping ¼ teaspoon salt to the bowl. Whisk in the remaining ½ cup olive oil, and the cream. Taste for balance and seasoning.

Cut each head of romaine in half lengthwise, and place them cut-side down on a cutting board. Make three long slices lengthwise, then turn the romaine and chop across the slices into ½-inch-sized pieces. Clean the lettuce, spin it dry, and place in a large mixing bowl.

Thinly slice the onion. Cut the cucumbers in half lengthwise, and cut them on the diagonal into ¼-inch-thick slices. Cut the cherry tomatoes in half. Add the onion, cucumbers, and tomatoes to the romaine, and toss with the dressing, the chopped parsley, toasted pita, half the feta, ¼ teaspoon salt, and some freshly ground pepper. Taste for balance and seasoning. Gently toss in the whole parsley and mint leaves, and arrange on six dinner plates. Sprinkle the remaining 2 ounces feta and the sumac over the top of the salads.

This is one of my all-time favorite A.O.C. salads, and one that I have probably eaten over a hundred times. Though the crispy pita adds an indulgent, rich crunch, the essence of this salad is very clean, calling for a wine that is similarly so. I've found that the best match for this dish is a white wine with a savory core and notes of bright-green herbs, like Assyrtiko from Greece, which is lean, refreshing, and kind of unfruity. The wine almost becomes an extension of the salad, creating a seamless connection between the two, while also allowing the sweetness of the tomatoes to shine through.

heirloom tomatoes with marinated labneh, purslane, and green harissa

Every summer, we obviously *have* to have an heirloom-tomato salad, so as the years go by I definitely feel the pressure to come up with new ways to show off these summer treasures. This version has a North African bent, using green harissa as the dressing—the green cousin of the classic condiment harissa, made with green (fresh) chiles rather than red (dried) ones and lots of fresh green herbs. The cumin and caraway give it an exotic, not-so-familiar note that I love. The harissa is spooned over the salad at the end, so the beautiful tomatoes and the bright harissa don't get mucky or murky-looking.

NOTE The labneh must hang in the cheesecloth for 3 days to dry out, so be sure to plan ahead.

Stem the cherry tomatoes, and cut them in half. Core the heirloom tomatoes. Cut half of them into wedges, and set them aside. Then, one by one, hold the remaining tomatoes on their sides and cut them into ¼-inch-thick slices. Season the slices with the fleur de sel and some pepper. Divide the slices among six dinner plates. Place the tomato wedges, cherry tomatoes, and the purslane in a large bowl, season with ½ teaspoon salt and a few grindings of pepper, and toss with the olive oil and the lemon juice. Taste for seasoning, and arrange the tomato wedges on the plates, piling them up in the center so the slices peek through. Carefully place three labneh balls on each salad, nestling them between the leaves. Spoon a generous amount of the green harissa over and around the tomatoes and cheese.

½ pint cherry tomatoes

2½ pounds heirloom tomatoes

1 teaspoon fleur de sel

1 bunch purslane, thick stems removed, to equal about 1 cup small sprigs, washed and dried

2 tablespoons extra-virgin olive oil

1 tablespoon freshly squeezed lemon juice

18 Marinated Labneh Balls (recipe follows)

Green Harissa (recipe follows)

Kosher salt and freshly ground black pepper

marinated labneh balls

Scant 2 tablespoons sliced
green garlic

2½ cups labneh

1 tablespoon freshly squeezed
lemon juice

1 cup plus 2 tablespoons
extra-virgin olive oil

3 sprigs thyme

2 chiles de árbol, broken in half

2 bay leaves, preferably fresh

Kosher salt

Labneh is the Middle Eastern term for strained yogurt that has a cheeselike consistency. Straining the yogurt removes the whey and results in a super-rich and creamy texture without the addition of any more fat or calories. "Greek yogurt" is made using the same process, which is why the nonfat version of this now popular yogurt is thicker and richer than even a full-fat traditional yogurt.

For this recipe, we pound green garlic, combine it with the labneh, and then strain *that*, to achieve a drier consistency, so we can then roll the cheeselike result into balls and marinate them. The labneh balls (for lack of a better term, and I can promise you I have tried to come up with one) look like little balls of mozzarella, but they have a dense texture and the bright, sour flavor of a very intense yogurt. This is another one of those recipes where I would say that, if you are going to the trouble to make it, make a bigger batch and use the remainder for other salads, mezze, and sandwiches. You can substitute scallions for the green garlic if you prefer.

NOTE Labneh is available at Middle Eastern markets and is worth seeking out, but if you can't find it, use a thick Greek yogurt.

Using a mortar and pestle, pound the green garlic with 1 teaspoon salt to a paste. Transfer to a medium bowl, and stir in the labneh, lemon juice, and 2 tablespoons olive oil. Taste for seasoning.

Cut a large square of cheesecloth, and place the labneh mixture at the center. Bring the corners of the cloth together to create a sack, and tie it closed with string.

Hang the sack in the refrigerator (you can tie the string to the upper rack or shelf), with a bowl underneath to catch the liquid, and leave it for 3 days.

When you are ready to shape the labneh balls, pour the remaining cup of olive oil into an 8-by-8-inch shallow earthen or ceramic dish. Add the thyme sprigs, chiles, and bay leaves. Open the cheesecloth sack and, using your hands, roll the labneh into 1-inch balls; place the balls carefully in the herb-scented olive oil as they are finished. Don't shake or agitate the dish too much or the balls will start to break and the oil will get cloudy. The labneh balls will keep at least a week in the oil. Reuse the oil to dress salads, brush on bread for grilling, or marinate more labneh balls.

green harissa

In this sauce, I substitute green versions of all the traditionally red ingredients in the North African condiment harissa.

MAKES ABOUT ¾ CUP

1 teaspoon cumin seeds

1 teaspoon caraway seeds

1 clove garlic

3 jalapeños, seeds removed but saved

1½ cups cilantro leaves, cleaned and dried

½ cup flat-leaf parsley leaves, cleaned and dried

⅔ cup extra-virgin olive oil

Kosher salt

Toast the cumin seeds in a small pan over medium-high heat for about 2 minutes, until they release their aroma and are lightly browned. Pound them coarsely in a mortar. Repeat with the caraway seeds, and transfer both seeds to a bowl. Pound the garlic with 1 teaspoon salt, and add to the bowl.

Place the jalapeños, cilantro, and parsley in the bowl of a food processor. Purée until finely minced. Add the garlic and cumin and caraway seeds, and then, with the machine running, slowly pour in the olive oil. Taste for balance and seasoning. If you would like it to be spicier, add some of the reserved jalapeño seeds.

The thing that I focus on when pairing wine with this salad is the delicious contrast between the über-sweetness of ripe heirloom tomatoes and the vibrant tang and creamy texture of the labneh. I shy away from wines that are too aggressive, such as Sauvignon Blanc, for fear that the acids in all these elements will clash and become overpowering. Sometimes you need restraint. For this reason, I veer toward a wine like Chablis, which has an inherent milky texture to mirror that of the labneh, and whose crisp mineral notes and clean acidity balance the sweetness of the tomatoes.

peach and arugula salad with burrata, cumin, and toasted almonds

½ cup raw almonds

1½ teaspoons cumin seeds

3 tablespoons red-wine vinegar

1 tablespoon freshly squeezed lemon juice

½ cup extra-virgin olive oil

3 large ripe peaches

1 pound burrata cheese

¼ cup thinly sliced shallots

½ pound arugula, washed and dried

¼ cup mint leaves, thinly sliced

Kosher salt and freshly ground black pepper

Do not bother making this salad unless you have perfectly ripe peaches. It's so simple that the peaches don't have anything to hide behind. But when the peaches are richly flavored (I can't stand a watery peach!), just tender, and oh so juicy, this is the best way to show them off.

Preheat the oven to 375°F.

Spread the almonds on a baking sheet, and toast for 8 to 10 minutes, until they're slightly darkened and smell nutty. Cool to room temperature, then roughly chop the almonds.

Toast the cumin seeds in a pan over medium heat for 2 to 3 minutes, until the seeds release their aroma and darken slightly. Pound half the cumin seeds to a fine powder, using a mortar and pestle.

Transfer this powder to a bowl with the remaining cumin seeds, ¼ teaspoon salt, red-wine vinegar, and lemon juice. Whisk in the olive oil. Taste for balance and seasoning.

Halve the peaches, remove the pits, and slice each half into four or five wedges.

Cut the burrata into six slices, then cut each piece in half. Season the burrata with a few grindings of black pepper.

In a large bowl, toss the peaches and sliced shallots with the dressing, and season with salt and pepper. Gently toss in the arugula, and taste for seasoning. Arrange the salad on six salad plates, tuck in the burrata slices, and scatter the sliced almonds and mint over the top.

The vibrant sweet peaches and savory cumin spice make the ideal partners for a Chardonnay from California's Sonoma Coast. This area, perched so close to the ocean, has, more than other regions in California, the ideal growing conditions for grapes like Chardonnay and Pinot Noir, allowing the wines to have a fresh, lively fruitiness alongside a racy acidity. The wines are vibrant and crisp, and when made with a small dose of new French oak, take on an exotic, aromatic spiciness that will be the perfect counter to the cumin's influence.

young escarole with anchovy dressing, pecorino, and torn croutons

This salad has some of the familiar flavors of a classic Caesar—croutons, crunchy greens, grated cheese, and, of course, anchovy—but my version is a little more pungent, with the bitterness of the escarole, the punch of mustard, and the starring role of the fish. I highly recommend buying anchovies in salt rather than oil. They are a little more work to rinse and fillet, but they are much less fishy and never mushy.

⅓ pound country white bread

1 cup plus 2 tablespoons extra-virgin olive oil

1 clove garlic

½ tablespoon Dijon mustard

1 tablespoon red-wine vinegar

2 tablespoons freshly squeezed lemon juice

4 salt-packed anchovies, rinsed, bones removed

4 heads young escarole, cores removed, leaves separated and cleaned, to yield ¾ pound cleaned greens

¾ cup coarsely grated Pecorino Romano (use the large holes on a box grater)

Kosher salt and freshly ground black pepper

Preheat the oven to 375°F.

Cut the crust off the bread, and tear the remaining loaf into rustic 1-inch pieces; you should have 3 cups croutons. Using your hands, toss the croutons with 2 tablespoons olive oil, squeezing the bread gently to help it absorb the oil. Toast on a baking sheet for 12 to 15 minutes, stirring a few times, until the croutons are golden brown and crispy on the outside but still a little soft and tender inside.

Using a mortar and pestle, pound the garlic and ¼ teaspoon salt to a paste. Transfer to a bowl, and stir in the mustard, vinegar, and lemon juice. Pound half the anchovies and add them to the bowl. Whisk in the remaining 1 cup of olive oil, and taste for balance and seasoning.

Slice the remaining 2 anchovies thinly on the diagonal.

Place the escarole and the croutons in a large salad bowl, and scatter the Pecorino over the leaves. Toss the salad with 1 cup dressing, ¼ teaspoon salt, and a few grindings of pepper. Taste for balance and seasoning.

Arrange the salad on six plates and tuck the anchovy slices into the leaves.

The bold flavors and punch of salty Pecorino Romano in this salad make it incredibly wine-friendly. A forceful, bright Sauvignon Blanc from the thematically appropriate Italian region of Alto Adige is the ideal choice, and it won't overpower the salad's ingredients. Instead, the wine's inherent vibrancy, its notes of racy citrus and bracing acidity, will marry perfectly with the sharpness of flavor in the vinaigrette and anchovy.

house-smoked black cod with endive, persimmon, and lemon cream

Persimmons are one of my favorite fruits, and I really do wait all year for their somewhat brief season. My favorite way to eat them is out of hand, like an apple. Just remember, there are two basic types of persimmons—the Fuyu type (you don't see their names often, but there are many, many interesting varieties within this broad category), which you can eat when they are hard, and the Hachiya type, which are more elongated and acorn-shaped and must be eaten very, very soft. This type is more often used in ice creams, cakes, and cookies. I love to freeze Hachiyas and then eat them with a spoon—easy instant frozen persimmon sorbet!

If you can make it to the Santa Monica Farmers Market on a Wednesday between July and January, you must track down Jeff Rieger and his lovely partner, Laurence, at Penryn Orchards' stand. I never knew how complex and overwhelming the world of fruit trees and fruit growing could be until I spent an afternoon chatting with them about the persimmons, Asian pears, and heirloom varieties of European pears that they grow. The man even grows bamboo shoots and practices the traditional Japanese art of drying persimmons, called *hoshigaki*. These dried treasures are like the Kobe beef of the fruit world—they are hung whole, regularly massaged, and cared for by hand until the fruit, whole and intact, is completely dried. *Hoshigaki* are a prized traditional gift in Japan and sell for about thirty-five dollars per pound. You can purchase some of Jeff and Laurence's fruits, preserves, and, of course, the *hoshigaki* at www.penrynorchard specialties.com.

Meeting growers like Jeff really inspires me to keep learning and creating, because they remind me how much more there is to do and discover in the world of food.

Anyway, back to this salad, I love the way the rich, sweet fall flavors of the persimmon complement the smoky, silky elegance of the smoked cod. The crisp crunch of the endive and rich yet acidic dressing make this salad a very special celebration of the season.

2 tablespoons finely diced shallots, plus 2 small shallots, thinly sliced

¼ cup freshly squeezed lemon juice

½ cup plus 2 tablespoons extra-virgin olive oil

¼ cup plus 1 tablespoon heavy cream

4 Belgian endives, cores removed, separated into spears

2 small Fuyu persimmons, thinly sliced

¾ pound House-Smoked Black Cod (recipe follows)

2 tablespoons flat-leaf parsley leaves

2 tablespoons ½-inch-snipped chives

Kosher salt and freshly ground black pepper

Place the diced shallots, lemon juice, and ¼ teaspoon salt in a bowl, and let sit for 5 minutes. Whisk in the olive oil. Gently stir in the cream, add a few grinds of pepper, and taste for balance and seasoning.

Place the endive spears, sliced shallots, and persimmon slices in a large bowl, season with salt and pepper, and pour three-quarters of the lemon dressing over them. Toss gently to coat the endive with the dressing. Taste for seasoning, and arrange the salad in a natural style on six plates. Think of building loose Lincoln Logs—cantilevering the endive spears on top of the ones below, so you are building height—but don't make it look too forced or geometrical.

Using your hands, pull the smoked cod into 1-inch chunks, tucking them among the endive leaves on each plate. Follow with the slices of persimmon, and then the parsley leaves and snipped chives. Spoon the remaining dressing over and around the salads.

house-smoked black cod

1 chile de árbol, crumbled

½ cup coarsely chopped fennel

½ cup coarsely chopped leek

Zest of 1 lemon

Zest of ½ orange

1 teaspoon black peppercorns

1 teaspoon fennel seeds

5 sprigs flat-leaf parsley

½ cup dark-brown sugar

1 cup kosher salt

1 pound Alaskan black cod, trimmed, skin on

3 cups wood chips, preferably applewood

Cooking is such a personal thing, and one of the things I love about working with so many different people over the years is that somehow *their* family histories end up becoming part of my own vernacular. Former A.O.C. Sous-Chef Aliza Miner is a particularly spirited, opinionated, and specific chef. Pretty much every sentence begins with "My grandmother used to make this thing" or "In Chicago" or "We Jews like to . . ." So, after a few years of working with her, I myself began to feel like a fiercely proud hyper-Jewish Chicago local. It was as if her grandmother had somehow become my grandmother, too, and I couldn't get enough beets, horseradish, pickles, and smoked fish. It was Aliza who developed our method of brining and smoking one of my all-time favorite fish in our wood oven. As with everything she cooks, the flavors are big, bold, and Old World, but her attention to detail and drive for perfection always ensured that the fish was perfectly cooked—so it was silky and smooth on the palate, just as black cod should be. It's very hard to say how long the fish needs to smoke: it's best to follow these guidelines and really pay attention, watching for the perfect moment when the fish goes from translucent to opaque.

Place the chile, chopped fennel, chopped leek, citrus zests, black peppercorns, fennel seeds, and parsley in a piece of cheesecloth, and tie into a sachet with string.

Place the sugar, salt, and the sachet in a large pot with 2 quarts water, and bring to a boil. Remove from the heat, and when the brine has cooled completely, place the cod skin-side up in the liquid, making sure it is completely submerged (you can place a saucer on the fish as a weight). Refrigerate for 6 hours.

Remove the cod from the brine, pat it dry with paper towels, place it skin-side down on a roasting rack set on a baking sheet, and leave in the refrigerator, uncovered, for 12 hours to air-dry.

One hour before you are ready to smoke the cod, take the fish out of the refrigerator and light the grill. Soak the wood chips in water for 20 minutes, strain, and discard the water. Wrap the wood chips up in a piece of aluminum foil, and poke the bundle all around with a fork.

When the coals are turning ash-colored, push them to one side of the grill and then add the wood-chip bundle to the coals. Let the chips smoke for about 5 minutes, and then place the roasting pan with fish on the colder side of the grill. Cover the grill and smoke the fish for 8 minutes, turn the roasting pan, and smoke another 8 minutes. Check for the next few minutes, until the cod is just firm and opaque. Cool completely.

I love this salad because of the play of the smoky, lusciously textured fish with the sweetness of the persimmon. The key to this pairing is finding a wine that has not only an inherent smokiness like that of the cod, but also a freshness, so that when the wine and food come together the flavors don't become muddied or overly heavy. A great white for this purpose is Pouilly-Fumé, Sauvignon Blanc from the Loire Valley, which is grown in mineral-laden soils that give the wine a light, smokelike back note and crisp, lean elegance. This salad could also handle a red wine, such as Carignan, from the southern regions of France, where the wines have an interesting balance of earthiness and red-fruit tones that will keep the pairing fresh and light.

arugula and autumn grapes with goat cheese, pecans, and saba vinaigrette

¾ cup pecan halves

½ pound seedless red or purple grapes

2 tablespoons finely diced shallots

3 tablespoons sherry vinegar

½ cup extra-virgin olive oil

Approximately 2 tablespoons saba

6 ounces arugula, cleaned and dried

¼ pound soft goat cheese

Kosher salt and freshly ground black pepper

The "secret ingredient" in this dish is the saba, a traditional Sardinian condiment made by cooking down unfermented grape must (the residue left over from winemaking) for many hours, to a dark, rich fruity syrup. In ancient times, honey and saba (or *mosto cotto,* as it is often called in Italy) were the only sweetening ingredients easily available for cooking, so they were used quite often.

The combination of the pounded fresh grapes and the darkly flavored grape-must reduction in the dressing really integrates the flavors of this salad and brings it together, ensuring that the *whole* salad has a "grapy" back note (and two types of grapiness—both raw and bright, and rich and reduced). That reiteration of flavor is what makes this salad so much more than arugula tossed with grapes in a standard vinaigrette.

Preheat the oven to 375°F.

Spread the pecans on a baking sheet, and toast for 8 to 10 minutes, until they're slightly darkened and smell nutty. When the nuts have cooled, chop them coarsely.

Crush ¼ cup grapes with a mortar and pestle. Cut the rest of the grapes in half.

Place the shallots, vinegar, crushed grapes, and ½ teaspoon salt in a bowl, and let sit for 5 minutes. Whisk in the olive oil and 1 tablespoon saba. Taste for balance and seasoning.

In a large salad bowl, toss the sliced grapes and arugula with the dressing, and season with salt and pepper. Arrange the salad on six chilled dinner plates. Tuck little clumps of the goat cheese in between the arugula leaves, sprinkle the pecans on top, and drizzle each salad with a little saba.

The key here is finding a wine that mirrors that same combination of ripeness, from the grapes and saba, and the rich and earthy flavors in the goat cheese and pecans. Godello, a grape variety from Galicia in northwestern Spain, makes an ideal pairing. The wine actually reminds me a bit of Chardonnay, because it can have a good deal of elegance and vibrant acidity and, when aged in oak, becomes deep, toasty, and complex. Aromas and flavors of golden melon and pear, along with a rich oiliness, make the wine work not only in terms of flavor profile, but texturally as well.

dandelion and roasted carrot salad
with black olives and ricotta salata

1 pound small carrots, ideally
    with tops attached

¾ cup extra-virgin olive oil

2 teaspoons thyme leaves

1½ teaspoons cumin seeds

3 tablespoons red-wine vinegar

1 tablespoon lemon juice,
    plus more as needed

¼ pound ricotta salata

3 ounces oil-cured black olives,
    pitted and thinly sliced

¼ cup thinly sliced shallots

3 ounces young dandelion
    greens, cleaned

Kosher salt and freshly ground
    black pepper

Dandelion is one of my favorite go-to greens. If you taste it raw and undressed, you might think I am crazy—it can be very bitter, quite pungent, and even a little tough sometimes. But, when it's dressed with an assertive vinaigrette and paired with bold-flavored ingredients, it really sings. This salad is a 101 on the balance of sweet (carrots), salty (ricotta and olives), acid (vinaigrette), and bitter (dandelion); and for the little je ne sais quoi factor, I love the crunch of the cumin seeds and the heat of the shallots.

Preheat the oven to 425°F.

Clean the carrots, leaving ¼ inch of the stems attached. Cut the carrots in half lengthwise. Toss the carrots with ¼ cup olive oil, the thyme, ½ teaspoon salt, and some freshly ground pepper. Preheat a heavy-duty baking sheet in the oven for 3 or 4 minutes. Remove the baking sheet from the oven, place the carrots on it, and roast them for about 20 minutes, until they are tender and a little caramelized. Set aside.

Meanwhile, make the cumin vinaigrette.

Toast the cumin seeds in a small pan over medium heat for 2 to 3 minutes, until they release their aroma. Pound half the seeds to a fine powder, using a mortar and pestle.

Transfer the cumin powder to a bowl, and add the whole cumin, ¼ teaspoon salt, the red-wine vinegar, and 1 tablespoon lemon juice. Whisk in remaining ½ cup olive oil. Taste for balance and seasoning

Place the ricotta salata flat-side down on a cutting board. Using a chef's knife, cut thin slices of the cheese.

In a large bowl, toss the carrots, olives, and shallots with three-fourths cup of the dressing to coat well. Add the dandelion, season with salt and pepper, and gently toss to coat the greens. Taste for balance and seasoning.

Arrange the salad on six dinner plates, and tuck the cheese into the leaves. Spoon a little more dressing over and around the salads if you like (I like!).

This is probably one of the most flavorful, perfectly fall-like salads I have ever eaten. The savory richness of the roasted carrots, along with the bitter greens, robust olives, and ricotta salata, beg to be paired with a powerful wine. And although we all tend to leave our pink-wine drinking to the summer months, this salad really pairs perfectly with a dark and hearty rosé. I'm thinking of the kind of rosé that looks like it should have been a light-bodied red, and that makes sense to drink when the weather turns cooler. Great examples can be found in Rosado from the Rioja region of Spain, and Rosato from Puglia in Italy, which are both made from hearty grape varieties and have a meatiness and firm tannin structure that can hold up to more full-flavored dishes.

DANDELION AND ROASTED CARROT SALAD   85

chopped salad dijonnaise with apples, bacon, roquefort, and walnuts

1 cup walnuts

½-pound slab applewood-
smoked bacon

2 large apples, such as Pink Lady,
Honeycrisp, or other firm,
crisp, and juicy varieties

1 extra-large egg yolk

1 tablespoon Dijon mustard

1½ tablespoons red-wine vinegar

1 tablespoon freshly squeezed
lemon juice, plus more
as needed

¾ cup extra-virgin olive oil

2 small heads romaine

1 small head radicchio

½ pound Belgian endive
(approximately 2 heads)

6 ounces Roquefort, crumbled

¼ cup chopped flat-leaf parsley

Kosher salt and freshly ground
black pepper

Everyone, including me, loves a chopped salad. This one is inspired by the flavors of Dijon—mustard, bacon, apples, walnuts, and parsley. I sometimes add chopped roasted chicken or steak to make a hearty main-course salad.

Preheat the oven to 375°F.

Spread the walnuts on a baking sheet, and toast for about 10 to 12 minutes, until they're golden brown and smell nutty. When the nuts have cooled, chop them coarsely.

Cut the bacon into ½-inch dice. Heat a large sauté pan over medium heat for 1 minute. Add the bacon, and cook for about 5 minutes, stirring frequently, until the bacon is tender and lightly crisped. Using a slotted spoon, remove the bacon to a plate lined with paper towels.

Place one of the apples on a cutting board with the stem pointed skyward. Cut ½-inch-thick slices until you reach the core. Rotate the apple 90 degrees and continue to cut ½-inch-thick slices. Repeat the rotating and slicing twice more, until you are left with a rectangular apple core. Discard it. Stack the slices and cut them into ½-inch dice. Repeat with the second apple.

Whisk the egg yolk in a medium bowl with the mustard, red-wine vinegar, 1 tablespoon lemon juice, ½ teaspoon of salt, and a pinch of pepper. Slowly whisk in the olive oil. Taste for balance and seasoning.

Cut each head of romaine in half lengthwise, and place cut-side down on a cutting board. Make ½-inch-thick slices lengthwise, then turn the romaine, and chop across the slices into ½-inch cubes. Wash and spin-dry the romaine. Use the same technique to chop the radicchio and the endive.

Place the chopped romaine, radicchio, and endive in a large salad bowl. Add the apples, bacon, Roquefort, walnuts, and parsley. Toss everything together with ¾ of the dressing. Taste for balance and seasoning, adding another squeeze of lemon juice if needed. Arrange on six large chilled dinner plates.

If I had to choose one word to describe this salad, it would be "pungent." The mustard vinaigrette and the Roquefort are a pretty powerful combination that makes for a perfect cold-weather starter. For a wine pairing, I take my cue from the geographical location of Dijon in the great French winemaking region of Burgundy. Because there is a good deal of richness from the combination of bacon and Roquefort, I like a white wine that is high in acid, to cut through these fatty elements. The trick here is to choose a wine with a touch of oakiness, like those from the appellation of Chassagne-Montrachet, where Chardonnay tends to be aged in a higher degree of new French oak. These wines display a toasted quality that softens the kick of the cheese while also highlighting the recipe's toasted walnuts.

CHOPPED SALAD DIJONNAISE   87

little gems with reed avocados, cara cara oranges, and cilantro

Cara Cara oranges are one of those wonders of the Santa Monica Farmers Market that we wait for all year. According to experts at UC Riverside, Cara Cara navel oranges are actually a mutation that occurred on a Washington navel orange tree in Venezuela in 1976. They look like regular oranges from the outside but have deep-pink flesh, almost the color of ruby grapefruits. Intensely flavorful and juicy, Cara Caras have a stone-fruit or cherry note to them. I love the way they pair with this creamy avocado dressing (a great recipe for when *all* your avocados are ripening at the same time), crispy lettuces, and cilantro leaves. You could, of course, substitute navel oranges, blood oranges, or ruby grapefruits in this salad.

3 or 4 small heads Little Gem lettuce (to yield 1 pound cleaned lettuce)

3 or 4 Cara Cara oranges

2 Reed avocados

¾ cup Avocado Dressing (recipe follows)

¼ cup cilantro leaves

1 teaspoon thinly sliced chile de árbol

NOTE If the chile de árbol is dry and brittle you can just crush or crumble it.

If the Little Gems have any tough or ugly outer leaves, remove them and discard. Carefully slice off the cores of the lettuces, discard, and separate the lettuce leaves. Clean the lettuces by submerging them in cold water. Spin-dry, and chill in the refrigerator. You should have 1 pound cleaned lettuce.

Cut the stem and blossom ends from the oranges. Place the oranges cut-side down on a cutting board. Following the contour of the fruit with your knife, remove the peel and cottony white pith, working from top to bottom, and rotating the fruit as you go. Then hold the oranges in your hand one at a time, and carefully slice between the membranes and the fruit to release the segments in between.

Cut the avocados in half lengthwise. Remove the pits, and peel. Cut the avocados into ¼-inch slices, and season with ½ teaspoon salt and freshly ground pepper.

Gently toss the Little Gems in a large bowl with ¾ cup dressing, ¼ teaspoon salt, and some pepper. Taste for balance and seasoning.

Arrange the lettuce on six large plates. Tuck the Cara Cara segments and avocado slices among the lettuce leaves. Scatter the cilantro leaves and chile over the top.

avocado dressing

1 soft Reed avocado, or 2 soft
  Hass avocados

3 tablespoons freshly squeezed
  lime juice (about 2 limes)

⅓ cup grape-seed oil

2 tablespoons heavy cream

Kosher salt and freshly ground
  black pepper

Chop the peeled and pitted avocado, and place it in a blender with the lime juice, ½ teaspoon salt, a few grindings of pepper, and ¼ cup water. With the blender running at medium speed, pour in the grape-seed oil and purée just until the mixture is completely emulsified. Turn off the blender immediately (overworking can cause the dressing to separate and become greasy). Remove to a medium bowl, stir in the cream, and taste for balance and seasoning.

Cara Cara oranges are particularly sweet and vibrant, with a flavor that is more candylike than that of any other citrus fruit I've tasted. Focusing on this quality in the fruit, as well as the bright hit of cilantro, is the key to finding the right wine pairing. I find that Chenin Blanc, with its citrusy, Creamsicle-like notes and glycerine minerality, works really well. Wines from France's Loire Valley, like Anjou and Savennières, are great examples, and when made slightly off-dry, are hallmarked by apple, pear, and honey flavors that are just the right partners for the avocado and young lettuces in this dish.

endive with beets, blood oranges, kumquats, and charmoula

Having grown up in southern California, I have a very emotional and seasonal attachment to kumquats. When we were little, my parents had a tradition of taking my sister and me to visit our aunt Gladys on Christmas Eve to try to distract us from our pent-up excitement about the onslaught of presents we were expecting the following morning.

Gladys Caruso lived in a house on the lake in Silver Lake, which at the time was very odd and quirky, and now would sell to a young hipster family for a couple million bucks. She had a kumquat orchard in her backyard, and part of the day's tradition was that Aunt Gladys would give us each a big paper grocery bag and let us pick (and take home!) as many kumquats as we could fit in those bags. Well, one year, my poor sister Jessica took the "pick one, eat one, pick one, eat one" strategy one step too far, and let's just say she has never eaten a kumquat since. I, on the other hand, have never lost my passion for kumquats. I love that really bright, sour burst when you first bite into one, and the intense sweet-bitterness and leathery texture of the skin itself.

For this salad, I wanted all that flavor in the vinaigrette—I actually did consider hand-squeezing the kumquats (wonder how many pantry cooks I would have lost with that move), but I decided instead to purée them with a little orange juice to make sure that the kumquat skin was a real player in the dressing. After that, the rest of the ingredients just made sense to me—the sweet, earthy nature of the vaguely North African-feeling beets seems just right for the spiced and slightly spicy charmoula. Endive is perfect for these types of salad, because the spears are such a great vehicle for holding dressings and ingredients. I prefer to eat this salad with my hands, picking up the spears like little tacos with all the goodies inside—nature's spoon, holding the perfect bite. The blood oranges are just a seasonal gilding of the lily.

2 pounds small or medium-sized beets

¾ cup plus 1 tablespoon extra-virgin olive oil

½ pound kumquats

6 tablespoons freshly squeezed orange juice

3 tablespoons sherry vinegar

3 large blood oranges

6 Belgian endives, cores removed, separated into spears

½ cup Charmoula (recipe follows)

Kosher salt and freshly ground black pepper

Preheat the oven to 400°F.

Clean the beets well, and toss them with 1 tablespoon olive oil and 1 teaspoon salt. Place the beets in a roasting pan with a splash of water in the bottom. Cover with foil, and roast for 50 to 60 minutes, until tender when pierced. (The roasting time will depend on the size and type of beet.) When the beets are done, carefully remove the foil. Let cool, and peel the beets by slipping the skins off with your fingers. Cut the beets into ½-inch wedges.

While the beets are roasting, thinly slice one-third of the kumquats, removing the seeds as you go along, until you have a heaping ½ cup of sliced kumquats. Cut the rest of the kumquats in half, and remove the seeds.

In a food processor, combine the halved kumquats, the orange juice, and ½ teaspoon salt, using the pulse function, until well blended. Add the vinegar, pulse once or twice, and then, with the machine running, pour in the remaining ¾ cup olive oil. Taste for balance and seasoning.

Toss the beets with 2 tablespoons kumquat dressing, salt, and pepper. Taste for balance and seasoning.

Slice the stem and blossom ends from the blood oranges. Place the blood oranges cut-side down on a cutting board and, following the contour of the fruit with your knife, remove the peel and white, cottony pith. Work from top to bottom, rotating the fruit as you go.

Slice each orange thinly, into 7 or 8 pinwheels.

Place the endive spears in a large bowl, and pour ⅔ cup kumquat dressing over them. Season with salt and pepper, and toss gently to coat the endive with the dressing. Taste for seasoning, and arrange the salad on six large plates.

Carefully tuck the beet wedges, blood-orange slices, and sliced kumquats in and around the endive spears. Spoon the charmoula over and around the salads.

charmoula

Charmoula is a classic North African condiment traditionally served with fish. It's the kind of sauce that is so good I can't help spooning it over almost anything—grilled fish, chicken, braised lamb, roasted and grilled vegetables—once I have some, so I always make a double batch.

MAKES ¾ CUP

NOTE I would never let my cooks do this, but you can make the charmoula more quickly and easily in a food processor!

Toast the cumin seeds in a small pan over medium-high heat for about 2 minutes, until the seeds release their aroma.

Using a mortar and pestle, pound the cumin, and transfer it to a medium bowl. Pound the garlic and a pinch of salt to a paste, and add to the cumin. Pound the cilantro and parsley, and add this to the garlic mixture. Pour the olive oil into the bowl, add the paprika and cayenne, and stir well. Stir in the rice-wine vinegar, lemon juice, and ¼ teaspoon salt. Taste for balance and seasoning.

1 tablespoon cumin seeds

1 clove garlic

1 cup coarsely chopped cilantro leaves

½ cup coarsely chopped flat-leaf parsley leaves

⅔ cup extra-virgin olive oil

½ tablespoon sweet paprika

Healthy pinch cayenne pepper

1 teaspoon rice-wine vinegar

2 tablespoons freshly squeezed lemon juice

Kosher salt

In my opinion, beets are fairly difficult to pair with wine. Aside from being sweet, they are also intensely earthy, with qualities much like the soil from which they were pulled. They have a strong mineral quality and an almost mossy flavor profile. When paired with a wine with too much acidity, the beets are resistant on the palate and just clash. To avoid this, I choose a wine like Riesling from Germany, which has soft fruit notes of mandarin orange and white peach, and enough acidity to keep the wine balanced but not bracing. The result here is that the gentle sweetness plays along with the sugary notes of the beets, while the wine's citrus flavors combine with those in the salad.

roasted kabocha squash with dates, parmesan, and pepitas

¾ cup pepitas

½ cup plus 1 teaspoon
   extra-virgin olive oil

2 pounds kabocha squash

1 tablespoon thyme leaves

3 ounces Parmigiano-Reggiano

6 ounces deglet noor dates

2 tablespoons freshly squeezed
   lemon juice

3 tablespoons sliced flat-leaf
   parsley

1 bunch dandelion greens,
   cleaned and dried

Kosher salt and freshly ground
   black pepper

This time of year, I just cannot get enough kabocha squash. It has such a dense texture and rich sweet-yet-starch flavor that I choose it over other winter squashes again and again. I love how the wedges stay intact when roasted and can be layered into this salad with some of my other favorite friends—dates, Parmigiano-Reggiano, dandelion, and pepitas.

Preheat the oven to 375°F.

Spread the pepitas on a baking sheet, and toast for about 10 minutes, stirring once or twice, until they smell nutty. Chop them coarsely and then toss with 1 teaspoon olive oil and a pinch of salt.

While the pepitas are toasting, cut the squash in half lengthwise and remove the seeds. Place the squash cut-side down on a cutting board, and use a sharp knife to remove the peel. Slice the squash lengthwise into 1-inch-thick wedges.

When the pepitas are done, turn the oven up to 425°F.

Toss the squash wedges with ¼ cup olive oil, 2 teaspoons salt, some pepper, and the thyme. Place the squash flat on a baking sheet, and roast in the oven for about 30 minutes, until tender when pierced.

Place the Parmigiano-Reggiano flat-side down on a cutting board. Using a chef's knife, cut into ¼-inch-thick slices. Stack the slices, and cut them into ¼-inch-thick "matchsticks." Finally, cut those matchsticks into ¼-inch cubes.

Pit the dates, and slice them thinly lengthwise, being careful not to let them stick together into one big date-ball.

Toss the dates in a shallow dish (to prevent the slices from sticking together) with remaining ¼ cup olive oil, the lemon juice, and parsley. Stir in the Parmigiano-Reggiano, and season with salt and pepper.

Arrange the warm squash on a platter with the dandelion greens. Spoon the date-Parmigiano relish over the top, and sprinkle the pepitas over salads.

The squash in this recipe is so distinctive that it has to be the driving force behind my wine pairing. Kabocha tastes like a drier version of pumpkin, with a touch of caramelized sweetness and thick, almost heavy texture. It reminds me of the white wines from the Rhône Valley, made from varieties like Marsanne and Roussanne, which have an oily texture, honeyed stone-fruit notes, and delicate acidity. These wines tend to finish fairly cleanly, with a background of aromatic spices like cardamom and ginger that will connect the wine to the sweetness of the squash and dates yet offset the bitterness of the dandelion.

fish

I love a perfectly grilled or roasted piece of super-fresh fish simply prepared and served with a wedge of lemon. I really do—it makes me feel nourished, healthy, and "clean," as we cooks like to say. But in reality, in the restaurant, the fish itself is the canvas for whatever flavors, vegetables, fruits, and grains I want to highlight and show off in the moment. Of course, the jumping-off point of that "moment" is the season—what is growing locally right then and there.

But there is also the mood and feeling of a season to consider—summer is hot, free, and brazen, whereas fall is more moody, brooding, and deep. I always try my best to honor the moods and feelings of the diner and the season, as well as the actual climate and produce growing outside. Does that sound crazy? What I mean is that summer food should be more simple and light and less involved, because we are hot and don't want to think so much about what we are eating—we want to be satisfied and indulged but in a more lighthearted way. In winter, on the other hand, we want the food to wrap us up like a blanket and comfort us. We crave deep, homey flavors and textures, richer sauces, and meats that fall off the bone.

When I am conceiving a fish dish, I think about the texture, flavor, and character of the fish itself. Halibut is the perfect foil for bright flavors, fresh herbs, and vibrant colors. Its mild, snow-white flesh pairs beautifully with carrot purée and asparagus in spring, and raw tomatoes with blue crab, arugula, and horseradish cream in the summer. I love the way halibut flakes and, when perfectly cooked, is just translucent in the center—it marries with those bright, clean flavors and complements but does not compete with or overpower them. Although Alaskan halibut is available March 15 to November 15, I find myself using it mostly in the spring and summer months.

Wild salmon is available May to September, and, boy, is there a celebration around here when it comes in. If you think salmon is that farmed, food-colored, flavorless stuff on the wedding buffet, you *need* to try the real deal. I always prefer my salmon grilled, because you get a great crust, nice smokiness, and—again, when cooked correctly—a tender and succulent flake thanks to the fattiness of the fish itself. Its brilliant color is matched by its bright, deeply sweet flavor, and, paired with sugary yet vegetal spring delights such as English peas, sugar snaps, fava beans, and summer produce such as corn, tomatoes, squash, peppers, and basil, it is perfection. Salmon also holds up well to strong flavors like anchovy, as well as briny olives and even preserved lemons. It's the fat in the fish that helps it stand up to these bold, salty, sharp, and acidic pairings.

Richer fall dishes need a sturdy and more full-flavored fish to carry their heavier ingredients. Black cod, one of my all-time favorite fish, has a rich silkiness that works well with winter squash and a sauce of Pedro Ximenez sherry and golden raisins. A milder fish would be overpowered, but the big flakes of the cod play off this rich Spanish-inspired sauce perfectly. Rock cod and sea bass are both meatier fish that work well with bold flavors like artichokes barigoule with braised bacon, and tomato rice with fried egg and salty, spicy sopressata.

In addition to thinking about the flavor of a particular fish, I always consider the size of the fillet. Large fish, like striped bass and halibut, can be cut into thick, chunkier portions, whereas Eastern black bass (another dreamy favorite) and pink snapper are thinner and hence more delicate. I like using snappers and other smaller fish, like orata or branzino, when I want the diner to get an equal amount of fish, sauce, and accompaniments in each bite, rather than a larger bite of fish with a smaller amount of sauce. It's funny: in the restaurant kitchen, we tend to taste the food with spoons rather than knives and forks, and there are certain dishes that work so well with a spoon—you cut right down through the whole and scoop up a little of each ingredient to make the perfect bite. Sometimes I have to remind myself that "normal" people eat with forks and knives and we had better taste the food that way, because that is how "they" will be tasting it. With a thick piece of salmon or bass, or with diver scallops, the dish is more about the fish glazed with a sauce and accompanied by the rest of the ingredients, whereas with a thinner piece of fish it's more about eating it all together. Neither one is right or wrong, it's just different—and by choosing which fish you use, and how the dish is plated, you are determining how your guests will experience the dish as a whole.

In all my cooking, I try to build a plate with contrasting and complementary ingredients that come together and integrate to create a whole that is greater than the sum of its parts. I consider the fish a major but equal player in these preparations, rather than the dominant member of the plate. The sauce, the vegetables, the grains, the greens, *and* the fish—they all bring something to the table (literally). And it's the delicate melding of flavors without muddling or muckiness, plus that balance *and* contrast of acidity, saltiness, texture, and flavor, that make a dish really work.

It's often the sauce or salsa on top of fish that ties a dish together. I like sauces to be spooned over the fish and then run down the sides and soak into the rest of the ingredients—so that the sauce is garnishing not just the fish itself but the whole plate. In Grilled Orata with Cauliflower, Fregola, and Persimmon-Pomegranate Salsa, the fall fruit sauce seasons not only the fish but the Sicilian couscous and the spiced curried cauliflower underneath it as well. There is a sort of three-way love fest going on between the vegetables and the fish, the vegetables and the sauce, and the sauce and the fish. If you remove any one of the ingredients, the combinations still work, and, funnily, the easiest part to lose is actually the fish. That's why I find it so easy to cook for vegetarians and vegans: these dishes are conceived in such a way that removing the protein may change the dish but what remains is inherently delicious and satisfying.

Whether there are three, or four, or five elements on the plate, the key is that the ingredients all work together, and that they are treated in a way, or presented in a way, that integrates and unifies them, so they are not just various ingredients that happen to be on the plate together. In California Sea Bass with Tomato Rice, Fried Egg, and Sopressata, sizzling the sopressata in olive oil before spooning it over the egg does the trick—the sopressata is warmed and crisped, and some of its fat and flavor go into the olive oil, making it more of a sauce that seasons the rice and sticks to the egg. Swirling soaked golden raisins into reduced Pedro Ximenez sherry before finishing the sauce with butter and pouring it over the Black Cod with Kabocha Squash accomplishes that same thing—it binds the ingredients together in a way that creates a comprehensive singular flavor.

With all this talk of creative process and balancing and melding flavors, I almost forgot to mention what is probably the single most important thing about cooking fish, and that is how you *actually* cook the fish. I like to start on a high heat and cook the fish about halfway, then lower the heat (or move the fish to a cooler part of the grill), turn the fish over, and let it coast gently until it is just translucent in the center (you can peek carefully inside the flakes of the fish until you get the hang of this). Using this method, you get a nice crispy sear or crust on the fish from the high heat, and then the slow-cooking lets the proteins relax and release (the same idea as letting meat "rest" before you slice it), and you get a softer, more tender texture from the flesh. Last, remember that the fish will continue to cook a little more once you take it off the grill or out of the pan—allow for this "carry-over cooking" by taking the fish off the heat source about thirty seconds *before* it's done.

One more important consideration when working with fish is assessing the sustainability of your choices. As a young aspiring chef, I never thought I would have to take this into account in my cooking, but now I truly must. As someone who purchases large quantities of meat, fish, produce, and groceries, I consider it my duty to pay great attention to how I am voting with my dollars. Ten years ago, when I first started getting really educated in the subject, our staff and guests didn't know what on earth I was talking about. It's amazing and wonderful how aware and concerned people have become in the last few years.

I was lucky enough to do an event at the Monterey Bay Aquarium many years ago—yes, a fish-cooking festival at an aquarium—and it was there that I learned all the issues of sustainable seafood and how to make the right choices regarding which fish to use and which to avoid. I love that the Monterey Bay Aquarium's message is not "stop eating fish" but "educate yourself and choose wisely."

From a sustainability viewpoint, there are a few major issues to consider when choosing what fish to prepare. First of all, are the fish "overfished"— meaning, are they being caught faster than they are able to reproduce, and is the rate at which they are being fished affecting the balance of the ocean and ecosystem in which they live? The sudden popularity of Chilean sea bass (which, by the way, is no more a sea bass than you or I) is the classic example of a fish (actually known as Patagonian toothfish) that has been illegally and unrestrictedly fished, a process that may potentially lead to extinction, because these fish are slow-growing and reproduce later in life.

Another major consideration is how the fish is caught. To use Chilean sea bass as an example again, the fishermen "bottom-trawl," which basically means they drag along the seafloor giant nets that, according to the Monterey Bay Aquarium, "catch everything in their path, including endangered sea turtles, juvenile fish and other unwanted species, resulting in wasteful by-catch. Dragging nets along the seafloor can damage or destroy fish habitat as well." Besides overfishing, habitat damage, and by-catch, one worrying thing is that, overall, the fishing industry is not very well regulated or managed. So I like to buy fish from Alaska and the well-managed fisheries of the East Coast of the United States. Wild striped bass and black bass were both once considered close to extinction, but now, with good quota systems and strict seasons, they are flourishing, and we get to enjoy them, just not all the time (sort of like tomatoes or blood oranges).

All these issues with wild seafood would make you think that farmed fish is the answer, but aquaculture has its own complex list of issues. The best choices are fish that are farmed in a self-contained system that does not affect the ecosystem of the ocean or lakes. Problems that sometimes arise with aquaculture are the escape of farmed fish into the wild, where they spread diseases; waste from the farms that gets dumped in the ocean; an excess of wild sealife used as feed to produce the farmed fish; the use of pesticides and antibiotics to "help" keep some of those fish "healthy."

From a taste perspective, I generally prefer wild fish, because I find some farmed fish to have a muddy taste or mealy texture. However, there are quite a few farmed fish I love as well—barramundi, arctic char, and rainbow trout, to name a few. You can learn more at www.seafoodwatch.org and even download and print their super-helpful pocket guide, which lists the fish that are the best choices and those to avoid.

All this seriousness aside, I hope you enjoy these recipes and learn some of the techniques and thought processes discussed here. And don't forget—please, please don't overcook your fish!

alaskan halibut with carrot purée, asparagus, and pistou

Basil is an obvious go-to herb in summer, but I really love the way its bright, green, almost aniselike flavor pairs with spring's sweet and vegetal produce. This recipe is really a template, so feel free to substitute whatever vegetables are most beautiful in the market. English peas, sugar snaps, fennel, and even young broccoli would be wonderful. I particularly love the way the crème fraîche and the pistou are separate on top of the fish, but then meld together into one creamy green sauce at the bottom of the plate. I try to control myself, but sometimes you just want cream *and* olive oil!

6 Alaskan halibut fillets, 5 to 6 ounces each

1 lemon, zested and reserved for juicing

1 tablespoon plus 1 teaspoon thyme leaves

2 tablespoons coarsely chopped flat-leaf parsley

¼ cup extra-virgin olive oil

1½ cups sliced spring onions, plus ½ cup sliced spring-onion tops

¾ pound thin asparagus, sliced on the diagonal into ¼-inch-thick pieces

3 tablespoons unsalted butter

4 ounces pea shoots

1 recipe Carrot Purée (recipe follows)

6 tablespoons crème fraîche

1 recipe Pistou (recipe follows)

Kosher salt and freshly ground black pepper

Season the fish with the grated lemon zest, 1 tablespoon thyme, and the parsley. Cover, and refrigerate at least 4 hours or overnight.

Remove the fish from the refrigerator 15 minutes before cooking, to bring it to room temperature.

Heat a large sauté pan over high heat for 2 minutes. (Depending on the size of your pan, you may need to cook the fish in batches, or in two pans.) Season the fish on both sides with salt and pepper. Swirl 2 tablespoons olive oil into the pan, and wait 1 minute. Carefully lay the fish in the pan, and cook for 3 to 4 minutes, until it's lightly browned. Turn the fish over, lower the heat to medium-low, and cook for a few more minutes, until it's almost cooked through. Be careful not to overcook the fish. When it's done, the fish will begin to flake and separate a little, and the center will still be slightly translucent. Remember, the halibut will continue to cook for a bit once you take it out of the pan. Transfer the halibut to a resting rack.

Heat a clean large sauté pan over medium heat for 1 minute. Add remaining 2 tablespoons olive oil, let heat for a moment, and then add the sliced spring onions, asparagus, ½ teaspoon salt, a pinch of pepper, and the remaining teaspoon thyme. Cook over medium heat 2 to 3 minutes, stirring, until the onions are translucent. Add the butter and 1 tablespoon water. Swirl the pan, and when the liquid comes to a simmer, toss in the pea shoots and onion tops. Immediately remove the pan from the heat, and squeeze a little lemon juice over the vegetables. Taste for seasoning.

Spoon dollops of warm carrot purée onto each of six plates, and then arrange the vegetables over the purée. Place the fish fillets at the center of the plates, and top each with a dollop of crème fraîche. Spoon the pistou over the crème fraîche and the fish, and around the plate.

carrot purée

2 pounds carrots, peeled, cut into ¼-inch rounds

Handful of basil stems (use the leaves for pistou)

¾ cup extra-virgin olive oil

1 cup diced white onion

Kosher salt and freshly ground black pepper

Steam the carrots with the basil stems for about 20 minutes, until tender. When the carrots are almost done, heat a Dutch oven over high heat for 1 minute. Pour in ½ cup olive oil, and add the onion. Season with 2 teaspoons salt and ¼ teaspoon freshly ground black pepper, and cook the onion for about 5 minutes, stirring often, until it's translucent. Add the steamed carrots, and cook for another 8 minutes, stirring and scraping the pan with a wooden spoon, until the carrots are lightly caramelized. Purée the mixture in a food processor until it's smooth. With the motor running, slowly pour in the remaining ¼ cup olive oil, and process until the oil is incorporated and the purée is very smooth. Taste for seasoning.

pistou

½ clove garlic

1 cup tightly packed basil leaves

2 tablespoons chopped flat-leaf parsley

½ cup extra-virgin olive oil

Kosher salt and freshly ground black pepper

Pistou is the Provençal version of pesto—no nuts, no cheese. I love swirling it into stewed shell beans, pastas, and soups this time of year. Makes a great spread for sandwiches as well—try stirring some into a little mayonnaise on a tomato sandwich. It's another one of those sauces that are so nice to just have around!

MAKES ¾ CUP

Using a mortar and pestle, pound the garlic with ¼ teaspoon kosher salt. Add a third of the basil leaves, and pound to a paste. Continue with the rest of the basil and the parsley. Stir in the olive oil, and season to taste with pepper and more salt if needed. It's also OK to use a food processor.

The carrot purée that accompanies the fish in this recipe has sweetness, but also a surprising richness and depth of flavor. When highlighted by the bright, herby pistou, this purée works really well with a wine that shows a similar contrast of sweet and savory on the palate. Austrian Grüner Veltliner is perfect, because it displays citrusy, Key-lime fruit notes alongside flavors of savory, bright-green herbs and white pepper. It truly embodies this concept of contrast on the palate, with a fruitiness and an oily texture that are in sync with those of the carrots, the delicate nature of the halibut, and an earthiness and spice that mirror the greener ingredients in the recipe.

trout wrapped in grape leaves with green rice, dill yogurt, and capers

This dish was inspired by my good friend and a fab farmer, Alex Weiser. Besides consistently having the best and most interesting variety of potatoes in southern California, Alex likes to keep us on our toes with special crops he takes under his wing and obsesses over for years. Alex and I love to joke that he named 2008, then 2009, and again 2010 the "year of the crosnes" before he had actually produced a real crop of the crinkly white tubers from the mint family that he fell in love with on a trip to France.

Romanesco was another one of Alex's pet projects, and I got right on board with his fascination with this Day-Glo relative of cauliflower, considered one of the best examples of a fractal found in nature. As W. K. Lang would describe it, romanesco's "geometric pattern is repeated at ever smaller scales to produce irregular shapes and surfaces that cannot be represented by classical geometry," and it is, in fact, quite visually stunning. Let's just say that the Pasadena Farmers' Market is abuzz with fascinated Caltech types who are more interested in this vegetable's structure than whether it would work better blanched or sautéed. (I love it sautéed with olive oil, garlic, and anchovy, tossed with pasta, and finished with breadcrumbs—but that's me!)

I digress, but my point is that I feel as if I'm in on these adventures with the farmers, and once the experiment finally works—meaning they have mountains of the given product to sell—I feel a happy obligation to cook with and therefore buy it. A few years back, I was seeking out grape leaves for a special Greek dinner we were doing, and I nagged and nagged Alex until he finally sent me a bunch (maybe just to shut me up!). Well, from that day on, whenever Alex saw me he would say, "Got loads of grape leaves now." So, to save face, and keep Alex happy, I came up with this trout wrapped in grape leaves.

The grape leaves made me think of Greece and the southernmost European points of the Mediterranean. I took some inspiration from a summer week my husband, David, and I spent on Pantelleria, the craggy volcanic island off the southern tip of Sicily, considered to grow the best capers in the world. Capers are the small green buds of caper bushes,

12 fresh grape leaves

6 Idaho trout, 8 ounces each, boned and butterflied

4 teaspoons grated lemon zest, plus 1 tablespoon lemon juice

1 tablespoon thyme leaves

½ cup plus 2 tablespoons extra-virgin olive oil

1 small sprig rosemary

1 chile de árbol

½ cup diced red onion

2 tablespoons salt-packed capers, soaked and drained

1 cup plain Greek yogurt

1 tablespoon freshly picked dill

½ clove garlic

1 recipe Green Rice (recipe follows)

2 tablespoons chopped flat-leaf parsley

¼ cup nasturtium petals (optional)

Kosher salt and freshly ground black pepper

which tend to grow best on rocky coasts. The capers from Pantelleria are actually an IGP (Indicazione Geografica Protetta) product—basically, an A.O.C. product that is called out for being particularly characteristic of its location. The designation specifies that capers from Pantelleria must be preserved in salt (rather than brine). Once you taste them, you will understand what capers are all about—fruity and floral with intense flavors of the rugged Mediterranean hillsides. For this dish, I made a little salsa with olive oil, stewed onions, lemon, parsley, and those glorious well-soaked capers, and spooned it over the grape-leaf-wrapped trout, herbaceous green rice, and a dollop of yogurt. When they are in season, I love to scatter nasturtium petals over this dish for a final spicy and beautiful flourish, though doing so is not necessary.

Clean the grape leaves well, and blanch them in boiling water for 1 minute. Drain and dry completely.

Light the grill 30 to 40 minutes before cooking.

Season the trout, inside and outside, with salt, pepper, 1 tablespoon lemon zest, and thyme. Lay 2 grape leaves, just overlapping, on a work surface, and place one fish at the center. Pick up the edges of the leaves closest to you and fold them over the top of the fish, and then roll the partially covered fish away from you to completely wrap it in the leaves. Repeat with each trout.

Meanwhile, heat a medium sauté pan over high heat for 2 minutes. Turn down the heat to medium, and add ½ cup olive oil, the rosemary, and the chile. When the rosemary and chile start to sizzle, add the onion. Turn the heat down to low, and let the onion stew gently for about 10 minutes, until tender. Add the capers, and turn off the heat.

Place the yogurt in a bowl. Using a mortar and pestle, pound the dill to a paste and add it to the bowl. Pound the garlic clove with ½ teaspoon salt, and add to the yogurt as well. Stir in the lemon juice and a pinch of pepper. Taste for balance and seasoning.

When the coals are broken down, red, and glowing, brush the wrapped trout with the remaining 2 tablespoons olive oil and season with salt and pepper. Grill the trout for 3 to 4 minutes on each side over medium heat, rotating the fish a quarter-turn as needed so the leaves do not burn. The trout should feel springy to the touch. You can also unwrap one of the fish to peek inside and check for doneness if you like.

Spoon the hot rice onto the center of six large dinner plates, and place the fish on top. Turn the heat back on under the caper sauce, and add the remaining 1 teaspoon lemon zest. When the sauce is sizzling, add the chopped parsley and taste for balance and seasoning. Dollop the yogurt onto each fish, and spoon the caper sauce over the fish and around the plate. Scatter the nasturtium petals if you are using them.

green rice

Bring the chicken stock and 1¼ cups water (or just 2¼ cups water) to a boil in a medium pot, and then turn off the heat.

Place the parsley, mint, chives, and cilantro in a blender. Add 1 cup of the hot liquid, and purée the herbs at medium speed. Pour in the rest of the liquid slowly, and purée at high speed for almost 2 minutes, until you have a very smooth, very green broth.

Toast the fennel seeds in a small pan over medium heat for 2 to 3 minutes, until they release their aroma and turn light golden brown. Pound them with a mortar and pestle.

Quickly rinse out the pot (if you used the chicken stock), and heat it over high heat for 2 minutes. Add the olive oil, diced fennel, onion, toasted fennel seeds, chile, and ½ teaspoon salt. Cook over medium-high heat for about 5 minutes, stirring often, until the onion and fennel are translucent. Add the rice, 1 teaspoon salt, and a pinch of pepper. Stir well, to coat the rice with the oil and vegetables. Add the herb broth and ½ teaspoon salt. Bring to a boil, and reduce the heat to a low simmer. Add the butter, cover, and cook the rice for 15 to 20 minutes, until tender. Turn off the heat, and leave the rice covered for 5 minutes. Then fluff the rice with a fork, and taste for seasoning.

1 cup chicken stock or water

½ cup packed flat-leaf parsley leaves

¼ cup packed mint leaves

2 tablespoons minced chives

¼ cup packed cilantro leaves

2 teaspoons fennel seeds

¼ cup plus 1 tablespoon extra-virgin olive oil

¾ cup finely diced fennel

¾ cup finely diced red onion

1 chile de árbol, crumbled

1½ cups white basmati rice

1 tablespoon unsalted butter

Kosher salt and freshly ground black pepper

The overall profile of this recipe is cool, with the bright yet delicate green notes in the rice and creamy yogurt. It does not overpower the palate but, rather, exudes freshness and clean earthiness. To work with this, I look for a white wine with delicate, not overly racy acidity, and fresh green herbal notes to mesh with those in the recipe. A great option for this is Pinot Gris, a grape variety that is grown throughout many European countries as well as New World regions like California, Oregon, and New Zealand. For this pairing, I recommend choosing one from Alsace or New Zealand, where Pinot Gris tends to show a touch of richness alongside a melonlike fruitiness and flinty mineral character.

roasted cod with artichokes barigoule, braised bacon, aïoli, and black olives

24 baby artichokes

½ cup plus 1 tablespoon
extra-virgin olive oil

1 sprig rosemary

1 cup sliced white onion

½ cup sliced carrots (cut in half
lengthwise, and then on the
diagonal)

¼ cup sliced garlic

1 chile de árbol, sliced

1 fresh bay leaf, sliced

2 teaspoons thyme leaves

1½ cups dry white wine

2 tablespoons freshly squeezed
lemon juice, plus ½ lemon
for juicing

½ pound Braised Bacon
(recipe follows)

6 fillets Eastern cod,
5 to 6 ounces each, skin on

½ cup pitted oil-cured black
olives, sliced in half

¼ cup sliced flat-leaf parsley
leaves

½ cup Aïoli (recipe follows)

Kosher salt and freshly ground
black pepper

This recipe is a lot of work. When I wrote my first book, *Sunday Suppers at Lucques,* I tried hard to balance simplifying recipes for home cooks with ensuring that those hard-core, serious home cooks were satisfied and didn't feel I was dumbing anything down. My solution in that book and in this one is to provide recipes of varying degrees of difficulty. So, if you are looking for a quick and easy one, turn the page; but if you are up for a pretty involved, really delicious ode to Provence, get your *mise en place* ready!

At A.O.C., we nestle the cod into the artichokes barigoule with chunks of braised bacon, and roast it all in the wood-burning oven. This way, the juices that are released as the fish is cooking are not lost, and instead meld with the white wine and olive oil from the artichokes barigoule to create a deeply flavored sauce. You can replicate this by baking the dish in a hot oven. The braised bacon lends a smoky note that mimics the smoke of the wood oven. I prefer to serve this dish family-style, from oven to table, for a dramatic rustic presentation. But unless you have a giant cazuela, you may need to split the ingredients into two baking dishes.

NOTE I love the braised bacon, but you can substitute slab bacon if you want to save a step.

NOTE If you want to prepare the artichokes ahead of time, you can place the artichokes in a bowl of cold water with a squeeze of lemon juice to prevent browning and leave them soaking for up to 4 hours.

NOTE If the chile de árbol is dry and brittle you can just crush or crumble it.

Cut off the top third of the artichokes, and remove the tough outer leaves until you reach the soft pale-yellow-green leaves. Using a paring knife, trim the bottom of the stem and cut any dark, bitter pieces away from where the stem meets the heart. Cut each artichoke in half, and remove the fuzzy choke if there is one.

Heat a large Dutch oven over high heat for 2 minutes. Pour ½ cup olive oil into the pan, add the rosemary sprig, and then add the onion, carrots, garlic, chile, bay leaf, and thyme. Stir to coat the vegetables in the oil, and cook for a few minutes. Add the artichokes, season with salt and pepper, and cook for 3 or 4 minutes, until the artichokes and onion are nicely glazed and the edges are just beginning to brown. Add the white wine, bring to a boil, and then cook for 3 minutes. Cover with a piece of parchment that fits directly on top of the vegetables. Cook over low heat at a gentle simmer for about 30 minutes, until the artichokes are tender and "al dente." Transfer to a large (12-inch round or equivalent) baking dish or cazuela, add the 2 tablespoons lemon juice, and taste for seasoning.

Preheat the oven to 450°F.

Slice the braised bacon into ⅜-inch-thick slices. Stack the slices in two piles, then cut the bacon crosswise into ⅜-inch-thick even-sided rectangles or *lardons*. Stir the *lardons* into the artichokes.

Season the cod with salt and pepper, and nestle the fillets, skin-side up, into the artichokes. Bake for 15 to 20 minutes, until the fish is just cooked through and the artichokes are bubbling. While the fish is cooking, toss the olives and parsley in a small bowl with the remaining 1 tablespoon olive oil and a squeeze of lemon juice.

As noted above, I like to serve this dish family-style: scatter the olives over the top of the whole dish, and pass a bowl of the aïoli at the table. You could also arrange servings on individual plates, top each with a dollop of aïoli, and scatter the olives over the plate, if you prefer.

braised bacon

Try slices of leftover braised bacon crisped up in a pan or in the oven with steamed green beans, or wilted kale or collards . . . maybe with a fried egg on top. . . . One of the best parts of this recipe is the sherry-and-bacon-fat-infused liquid that it creates. Use it to finish pastas as you would use stock or pasta water, or add it to braises and ragouts.

3 tablespoons extra-virgin olive oil

1 cup diced onion

⅓ cup diced carrot

⅓ cup diced celery

2 cups sherry

6 cups chicken stock

2 pounds slab bacon

2 fresh or dried bay leaves

1 teaspoon black peppercorns

4 sprigs thyme

4 sprigs flat-leaf parsley

Preheat the oven to 325°F.

Heat a large Dutch oven over high heat for 2 minutes. Pour in the olive oil, add the onion, carrot, and celery, and sauté about 5 minutes, stirring often, until the vegetables start to caramelize.

Pour in the sherry, and reduce by half, about 5 minutes. Add the chicken stock, and bring to a boil.

Turn off the heat, and add the bacon, bay leaves, peppercorns, thyme, and parsley. Cover the pan with a tight-fitting lid, and braise in the oven for about 3½ hours.

The bacon is done when it will yield easily to a knife inserted into the center.

Let the bacon rest for 10 minutes in the juices, and then carefully transfer it to a baking sheet.

Strain the broth into a container, and let cool. Skim the fat that rises to the top and discard it. Reserve the broth for other uses (see the headnote).

aïoli

1 extra-large egg yolk
½ cup grape-seed oil
½ cup extra-virgin olive oil
1 small clove garlic
½ lemon, for juicing
Pinch cayenne pepper
Kosher salt

Place the yolk in a stainless-steel bowl. Begin whisking in the grape-seed oil, drop by drop. Once the mixture has thickened and emulsified, you can whisk in the remaining grape-seed and olive oils in a slow, steady stream. If the mixture gets too thick, add a drop or two of water.

Pound the garlic with ¼ teaspoon salt with a mortar and pestle. Whisk the garlic paste into the aïoli. Season with another ¼ teaspoon salt, a squeeze of lemon juice, and the cayenne. Taste for balance and seasoning. If the aïoli seems thick and gloppy, thin it with a little water. In addition to thinning the aïoli, this will also make it creamier.

Most people recommend shying away from artichokes when it comes to wine pairing, because artichokes have a tendency to neutralize the palate and render everything that touches it tasteless. Fortunately for me, I have never encountered this "phenomenon" when working with Suzanne: her recipes are so bold in flavor and texturally complex that the artichoke taboo just doesn't apply. This recipe is a perfect example, with its combination of smokiness in the bacon and fleshiness that comes from the olive oil and aïoli. It's a fish dish that is rich enough to need a red wine with depth of flavor, as well as a good dose of acidity to keep the pairing vibrant. I like Cabernet Franc, especially when it's from the Loire Valley, where the wines are fairly restrained in concentration and body, but deep enough in fruit and earthy flavors to feel hearty. These wines typically show an undercurrent of green-pepper and tomato-stem notes that will play well with the recipe's vegetable ingredients.

wild salmon with spinach soubise, wilted leeks, and meyer lemon butter

The Meyer-lemon "butter" in this salmon preparation is actually a classic *beurre blanc* (a traditional white butter sauce from Brittany, France) with wilted leeks and Meyer lemon stirred in at the end. Once you have the hang of this sauce, you can flavor and season it so many ways. Here it's spooned over the vibrant salmon and the bright-green soubise—it's rich but still springy, and the Meyer lemon gives it a great burst of acid.

Season the salmon with the zest, thyme leaves, and parsley. Cover, and refrigerate for at least 4 hours.

Remove the fish from the refrigerator 15 minutes before cooking, to bring it to room temperature.

Slice the stem and blossom ends from the Meyer lemon. Stand the lemon on one end, and cut it vertically into ⅛-inch slices. Stack the slices in small piles on a cutting board, and cut them lengthwise into ⅛-inch-thick matchsticks. Line up the matchsticks, and cut them into ⅛-inch cubes. You will need ¼ cup diced lemon.

Place the shallots, white wine, Meyer-lemon juice, bay leaf, peppercorns, and thyme sprigs in a medium nonreactive saucepan, and bring to a boil over medium-high heat. Cook for about 5 minutes, until the liquid is reduced to 2 tablespoons, and then add the cream. Turn the heat down to medium-low, and cook for about another 5 minutes, until the cream is reduced by half and is thickened and glossy. Slowly add the butter, whisking constantly, until it is completely incorporated.

Strain the butter sauce into a clean saucepan, and add the leeks, ½ teaspoon salt, and a few grindings of black pepper. Cook over low heat for a minute or two, until the leeks are wilted. Stir in the diced Meyer lemon, and taste for balance and seasoning. Keep the sauce warm.

Heat a large sauté pan over high heat for 2 minutes. (Depending on the size of your pan, you may need to cook the fish in batches.) Season the fish with salt and pepper on both sides. Swirl the olive oil into the pan, and wait 1 minute. Carefully lay the fish in the pan skin-side down, and cook for 3 to 4 minutes, until the skin is crisp. Turn the fish over, lower the heat to

6 fillets wild salmon,
    5 to 6 ounces each, skin on

1 tablespoon Meyer lemon zest

1 tablespoon thyme leaves,
    plus 2 sprigs thyme

2 tablespoons chopped flat-leaf
    parsley

1 whole Meyer lemon

3 tablespoons finely diced
    shallots

1 cup dry white wine

¼ cup Meyer lemon juice

1 bay leaf, fresh if possible

2 black peppercorns

½ cup heavy cream

10 tablespoons unsalted butter,
    cut into small cubes

¾ cup thinly sliced leeks

2 to 4 tablespoons extra-virgin
    olive oil

1 recipe Spinach Soubise
    (recipe follows)

Kosher salt and freshly ground
    black pepper

medium-low, and cook for another minute or two, until the salmon is still a little rare in the center. Remember, the fish will continue to cook a bit more once you take it out of the pan.

Spoon the hot spinach soubise onto the center of six large dinner plates. Place the salmon on top, skin-side up, and spoon a few tablespoons of the Meyer-lemon butter over the fish and around the soubise.

spinach soubise

4 tablespoons unsalted butter

1 cup diced white onion, plus 6 cups thinly sliced white onions (about 1½ pounds total)

1 tablespoon thyme leaves

¼ cup Arborio rice

½ pound spinach, cleaned, plus 2 cups thinly sliced spinach

¼ cup heavy cream

Kosher salt and ¼ teaspoon freshly ground black pepper

Sometimes "soubise" refers to a very reduced onion purée; other times it calls for onion purée to be folded into béchamel. Honestly, I do not love either of those versions. *My* beloved "soubise" is actually based on a Julia Child recipe from *Mastering the Art of French Cooking*—a book I was basically raised on as my mother worked her way through it during my delicious childhood. In Julia's book the recipe is actually called Braised Rice and Onions. I have tweaked this recipe in more ways than you can imagine.

I have stirred green garlic, sweet-pea purée, any number of cheeses, sorrel, and, in this case, spinach into Julia's luscious union of tons of onions and a tiny bit of rice. I explain it to my staff as "reverse risotto," where the onion and rice switch places in their importance. The key for this soubise, unlike the onion-purée one, is not to get any color on the onions at all, stewing them ever so gently, then covering them and steaming them with the rice in the oven, so their sweet natural juices come out and bind with that tiny bit of starch from the rice.

Preheat the oven to 350°F.

Heat a large ovenproof saucepan or Dutch oven over medium heat for 1 minute. Add the butter, and when it foams, add the diced and sliced onions, thyme, 2 teaspoons salt, and the white pepper. Turn the heat down to medium-low, and cook the onions gently for about 10 minutes, stirring often. They should soften and wilt but not be allowed to color at all.

While the onions are cooking, bring a small pot of water to a boil. Cook the rice for 5 minutes in the boiling water, and drain well. Stir the blanched rice into the onions.

Remove the pot from the heat. Cover it with aluminum foil and a tight-fitting lid. Cook in the oven for 30 minutes.

While the soubise is cooking, bring a large pot of heavily salted water to a boil. Blanch the ½ pound spinach for 30 seconds, and cool in a bowl of ice water. Squeeze out all the excess water, and purée in a food processor. You will need to add a little water (about 2 to 4 tablespoons) to get the purée going; just be careful to add the smallest amount necessary.

Remove the soubise from the oven, and let it "rest," covered, about 15 minutes.

Just before serving, uncover the soubise, and heat it over medium heat, stirring once or twice. When the soubise is hot, stir in the spinach purée, sliced spinach, and cream. Taste for seasoning.

The spinach soubise in this recipe is luscious and fairly unctuous. In order to tame its richness and incorporate the lemon butter into the pairing, the best option would be to choose a wine that has a good dose of lemony citrus and enough acidity to balance it all. Chardonnay from the Mâconnais, in the southern region of Burgundy, works well for this purpose. The wines, labeled as Mâcon or Mâcon-Villages, and particularly those from warmer vintages such as 2003, 2005, and 2009, tend to show a bit more tropical fruit and bright citrus than others, which gives them a deep flavor profile and vibrancy. This racy fruit quality will help in lightening the weight of the soubise on the palate while meshing with the tang of the citrus butter.

grilled arctic char with arugula and cherry tomato—anchovy brown butter

1 lemon, zested, and 4 teaspoons juice

6 fillets arctic char, 5 to 6 ounces each, skin on

1 tablespoon thyme leaves

¼ cup chopped flat-leaf parsley

1½ pounds heirloom tomatoes

2 tablespoons sliced basil, green and opal if possible

4 ounces arugula, cleaned and dried

¼ cup extra-virgin olive oil

8 tablespoons unsalted butter

1½ teaspoons minced anchovy (I highly recommend salt-cured anchovies)

¾ pint small cherry tomatoes, cut in half

Kosher salt and freshly ground black pepper

On a hot summer evening, when you can't imagine being able to eat anything, this light but satisfying dish should do the trick. I love big salads with grilled fish or meat, and sauces that then dress and half wilt the salad to bring the whole dish together. Arugula, tomatoes, anchovies, and basil work well with the richness of the arctic char, but this dish would also be great with wild salmon if it's available. Arctic char, related to salmon and trout, has characteristics of both, although I find it to be much closer to salmon. Most of the char in the United States is farmed and is considered a "Best Choice" by the Monterey Bay Aquarium's Seafood Watch program, because it's farmed in an ecologically responsible manner, in closed, recirculating, land-based systems.

This cherry tomato–brown-butter sauce is my go-to quick and easy sauce for summer. The only trick is to make sure the butter is properly browned and hot, so that when you drop the cherry tomatoes into it they pop and sizzle, getting glazed and a little seared in the butter while releasing their juices to create an integrated sauce. This Provençal-inspired version has anchovies, thyme, lemon, and parsley.

Grate zest from the lemon, and season the char with the lemon zest, thyme, and 2 tablespoons parsley. Cover, and refrigerate for at least 4 hours.

Light the grill 30 to 40 minutes ahead of time and take the char out of the refrigerator, so it comes to room temperature.

Core the heirloom tomatoes, hold them on their sides, one by one, and cut them into ¼-inch-thick slices. Season the slices with salt and pepper, and scatter the basil over them. Arrange a few slices of tomato on each of six large dinner plates.

Toss the arugula in a large bowl with 2 tablespoons olive oil, 2 teaspoons lemon juice, salt, and pepper. Arrange two-thirds of the salad on the plates in a natural style, followed by the remaining tomatoes, and finally the rest of the arugula.

When the coals are broken down, red, and glowing, brush the char with the remaining 2 tablespoons olive oil, and season with salt and pepper. Place the fish on the grill skin-side down, and cook for 3 to 4 minutes, rotating the fish once after a couple of minutes, to get the skin crispy. Turn the fish over, and cook another minute or so, until medium-rare. Place the fish, skin-side up, on top of the arugula-and-tomato salad.

While the fish is cooking, place the butter in a medium sauté pan. Cook for a few minutes over high heat, until it starts to brown and smells nutty, and then add the anchovy, cherry tomatoes, ¾ teaspoon salt, and a few grindings of black pepper. Cook for 30 seconds, shaking the pan, until the tomatoes release some of their juice. Squeeze 2 teaspoons lemon juice into the pan, and taste for balance and seasoning. Stir in the remaining 2 tablespoons parsley. Spoon the sauce over the fish and around the salad.

The cherry tomato butter in this recipe gives the fish a really nutty, deep complexity. You experience not only the sweetness of the tomatoes, but also their more earthy aspect, with touches of green tomato leaf and a hint of bitterness from their skins. These secondary flavors are akin to those in Cabernet Franc, a Bordeaux grape variety that is also grown in California's Napa Valley. These wines can show dark berry notes and hints of chocolate when made in a more concentrated style, but when made lighter they become something totally different, taking on a bright red fruit profile and showing a good deal of green pepper and tomato leaf.

grilled snapper with couscous, apricots, yogurt, and pistachio aillade

In summer, I have a hard time not putting fruit on everything—it's almost not fair that there are so many delicious, juicy delights, *all* ripe at the same time. Roasting and grilling fruit is a great way to transform it into a saucy element for main courses. The roasted apricots in this dish are bursting with sweet, intensified juices that glaze the fish when you cut into them. I love the combination of pistachios, stone fruit, and yogurt. The saffron couscous pairs well with the honey, clove, and star anise in the syrup in which the apricots are roasted, and is also perfect to soak up all the sweet, sour, nut-oily juices on the plate.

Season the fish with the zest, 1 tablespoon thyme, and parsley. Cover, and refrigerate for at least 4 hours.

Thirty to 40 minutes before cooking, preheat the oven to 375°F, light the grill, and take the snapper out of the refrigerator.

Place the orange juice, honey, cloves, star anise, and lemon juice in a medium nonreactive pot, and reduce over medium heat by half.

Cut the apricots in half, and remove the pits. Place them cut-side up on a work surface, and season with salt, pepper, and the remaining 2 teaspoons thyme.

Heat a large ovenproof sauté pan over medium-high heat for 1 minute. Swirl in 2 tablespoons olive oil, and carefully place the apricots in the pan cut-side down. Cook for 2 or 3 minutes, until slightly caramelized, and then turn the apricots over and turn off the heat. Spoon the syrup over the apricots, and place the pan in the oven. Bake for 10 to 15 minutes, until the apricots are tender and nicely glazed.

When the coals are broken down, red, and glowing, brush the snapper with remaining 2 tablespoons olive oil, and season with salt and pepper. Place the fish on the grill skin-side down, and cook for 3 to 4 minutes, rotating the fish once, after a couple of minutes, to get the skin crispy. Turn the fish over, and cook for a few more minutes on the other side. Be careful not to overcook the snapper. When it's done, the fish will begin to flake and separate a little and

6 fillets snapper, 5 to 6 ounces each, skin on

1 tablespoon grated orange zest

1 tablespoon plus 2 teaspoons thyme leaves

2 tablespoons chopped flat-leaf parsley

½ cup freshly squeezed orange juice

2 tablespoons honey

A few whole cloves

1 star anise

1 tablespoon freshly squeezed lemon juice

9 small apricots

¼ cup extra-virgin olive oil

1 recipe Couscous (recipe follows)

2 ounces mizuna

½ cup plain good-quality yogurt

1 recipe Pistachio Aillade (recipe follows)

Kosher salt and freshly ground black pepper

the center will be slightly translucent. Remember, the snapper will continue to cook a little more once you take it off the grill.

Spoon the hot couscous onto the center of six dinner plates. Tuck a few mizuna leaves into the couscous, and place the snapper on top, skin-side up. Arrange the hot apricots around the fish and the couscous, and dollop the fish with yogurt. Spoon the pistachio aillade over and around the plate and serve the rest at the table.

couscous

¼ teaspoon saffron threads

3 tablespoons extra-virgin olive oil

1 cup finely diced yellow onion

2 cups couscous

½ cup sliced scallions

Kosher salt

Toast the saffron in a small pan over medium heat until it just dries and becomes brittle. Pound the saffron to a fine powder in a mortar. Pour the olive oil into the mortar, and stir it well to incorporate the saffron.

Heat a medium saucepot over medium heat for 2 minutes, and add the saffron-infused olive oil. Add the diced onion, and cook gently for about 5 minutes, until translucent. Meanwhile, place the couscous, the scallions, and 1½ teaspoons salt in a medium bowl, and stir to combine.

Add 2 cups water to the pot with the saffron onions, and bring to a boil. Pour the liquid over the couscous, stir with a fork, and immediately cover the bowl tightly with plastic wrap. Let sit for at least 15 minutes.

When you are ready to serve, remove the plastic wrap and fluff the couscous with a fork.

pistachio aillade

This is one of my all-time favorite sauces. I love it so much that I actually came up with a sweet version to serve with desserts, too! (See page 300.) You can make it in advance, but if you do, don't add the zest and juices until the last minute or they will make the nuts soggy. This pistachio aillade is especially delicious made with Santa Barbara Pistachio Company's bright-green local nuts—available at www.santabar barapistachios.com.

Preheat the oven to 375°F.

Spread the pistachios on a baking sheet, and toast for 5 minutes, until they dry out just a little—you don't want them as toasted as usual, because that would make the aillade dark.

Pound the garlic and ¼ teaspoon salt in a mortar and pestle.

In a food processor, chop the pistachios roughly, and then add the garlic. With the machine running, pour in half the olive oil. Transfer to a medium bowl.

Stir in the remaining ¼ cup olive oil, the orange zest, 1 tablespoon of the orange juice, 1 tablespoon lemon juice, ¼ teaspoon salt, and a few grinds of pepper. Taste for balance and seasoning.

1 cup shelled pistachios, preferably from Santa Barbara Pistachio Company

1 small clove garlic, or ½ large clove

½ cup extra-virgin olive oil

Grated zest and juice of ½ orange

1 tablespoon freshly squeezed lemon juice

Kosher salt and freshly ground black pepper

When I think of dishes with this kind of Moroccan influence, I am immediately drawn to the south of France, North Africa's neighbor across the sea, and I think about the rosés and other wines from the region of Cassis. This stunningly beautiful region features dramatic coastal vistas and turns out elegant wines made from Marsanne, Clairette, Ugni Blanc, and Sauvignon Blanc. These wines tend to show bright stone-fruit notes, exotic aromatics of cardamom and ginger, and low levels of acidity. Their delicate spiciness really enhances the flavors in the apricots and pistachios, and their softness of texture reflects that of the dish itself.

pan-roasted halibut with blue crab, early girls, and horseradish crème fraîche

The funny thing about our crazy southern-California growing situation is that Early Girl tomatoes often aren't actually early at all! But I do love them for their straightforward, no-nonsense look and taste, unlike their glamorous and precious heirloom counterparts. This dish is another hot-weather crowd pleaser that requires very little actual cooking and really satisfies. To make it even easier, you can prepare the vinaigrette and horseradish crème fraîche several hours in advance. If you want a still lighter version, try stuffing the Early Girls with the crab mixture and topping them with the horseradish crème fraîche for a light summer lunch or first course, without the halibut.

Season the halibut with the lemon zest, thyme, and 2 tablespoons chopped parsley. Cover, and refrigerate at least for 4 hours or overnight.

Remove the fish from the refrigerator 15 minutes before cooking, to bring it to room temperature.

Place the diced shallot, both vinegars, and ½ teaspoon salt in a bowl, and let sit for 5 minutes. Whisk in 6 tablespoons olive oil and set aside.

In a medium bowl, toss the crab gently with 1 tablespoon crème fraîche, the lemon juice, 1 tablespoon olive oil, and the remaining 2 tablespoons chopped parsley. Taste for balance and seasoning (the crab may or may not need salt).

Combine the remaining crème fraîche, horseradish, ¼ teaspoon salt, and a little pepper in a small bowl. Taste for seasoning, and refrigerate.

Core the tomatoes, and slice them into ½-inch-thick round slices. (There should be about 18 slices.) Spread the slices on a cutting board or plate, and season them with salt and pepper.

Season the fish with salt and pepper. Heat a large sauté pan over high heat for 2 minutes. (You may need to cook the fish in batches or in two pans.) Swirl in the remaining 2 tablespoons olive oil, and carefully lay the fish in the pan. It will smoke, but resist the temptation to move the fish. Cook for 3 to 4 minutes, until it's browned. Turn the fish over, lower the heat to medium-low, and cook for a few more minutes, until it's just cooked through. Be careful not

Ingredients

6 fillets halibut, 5 to 6 ounces each

1 tablespoon grated lemon zest plus 4 tablespoons freshly squeezed juice

1 tablespoon thyme leaves

4 tablespoons finely chopped flat-leaf parsley

1 tablespoon finely diced shallot

1½ tablespoons red-wine vinegar

1 tablespoon balsamic vinegar

½ cup plus 1 tablespoon extra-virgin olive oil

¾ pound steamed picked-over blue crabmeat

¾ cup crème fraîche

1 tablespoon prepared horseradish

2 pounds Early Girl, beefsteak, or heirloom tomatoes

2 ounces arugula, cleaned and dried (about 1 bunch)

Kosher salt and freshly ground black pepper

to overcook the fish. When it's done, it will begin to flake and separate a little, and the center will still be slightly translucent. Remember, the halibut will continue to cook a bit more once you take it out of the pan.

While the fish is cooking, arrange the sliced tomatoes on six large dinner plates. Tuck the leaves of arugula between and around the tomatoes in a natural style. Spoon the vinaigrette over the tomatoes and arugula. Place the halibut at the center, and arrange spoonfuls of crab on top of the fish. Dollop each fillet with a heaping tablespoon of the horseradish crème fraîche, and pass the rest at the table (chances are it will all be gone by the end of the meal!).

When pairing a wine with crab, I usually look for one that has a brininess and flavor profile similar to that of the fish itself. A great example of this, and one that would be a perfect complement to this dish, is Vermentino, grown on the islands of Corsica and Sardinia, as well as in Liguria, where it is known instead as Pigato. I particularly like the wines that are produced in the Corsican region of Patrimonio. These wines show bright stone-fruit notes—something that will work nicely with the sweet tomatoes—and a clean, salty, almost seaside quality that will highlight the flavors of the sea in the blue crab.

california sea bass with tomato rice, fried egg, and sopressata

I love bacon and eggs. Pretty much any version, or any excuse to eat either of those things, is good with me. So this dish makes perfect sense to me. Start with slightly soupy, richly flavored tomato rice, add a meaty piece of grilled bass, top it with a sunny-side-up egg, and spoon over it some sizzling spicy sopressata. I knew I would love it but was happily surprised when it became kind of a cult hit at the restaurant.

Season the fish with the lemon zest, thyme, Aleppo pepper, and 2 tablespoons parsley. Cover, and refrigerate for at least 4 hours.

Light the grill 30 to 40 minutes before you're ready to cook the bass and take the fish out of the refrigerator, to bring it to room temperature.

Stack the sliced sopressata, and cut into long ½-inch-thick strips. Heat a medium sauté pan over medium heat for 2 minutes, swirl in 2 tablespoons olive oil and add the sopressata. Cook for 2 minutes, stirring often, until the sopressata is crispy. Turn off the heat, and stir in the paprika and 1 tablespoon parsley.

When the coals are broken down, red, and glowing, season the bass with salt and a little pepper, and brush with about 2 tablespoons olive oil.

Place the fish on the grill skin-side down, and cook for 3 to 4 minutes, rotating the fish once after a couple of minutes to get the skin crispy. Turn the fish over, and cook for a few more minutes on the other side. When it's done, the fish will begin to flake and separate a little, and the center will be slightly translucent. Remember, the bass will continue to cook a little more once you take it off the grill.

Heat two nonstick or cast-iron pans over high heat for 2 minutes. Swirl 2 tablespoons olive oil and crack 3 eggs into each pan. Turn off the heat, and season the eggs with salt and pepper. The eggs should cook slowly and completely from the heat of the pans.

Stir the remaining 2 tablespoons parsley into the hot rice, taste for seasoning, and spoon it onto the center of six large, shallow bowls or plates. Arrange the fish on the rice, skin-side up, squeeze a few drops of lemon juice on the fish, and use a spatula to place a sunny-side-up egg carefully on top. Spoon the crispy sopressata onto the egg, and scatter the opal basil on each plate.

6 fillets California sea bass, 5 to 6 ounces each, skin on

1 tablespoon finely grated lemon zest, plus ½ lemon for juicing

1 tablespoon thyme leaves

1 tablespoon crushed Aleppo pepper

5 tablespoons chopped flat-leaf parsley

3 ounces thickly sliced sopressata

½ cup extra-virgin olive oil

1 teaspoon smoked paprika

6 extra-large eggs

1 recipe Tomato Rice (recipe follows)

2 tablespoons sliced opal basil

Kosher salt and freshly ground black pepper

tomato rice

After we've spent months longing for and dreaming of summer and its produce, there comes that moment in late August when we are suddenly inundated with summer squash, basil, eggplant, and tomatoes. This Portuguese-inspired tomato rice is the perfect way to clear your kitchen counter of those baskets of almost overripe tomatoes. It's like the rice version of *pappa pomodoro,* a thick Italian bread soup or porridge, which I also love. It's comforting and warm without being too heavy for the summer months. I think I must have been a European peasant in my last life!

NOTE If the chile de árbol is dry and brittle you can just crush or crumble it.

Blanch the tomatoes in boiling water for 30 seconds. Cool the tomatoes in a bowl of ice water for a few minutes, and then use your fingers to slip off their skins. Remove the cores, and cut each tomato in half horizontally. Squeeze the tomato halves cut-side down over a strainer set in a bowl. Scoop the seeds out with your fingers and discard them. Chop the tomatoes coarsely and reserve the juice.

Heat a medium saucepan over high heat for 1 minute. Add the olive oil, the rosemary sprig, and the chile. Let them sizzle in the oil about 1 minute, and then stir in the onion, garlic, thyme, 1 teaspoon salt, and some pepper. Turn down the heat to medium, and cook about 5 minutes, until the onion is translucent. Add the tomatoes, tomato juices, and 1 teaspoon salt, and cook another 20 minutes, stirring frequently, until the sauce thickens and looks like a thin marinara sauce.

Add the stock to the pot, bring to a boil, and stir in the rice. Return to a boil, then turn down the heat to low, cover the pot, and simmer for about 12 minutes, until the rice is tender. Taste for seasoning.

4 pounds ripe red tomatoes

¼ cup extra-virgin olive oil

1 small sprig rosemary

1 chile de árbol, sliced

1½ cups finely diced yellow onion

2 teaspoons minced garlic

2 teaspoons thyme leaves

2 cups chicken stock

1½ cups basmati or long-grain rice

Kosher salt and freshly ground black pepper

The savory spiciness of this recipe and its Italian inspiration take my mind to the island of Sicily, and the bright, mineral-rich red wines of the region of Etna. Wines from this area, made from varieties like Nerello Mascalese and Nero d'Avola, are characteristically bright, elegant, and high in acid. These wines are dominated by red and black fruit tones and, depending on the amount of oak aging, a velvety texture and grip. They have a background of tarlike mineral notes from the area's volcanic soils, which give the wine a savory, gamy quality reflective of the flavors in the crispy sopressata and tomato.

alaskan black cod with kabocha squash, golden raisins, and pedro ximenez

6 fillets black cod, 5 to 6 ounces each, bones removed, skin on

1 tablespoon grated lemon zest

1 tablespoon thyme leaves

2 tablespoons chopped flat-leaf parsley

½ cup golden raisins

¼ cup Pedro Ximenez sherry

2 tablespoons dry sherry

1 bunch green Swiss chard, cleaned, center ribs removed

¼ cup extra-virgin olive oil

1 recipe Kabocha Squash Purée (recipe follows)

8 tablespoons unsalted butter

1 tablespoon sliced sage

Kosher salt and freshly ground black pepper

When I first conceived of this dish, I was worried that although I was excited about the combination of some of my favorite ingredients, there might be too much sweetness going on for it to all work. I loved the idea of the wood-cask flavor of sherry paired with the deep earthiness of kabocha squash. And I had high hopes for the combination of golden raisins with one of the world's greatest uses of grapes—Pedro Ximenez sherry. Fortunately, the sage in the kabocha-squash purée, the savory Swiss chard, the silky, luscious black cod, and the right amount of salt provided enough savory flavors to bring the whole dish together in glorious balance.

When choosing black cod or sablefish, I always seek out fish from Alaska. Actually, Alaskan seafood is always a good bet, because that area boasts one of the world's best-managed fisheries, which means you can count on ecologically and sustainably soundly caught fish.

Season the fish with the lemon zest, thyme, and parsley. Cover, and refrigerate for at least 4 hours or overnight.

Remove the fish from the refrigerator 15 minutes before cooking, to bring it to room temperature.

Place the raisins in a small bowl, and pour boiling hot water over them to cover. Let them sit for 10 minutes, strain, dry the bowl, and return the raisins to the bowl. Pour the Pedro Ximenez and dry sherry over the raisins, and let sit for at least 30 minutes.

Heat a large sauté pan over high heat for 2 minutes. Tear the Swiss chard into large pieces. Add to the pan 2 tablespoons olive oil, the Swiss chard, ¼ teaspoon salt, and a few grindings of pepper. Cook for a few minutes, stirring often, until the greens are tender. Keep warm.

Heat another large sauté pan over high heat for 2 minutes. (Depending on the size of your pan, you may need to cook the fish in two pans or two batches.) Season the fish with salt and pepper on both sides. Swirl in the remaining 2 tablespoons olive oil, and wait 1 minute. Carefully lay the fish in the pan skin-side down, and cook for 3 to 4 minutes, until the skin is crisp. Turn the fish over, lower the heat to medium-low, and cook for a few more minutes, until it's just cooked through. Be careful not to overcook the fish. When it's done, the fish will begin to flake and separate a little. Remember, the fish will continue to cook a little more once you take it out of the pan.

Spoon the hot kabocha-squash purée onto the center of six large dinner plates, and arrange the Swiss chard around the purée. Place the fish on top.

Wipe out the fish pan with paper towels, and return it to the stove over medium-high heat.

Add the butter, and cook a few minutes, swirling the pan occasionally, until the butter browns and smells nutty. Turn the heat down to low, and add the raisins, both sherries, ½ teaspoon salt, and a few grindings of pepper. Cook a minute or two, until the sauce is emulsified and the consistency is syrupy. Add the sage, taste for balance and seasoning, and spoon the raisin sauce over the fish.

kabocha squash purée

1 small kabocha squash, peeled and cut into 2-inch chunks

¼ cup extra-virgin olive oil

1 tablespoon thyme leaves

1 cup heavy cream

8 tablespoons unsalted butter

2 tablespoons sliced sage

Kosher salt and freshly ground black pepper

I like the richness and textural surpise you get from roasting the squash before puréeing it. Yes, it's an extra step, but so worth it in my opinion.

Preheat the oven to 425°F.

Toss the squash chunks with the olive oil, 1 tablespoon salt, some pepper, and the thyme. Place the squash on a baking sheet, and roast in the oven for about 30 minutes, until tender when pierced.

Warm the cream, and set aside.

Cook the butter in a medium saucepan over medium heat about 5 minutes, shaking the pan occasionally, until the butter browns and smells nutty. Once the butter has browned, remove the pan from the heat and wait a minute or two. Add the sage to the pan. (Be careful—the butter might foam up a little, and it's very hot.)

Place half the cooked squash, half the butter, and half the cream in a food processor, and purée completely to a smooth consistency. Transfer to a large mixing bowl. Place the remaining squash, butter, and cream in the food processor, and use the pulse function to process to a chunky consistency. Add to the bowl, and fold the two batches of squash purée together with a rubber spatula. Taste for seasoning.

This dish has a beautiful earthiness and a dose of richness that is perfect for the cool fall months. The nutty Pedro Ximenez, golden raisins, and sweet kabocha beg for a wine with similar qualities, like the unusual white wine of the Jura. This is a region located between Burgundy and Switzerland, where the Chardonnay and Savagnin grapes are fermented and aged in the same manner as sherry, allowing the wine to develop a relatively dark color and nutty flavor. The wines display notes of exotic spices along with ginger and honey, resulting in an interesting tension, reflective of the flavor profiles in this recipe.

fried oysters with celery root rémoulade and watercress

Our opening chef, the infamous Julie Robles, came up with this dish to celebrate her love of New Orleans. I thought I had worked in a lot of places, but I swear, Julie has worked in at least one restaurant in practically every state! You could play culinary six degrees of separation with most of the great chefs in the country and would quickly be led to Julie. She worked for Thomas Keller at Checkers in downtown L.A. long before he had even thought of Yountville. She chugged it out on the brunch line at Mr. B's Bistro in New Orleans. And, boy, does she have stories to tell. Julie *is* the restaurant business, through and through—tough but caring, incredibly quick-witted, and fierce but loving. In fact, when I first met my husband, David Lentz, I told Julie, "You're going to like him, he's kind of like a boy version of you!"

NOTE You can use good-quality shucked oysters for this dish if you don't feel like shucking them yourself.

2 pounds celery root

1 to 1¼ cups Rémoulade (recipe follows)

2 to 3 quarts vegetable oil, for frying

1 pound shucked good-sized oysters (we use Willapa Bay, from Washington State)

½ recipe Tempura Batter (recipe follows)

1 Meyer lemon, thinly sliced, plus ½ lemon for juicing

1 bunch watercress, cleaned and dried, tough stems removed

Kosher salt and freshly ground black pepper

Place the celery root on its side and, using a sharp knife, cut the top and bottom from the vegetable. Stand the celery root upright on the cutting board. Following the shape of the root, remove the skin, working from top to bottom, rotating the celery root as you go. Rinse the celery root and dry it well.

Using a mandoline, cut the peeled celery root into fine (⅛-inch) julienne strips. Transfer to a large bowl, pour ¾ cup rémoulade over the celery root, and toss very well, to coat completely. Taste for balance and seasoning.

Heat the oil to 350°F on a deep-frying thermometer, over medium heat, in a heavy, wide-bottomed pan.

Dry the oysters on paper towels. One by one, dip the oysters into the tempura batter, shake off the excess, and gently drop them into the hot oil. Cook the oysters until they're golden brown, about 2 minutes on each side, drain on paper towels, squeeze a little lemon juice over the top, and season lightly with salt and pepper.

Gently toss the watercress into the celery-root rémoulade, and arrange the salad on six large plates. Twist Meyer lemon slices (about three per plate), and tuck them into the salads. Arrange three fried oysters on each salad, and dollop with a little more rémoulade. Or serve family-style, and let everyone just fight over them!

rémoulade

1 extra-large egg yolk

½ cup grape-seed oil

½ cup extra-virgin olive oil

2½ teaspoons red-wine vinegar

1 tablespoon freshly squeezed
  lemon juice

½ tablespoon whole-grain
  mustard

½ tablespoon Dijon mustard

1 tablespoon finely minced
  shallot

1 tablespoon chopped capers

2 tablespoons chopped
  cornichons

1 tablespoon finely minced
  flat-leaf parsley

½ tablespoon finely minced
  tarragon

½ tablespoon finely minced
  chives

Pinch cayenne pepper

Kosher salt and freshly ground
  black pepper

It's hard to make a small batch of this Über-bistro classic sauce, because it starts with a mayonnaise, which is very difficult to make with less than one egg and 1 cup of oil. I would recommend making the recipe and planning to use this herb-spiked sauce of capers, mustard, and cornichons on grilled fish or a sandwich the next day. Think French tartar sauce! The rémoulade will be good for a couple of days if kept covered and refrigerated.

MAKES 2½ CUPS

Place the yolk in a stainless-steel bowl. Begin whisking in the grape-seed oil, drop by drop. Once the mixture has thickened and emulsified, you can whisk in the remaining grape-seed and olive oils in a slow, steady stream. If the mixture gets too thick, add a drop or two of water.

Stir in the remaining ingredients, seasoning with 1 teaspoon salt and a pinch of black pepper. Thin to a creamy texture by stirring in a tablespoon or so of water if necessary. Taste for balance and seasoning.

tempura batter

This recipe is courtesy of my handsome husband, David Lentz, of The Hungry Cat restaurants.

MAKES 3 CUPS

1 extra-large egg

1¼ cups very cold soda water

1 cup all-purpose flour

Pinch cayenne pepper

Kosher salt

Whisk the egg and soda water together in a medium bowl.

Sift the flour into a large bowl, and stir in 2 teaspoons salt and the cayenne. Make a well in the center of the dry ingredients. Slowly pour the liquid into the well, whisking all the time at the center. Once the batter starts to incorporate, bring in more dry ingredients, working from the center out. Keep the batter very cold.

Pairing wine with oysters when they are fried is slightly different from when they are raw. When they're raw and served on the half-shell, the ultimate pairing is with a clean, dry, high-acid white, something that matches the light, briny flavor profile of the fish. When fried, oysters take on a more intense flavor profile, becoming meaty and rich, with a deeper flavor. This is the perfect opportunity to take the wine selection in a more exciting direction, toward something sparkling and vibrant, like champagne. Just as frying takes the oyster to a new place, so do the bubbles, elevating the wine to be more exciting on the palate. For this recipe, I would opt for a blanc de blancs, a champagne made entirely from Chardonnay, which tends to be brighter and more mineral-intensive and can hold up to the bigger, fleshier flavor of the oyster.

grilled orata with cauliflower, fregola, and persimmon-pomegranate salsa

6 fillets orata, 5 to 6 ounces each, skin on

1 tablespoon grated lemon zest

1 tablespoon thyme leaves

2 tablespoons chopped flat-leaf parsley

1½ cups *fregola sarda,* or Italian couscous

½ recipe Roasted Cauliflower with Curry and Red Vinegar (page 274)

¼ cup extra-virgin olive oil

1 cup cooked chickpeas (recipe follows)

2 tablespoons sliced cilantro leaves

2 ounces mizuna

1 recipe Persimmon-Pomegranate Salsa (recipe follows)

Kosher salt and freshly ground black pepper

The curried cauliflower in the wood-burning oven chapter (see page 274) is one of my all-time favorite recipes—it's in the category of most beloved foods, along with farro, young broccoli sautéed with garlic and chile, rib-eye steaks, and pasta with butter and Parmesan. So, of course, I had to find another way to use and therefore eat it. Chewy, toasty Sardinian couscous, or *fregola,* is the perfect vehicle for soaking up all the cauliflower's spices and oily juices. Topped with a salsa of perfectly matched persimmons and pomegranate (what would these two do without each other?), it's a really satisfying and yet refreshing fall meal.

NOTE If you can't find *fregola,* or Italian couscous, you can substitute Israeli couscous. If you're using standard couscous, cook using the technique on page 120.

Season the fish with the zest, thyme, and parsley. Cover, and refrigerate for at least 4 hours.

Light the grill 30 to 40 minutes before cooking, and take the orata out of the refrigerator.

Bring a pot of heavily salted water to a boil over high heat. Add the *fregola* and cook for 8 to 10 minutes, until tender but still al dente. Drain the *fregola,* and cool on a baking sheet.

Roughly chop the curried cauliflower.

Heat a large sauté pan over high heat for 2 minutes. Swirl in 2 tablespoons olive oil, and add the *fregola,* ¼ teaspoon salt, and a few grindings of pepper. Cook for about 5 minutes, stirring occasionally with a wooden spoon, scraping the bottom of the pan as the *fregola* starts to crisp. Stir in the chickpeas and the curried cauliflower, and cook for another 4 to 5 minutes, stirring often to combine well and heat all the ingredients through. Keep warm in the oven while you cook the fish.

When the coals are broken down, red, and glowing, brush the orata with the remaining 2 tablespoons olive oil, and season with salt and pepper.

Place the fish on the grill skin-side down, and cook for 3 to 4 minutes, rotating the fish once after a couple of minutes to get the skin crispy. Turn the fish over, and cook for a few minutes on the other side. Be careful not to overcook the orata. When it's done, the fish will begin to flake and separate a little, and the center will be slightly translucent. Remember, the orata will continue to cook a little more once you take it off the grill.

Stir the cilantro into the *fregola,* and taste for balance and seasoning. Spoon onto the center of six large dinner plates. Tuck a few leaves of mizuna into the *fregola,* and place the orata on top. Spoon the persimmon-pomegranate salsa over the fish and around the plate.

chickpeas

I prefer to cook my own chickpeas, but in a pinch you can use good-quality canned chickpeas. Just drain them and sizzle them in some olive oil with the seasonings listed below.

Heat a medium pot over high heat for 2 minutes. Pour in the olive oil, wait a minute, and then add the onion, garlic, chile, thyme, and bay leaf. Cook for a minute or two, until the onion is wilted, and then add the chickpeas, paprika, cayenne, and cinnamon stick. Stir for a few minutes, coating the chickpeas with the oil and spices.

Cover with water by 3 inches, and bring to a boil over high heat. Turn the heat down to low, and place a paper towel on top of the chickpeas, to keep them under the surface.

Simmer for 30 minutes, and then add 2½ teaspoons salt. Continue cooking on a low simmer for about 1 hour, until the chickpeas are tender. While they cook, add water as necessary. When they are done, taste for seasoning, and cool the chickpeas in their juices.

¼ cup extra-virgin olive oil

½ cup diced onion

3 cloves garlic, smashed

1 chile de árbol, crumbled

1 teaspoon thyme

1 bay leaf

1½ cups dried chickpeas
(see Sources)

1 teaspoon sweet paprika

Healthy pinch cayenne pepper

1 cinnamon stick

Kosher salt

persimmon-pomegranate salsa

3 tablespoons finely diced
    shallots

2 tablespoons freshly squeezed
    lemon juice, or more as
    needed

1½ tablespoons pomegranate
    molasses

⅔ cup extra-virgin olive oil

½ cup pomegranate seeds

½ cup diced, peeled ripe
    persimmon

2 tablespoons sliced cilantro
    leaves

Kosher salt and freshly ground
    black pepper

The combination of persimmon and pomegranate is the essence of fall—sweet, earthy, vibrant. Persimmon even seems to have notes of natural pumpkin-pie spices. I love the way its rich denseness is balanced by the burst of acidity and crush of the pomegranate seeds. And, seriously, what would you *not* want to eat this with? Spoon it over fresh ricotta, burrata, or triple cream, grilled quail or duck, roasted winter squash, sautéed kale, or even a simple green salad.

Place the shallots, lemon juice, and ¼ teaspoon salt in a small bowl, and let sit 5 minutes.

Whisk in the pomegranate molasses and then the olive oil. Stir in the pomegranate seeds, persimmon, a few grinds of pepper, and the cilantro. Taste for balance and seasoning, adding a little more salt and lemon if needed.

The vegetables and grains accompanying the fish in this recipe make for a hearty, chewy, earthy-sweet combination of flavors and textures that is the ideal partner to a light-bodied, high-acid red wine, like Barbera. This wine, from the fog-laden Piemonte regions of Alba and Asti in Italy, shows bright red, tart notes akin to the taste of the pomegranate, a deep mineral-like earthiness, and firm acid structure. The wine's depth of flavor and structure will complement the *fregola* and vegetal notes in the cauliflower as well.

albacore crudo with avocado, cucumber, and ruby grapefruit

Dennis Kelly, our former chef at Tavern, created this dish. Though Dennis never actually worked at A.O.C., he did time at Lucques in the old days, and he has a beautiful baby boy with former A.O.C. Sous-Chef Melody Bishop, so he is definitely part of the A.O.C. extended and rather incestuous restaurant family.

I will never forget the day I met Dennis. It was at Lucques in 2003 or so, and we were desperate for a great line cook. When Dennis's résumé and cover letter arrived via fax (yes, it was the old days), I got really excited at the prospect of what sounded like a really solid East Coast, old-school cook from Cape Cod. We chatted on the phone, and, from what I could understand through his very thick, almost parody Boston accent, it seemed like a good fit. He had grown up on "the Cape," eating all kinds of fish and working at various clam shacks and fish houses, before moving on to some serious restaurants in Boston. It sounded as if he had everything I look for in a cook—a real connection to eating and food itself, a great work ethic (I mean, those clam shacks have to be rough in the summer, right?), and dedication to serious cooking.

Well, the day came for his interview, and around 4 p.m., the hostess buzzed back to the kitchen, "Suzanne, Dennis Kelly is here to see you." I walked out front, looked around the empty dining room, and all I saw was a slight, reserved-looking young Asian man sitting on the sofa. I made a not-so-inconspicuous circle around the dining room and went back to the kitchen. I called the hostess, "Where is Dennis Kelly?" "He's on the sofa," she replied. Hmm, I thought, how could this be? Where was my hulking, rough-around-the-edges, fisherman-type interviewee?

I got my nerve up and went back out to the dining room. When I said hello in my most nervous and exploratory way, Dennis replied, "Oh, hey, hi, how ya doin'?" And there it was, that big booming Boston voice from the phone interview. As it turns out, Dennis was born in Korea and left on the steps of a church as an infant, and it was the Kellys—the nicest, most Irish, most Cape Cod folks you could ever imagine—who adopted him!

In this dish, Dennis wanted to showcase a couple of farmer Peter

2 ruby grapefruits

2 tablespoons finely diced shallots

¼ cup freshly squeezed lime juice, plus 1 teaspoon fine zest

½ cup extra-virgin olive oil

2 tablespoons seeded, diced jalapeños (1 large)

1 medium-sized Persian cucumber, diced to ¼ cup

2 ripe medium avocados

12 ounces (¾ pound) cleaned sushi-grade albacore or hamachi

1 bunch watercress, stemmed, cleaned, and dried

2 tablespoons sliced cilantro

Kosher salt and freshly ground black pepper

Cut the stem and blossom ends from the grapefruits, and place them cut-side down on a cutting board. Following the contour of the fruit with your knife, remove the peel and cottony white pith, working from top to bottom, and rotating the fruit as you go. Then hold the grapefruits in your hand, one at a time, and carefully slice between the membranes and the fruit to release the segments in between. Carefully cut each segment into four pieces, and place them in a medium bowl.

Add the shallots, 3 tablespoons lime juice, and ½ teaspoon salt to the grapefruit, and let sit for 5 minutes. Whisk in 6 tablespoons olive oil, and stir in the jalapeños and cucumber. Taste for balance and seasoning.

Cut the avocados into quarters lengthwise. Remove the pit and peel, and cut the avocado into chunks. In a food processor, purée the avocado to a smooth consistency with remaining 1 tablespoon lime juice and 2 tablespoons olive oil, and 1 teaspoon salt and some pepper. Taste for balance and seasoning.

Cut the fish into ¼-inch-thick slices against the grain.

Spoon the avocado purée onto six plates, and spread it with the back of a spoon. Scatter the watercress over the purée. Season the fish with the lime zest, salt, and pepper. Arrange the albacore slices overlapping over the avocado purée. Spoon the cucumber-grapefruit salsa over and around the fish, and sprinkle the sliced cilantro over the top.

This is a light, fresh, and fruity crudo that really needs to be paired with an equally delicate wine, like a dry Riesling. Domestic versions have given Riesling the dubious reputation of being a sweet, syrupy, cheap wine. In truth, Riesling is one of the most versatile grape varieties, and is at the heart of some of the world's most complex low-alcohol wines. Germany and Austria are the best-known regions for Riesling production, though many New World areas are making outstanding wine. Here I would look for a Riesling from New Zealand or Australia, where the wines have the characteristic diesel and tar on the nose and brightening acidity in the finish, but are just a smidge rich in the mid-palate, creating a synergy of flavor and texture with those in the avocado and citrus.

black bass with fennel purée, winter citrus, and green olives in green harissa

3 pounds mixed citrus fruit (pomelos, oro blancos, grapefruits, mandelos, Cara Cara oranges, navel oranges)

6 fillets black bass, 5 to 6 ounces each, skin on

1 tablespoon thyme leaves

2 tablespoons chopped flat-leaf parsley

¾ cup Castelvetrano or Lucques olives

½ cup Green Harissa (page 75)

½ lime, for juicing

2 tablespoons extra-virgin olive oil

1 teaspoon sugar

1 chile de árbol, crumbled

4 tablespoons unsalted butter

1 recipe Fennel Purée (recipe follows)

Kosher salt and freshly ground black pepper

I love this dish so much that, when I was lucky enough to cook for President Obama, it was one of the dishes I served him. Citrus and olives are a pretty classic combination, but in this preparation I stir bulbous, juicy, bright-green Castelvetrano olives into a spiced green harissa and spoon that over a citrus sauce made with reduced citrus juices, chile, a pinch of sugar, butter, and assorted citrus segments. All this over a smooth fennel purée and a nice piece of seared black bass is a heavenly (and presidential) winter dish.

Finely grate 1 tablespoon zest from some of the citrus, and season the fish with zest, thyme, and parsley. Cover, and refrigerate for at least 4 hours.

Light the grill 30 to 40 minutes before cooking and remove the fish from the refrigerator, to bring it to room temperature.

Cut the stem and blossom ends from the fruit. Place the citrus cut-side down on a cutting board. Following the contour of the fruit with your knife, remove the peel and cottony white pith, working from top to bottom, and rotating the fruit as you go. Then hold each piece of fruit in your hand, one at a time, and carefully slice between the membranes and the fruit to release the segments in between. Discard all seeds. Reserve 1½ cups juice for the sauce.

To pit the olives, place them on a kitchen towel, and wrap the towel around to cover the top of the olives as well. Tap the olives very gently with a mallet or rolling pin, uncover the cloth, and remove the pits.

Toss the pitted olives in ½ cup of the green harissa, and season with a squeeze of lime juice.

When the coals are broken down, red, and glowing, brush the bass with the olive oil, and season with salt and pepper. Place the fish on the grill skin-side down, and cook for 3 to 4 minutes, rotating the fish once after a couple of minutes to crisp the skin. Turn the bass over, and cook for another few minutes, until just cooked through. When it's done, the fish will begin to flake and separate a little, and the center will be slightly translucent. Remember, the bass will continue to cook a little more once you take it off the grill.

While the fish is cooking, pour the citrus juice, sugar, and chile into a large sauté pan, and bring to a boil over high heat. When the juice has reduced by two-thirds, turn the heat down to low, and quickly whisk in the butter, ¼ teaspoon salt, and a pinch of freshly ground pepper. Swirl the pan to incorporate the butter as it melts. Add the citrus segments, swirl the pan for another 30 seconds, then remove from the heat. Taste for seasoning.

Spoon ½ cup hot fennel purée onto the center of each of six large dinner plates. Place the grilled fish on top, and spoon the citrus sauce over the fish and around the plate. Top with the green olives in green harissa.

fennel purée

½ cup Pernod

1 tablespoon extra-virgin olive oil

1 cup sliced fennel
(approximately 1 large bulb)

½ cup heavy cream

¾ pound Yukon Gold potatoes

Kosher salt and freshly ground
black pepper

Pour the Pernod into a nonreactive pan, place on the stove over low heat, and reduce to ¼ cup.

Heat a medium sauté pan over high heat for 1 minute. Pour in the olive oil, and add the fennel, ½ teaspoon salt, and a few grindings of pepper. Turn the heat down to medium-low, and gently cook for about 10 minutes, stirring often, until the fennel softens. Add the cream, and gently simmer for another 5 minutes, until the fennel is completely soft. Transfer to a blender, and purée.

Meanwhile, bring a large pot of salted water to a boil over high heat. Peel the potatoes, and cut them into 2-inch chunks. When the water boils, add the potatoes, turn down to a simmer, and cook for about 15 minutes, until the potatoes are tender. Drain the potatoes, and pass them through a food mill or a potato ricer.

Fold the fennel cream, the reduced Pernod, and 1 teaspoon salt into the riced potatoes. Taste for seasoning, and pass the purée through a fine-mesh *tamis* for a very silky purée (or serve as is for a more rustic consistency).

The juxtaposition of flavors in this dish makes it fantastically wine-friendly, the highs and lows of flavor providing a complex experience on the palate. I like to pair this dish with Roussanne, a white Rhône variety that has a rich, unctuous texture and a dark-golden color. On its own, or blended with other grape varieties, the wine has a delicate spiciness and really earthy, lanolinlike quality that, when paired with this dish, reflects not just the layer of flavors in the fennel purée but also those of the citrus fruits.

atlantic sea scallops with saffron potatoes and blood orange—meyer lemon salsa

I love the colors of this Sicilian-inspired dish—the deep-red, orange, and yellow tones of the salsa spooned over those white scallops and over the mounds of sienna-hued potatoes remind me of an Italian vacation. I was never a big fan of scallops until I tasted the super-sweet, succulent, meaty East Coast diver-caught ones we are lucky enough to get from Steve Connolly in Gloucester, Massachusetts. Seek them out—they are so worth it! This preparation would also work beautifully with halibut, sole, or other white flaky fish.

NOTE Mexican diver-caught scallops are a good alternative to the Atlantic sea scallops.

Remove the rosemary leaves from the branches except for 2 inches at the bottom of each. Cut the leafless end of each branch at an angle with a sharp knife to make a point and coarsely chop the picked rosemary leaves.

Season the scallops with the lemon zest and 1½ tablespoons chopped rosemary. Skewer three scallops onto each rosemary branch. Cover and refrigerate.

Place the shallots, champagne vinegar, and a healthy pinch of salt in a small bowl, and let sit for 5 minutes.

Cut away the stem and blossom ends from the Meyer lemons. Stand the lemons on one end, and cut them vertically into ⅛-inch slices (keeping the rinds on). Stack the slices in small piles on a cutting board, and cut them lengthwise into ⅛-inch-thick matchsticks. Line up the matchsticks, and cut them into ⅛-inch cubes.

Cut away the stem and blossom ends from two blood oranges. Place the oranges cut-side down on a cutting board. Following the contour of the fruit with your knife, remove the peel and cottony white pith, working from top to bottom, and rotating the fruit as you go. Then hold the oranges in your hand, one at a time, and carefully slice between the membranes and the fruit to release the segments in between.

Add the diced lemon, blood-orange segments, their juices, and the juice

6 branches rosemary, about 7 to 8 inches long

18 Atlantic sea scallops, each about 2 ounces

1 tablespoon Meyer lemon zest

2 tablespoons finely diced shallots

1 tablespoon champagne vinegar

2 Meyer lemons

3 large blood oranges

1 cup extra-virgin olive oil

1 tablespoon sliced mint

1 teaspoon saffron threads

2 pounds Yukon Gold potatoes, peeled and cut into 1½-inch chunks

1 cup diced red onion

1 tablespoon thyme leaves

1 chile de árbol, crumbled

2 ounces young dandelion greens or arugula

Kosher salt and freshly ground black pepper

of the remaining orange to the shallot mixture. Stir in ½ cup olive oil, the mint, ½ teaspoon salt, and a few grinds of pepper.

Light the grill 30 to 40 minutes before cooking, and take the scallops out of the refrigerator.

Place the saffron in a small bowl, and pour 1 cup warm water over it.

Heat a large Dutch oven over high heat for 1 minute. Swirl in ¼ cup olive oil, and wait 1 minute. Add the onion, thyme, chile, ½ teaspoon salt, and a few grindings of black pepper. Reduce the heat to medium, and sauté for about 3 minutes, stirring often, until the onion is translucent. Turn up the heat to medium-high. Add the potatoes and 2 tablespoons of olive oil, and season with 1 teaspoon salt and a few grindings of pepper. Don't stir the pan for a couple of minutes while the potato edges sear in the hot oil and form a nice crust. Lift and tilt the pan to distribute the oil evenly. After 3 to 4 minutes, firmly shake the pan to loosen the potatoes. Turn with a wooden spoon and cook for another 3 minutes, stirring to coat with the onions.

Add the saffron water. Stir to combine, cover the pot, reduce the heat to low, and let simmer for about 25 minutes, until the potatoes are nicely glazed and tender when poked with a paring knife. If at any point the liquid starts to dry up, add a little more water. The saffron potatoes should be glazed, neither dry nor soupy. Turn off heat, and put the lid halfway on.

When the coals are broken down, red, and glowing, brush the scallops with remaining 2 tablespoons olive oil, and season with salt and pepper on both sides. Place the skewered scallops on the grill, and cook for 4 minutes, rotating once to create crosshatch marks and a browned crust. Flip the scallops, move them to a cooler side of the grill, and cook for another 1 to 2 minutes, until they're medium-rare.

Spoon the hot saffron potatoes into the center of six dinner plates, scatter the dandelion, and place the scallop skewers on top. Spoon the blood-orange–Meyer-lemon salsa over the scallops.

There is an aromatic, fairly exotic quality to this dish, given the saffron in the potatoes and the rich citrus butter. As a result, red wine is more appropriate for these scallops, which I normally pair with white wine. The key in this case is to find a red with similar aromatics and spicy fruit notes, like Pinot Noir from California's Central Coast. The region's proximity to the ocean keeps the climate cool and the growing season long, resulting in wines with bright red fruit notes, cola undertones, and racy acidity.

pink snapper with coconut rice, peanuts, and kumquat sambal

One of our loveliest A.O.C. cooks ever is a Texan beauty named Melody Bishop. Melody is quite an anomaly in a professional kitchen—soft-spoken, ladylike, über-polite, and with never a curse word passing her lips. She started out on the production side of Hollywood—another career path littered with big egos, lots of drama, and a fair share of F-bombs—but then, somehow, found herself cooking her way through Thailand for more than a year. She has an amazing palate and a wonderful way of integrating those Thai flavors with the food we produce every day. When we opened Tavern, Melody was promoted to sous-chef and she began making bowlfuls of delicious Thai noodles, Thai beef salads, and this delicious coconut rice that I just can't get enough of!

"Sambal" is a term used to describe a myriad of Southeast Asian chile sauces or condiments. As with the harissas, charmoulas, and gazpachos of the world, there are probably as many recipes as there are serious cooks. My husband, David, and I honeymooned in Thailand and have spent quite a bit of time in Singapore as well, where we both became addicted to the many versions of sambal. You can buy many sambals in Asian markets, but I played around and came up with my own, very inauthentic, but delicious version for this recipe. I love the crunch of the peanuts and the chewy, rindy, acidic punch of pure citrus from the sizzling slices of kumquat.

Season the fish with the lime zest and 2 tablespoons cilantro. Cover, and refrigerate for at least 4 hours.

Light the grill 30 to 40 minutes before you're ready to cook and remove the fish from the refrigerator, to let it come to room temperature.

Preheat the oven to 375°F.

To make the sambal, heat a medium sauté pan over high heat for 2 minutes. Swirl in 3 tablespoons grape-seed oil, and add the bell pepper. Cook for about 4 minutes, stirring often, and then add the ground chile, and turn the heat down to medium. Cook for another few minutes, until the pepper begins

6 fillets pink snapper,
    5 to 6 ounces each, skin on

1 tablespoon grated lime zest plus
    ½ lime for juice

6 tablespoons sliced cilantro

7 tablespoons grape-seed oil, plus
    more, if needed

1 cup finely diced red bell pepper

1 teaspoon ground chile de árbol

3 tablespoons finely diced
    shallots

1 teaspoon minced garlic

¼ teaspoon sugar

½ teaspoon shrimp paste (see
    Sources)

1 canned tomato, preferably
    San Marzano or Muir Glen,
    chopped

½ cup Spanish peanuts

2 tablespoons extra-virgin
    olive oil

2 teaspoons grated fresh ginger

9 kumquats, thinly sliced, seeds
    removed

1 recipe Coconut Rice
    (recipe follows)

¼ cup sliced scallions, or
    2 ounces mizuna, cleaned
    and dried

Kosher salt and freshly ground
    black pepper

to caramelize, adding another tablespoon of oil if the pan starts to look dry. Add 2 tablespoons shallots and the garlic, season with a heaping ½ teaspoon salt and the sugar, and cook for another 3 or 4 minutes, until the shallots are translucent and beginning to caramelize. Add the shrimp paste, and use a wooden spoon to break it up and help it toast in the oil and combine with the pepper. Once the shrimp paste has become integrated with the pepper, add the tomato to the pan, turn up the heat to medium-high, and cook for another 5 minutes, until the tomato is cooked down and glazes the pepper. Cool for a few minutes, and then purée in a food processor fitted with a metal blade.

While the sambal is cooking, spread the peanuts on a baking sheet and toast for about 5 minutes, stirring once or twice, until they smell nutty.

When the coals are broken down, red, and glowing, brush the fish with the olive oil, and season with salt and pepper on both sides. Place the fish on the grill, skin-side down, and cook for 2 to 3 minutes, rotating the fish once, until it's nicely colored on the first side. Turn the fish over, and cook for a few more minutes, until it's just barely cooked through.

While the fish is cooking, heat ¼ cup grape-seed oil in a medium sauté pan over high heat for 30 seconds. Add the ginger, let it cook for 1 minute, then add the remaining tablespoon shallots to the pan and season with salt and pepper.

When the shallots and ginger are sizzling in the oil, add the sambal, the kumquats, the peanuts, and a squeeze of lime juice. Stir well to combine, and taste for balance and seasoning. Cook for a minute more, turn off the heat, and add the remaining ¼ cup cilantro.

Spoon approximately ½ cup hot coconut rice onto the center of each of six dinner plates. Scatter the sliced scallions or mizuna over the rice, and place the fish, skin-side up, on top. Spoon generous amounts of kumquat sambal over the fish, letting it soak down into the rice.

coconut rice

2 cups jasmine or Thai sweet rice

One 13.5-ounce can unsweetened coconut milk

⅓ cup palm sugar (available at Asian markets or online), or ¼ cup granulated sugar

Kosher salt

Cover the rice with 2 cups water, and set aside to soak at room temperature for 24 hours (in a pinch, you can soak it for 6 hours, but 24 is best). Drain the rice, and rinse it three times in a fine colander. Cut a square of cheesecloth, and moisten with water. Unfold the cheesecloth to a double layer, lay it across a vegetable steamer set in a medium pot, and fill the pot with water until it is just below the level of the steamer basket.

Remove the steamer basket from the pot, and place the rice in the basket. Bring the water to a boil over medium heat, and reduce to a simmer. Place the steamer basket in the pot, and cover tightly. Steam for about 15 minutes, until tender, and then immediately remove the steamer basket and transfer the rice to a heatproof dish. Discard the cheesecloth, and cover the dish tightly with plastic wrap until you are ready to serve.

Meanwhile, bring the coconut milk, palm sugar, and 2½ teaspoons salt to a boil over medium heat; boil, stirring frequently, for about 3 minutes. When the salt and sugar have dissolved pour the coconut mixture over the rice. Let sit for 5 minutes while the rice absorbs the coconut milk. Stir and taste for seasoning before serving.

The key in pairing a wine with this complex and exotic recipe is to choose one that won't be overwhelmed by the sambal's heat. For this, I always opt for a white wine with a touch of sweetness, like Rieslings from Germany. These wines are fresh, bright, and light with hints of white flowers that work well with the sweet rice. The fruitiness of the wine also serves to soften the heat of the chile, while the chile conversely calms the sweetness in the wine.

wild striped bass with roasted beets, watercress, and blood orange butter

Being pregnant and being a chef do not necessarily go hand in hand. Of course, there are the 12 hours or more on your feet, the bending down to open the oven (and feeling as if your insides are going to fall out), and the dreaded smell of veal stock, meat, bones, and pretty much everything else in the kitchen. When I was pregnant with my twins, it was really bad. Suddenly I hated everything I used to love—tomatoes, garlic, bread, for God's sake, and even water! Literally, I could not stand the taste of water.

My second (and singleton) pregnancy was much more civilized—there was no vomiting, and I could actually walk into the restaurant and not howl, "Who on earth is cooking short ribs? Disgusting!" No, with Charles I just wanted everything raw and cold, and I took the customers along on this little clean, raw diet with me. I didn't do it on purpose; it was just that the only food I could think about eating, or *anyone's* wanting to eat, was cold, and I mean ice-cold, crunchy, fresh, and made up mostly of vegetables and fruit. This bass dish was one of my favorite creations from that era, and I happily eat it now, in my not-pregnant state.

The foundation of this dish is a very bright, slightly acidic beet purée made by simply blending roasted beets with cilantro, shallots, and red-wine vinegar. I'm sure if I had come up with this when I was not pregnant it would have had olive oil in it! The purée is topped with a salad of wedges of roasted beets, slices of blood orange, watercress, and the grilled fish. Then I spoon over it my go-to winter citrus sauce—blood-orange juice reduced with a little sugar, chile, and salt, and finished with a little butter (to cut the acid and give a creamy, unctuous texture) and blood-orange segments. Use this technique with any citrus to make glazy, rich, yet refreshing sauces all season long.

6 fillets wild striped bass, 5 to 6 ounces each, skin on

3 blood oranges, plus 1 cup freshly squeezed juice, and 1 tablespoon zest

1 tablespoon thyme leaves

2 tablespoons chopped flat-leaf parsley

2 bunches small mixed-colored beets

6 tablespoons extra-virgin olive oil

2 pounds large red beets

2 tablespoons chopped cilantro

Heaping ¼ cup diced shallots

2 tablespoons red-wine vinegar

1 bunch watercress, cleaned, tough stems removed

¼ cup mint leaves

1 tablespoon freshly squeezed lemon juice

1 teaspoon sugar

1 chile de árbol, crumbled

4 tablespoons unsalted butter

Kosher salt and freshly ground black pepper

Season the fish with the orange zest, thyme, and parsley. Cover, and refrigerate for at least 4 hours.

Preheat the oven to 400°F.

Cut off the beet greens from the small beets, leaving ½ inch of the stems still attached. Clean the small beets well, and toss them with 1 tablespoon olive oil and 1 teaspoon salt. Place the small beets in a roasting pan with a splash of water in the bottom. Repeat the procedure with the large beets in a separate roasting pan.

Cover both pans tightly with foil, and roast, until they're tender when pierced. The small beets will take about 40 minutes, the large beets longer. When the beets are done, carefully remove the foil. Let cool, and peel the beets by slipping off the skins with your fingers. Cut the small, mixed-colored beets into ½-inch wedges, and cut the large red beets into eight pieces each.

Place the large red beets in a blender with the cilantro, shallots, red-wine vinegar, ¼ cup water, 1 teaspoon salt, and some freshly ground pepper. Purée to a smooth, velvety texture, the consistency of mashed potatoes. I like to serve the beet purée at room temperature.

Remove the fish from the refrigerator 15 minutes before cooking, to bring it to room temperature.

Cut the stem and blossom ends from the blood oranges. Place the oranges cut-side down on a cutting board. Following the contour of the fruit with your knife, remove the peel and cottony white pith, working from top to bottom, and rotating the fruit as you go. Then hold the oranges in your hand, one at a time, and carefully slice between the membranes and the fruit to release the segments in between. Place the orange segments in a small bowl.

Heat a large sauté pan over high heat for 2 minutes. (Depending on the size of your pan, you may need to cook the fish in batches or use two pans.) Season the fish with salt and pepper on both sides. Swirl in 2 tablespoons olive oil, and wait for 1 minute. Carefully lay the fish in the pan skin-side down, and cook for 3 to 4 minutes, until the skin is crisp. Turn the fish over, lower the heat to medium-low, and cook for a few more minutes, until the bass is almost cooked through. Be careful not to overcook the fish. When it's done, the fish will begin to flake and separate a little, and the center will still be slightly translucent. Remember, the fish will continue to cook a bit more once you take it out of the pan.

Toss the small beet wedges, the watercress, and the mint in a large bowl with the lemon juice, 3 tablespoons olive oil, 1 teaspoon salt, and a few grinds of pepper. Taste for balance and seasoning.

Wipe out the pan, and return it to the stove over medium-high heat. Add the blood-orange juice (plus any juice from the bowl of orange segments), sugar, and chile, and bring to a boil. When the juice has reduced by two-thirds, turn the heat down to low, and quickly whisk in the butter, ¼ teaspoon salt, and a pinch of freshly ground pepper. Swirl the pan to incorporate the butter as it melts. Add the orange segments, swirl the pan for another 30 seconds, then remove from the heat. Taste for seasoning.

Spoon the beet purée onto the center of six dinner plates. Drag the back of the spoon through the purée, starting at the center, spreading it nicely across the plate. Arrange the watercress-and-beet salad at the center of the plates, leaving some of the beet purée showing. Place the fish, skin-side up, on top of the salad, and spoon the blood-orange sauce over the fish and around the plate.

Although this is a winter recipe, the freshness and bright fruitiness of the beets and blood orange make it a refreshingly light cold-weather preparation. For pairing, it works really well with fairly fruity wines, both white and red, that reflect the flavors of the blood oranges and beets. Elegant, high-acid Chardonnay from California's Central Coast works well, because it tends to show bright citrus notes and cool, coastal sea essences that mirror the depth of flavor in the blood orange. Likewise, Pinot Noir from the same region shows red-cherry fruit notes and touches of orange oil that work similarly well.

meat

Meat, meat, meat. In my first book, *Sunday Suppers at Lucques,* I made a comment that I could be a vegetarian if I could just have a little bacon and steak every once in a while. Now, in reality, as much as I would like for that to be true, I just love meat too much ever to give it up.

There is nothing like the crust of a perfectly grilled steak, that caramelized exterior that hides the juicy, bloody, tender interior of pure protein. It's the smell, the texture—that chew that gives way to tenderness—and the way you feel after you eat it. I think I must have been a cavewoman in an earlier life, because there is nothing I crave and nothing that satisfies quite like red, red meat. Oh, and pork, did I mention pork? I mean, life without bacon? Can you imagine it? Not I.

Oddly, the other reason I love meat so much is that, like fish, it's such a perfect partner for so many grains, fruits, and vegetables. I know that sounds silly, but for me, that canvas of protein is what carries the vegetables, starches, sauces, and grains. When I'm thinking up a new dish, I usually do start with the produce, and as I'm figuring out how I would like to prepare it, I start thinking of what meat (or fish) would go well with it—rather than the other way around.

Delicate green spring vegetables work beautifully with the subtle, slightly gamy flavor of lamb. Summer vegetables are a natural with beef and the more neutral palate of chicken. Pork works beautifully with anything sweet—corn, winter squash, and long-cooked kale—because it has its own natural sweetness. Duck and quail, as well as pork, are particularly good with summer and fall fruits—peaches, plums, apples, pears, and pomegranate all work well. I do find that, for the most part, I save citrus for fish dishes, with a few exceptions, such as Kumquat Sambal, which I love on grilled pork and duck, or Grilled Duck Breast with Preserved Citrus Peel and Sweet Potato Purée.

"What's your favorite thing to cook?" is the eternal dreaded question in my life. To me, it's one of those open-ended, super-general, super-boring questions, like "What's your favorite color?" (Some guy actually did ask me that on a date a million years ago.) At least for me, there is no real answer—there is not one dish or protein or vegetable that is my "favorite" thing to cook. In fact, I much prefer cooking different things different ways and mixing it up. And sometimes that drive to "mix it up" and do things differently can lead to fun and delicious places.

That said, Caroline always says I have a "way" with chicken. It's a funny statement, but I think she means that you sort of expect chicken to be boring, and therefore I take great pains to make it interesting. There is, of course, the proper cooking technique as well (are you tired of hearing me say that yet?). But I actually find chicken to be really fun to cook, because it's very versatile, and it takes on lots of different flavors very well. One of the classic dishes at Lucques, from our opening menu, was a riff on Julia Child's Poulet Grillé à la Diable, called Devil's Chicken, for which I marinated chicken thighs in a delicious mixture of mustard, shallots, and vermouth, and then baked them in a cazuela on a bed of potatoes and leeks. At A.O.C. and in this book, in Mustard-Grilled Chicken with Spinach, Pine Nuts, Pecorino, and Soft Egg, I use that same mustard mixture to marinate boned chicken legs, then grill them and serve over a savory pecorino pudding and mustard-dressed spinach salad, topped with grated pecorino, mustard breadcrumbs, and a soft-cooked egg. This dish is pretty much a case study for reinforcing and repeating the same flavor a few times in a single dish. The mustard marinade bubbles and cooks onto the chicken skin, making it very different from the smooth "raw" Dijon flavor in the spinach-salad dressing, and the breadcrumbs are tossed with brown butter and mustard before being baked, so they have yet another version of mustard flavor. Rather than being too much, these multiple reiterations of the same base flavor knit the dish together into its very integrated whole.

I guess one thing to know about cooking is that, like learning a language, the more you practice, the bigger your vocabulary becomes. People sometimes ask me, "How do you come up with all these new dishes all the time?" Well, the truth is that it's one long continuous riff on something I tasted, or did before, or tweaked, or thought of one night in my sleep, and on and on. For example, after that mustard-chicken dish, I played around with doing the same thing using harissa, marinating the chicken in the harissa before grilling it, making a dandelion salad with a harissa dressing to go with it, and so on. Most ideas don't come out of nowhere, so it's all about building more and more blocks for your foundation, to grow into more and more dishes and preparations.

Having the freedom and confidence to play around, think outside the box, and try something new is what makes you a great creative cook. One of my oldest friends, Mike Chessler, is a perfect example of someone who got to the point of no longer being a prisoner of recipes and instead started to write his own. Mike is a Harvard-educated TV writer and producer, and one of the smartest, most OCD, and hilarious people I know. He was a vegetarian for a lot of my early culinary years, until, one moment, sitting at Lucques after a big birthday, he asked himself, "Why am I limiting myself when there is so much good-tasting food out there?" From that moment on, Mike embraced his newfound inner carnivore as a diner, but also as a cook, to a degree I have not quite seen before. As with everything he engages, Mike got into eating, and particularly cooking, seriously, intensely, and passionately.

For all his oddball qualities and humor, Mike is, let's just say, rigid—oh, and a perfectionist—so when he follows a recipe it is to a T, and maybe even to T's that aren't actually there, because the rest of us aren't smart enough to think of them. Having literally cooked every single dish from *Sunday Suppers at Lucques,* Mike took to coming in for dinner and then e-mailing me for recipes. It was spring last year when he asked me how to make the Fava Bean Purée with Burrata and Fava Bean Pesto that he had enjoyed one night at A.O.C. A few days later, I got the call. I picked up the phone in fear. Oh no, I thought, what tiny step did I leave out that seemed so obvious to me, or what timing or ¼ teaspoon was off? And then I heard it, the moment I had not ever imagined happening: Mike Chessler's culinary epiphany. "Hey, so, Sue, I got this really beautiful green garlic at the Sunday Hollywood market, and pine nuts are so expensive right now, so do you think I could substitute green garlic for the regular garlic, and pistachios for pine nuts, in the pesto?" I nearly dropped my whisk! Mike Chessler—the most anal, OCD, hypercritical, and uptight person I know—*got* it. He finally understood what it was all about, that the idea is to follow recipes to learn *how* to cook and the ideas behind flavor combinations and pairings, but that the goal is exactly what Mike achieved—he had spread his wings and was able to think outside the lines in the cookbooks and was doing his own thing!

For me, in a restaurant kitchen, it is, in fact, sometimes limitations that lead to new creations. As is so often the case in cooking, necessity is what breeds invention. Take lamb, for example—though I love rack of lamb, in all honesty the beautiful Colorado product that I want to cook is so expensive that I can really serve it only for New Year's Eve and other special events. Because I wanted to keep our menu prices in check, I started playing around with different ways to use the less expensive cuts of that gorgeous Colorado lamb. I found that lamb sirloin was particularly flavorful and easier to work with than a whole lamb leg (which I also love for large parties or gatherings). The sirloin has all the flavor of the leg, but it's even moister and juicer, and it doesn't have as much sinew to deal with. I found that marinating the lamb sirloin with garlic and herbs, grilling it, and then slow-roasting it under a mound of herbs and butter, basting it as it cooks, produced an unbelievably tender and succulent result.

Having come up with this newly beloved way to roast a smaller piece of lamb, I immediately turned my attention to finding something different to do with it. In France, the leg and sirloin are often cut into steaks and grilled—they are rustic and flavorful, smoky and charred on the outside—but from a restaurant perspective, they are a little inconsistent, and often too chewy to keep the average Angeleno happy. Bemoaning that one day, I had an idea. What if we cut that same lamb sirloin into thin slices, or paillards, grilled them super-quickly (just a minute or two per side), and layered them with a warm spinach salad with mustard, potatoes, and bacon, or on top of risotto carbonara with pea shoots and chanterelles? I tried it, and instantly loved it. We are so used to having lamb leg or sirloin sliced that it's a nice textural surprise to have the thin slices of flash-cooked lamb, and it's fun to layer those slices into a dish rather than fanning them out, as we do with the slow-roasted lamb.

Moving on to the shoulder and butt of the beast, braising or confiting (braising meat in its own fat) works best with these more muscular, working parts of the animal. Braising imparts flavor to the dish on so many levels—with the marinade, the mirepoix, the choice of wine and vinegar and stock to braise them in—and, best of all, you have both cooked meat *and* a delicious sauce when you are done.

Playing around with different spices and traditional seasonings for your braise creates dishes with particular flavor profiles. Garlic, rosemary, thyme, and lemon zest go into the marinade for pork cheeks to be braised with mirepoix, sherry, and veal stock. I love thyme in almost everything, but rosemary is a little trickier to work with. The key is not to overuse it, and I think, in a way, it has gotten a bad rap because, when you do use too much, the result can be sort of medicinal and overwhelming. Used judiciously, rosemary gives a deep, pungent feeling of hillsides—think Provence, Tuscany, and, of course, the Hollywood Hills!

In all seriousness, I grew up playing on the craggy, overgrown hillside behind our house that was full of foxtails, dried grasses, wild fennel, and some sort of wild savory that smelled like a cross between thyme and mint—I used to come in for dinner smelling like a sweaty sachet of *herbes de Provence*! When I smell those scents, I am immediately transported to long summer afternoons, childhood freedoms, and rugged Mediterranean lands. So, anyway, my point is not to use too much rosemary, but do, please, use it! We have a ton growing in our backyard now, and just a few sprigs scattered over a roasting chicken or pork loin can change the whole thing from boring to ethereal. I laugh at how many times people come in the kitchen and say, "What on earth are you cooking? It smells amazing!" And so often it's a simple roast with herbs and olive oil.

Those choices you make—the marinade, spices, vegetables, wine, and stock—they all come together to make the ultimate flavor and personality of a dish. Duck legs braised with Madeira are deeply flavored, fruity, and almost dusky, like the Portuguese fortified wine in which they are braised. And for me, the gamy notes of the duck and the aged and somewhat dark oxidized wine-cask flavor of the Madeira are perfect for fall and work beautifully with the super-earthy deep-green notes of the kale stuffing, the starchiness of the chestnut, and the brown-sugar sweetness of the dates in Braised Duck with Madeira, Kale Stuffing, and Dates.

Though braised meats are an obvious pick for fall and winter, sometimes they can work for summer, too. Pork belly braised in sherry . . . Wait a minute, I have to stop myself. What is it about me and sherry (and sherry vinegar, now that I mention it)? I must say that sherry is the wine I turn to most often in the kitchen for braising and sauces. Of course, I love red wine and can't imagine braising meat for Beef Brisket with Long-Cooked Romano Beans and Black Olive Aïoli, or Coq au Vin with Bacon, Potato Purée, Cipollini Onions, and Black Trumpets without it. But red wine gives a great big, dark, hearty result, whereas sometimes I want something a little more subtle, and white wine just isn't quite enough. Sherry has deep but almost exotic notes—somewhat nutty and sweet, and very much tasting of the cask. I think what I like most about it is how well it blends with other flavors without overpowering them.

Back to that Crispy Pork Belly with Peaches, Ricotta Salata, and Abbamele I was starting to write about: The sherry gives a real backbone and nice richness to the pork that you wouldn't get from white wine, but also doesn't overpower and make it as heavy as it would be with red wine. Especially because the pork is going to be paired with peaches, that lovely, subtle, slightly sweet flavor is really perfect.

Of course, sausage making is the ultimate way to work whatever flavors you like into your creation. Roasted red peppers, garlic, crushed chiles, paprika, oregano, and red wine are used to marinate chunks of lamb shoulder to make Lamb Merguez with Eggplant Jam, Roasted Cherry Tomatoes, and Green Olives. And do not let the process intimidate you. Making sausages is actually easy, once you have the fundamental method down. You basically marinate chunks of meat with fat and seasonings, and then grind them up! The key is to work with everything very cold, not to overwork the meat, and, of course, to season properly. At home, I often forgo the stuffing part and just shape the sausage meat into patties, wrap them with caul fat (or not), and sauté them in a cast-iron pan. I always make a double batch, and use leftover sausage meat in ragouts with rapini or shell beans over soft, cheesy polenta, or throw little golf-ball-sized pieces into hot olive oil as a start for a simple pasta dish.

Braising and sausage making obviously have their place, but there are times when I just want a simple and pure piece of grilled or pan-seared meat. In my mind, steak is one of those foods not to be messed with. Salt, pepper, olive oil, a nice hot grill, and you are done—there is no reason to play around or change it up, it's perfect, so just leave it alone. I feel the same way about a perfectly cooked duck or chicken breast, or a lovely charred pork chop—sometimes it really is just all about the meat.

As with produce and seafood, choosing where your meat comes from is very important. Look for small local farms and ranches, and producers that don't use antibiotics or hormones in their meat production. Recently, I have done some work with The Pew Charitable Trusts to try to bring public awareness to the routine overuse of antibiotics in industrial farming. The overuse of these drugs in healthy animals has led to a rise in antibiotic-resistant "superbugs," which kill over ninety-nine thousand Americans per year. It's scary stuff, and worth paying great attention to—and, of course, well-raised livestock, just like fruits and vegetables, tends to taste better, too.

mustard-grilled chicken with spinach, pine nuts, pecorino, and soft egg

I basically *always* want some sort of greens on my plate. I try to fool myself when I'm coming up with new dishes and my chefs ask me, "Do you want some arugula or dandelion on the plate?" "Oh no," I often reply, but when I actually taste the whole dish together, I want that break or reprieve that you can get only from something bright, green, and raw. So this dish is heaven for me—it's not just a few leaves of green but a whole spinach salad, sandwiched between the rich pecorino pudding and the hot, mustard-crusted chicken. Oh, and the egg—did I mention the egg? Tell your family or guests to cut right through the egg to release the silky, runny yolk inside, and let it further dress the salad and bathe the whole plate. This is definitely one of those moments when all the juices and flavors for all the components (chicken, spinach, mustard dressing, egg, and cheese) meld together to a dreamy whole.

2 tablespoons unsalted butter

½ cup finely diced shallots

1 teaspoon thyme leaves

½ cup dry vermouth

½ cup plus 1 tablespoon Dijon mustard

7 extra-large eggs

2 teaspoons chopped fresh tarragon

6 large chicken legs with thigh attached, boned (or substitute chicken breasts)

1 extra-large egg yolk

1½ tablespoons red-wine vinegar

1 lemon, for juicing

¾ cup plus 2 tablespoons extra-virgin olive oil

½ cup pine nuts

6 ounces baby spinach, cleaned and dried

1 recipe Mustard Breadcrumbs (recipe follows)

¾ cup thin diagonal slices of spring onions (white and green parts)

1 recipe Pecorino Pudding (recipe follows)

½ cup grated pecorino

Kosher salt and freshly ground black pepper

NOTE There are a lot of components to this dish but you can make the pecorino pudding and marinate the chicken the day before. The mustard dressing, mustard breadcrumbs, and toasted pine nuts can be done in advance as well. So, when you are ready to serve, you can just concentrate on grilling the chicken, tossing the salad, and cooking those gorgeous eggs.

Preheat the oven to 375°F.

For the chicken marinade, heat a small sauté pan over medium heat for 1 minute. Swirl in the butter, and when it foams, add the diced shallots and the thyme; sauté for about 2 minutes, until the shallots are translucent. Add the vermouth, and reduce by half. Transfer to a baking dish, and let cool a few minutes. Whisk in ½ cup Dijon mustard, 1 egg, the chopped tarragon, and a pinch of black pepper.

Place the chicken legs between two pieces of plastic wrap, and pound them with a mallet to an even ½-inch thickness. Remove from the plastic wrap, and slather the chicken with the marinade, making sure to coat both sides well. Refrigerate for at least 4 hours.

Whisk the egg yolk in a small bowl with the remaining 1 tablespoon Dijon mustard, the red-wine vinegar, 1 tablespoon lemon juice, ½ teaspoon salt, and a pinch of pepper. Slowly whisk in ¾ cup olive oil. Thin the vinaigrette with 1 teaspoon water or more if needed. Taste for balance and seasoning.

Light the grill 30 to 40 minutes before you're ready to cook the chicken and take the chicken out of the refrigerator to let it come to room temperature.

Spread the pine nuts on a baking sheet, and toast in the oven for 4 to 5 minutes, until they're lightly browned and smell nutty. (Keep a close eye, because pine nuts are expensive and they burn quickly!) When the pine nuts have cooled, coarsely chop them.

Meanwhile, carefully lower the remaining six eggs into a pot of boiling water. Cook for exactly 6 minutes, and cool immediately in a bowl of ice water. When the eggs have cooled, peel them.

Place the spinach, half the pine nuts, half the breadcrumbs, and the spring onions in a large bowl.

When the coals are broken down, red, and glowing, place the soft-cooked eggs in the oven to heat up.

Drizzle the chicken with the remaining 2 tablespoons olive oil, and place it on the grill skin-side down. Cook for 4 to 5 minutes, rotating once or twice after a couple of minutes to get the skin crispy. (The chicken will stick to the grill at first, but it will eventually release.) When the skin side is nicely crisped, turn the chicken over, and cook for a few minutes on the other side, until it's just cooked through.

Pour ½ cup of the mustard vinaigrette over the salad, and season with salt, pepper, and a squeeze of lemon. Toss well, and taste for balance and seasoning.

Spoon the hot pecorino pudding onto the center of six dinner plates. Arrange the spinach salad on top of the pudding, and place the chicken on top. Carefully balance an egg on top of each piece of chicken. Drizzle with ¼ cup mustard vinaigrette, and sprinkle the remaining pine nuts and breadcrumbs and the grated pecorino over the top.

mustard breadcrumbs

1 cup fresh breadcrumbs
2 tablespoons unsalted butter
1 tablespoon Dijon mustard
1 teaspoon thyme leaves
1 teaspoon chopped flat-leaf parsley

Preheat the oven to 375°F.

Place the breadcrumbs in a medium bowl. Heat a small sauté pan over medium heat for 1 minute. Add the butter, and when it foams, whisk in the mustard, thyme, and parsley. Remove from the heat, let cool for a few minutes, and then pour the mustard butter over the breadcrumbs, tossing to coat them well. Transfer the breadcrumbs to a baking sheet, and toast them for 10 to 12 minutes, stirring often, until they're golden brown and crispy.

pecorino pudding

Preheat the oven to 350°F.

Heat a medium pot over medium heat for 1 minute. Add the butter, and when it foams, whisk in the flour, 1 tablespoon at a time, and cook for about 5 minutes, being careful not to let the flour brown. Slowly pour in the milk and cream, whisking constantly to incorporate it. The butter and flour will seize up and get pasty at first. Continue whisking vigorously as you add the liquid, and the mixture will become smooth. Cook for a few more minutes, until warm to the touch. Remove the pan from the heat.

Whisk the egg and egg yolk together in a small bowl. Slowly drizzle the eggs into the cream mixture, whisking continuously until combined. Stir in the cheese, and season with a heaping ½ teaspoon salt. Pour the mixture into an 8-by-6-inch (or equivalent) baking dish, and cover lightly with foil. Place the baking dish in a roasting pan, and add hot water to the pan until it comes halfway up the outside of the baking dish. Place the pan in the oven, and bake for about 1 hour, until the pudding is just set. If you make the pudding ahead of time, be sure to take it out of the refrigerator to reach room temperature. When it does, heat it in a 350°F oven for about 20 minutes, until it is heated through and starts to brown slightly on top.

3 tablespoons unsalted butter

¼ cup plus 2 tablespoons all-purpose flour

1¾ cups whole milk

⅔ cup heavy cream

1 extra-large egg

1 extra-large egg yolk

1¼ cups grated Pecorino Romano

Kosher salt

This chicken preparation has a super-bright, savory quality from the combination of the mustard, pecorino, and puckery vinaigrette. For pairing, I look for a wine with high-toned red fruit notes and bright acidity, essentially to mirror the spikiness of flavor in the recipe. Grenache, when made in a lean, elegant style, is a great option: it has the lightness of body and acidity that I'm looking for, as well as a good amount of cherry fruit notes to keep the combination from becoming too acidic. This spicy incarnation of Grenache, which is bright red in color, translucent in the glass, and light on the palate, can be found in cooler climates such as California's Central Coast and in the cooler areas of France's Rhône Valley.

grilled pork chops with cornbread-chorizo stuffing and poached cherries

At the restaurant, we use "country-style pork chops," which are cut from the fattier, shoulder end of the pork loin. They are more oddly shaped and marbled with fat than the pristine-looking center-cut chops. But I love the way the fat crisps up and crackles on the grill, and in the end these chops are a little more rustic, shall we say, but also juicier and gamier—in a good way!

What could be a better accompaniment to pork than more pork? For better or for worse, it makes total sense in my brain. The stuffing is made half with country-style croutons and half with cornbread tossed with stewed onions and crispy Mexican-style chorizo. The cherry compote spooned over the top completes that "love fest" we are always looking for—the sweet complement to the spicy and very savory chorizo.

Season the pork chops with the thyme, chopped rosemary, and 2 tablespoons olive oil. Cover, and refrigerate for at least 4 hours, preferably overnight.

Light the grill 30 to 40 minutes before cooking. Remove the pork chops from the refrigerator, and bring them to room temperature.

Preheat the oven to 375°F.

Tear the cornbread into 1½-inch rustic pieces, and place them in a large bowl.

Heat a large sauté pan over high heat for 1 minute. Add the remaining ¼ cup olive oil, the rosemary sprig, and the chile, and let them sizzle in the oil for about 1 minute. Stir in the onions and garlic, and season with salt and pepper. Turn the heat down to medium, and cook for about 10 minutes, until the onions are translucent. Pour the mixture over the cornbread.

While the onions are cooking, heat a medium sauté pan over high heat for 2 minutes. Crumble the chorizo into the pan, and sauté for about 8 minutes, until the sausage is crisp and cooked through. Drain the chorizo of excess oil, and add it to the bowl with the cornbread and onions. Add the parsley, and stir to combine well. Taste for seasoning, and transfer to a 9-by-9-inch (or equivalent) baking dish.

Place the stuffing in the oven 15 minutes before you plan to serve.

6 country-style pork chops, 10 ounces each

2 tablespoons thyme leaves

1 tablespoon chopped rosemary, plus 1 small sprig rosemary

6 tablespoons extra-virgin olive oil

¾ recipe Cornbread (recipe follows)

1 chile de árbol, broken in half

2 cups finely diced onions

1 tablespoon minced garlic

1 pound fresh Mexican chorizo, casing removed

¼ cup chopped flat-leaf parsley

1¼ cups Poached Cherries (page 29)

2 tablespoons unsalted butter

2 ounces dandelion greens, cleaned and dried

Kosher salt and freshly ground black pepper

When the coals are broken down, red, and glowing, season both sides of the pork chops generously with salt and pepper. Place the chops on the grill, and cook for 4 to 5 minutes per side, rotating once or twice, to sear them nicely. Cook until medium.

Bring the poached cherries to a boil over medium heat, and swirl in the butter.

Remove the stuffing from the oven, spoon it evenly onto six dinner plates, and scatter a few leaves of dandelion on top. Place the pork chops on the stuffing, and spoon the hot poached cherries over the top.

cornbread

I love this recipe so much that I just have to keep coming up with more and more reasons and ways to use it! You will have half a cornbread left over if you are making the cornbread-chorizo stuffing, but don't worry; toasted or grilled and buttered, it will not last long!

Preheat the oven to 400°F.

Heat a 10-inch cast-iron pan over medium heat for 1 minute. Add 8 tablespoons (1 stick) butter, and cook for 4 to 5 minutes, swirling the pan often, until the butter browns and smells nutty. Turn off the heat.

Combine the cornmeal, flour, sugar, baking powder, baking soda, and salt in a large bowl. Make a well in the center of the dry ingredients.

Whisk together the eggs, buttermilk, and honey in another bowl. Pour the liquid into the well, and gently whisk until just combined. (Don't overwork the batter.) Fold in the brown butter.

Return the cast-iron pan to the stove over medium-high heat. Swirl in the remaining 2 tablespoons butter, and when it foams, pour the batter into the pan. Transfer the pan immediately to the oven, and bake for 25 to 30 minutes, until golden brown and set.

10 tablespoons unsalted butter, cut into single tablespoons

2 cups cornmeal

2 cups all-purpose flour

¼ cup sugar

1 tablespoon baking powder

¼ teaspoon baking soda

1 tablespoon kosher salt

2 extra-large eggs

2½ cups buttermilk

3 tablespoons honey

The minute a recipe features cherries, I turn straight to Pinot Noir for a wine accompaniment. Pinot is a variety that is so tied to the flavor profile of red and black cherries that it is hard to find a better match. For this dish, I would opt for one from California's Santa Lucia Highlands region, an area that is producing some of the best Pinot Noir in California. These wines tend to be fairly opulent in flavor, with concentrated, full red-cherry notes and fleshy texture. The wine's complex layers of earth and spice will complement the flavors in the stuffing, while fruit and acid structure will keep the pairing fresh and bright.

lamb paillards with risotto carbonara, english peas, and chanterelles

1¾ pounds lamb top sirloin

3½ cups chicken stock

7 tablespoons extra-virgin olive oil

2 ounces finely diced applewood-smoked bacon

2 ounces finely diced guanciale

2 ounces finely diced pancetta

1 cup finely diced white onion

1 tablespoon minced garlic

1 tablespoon thyme leaves

1½ cups high-quality Arborio rice

¼ cup white wine

1 cup freshly shucked English peas (from just over 1 pound in the pod)

6 extra-large egg yolks, beaten

½ cup grated Parmigiano-Reggiano

2 tablespoons chopped flat-leaf parsley

2 tablespoons unsalted butter

¾ pound chanterelles, cleaned

3 ounces pea shoots, cleaned

Kosher salt and freshly ground black pepper

My younger son, Charles, is really the old soul in our family. In a house of madness and mayhem, it is a bit odd that the 4-year-old is the one who is at peace with whatever happens to be going on. After he slides down our backyard hillside when everyone is too distracted to think about where he is, he's the first one to come report the accident, and always with a smile and a reassuring "It's OK, Mommy, I'm fine, really!"

And Charles can eat. This pint-sized boy has the appetite of a 16-year-old football star. I shudder to think how I will keep the refrigerator stocked when he actually reaches his teens. Now, Charlie likes his veggie wraps and loves seaweed, but in his heart of hearts I think he's a meat-and-potatoes guy. He loves steak, pork chops, pasta, and baked potatoes. Literally every morning, when I ask what he wants for breakfast, he replies in his perfect 4-year-old lispy, cartoon voice, "Bacon and eggs!" He is definitely his mother's son! And you can imagine his delight when it finally hit me to cook spaghetti carbonara for him. "Bacon and eggs and pasta for dinner!" he cried—it was better than Disneyland! As I was making what is now Charlie's favorite meal, it occurred to me, why limit this dream of bathing starch in bacon, egg yolks, and cheese to pasta? Why not spread the salty, fatty, unctuous love along to risotto?

In this dish, the English peas bring a lovely spring flourish to the rich risotto, and the pea shoots wilted in with the chanterelles reinforce that pea flavor. This dish would be delicious with roasted rack of lamb as well.

Cut the lamb against the grain into 1½-inch-thick pieces, weighing approximately 1½ ounces each (or have your butcher do this for you). Pound the lamb between sheets of plastic wrap to ⅛-inch thickness.

Light the grill 30 to 40 minutes before you are ready to cook the lamb, and then start the risotto and chanterelles.

Bring the chicken stock and 3 cups water to a boil over high heat. Then turn off the heat.

Heat a large Dutch oven or other heavy-bottomed pot over medium-high heat for 2 minutes. Swirl in 2 tablespoons olive oil, and add the bacon, guanciale, and pancetta, and cook about 5 minutes, stirring often, until the pork mixture is slightly crisped but still tender. Add the onion, garlic, and 2 teaspoons thyme to the bacon, and cook for about 5 minutes, stirring often, until the onion is translucent. Stir in the rice, 1 teaspoon salt, and a pinch of pepper. Cook, stirring continuously, until the rice just begins to toast and each grain of rice has a white dot at its center.

Pour in the white wine, and once it has evaporated, quickly add 1 cup of the hot stock, stirring continuously. When the stock is completely absorbed, begin adding the liquid in 1-cup batches, stirring continuously with a wooden spoon in a rhythmic back-and-forth motion. Wait for each batch of liquid to be absorbed before adding the next. The rice should be bubbling and quickly absorbing the stock. After about 15 minutes, taste the rice for doneness. It should be slightly but not too al dente. The risotto may need a little more liquid and more time, so keep cooking until it's done. It should be neither soupy nor dry; each grain of rice should be coated in a flavorful, starchy "sauce."

When the rice is almost done, stir in the peas, cook for a minute or two, and then turn off the heat. Quickly stir in the egg yolks, the Parmigiano-Reggiano, the parsley, and 1 tablespoon butter, and taste for seasoning. The rice will keep absorbing liquid, so add a little more stock if necessary.

While the risotto is cooking, you can sauté the chanterelles (if this seems like too much, you can sauté the mushrooms first, turn off the heat, and leave them in the pan to finish after the risotto is done).

Heat a large sauté pan over high heat for 2 minutes. Add 2 tablespoons olive oil, and heat for another minute. Swirl in the remaining 1 tablespoon butter, and when it foams, add the chanterelles, the remaining 1 teaspoon thyme, ½ teaspoon salt, and a healthy pinch of pepper. Sauté the mushrooms for about 5 minutes, stirring occasionally, until they're tender and a little crispy. Don't be tempted to move them around in the pan too much in the beginning; let them sear a bit before stirring. Turn off the heat, and leave the chanterelles in the pan until you are ready to serve.

When the coals are broken down, red, and glowing, season the lamb with salt and pepper, and brush with the remaining 3 tablespoons olive oil.

Grill the lamb paillards for 2 to 3 minutes on the first side, and then just 1 minute or so on the second side. They should have nice color but still be medium-rare. Transfer them to a resting rack.

Turn the flame up under the chanterelles; when they are hot, add the pea shoots, and toss them until just wilted.

Spoon the risotto onto six dinner plates. Arrange half the chanterelles and pea shoots over the risotto, and then layer the lamb paillards onto each dish; top with the remaining chanterelles and pea shoots.

Don't let the season fool you. Although this is a spring recipe, it's fairly hearty and full-flavored. The ideal pairing is one that has some substance and weight to match that of the dish, as well as acidity to keep it all balanced. And with the Italian influence, a wine from Tuscany is very appropriate. The beauty of "Super Tuscan" wines is that they have a good deal of body and dark fruit from the addition of Bordeaux varieties such as Cabernet Sauvignon and Merlot, which in themselves are great partners for the lamb, but also feature Sangiovese, which gives them the acidic structure and brightness to cut through the richness of the carbonara.

veal saltimbocca with mortadella, mozzarella, sage, and marsala

This hybrid of a saltimbocca and a Milanese was on our opening menu at A.O.C. It was 2002, and we were just beginning to be able to get real Italian mortadella imported to this country. (Don't get me started on the government's trying to "protect" us from ancient culinary delights that have been prized for centuries by cultures that have somehow managed to survive despite the nonexistence of the health department and the FDA.) Anyway, I wanted to do a riff on saltimbocca, a classic Italian preparation in which sage leaves and thin slices of prosciutto are attached with toothpicks to thin pieces of meat (usually veal), and then sautéed until they deliciously "jump in your mouth"—or "*saltano*" in your "*bocca.*"

Of course, being the lily gilder that I am, I wanted to add some sort of melty cheese and breadcrumbs. Sometimes I am good at paring things down, but this was not one of those moments. I sliced a little pocket into the veal medallions, layered in all those slutty treats—the mortadella, the mozzarella, and the sage—closed up the little packets, dredged them in flour-egg-breadcrumbs, and sautéed them until the breadcrumbs were crispy and the cheese melted and oozing out the side. Pretty darn delicious, I must say.

2¼ pounds veal top round

6 thin slices mortadella or prosciutto di Parma

10 ounces fresh mozzarella

12 sage leaves

1 cup all-purpose flour

2 extra-large eggs

4½ cups fresh breadcrumbs, finely ground

¼ cup extra-virgin olive oil

8 tablespoons unsalted butter

3 tablespoons Marsala

1 tablespoon chicken stock

1 recipe Celery Root Purée (recipe follows)

2 ounces dandelion greens

2 tablespoons chopped flat-leaf parsley

Kosher salt and freshly ground black pepper

Cut the veal against the grain into ½-inch-thick slices. Cut the slices into twenty-four 1½-ounce pieces (or have your butcher do this for you). Pound the veal between sheets of plastic wrap to ⅛-inch thickness. Season the veal on both sides with salt and pepper.

Lay 12 of the veal pieces on a cutting board or work surface. Cut the mortadella (or prosciutto) and the mozzarella into pieces just smaller than the veal. Place one piece of prosciutto, followed by one piece of mozzarella, and then one sage leaf on top of each of the 12 pieces of veal. Top with another piece of veal, and "seal" the edges with your fingers.

Place the flour on a plate or in a pie pan. Beat the eggs in a shallow bowl. Place the breadcrumbs in a shallow baking dish. Line the three dishes up in a row.

Carefully dredge the veal packets in the flour, then the egg, and then the breadcrumbs.

Heat two sauté pans over high heat for 2 minutes. Swirl 2 tablespoons olive oil into each pan, and wait a minute. Place six veal packets in each pan. Cook for 3 minutes, and then add 1 tablespoon butter to each pan. Cook for another minute, and when the crumbs are golden brown, carefully turn each piece of veal over. Turn the heat down to medium, and cook for a few more minutes, until the second side is golden brown. Remove to a baking sheet.

Wipe out one of the pans, and return it to the stove over medium heat. Add the remaining 6 tablespoons butter, and cook until it's brown and smells nutty. Turn off the heat, and add the Marsala. Swirl the pan to combine the Marsala with the butter, add the chicken stock, and season with salt and pepper to taste. (Be careful not to burn your tongue!) Spoon the hot celery-root purée onto the center of six large dinner plates. Scatter the dandelion greens over the purée, and arrange two veal saltimboccas on each plate. Stir the parsley into the Marsala brown butter, and spoon the sauce over the veal.

celery root purée

Place the celery root on its side and, using a sharp knife, cut the top and bottom from the vegetable. Stand the celery root upright on the cutting board. Following the shape of the root, remove the skin, working it from top to bottom, rotating the celery root as you go. Rinse the celery root and dry it well. Cut it into 1-inch chunks, and place the chunks in a large, heavy-bottomed pot. Peel the potatoes, cut them into ½-inch chunks, and add to the pot with the celery root. Add 2 teaspoons salt, and fill the pot with cold water. Bring the celery root and potatoes to a boil over high heat, turn down the heat to low, and simmer for about 20 minutes, until tender.

When the vegetables are cooked through, strain them, and set them aside to cool for 10 minutes or so. Rinse out the pot, and dry it well. Heat the cream and milk together in a small saucepan, then turn off the heat. Pass the celery root and potato through a food mill or potato ricer and into the heavy-bottomed pot. Heat them over medium heat a few minutes, stirring continuously with a wooden spoon, to dry them out a little. Add the butter slowly, stirring constantly. Season with 2 teaspoons salt and some black pepper.

When all the butter has been incorporated, slowly stir in the warm cream mixture until you have a smooth purée. Taste for seasoning. Pass the purée through a fine-mesh *tamis* twice for a smoother texture, or serve as is for a more rustic purée.

1½ pounds celery root
1½ pounds russet potatoes
½ cup heavy cream
½ cup whole milk
4 ounces unsalted butter
Kosher salt and freshly ground
   black pepper

The intense flavors and saltiness in this saltimbocca preparation beg to be paired with a wine of equal vibrancy and punch. I like Barbera d'Alba for this, because not only is it regionally thematic, but it is a great example of how well Italian wine and ingredients work together. Barbera shows bold, bright red cherry notes, as well as elements of dark-green herbs and a characteristic astringency. The flavors and textures are aggressive yet balanced. When combined with the ingredients of this dish, the fruity aspect of the wine works to pull out the sweeter flavors in the mortadella and cheese while also cutting through their saltiness. The herbal quality of the wine mirrors that of the veal, and the wine's acidity keeps the pairing exciting on the palate.

grilled hanger steak with sweet peppers, cherry tomatoes, and chimichurri

3 pounds hanger steak

3 teaspoons thinly sliced chile de árbol

1 tablespoon cracked black pepper

2 tablespoons plus 1 teaspoon thyme leaves

1 fresh jalapeño

1 teaspoon oregano

½ teaspoon rosemary leaves

1 bay leaf

1 cup extra-virgin olive oil, plus 3 tablespoons or so for brushing the steak

1 tablespoon red-wine vinegar

1½ teaspoons sweet paprika

6 large bell peppers (about 3 pounds), julienned

¼ cup sliced garlic

6 ounces cleaned arugula

2 tablespoons freshly squeezed lemon juice

½ pint cherry tomatoes, cut in half

1 tablespoon chopped flat-leaf parsley

Kosher salt and freshly ground black pepper

Many years ago, right after my father passed away, my friend the punk-rock chef guru Fred Eric invited me to assist him at a cooking festival in Rio de Janeiro. I have to say it was one of the wackiest of all my culinary adventures *ever.* It turns out that the man who arranged the whole event was a raging cocaine fiend and had not *actually* "arranged" anything at all! Well, that's not completely true. We did have hotel rooms and what looked like an amazing itinerary. But, the first day, Fred and I stood outside our hotel for 4 hours waiting for a mysterious culinary expert who was supposed to take us to the market and then on to our host restaurant to prep for the first event, which was, of course, that evening. Long story short, the host restaurant didn't exist, and the crazy coked-up guy placed us at some friend's restaurant, where they plied us with Caipirinhas made with Bolivian coca-leaf liquor and tried to make us cook—let's just say things got *very* ugly from there on out.

As soon as I got over the once-horrifying, now hilarious moments, I remembered having some of the most delicious meat of my life served in more ways than you can imagine—roasted on long skewers, in outdoor pits, and jury-rigged barbecues at the town market. As much as I was craving salads and vegetables after a few days, I told myself, when in South America, just indulge your inner carnivore. One of the most delicious ways to do that is with grilled steak seasoned with a traditional Argentinian warmed herb-and-olive-oil sauce called chimichurri.

As you may have realized by now, I am on the constant prowl for new olive-oil-and-herb-based sauces. Something about the way that silky olive oil and the brightness and power-packed flavor of fresh herbs meld with meat juices is so perfectly balanced for my palate. The oil turns the natural juices into a sauce, and the herbs lift and counter the richness of the meat. But, whereas I tend toward the "soft" herbs, such as parsley, mint, and cilantro, in my herb salsas, chimichurri is made with tougher, more sturdy, dark-and-earthy-flavored members of the herb family. Rosemary, thyme, oregano, and even bay leaf are minced and warmed in olive oil with charred jalapeño and red-wine vinegar. This is a strong, bold gaucho to pistou's delicate mademoiselle.

NOTE If the chiles de árbol are dry and brittle you can just crush or crumble them.

Light the grill.

Trim the hanger steak of excess fat and sinew, if any (it doesn't usually need much trimming). At least an hour before serving, season the hanger steak with 2 teaspoons sliced chile, the cracked black pepper, and 1 tablespoon thyme. Leave out to bring to room temperature. (Or, of course, you can refrigerate for later. Just make sure to take the meat out at least an hour before serving.)

To make the chimichurri, char the jalapeño on all sides on a medium-hot grill, or on the burner of a gas stove, or in the broiler, until it is completely blackened. Place it in a small paper bag, and close it tightly (peppers can leak, so place the bag on a plate). Let the pepper steam for about 10 minutes, and then remove the seeds and mince the flesh of the jalapeño, including the charred skin, and place them in a medium sauté pan with ½ cup olive oil.

Mince the oregano, rosemary, bay leaf, and 1 teaspoon thyme. Bring the jalapeño in oil to a simmer over medium-low heat, and then remove from the heat, and add the minced herbs, the vinegar, and the paprika. Leave the chimichurri in the pan, off the heat, and let the herbs infuse for at least 1 hour.

Meanwhile, stew the peppers. Heat a large sauté pan over high heat for 1 minute. Swirl in ½ cup olive oil, and then add the bell peppers. Season with remaining 1 tablespoon thyme, 1 tablespoon salt, and 1 teaspoon ground pepper. Turn the heat down to medium, and sauté for 3 to 4 minutes, until the peppers start to wilt. Add the sliced garlic and the remaining 1 teaspoon sliced árbol chile, and cook for another 10 minutes, stirring often, until the peppers are completely tender. Turn off the heat.

When the coals are broken down, red, and glowing, season the steak generously with salt, and brush it lightly with 3 tablespoons olive oil. Place the meat on the hottest part of the grill, to get a nice sear on the outside. Cook for about 3 minutes, turn the meat a quarter-turn, and cook for another minute or two. Turn the meat over, and move it to a cooler spot on the grill. Cook for another minute or two for medium-rare. Rest the steaks on a wire rack set over a baking sheet for 5 minutes.

In a large salad bowl, gently toss the arugula with the warm peppers,

1 tablespoon lemon juice, salt, and pepper. Taste for balance and seasoning, and divide among six large dinner plates. Set the pan with the chimichurri on the stove over medium-high heat. When it starts to boil, add the cherry tomatoes, and season with salt and pepper. Cook for 30 seconds, shaking the pan, as the tomatoes blister a little and release their juices, then add the remaining 1 tablespoon lemon juice, and toss in the parsley. Remove from the heat and taste for seasoning. Slice the steak against the grain, lay the slices over the arugula, and spoon the sizzling cherry tomatoes in chimichurri over the steak and around the plate.

I love the Argentinian influence on this dish and am, of course, drawn to that country's dark and seductive wines for pairing. The Mendoza region produces outstanding Malbec, which is a really fabulous accompaniment to grilled meat. Malbec tends to show deep cocoa-infused black fruit notes with touches of smokiness and grippy tannins. These darker aspects of the wine are very much like the sweet charred flavors of the steak itself. The wine also tends to show a good dose of acid, which will work seamlessly with the bright-green herbs in the chimichurri and the tomato.

crispy pork belly with peaches, ricotta salata, and abbamele

I guess, officially, pork belly would be in the rich, heavy, save-it-for-fall-and-winter department, but in this preparation—because it's served with raw peaches, lots of dandelion greens, and shavings of bright white ricotta salata—it really works for summer. Searing the braised, tender fatty belly gives it a contrast of texture and brings the stewed meat to life. I find this contrast of caramelized crispy crust to be essential to cooking a truly great braised meat. Whether it's short ribs, beef brisket, lamb daube, or pork stew, letting the soft, tender meat cook uncovered at a higher heat (or, in this case, crisping it in a pan on the stove) elevates bistro comfort food to another level.

Abbamele is an ancient Sardinian specialty made by pressing all the honey and bee pollen out of specially selected honeycombs and then cooking that mixture down to a syrupy consistency in copper pots. Its earthy sweetness works beautifully with the rich, fatty pork, the sweet almond notes of the peaches, and the dry, salty ricotta.

> **NOTE** Pork belly is very fatty—it is the belly of a pig, after all! It's delicious, and I encourage it once in a while, but I just want to make sure you know what you are getting into and are not surprised when you purchase it or after you cook it. Yes! It is fatty!

> **NOTE** If the chiles de árbol are dry and brittle you can just crush or crumble them.

Place the pork belly in a baking dish, and season it on both sides with the thyme leaves, cracked black pepper, chile, and fleur de sel, and let sit at least 1 hour.

Preheat the oven to 325°F.

Heat a large Dutch oven over high heat for 3 minutes. Pour in 2 tablespoons olive oil, and wait for a minute or two. Carefully place the pork belly in the pan, and sear until well browned and caramelized on all sides; this will probably take at least 10 minutes. Remove the seared belly to a baking sheet.

Turn the heat down to medium, and add 2 tablespoons olive oil, the

---

3-pound slab pork belly

3 tablespoons thyme leaves, plus 5 sprigs thyme

3 tablespoons cracked black pepper

1 tablespoon sliced chile de árbol

3½ tablespoons fleur de sel

¼ cup plus 3 tablespoons extra-virgin olive oil

1 cup diced onion

¼ cup diced celery

¼ cup diced carrot

1 cup sherry

6 cups veal stock

5 sprigs flat-leaf parsley

2 bay leaves (fresh or dried)

3 large ripe peaches

⅓-pound chunk ricotta salata

1 bunch dandelion greens, cleaned and dried

Approximately 3 tablespoons abbamele (see Sources)

Kosher salt and freshly ground black pepper

onion, celery, and carrot. Stir with a wooden spoon, scraping up all the tasty crusty bits left in the pan. Cook for 6 to 8 minutes, until the vegetables start to caramelize.

Pour in the sherry, and reduce by half, about 5 minutes. Add the stock, and bring to a boil.

Turn off the heat, add the pork to the pot, and tuck the thyme sprigs, parsley sprigs, and bay leaves around the meat. The liquid should come almost to the top of the belly, leaving the top exposed. Cover the pan with aluminum foil and a tight-fitting lid. Braise in the oven for about 3½ hours, until the belly is tender and will yield easily to a paring knife.

Cool the belly to lukewarm in the braising juices, then remove the meat from the broth. Strain the liquid, and chill the meat completely. Cut the cold pork belly into 6-ounce rectangles, and then cut those rectangles lengthwise into triangles. The best way to do this is to weigh the whole cooked pork belly and divide by six, and you will know how many triangles you can get out of that one piece.

Thirty minutes before you are ready to serve, heat a large sauté pan over high heat for 3 minutes. Pour in the remaining 3 tablespoons olive oil, and wait a minute or two, until the pan is very hot and almost smoking. Place the pork-belly triangles in the pan, and sear on all sides until they are crispy and dark golden brown; this may take about 15 minutes. Depending on the size of your pan, you may need to use two pans or work in batches.

Meanwhile, reheat the strained braising juices, and reduce slightly over medium-high heat. Cut the peaches in half, and cut each half into three wedges. Place the ricotta salata flat-side down on a cutting board, and, using a chef's knife, carefully cut ⅛-inch-thick slices of cheese. (You can cut the peaches and cheese before you start searing the pork triangles if you prefer.)

Place two pieces of pork belly, one leaning loosely up against the other, at the center of each of six large dinner plates. Arrange three wedges of peach artfully on each plate—I like to lay one on its "back," another resting up against the pork, and one on top. Weave the dandelion between the pork and the peaches (if the dandelion leaves are big, you can tear them in half). Place the slices of cheese loosely on top of the leaves, peaches, and pork.

Gently spoon the hot sauce developed from the braising liquid over the pork, and a little around the plate. Drizzle with the abbamele.

Although this recipe has a good amount of richness from the pork belly itself, it has a clean and elegant quality, in good part from the addition of the fresh peaches and the dry ricotta. The key to pairing wine with this recipe is finding one that has a soft, plumlike fruitiness to play off of the meat and peaches, as well as a healthy amount of acidity to cut through the fattiness of the meat. Syrah from California's Central Coast is a great option, because these wines show fig and ripe black fruit notes alongside savory herb and olive elements. The area's cool climate allows these wines to retain the necessary acidity to keep them balanced as well as provide a gamy brightness that is ideal for pairing with the pork.

slow-roasted lamb sirloin with skordalia, lima purée, and cucumber yogurt

Skordalia is a classic purée in Greek cooking—made with lots of garlic, potato, almonds (sometimes walnuts are substituted), and plenty of olive oil. It is classically served with fish—you could prepare this exact same dish with a meaty white fish or wild salmon, and it would be lovely—but I just love it with slow-roasted lamb. The lima purée and skordalia have similar textures but such different flavors, which is a nice surprise for the palate. To complete this dish, I really took the cue from the Greeks—slicing cucumbers and coating them with yogurt for a bright, creamy, and cooling topping for this summer dish.

Season the lamb with 1 tablespoon thyme leaves, the rosemary leaves, and the smashed garlic. Let sit at least an hour, or cover and refrigerate if you are not cooking right away. Remember to take the lamb out of the refrigerator at least 1 hour before cooking, to bring it to room temperature.

Bring a medium pot of salted water to a boil, and blanch the lima beans for about 3 minutes, until they're just tender.

Drain the pot, rinse it out, and return it to the stove over high heat for 1 minute. Swirl in ½ cup olive oil, turn the heat down to low, and add 1 small sprig rosemary and the crumbled chile. When the rosemary begins to sizzle, add the onion, the minced garlic, and the remaining ½ tablespoon thyme, and sauté over medium heat for 3 to 4 minutes, until the onion is translucent. Add the lima beans and ½ teaspoon salt, and stew gently for 5 to 7 minutes, until the beans are soft but not mushy. Strain the beans, setting aside ½ cup of them, and reserve the oil. Discard the rosemary sprig and chile.

Place the beans (except the reserved ½ cup) in the bowl of a food processor fitted with a metal blade and purée. With the motor running, slowly pour in some of the reserved oil, until the mixture has a smooth consistency. You may not need all the oil, so save it to drizzle over toasted bread, add to sautéed vegetables, or spoon over sliced tomatoes. Season with salt, pepper, and a squeeze of lemon juice to taste.

Preheat the oven to 325°F.

3 pounds lamb sirloin

1½ tablespoons thyme leaves, plus 6 sprigs thyme

1 tablespoon rosemary leaves, plus 3 sprigs rosemary, broken into 3-inch pieces

7 smashed cloves garlic, plus 1 tablespoon minced garlic

2½ cups fresh lima beans (from approximately 2½ pounds in the pod)

½ cup plus 2 tablespoons extra-virgin olive oil

1 dried chile de árbol, crumbled

¼ cup finely diced onion

½ lemon, for juicing

3 tablespoons unsalted butter, sliced into ¼-inch pieces

2 small Persian hothouse cucumbers, or 1 European-style cucumber

¾ cup good-quality low-fat plain yogurt (I use half Greek and half Straus)

1 recipe Skordalia (recipe follows)

6 mint leaves, thinly sliced

Kosher salt and freshly ground black pepper

Heat a large sauté pan over high heat for 3 minutes. Season the lamb with salt and pepper. Swirl the remaining 2 tablespoons oil into the pan, and wait for a minute or two. Place the lamb in the pan, and sear it on all sides until well browned and caramelized.

Transfer the lamb to a roasting rack. Arrange the sliced butter and the thyme sprigs, the remaining rosemary sprigs, and the garlic from the marinade on top of the lamb.

Roast the lamb for about 40 minutes, until a thermometer inserted into the center reads 135°F (for a rare-ish medium-rare). Let the lamb rest for at least 10 minutes before slicing. Pour the buttery juices left in the pan over the lamb, and then thinly cut the roast into ¼-inch-thick slices.

While the lamb is cooking, cut the cucumbers in half lengthwise, thinly slice them, and transfer them to a medium bowl. Stir in the yogurt, 1 teaspoon lemon juice, the reserved lima beans, ½ teaspoon salt, and a pinch of pepper. Taste for balance and seasoning.

Spread the skordalia on six large dinner plates. Fan the lamb slices over the skordalia, dollop the warm lima purée onto the meat, spoon the cucumber-yogurt mixture over the top and around the plate, and sprinkle with the sliced mint.

skordalia

2 pounds russet potatoes

2 cloves garlic, smashed

¼ cup whole blanched almonds

⅔ cup extra-virgin olive oil

2 teaspoons freshly squeezed
lemon juice

1 tablespoon white-wine or
champagne vinegar

Kosher salt and freshly ground
black pepper

Place the potatoes, whole and unpeeled, in a large saucepan. Add 2 tablespoons salt, and fill the pot with cold water. Bring the potatoes to a boil over high heat, turn down the heat to low, and simmer for about 45 minutes, until tender.

When the potatoes are cooked through, strain them, and set them aside to cool for 10 minutes or so. When the potatoes have cooled, peel them and pass them through a food mill or potato ricer set over a large mixing bowl.

Pound the smashed garlic cloves with 1 teaspoon salt, using a mortar and pestle.

Transfer the pounded garlic mixture to the bowl of a food processor fitted with a metal blade. Add the almonds and the olive oil, and purée until smooth.

Transfer to the bowl with the potatoes, and season with 2 teaspoons salt, 3 tablespoons water, the lemon juice, the vinegar, and a healthy pinch of pepper. Taste for balance and seasoning. I like to serve the skordalia at room temperature.

It is hard to find a more perfect dish to pair a Greek red wine with than this garlicky lamb. Wines made from indigenous varieties, such as Aghiorghitiko, Xinomavro, and Mandilaria, tend to show dark fruit notes and savory, smoky flavors that work perfectly with gamy meat like lamb and the herbaceous ingredients in the other components of this recipe. When a high-quality Greek wine is not readily available, another great option would be one made from Cabernet Franc from Bordeaux, California, or even from the East Coast of the United States. These wines show intense, velvety blackberry and dark green herbal components that will work with the lamb in much the same way as a Greek varietal.

grilled chicken with fresh garbanzos, corn, and chile-cumin butter

The first time I ever saw fresh garbanzo beans, they were still on the branches, in a giant pile at James Birch's Flora Bella Farm's stand at the Santa Monica Farmers Market. I almost walked right by them, thinking it was James's compost pile, or some sort of odd hay-and-wheat project he might have going on. But James knows me well enough to know that I would soon be smitten by the fresh green version of one of my favorite legumes.

Fresh garbanzos are popular in Mexico, India, and the Middle East, so it's funny that, as many chickpeas as we grow here in California, it's rare to find them in their fresh, pre-dried state.

Now, the season for these green beauties is very short, and they are a lot of work—so, of course, I love them! You should see the prep cooks' faces when they see the truckloads of them at the back door. As I always advise, with tedious and time-consuming projects like this, pour yourself a glass of wine, grab a friend or family member, and picture yourself as an old European grandmother, sitting around the town fountain, peeling garlic and gossiping—it's actually a nice way to pass an hour or so one afternoon.

In this dish, a sort of Mexican fresh-garbanzo-inspired succotash is topped with grilled chicken and seasoned with lime and a delicious chile-cumin butter made with crushed ancho and árbol chiles and toasted cumin. Lamb's-quarter is an edible weed popular in India but often picked and thrown out by irritated gardeners and farmers in the United States. It's actually quite delicious and nutritious, with a lovely mineral-like taste and wonderful texture. You can steam or sauté it, but I prefer to wilt it into vegetable sautés such as this succotash. If you can't find lamb's-quarter, substitute torn or julienned leaves of Swiss chard, young spinach, or a more delicate kale.

6 boneless chicken breasts, 6 to 8 ounces each, ideally airline breasts (with drumette attached)

1 tablespoon thyme leaves

¼ cup sliced flat-leaf parsley

2 limes

2 pounds fresh garbanzo beans on the branch, or 2 cups shucked (to yield 1 cup peeled beans)

¼ cup extra-virgin olive oil

2½ cups fresh corn (from 3 or 4 ears)

2 cups sliced summer squash

1 recipe Chile-Cumin Butter (recipe follows)

½ pint cherry tomatoes, cut in half

1½ cups cleaned lamb's-quarter (½ bunch)

½ cup sliced spring onions

Kosher salt and freshly ground black pepper

Season the chicken with the thyme, 2 tablespoons parsley, and the zest of one lime. Cover, and refrigerate for at least 4 hours or overnight.

Light the grill 30 to 40 minutes before you are ready to cook the chicken, and remove the chicken from the refrigerator, to bring it to room temperature.

Pluck the garbanzo beans from the branches, and then peel open each pod to release the bright-green fresh chickpea inside. Blanch the garbanzos in boiling salted water for 1 minute, cool in ice water, and set aside.

When the coals are broken down, red, and glowing, brush the chicken breasts with 2 tablespoons olive oil, and season with salt and pepper. Place the chicken on a medium-hot part of the grill skin-side down, and cook for 3 to 4 minutes, rotating once after a couple of minutes, to get the skin crispy. Turn the chicken over, and move it to a cooler spot on the grill. Cook the chicken for another minute or so, until just cooked through and springy to the touch. Transfer the chicken to a resting rack.

Meanwhile, heat a large sauté pan over high heat for 1 minute. Swirl in the remaining 2 tablespoons olive oil, and wait for a minute. Add the corn and squash to the pan; season with 1 teaspoon salt and some freshly ground pepper. Sauté for 1 minute, then add 3 tablespoons chile-cumin butter and the garbanzos, and toss very well, to coat all the vegetables with the butter. Add the cherry tomatoes and another ½ teaspoon salt. Cook for 1 minute more, and then add the lambs'-quarter, spring onions, and the remaining 2 tablespoons parsley. Toss, just to wilt the greens and combine the ingredients. Squeeze in some lime juice, taste for seasoning, and spoon onto six large dinner plates.

Place the chicken breasts on the greens, and top each one with a dollop of chile-cumin butter.

chile-cumin butter

Remove and discard the stems and seeds from the chiles, and then soak them in hot water for 15 minutes to soften. Drain the chiles, and pat dry with paper towels.

Meanwhile, toast the cumin seeds in a small pan over medium-high heat for about 2 minutes, until the seeds release their aroma. Using a mortar and pestle, pound the cumin, garlic, and ¼ teaspoon salt to a paste. Transfer to a medium bowl.

Pound the chiles in the mortar, and transfer to the bowl as well. Add the softened butter, and whisk together well to incorporate completely. Taste for seasoning and heat.

2 ancho chiles

2 chiles de árbol

1 teaspoon cumin seeds

2 small cloves garlic

4 ounces unsalted butter, softened

Kosher salt

There is a definite South American influence in this recipe, between the corn, chile, and cumin, making it an ideal match for some of the lighter-bodied wines coming from Argentina, Chile, and even Uruguay. Chilean wine made from Carménère is a particularly good option here. Rather than being dark and rich, like most wines from hot Latin regions, these wines tend to be lighter in body, displaying flavors of bright red cherry, smoke, and savory herbs that will be in balance with the relative lightness of this preparation.

grilled quail with couscous, walnuts, and pomegranate salsa

1 tablespoon cumin seeds

1 tablespoon coriander seeds

12 semi-boneless quail

1 tablespoon crushed Aleppo
    pepper

3 tablespoons chopped cilantro,
    plus ¼ cup whole cilantro
    leaves

9 tablespoons extra-virgin
    olive oil

½ cup walnuts

3 tablespoons finely diced
    shallots

1 teaspoon freshly squeezed
    lemon juice

1 tablespoon pomegranate
    molasses

½ cup pomegranate seeds

4 ounces mizuna
    or watercress (2 bunches)

¼ cup sliced spring onions or
    scallions

2 teaspoons freshly squeezed
    lime juice

1 recipe Saffron Couscous
    (recipe follows)

Kosher salt and freshly ground
    black pepper

Between the saffron couscous, the walnuts, and the pomegranate molasses, this quail dish has a lovely subtle Middle or Far Eastern vibe. Pomegranate seeds are the jewels of fall, and I just can't help spooning them over everything in celebration of cooler, shorter days and that chill in the air. This dish would go beautifully with the Turmeric-Spiced Root Vegetables with Kaffir Lime Yogurt and Mint Chutney, and Roasted Kabocha Squash with Dates, Parmesan, and Pepitas.

Toast the cumin seeds in a small pan for a few minutes, until the seeds release their aroma and are lightly browned. Using a mortar and pestle, pound them well. Repeat with the coriander seeds.

Using your hands, season the quail with the cumin, coriander, Aleppo pepper, 2 tablespoons chopped cilantro, and 3 tablespoons olive oil. Cover, and refrigerate if you are not cooking them within the next hour or so.

Light the grill 30 to 40 minutes before you're ready to cook.

Preheat the oven to 375°F.

Spread the walnuts on a baking sheet, and toast for 8 to 10 minutes, until they are golden brown and smell nutty.

While the nuts are toasting, place the shallots, lemon juice, and ¼ teaspoon salt in a small bowl, and let sit for 5 minutes. Whisk in the pomegranate molasses, pomegranate seeds, ¼ cup olive oil, and the remaining tablespoon chopped cilantro.

When the nuts have cooled, chop them coarsely and add them to the pomegranate salsa.

When the coals are broken down, red, and glowing, season the quail with salt and pepper. Tuck the wing tips behind the wing joints. Place the quail breast-side down on the grill. Cook for 3 to 4 minutes, rotating the birds a few times, until the skin crisps. Turn the quail over and cook them for another 2 to 3 minutes or so, until the meat is just rosy. Peek inside the legs to check for doneness. The legs should be just cooked through—the meat will release from the bones when you give them a little squeeze—and the breast should be rosy pink, just over medium-rare. Remember, they will continue to cook off the grill.

In a large bowl, toss the mizuna, spring onions, and whole cilantro leaves with the lime juice, remaining 2 tablespoons olive oil, ¼ teaspoon salt, and some pepper.

Spoon the couscous onto six large dinner plates, and arrange the salad on top. Place the quail on the salad, and spoon the pomegranate salsa over and around the quail.

saffron couscous

Toast the saffron threads in a small pan over medium heat, just until they dry and become brittle. Pound the saffron with a mortar and pestle to a fine powder. Add the butter, and use a rubber spatula to incorporate it, making sure to "pick up" all the saffron from inside the mortar.

Place the couscous, saffron butter, spring onions, cilantro, cayenne, 1 teaspoon salt, and some pepper in a medium heatproof bowl, and stir to combine.

Bring the water or stock to a boil, and pour it over the couscous. Stir with a fork, and immediately cover the bowl tightly with plastic wrap.

Let sit at least 15 minutes.

When ready to serve, carefully uncover the bowl, and fluff the couscous with a fork. Taste for seasoning.

½ teaspoon saffron threads

1 tablespoon unsalted butter, softened

2 cups couscous

1 cup sliced spring onions or scallions

2 tablespoons chopped cilantro

Pinch cayenne pepper

2 cups chicken stock or water, or a combination

Kosher salt and freshly ground black pepper

In searching for a wine pairing here, I look to the sweet-and-sour quality that the pomegranate salsa brings to the savory base of the quail and couscous. Pinot Noirs from regions like Chambolle-Musigny and Savigny-les-Beaune work really well with this recipe: these wines tend to be light in body and lacy in texture, and express the red-fruit and rose-hips aspects of the variety. The high-toned brightness and body of the wine will balance the gamy quality of the quail and highlight the earthiness in the combination of couscous and walnuts.

lamb merguez with eggplant jam, roasted cherry tomatoes, and green olives

12 ounces red bell peppers,
   or ¾ cup roasted peppers

2 pounds lamb shoulder, cleaned,
   cut into 1-inch chunks

½ pound pork fatback, cut into
   ½-inch chunks

1 teaspoon sugar

½ teaspoon crushed chile flakes

1 teaspoon minced garlic

1 tablespoon Spanish paprika

1 tablespoon fresh oregano leaves

2 tablespoons chilled red wine

2 tablespoons ice water

5 feet lamb casings, soaked in
   cold water

½ pint cherry tomatoes

1 teaspoon thyme leaves

½ cup extra-virgin olive oil

4 ounces Castelvetrano olives

2 tablespoons finely diced
   shallots

2 tablespoons plus 2 teaspoons
   freshly squeezed lemon juice

2 tablespoons chopped flat-leaf
   parsley

3 cups Eggplant Jam
   (recipe follows)

2 ounces dandelion greens

Kosher salt and freshly ground
   black pepper

My husband, David Lentz, developed this recipe for the North African–style lamb sausages called "merguez." It always reminds me of our exotic, pre-children travel adventures in Tunisia. It was September 2001, and we had just popped over the Mediterranean from Sicily in a plane that looked as if it were held together with masking tape, chewing gum, and sweat. None of the seatbelts matched, half the tray tables were missing, and a few of the windows sure looked dangerously cracked. To top it off, David hates to fly, so you can imagine the ride.

Tunis was gorgeous and fascinating. I remember feasting on merguez, harissa, olives, chickpeas, braised goat, and tuna belly that was so fatty it had to be served medium well or you wouldn't have been able to cut it—literally the most delicious piece of fish in my life. The spices, smells, and sounds of that market—with the headless chickens running around, and whole animals hanging in the heat—still permeate my mind.

David and I weren't even married yet and had not figured out the roles that are now so obvious in our daily lives. I am the goofy, over-excited, usually too-nice eternal optimist, and David is the cautious, critical, and chronically worried one, who always thinks someone is breaking into the house at night. As we drove around Tunisia in our run-down rental car, I was thrilled how well my French seemed to have come back, how everyone was so nice to me, how delicious the street food looked, and generally how comfortable I felt in this very foreign country. David, on the other hand, couldn't stop looking over his shoulder. "Something just feels weird," he would say, "like these packs of men are all looking at me like they hate my very being." At an off-the-radar beachside town that I was so proud of finding, David literally made me check us *out* of a hotel just as soon as we had checked in, because he saw groups of men by the pool looking "hateful and suspicious, like they want to kill me."

"Wow," I thought to myself, "David is being seriously paranoid and closed-minded. I mean, really, he doesn't actually think they hate us just because we are American, does he?" Well, we flew home September 9, 2001—through Boston, no less—and two days later, on that fateful and horrible day, suddenly David didn't seem so unperceptive and crazy anymore. I still have wonderful memories of that trip, even though they were changed by the course of history. And I still love merguez. Here it's served with an eggplant jam and topped with roasted cherry tomatoes and green olives.

NOTE You can ask your butcher to grind the lamb and fatback for you. If you do this, process the marinating ingredients (roasted peppers, sugar, salt, and spices) to a purée, gently combine with the ground meat, and marinate in the refrigerator for at least 4 hours. And if you don't feel like stuffing the sausage, you can shape the merguez into patties and cook them in a hot cast-iron pan.

Char the peppers on a medium-hot grill, or on the burners of a gas stove, or in the broiler, until all sides are just blackened (you want to char the skin of the peppers without burning the flesh underneath). Place the peppers in a large paper bag, close it tightly, and let them steam for at least 15 minutes. (They sometimes leak, so put the closed bag on a plate.)

Open the bag of roasted peppers, and let them cool slightly. Peel each one carefully. Do not run them under water or you will lose all their delicious juices. Work over a strainer set in a bowl to catch their juices. Tear the peppers in half lengthwise, along their natural seam, and remove the seeds and membranes. Purée the peppers and their juices in a food processor. It should yield ¾ cup.

In a large mixing bowl, combine the roasted peppers, lamb, fatback, sugar, chile flakes, garlic, paprika, oregano, 2 tablespoons salt, and ½ teaspoon pepper. Mix well, cover, and chill for at least 4 hours or overnight.

Preheat the oven to 400°F.

Grind the meat through the small die into a bowl set in ice. Transfer to a stand mixer and, using the paddle attachment, add the wine and ice water, and mix until the sausage is emulsified. Using a sausage stuffer, stuff the meat into the lamb casings and shape into 5-inch-long sausages.

Light the grill 30 to 40 minutes before cooking, and remove the merguez from the refrigerator.

Remove the stems from the cherry tomatoes, and toss them in a medium bowl with the thyme, 2 tablespoons olive oil, salt, and pepper. Roast them in the oven for about 15 minutes, until they are blistered but still plump.

Place the olives on one side of a kitchen towel, wrapping the towel around to cover the top of the olives as well. Tap the olives very gently with a mallet or rolling pin, uncover the cloth, and remove the pits one at a time.

Place the shallots and lemon juice in a small bowl, and let sit 5 minutes. Stir the pitted olives, 5 tablespoons olive oil, and the chopped parsley into the shallots. Taste for balance and seasoning.

When the coals are broken down, red, and glowing, brush the sausages with the remaining 1 tablespoon olive oil.

Place the sausages on the grill, and cook for about 3 minutes. Turn the sausages a quarter-turn, and cook for another minute or two. When they are nicely seared, turn the sausages over and cook for 2 to 3 minutes, until they are just medium.

Spoon some hot eggplant jam (about ½ cup per person) onto six large dinner plates. Scatter a few dandelion greens and arrange the merguez on top. Place the roasted cherry tomatoes over and around the sausages and spoon over the green olive salsa.

eggplant jam

Cut the eggplants into ½-inch-thick slices, score each slice, and season with 1 tablespoon salt. Let sit 10 minutes, and then dry with paper towels. Heat two large sauté pans over high heat for 2 minutes (you may need to do this in batches). Swirl 3 tablespoons olive oil into each pan, and wait 1 minute. Add the eggplant to the pans in a single layer. Once the slices start to color, turn the eggplant over and cook for another 3 to 4 minutes, until tender and golden. Transfer to a paper-towel-lined baking sheet.

Cut the eggplant into ½-inch chunks, and toss in a large bowl with the paprika, cayenne, and 2 teaspoons salt. Pound the garlic with a mortar and pestle, with a pinch of salt, and add it to the eggplant with the chopped cilantro. Taste for seasoning.

Cut an "X" on the bottom of each tomato, and blanch them in boiling water for 30 seconds. Cool the tomatoes in a bowl of ice water, and then use your fingers to slip off their skins. Remove the cores, and cut each tomato in half horizontally. Squeeze the tomato halves cut-side down over a strainer set in a bowl. Scoop the seeds out with your fingers, and discard them. Chop the tomatoes coarsely, and reserve the juice.

Heat a medium-large sauté pan over medium-high heat for 1 minute. Swirl in 2 tablespoons olive oil, add the rosemary and chiles, and heat for another minute. Add the onion, season with 2 teaspoons salt and some pepper, and sauté for 3 to 4 minutes, until the onion is translucent. Add the chopped tomatoes, their juices, the sugar, and the vinegar. Season with 2 teaspoons salt, and cook for 10 to 12 minutes, until most of the liquid has evaporated and the tomatoes are cooked. Add the eggplant to the pan, turn up the heat, and cook for another 6 to 8 minutes, stirring often until well integrated and jammy in texture.

2 pounds globe eggplants (about 2 medium)

About ½ cup extra-virgin olive oil

1½ teaspoons smoked paprika

¼ teaspoon cayenne pepper

2 cloves garlic

¼ cup chopped cilantro

2 pounds ripe tomatoes (about 6 medium)

1 small sprig rosemary

2 chiles de árbol, crumbled

1 cup diced onion

1 teaspoon sugar

1 tablespoon red-wine vinegar

Kosher salt and freshly ground black pepper

Although I would normally look to Syrah for this pairing, the North African influence in the sausage steers me across the sea to Spain, to the wine region of Priorat, instead. Wines from this dry, hot area are loaded with black fruitiness and intense mineral concentration from the region's slate-rich soils. These wines balance a deep richness that will complement the sweetness in the meat and tomatoes, with an earthy, tarlike quality that will mirror that of the black olives.

braised duck with madeira, kale stuffing, and dates

This recipe tortured me for a while. My first thought about this deeply fall duck braise was to make a stuffing with kale, dates, and chestnuts to accompany it. But once I tried it out, I was disappointed. Though the chestnuts worked beautifully with the bitterness and earthiness of the kale, somehow the oomph of both the chestnuts and the dates was diminished, muted. I tried taking the dates and chestnuts out of the stuffing and serving them on top of the duck instead, glazed in a little brown butter. Well, that was delicious, but now my stuffing had sort of lost its mojo. I put the dates back in the stuffing, but when I tasted it that time, with the Madeira and the softened dates in the stuffing, the whole thing just seemed too sweet.

Finally, after much agonizing (are you feeling my pain?), I realized that the best solution was to use the chestnuts twice—in the stuffing, and then again glazed with the dates, on top of the duck—and to use the dates only once, on top rather than in the stuffing. Phew, sometimes it comes so easy, but this time was a little bit of hell. Luckily, I am very happy with the result and hope you will be, too.

NOTE You will need 1½ cups chopped chestnuts total for this dish (1 cup for the stuffing and another ½ cup for the finished dish). Be careful when you slice the dates to lay them out carefully so they don't all stick together. I have listed the measurement in ounces, because if you pack the sliced dates into a measuring cup they will all clump together. The idea behind sizzling them in the butter (besides that butter is delicious) is that each little slice of date will get glazed and develop a sort of skin that will keep it separate from the other date slices. This way, you have a nice texture of chew or bite on the outside of the date, and tender softness on the inside.

Trim the excess fat from the duck legs. Season them with the thyme leaves, 1 teaspoon salt, and several grinds of pepper. Let them sit at room temperature for at least 1 hour before cooking.

Heat a large sauté pan over high heat for 2 minutes. Swirl in the olive oil, and wait for 1 minute. Place the duck legs in the pan skin-side down, and cook

6 large duck legs, 8 to 10 ounces each

1 tablespoon thyme leaves, plus 6 whole sprigs thyme

2 tablespoons extra-virgin olive oil

1½ cups diced onions

½ cup diced carrot

½ cup diced celery

1 fresh bay leaf

2½ cups Madeira

3 to 4 cups chicken or duck stock

6 ounces deglet noor dates, or another dry variety

1 recipe Kale Stuffing (recipe follows)

6 tablespoons unsalted butter

½ cup chopped chestnuts

2 tablespoons sliced flat-leaf parsley

Kosher salt and freshly ground black pepper

for 8 to 10 minutes, until the skin is deep golden brown and crispy. (If your pan is too small to fit all the legs, brown them in two pans or in batches, so you don't crowd them.) Turn the duck legs over, reduce the heat to medium, and cook for 2 minutes on the other side. Move the duck skin-side up to a Dutch oven or a 13-by-9-inch glass baking dish. (The duck legs should fit snugly as a single layer in the pan.)

Remove half the fat (reserve it for sautéing potatoes, if you like), and return the pan to the stove over medium heat. Add the onion, carrot, celery, thyme sprigs, bay leaf, and a pinch of pepper. Cook for about 10 minutes, stirring often with a wooden spoon to scrape up all the crusty bits.

Preheat the oven to 325°F.

When the vegetables are nicely browned and caramelized, add the Madeira. Turn the heat up to high, bring the liquid to a boil, and cook for 6 to 8 minutes, until reduced by half. Add 3 cups stock, and bring it to a boil. Turn down the heat to low, and simmer for 5 minutes.

Pour the broth and vegetables over the duck, and then scrape the vegetables that have fallen on top of the duck back into the broth. The liquid should not quite cover the duck (add more stock if necessary). Cover the pan very tightly with aluminum foil and a tight-fitting lid if you have one. Braise in the oven for about 2½ hours, until the duck is very tender.

To check for doneness, carefully remove the lid and foil, and pierce a piece of duck with a paring knife. When the meat is done, it will yield easily and be tender but not quite falling off the bone.

Turn up the oven to 400°F.

Carefully transfer the duck to a baking sheet. Bake for 10 to 15 minutes, to crisp up the skin.

Strain the broth into a saucepan, pressing down on the vegetables with a spoon to extract all the juices. Skim the top layer of fat from the sauce. Reduce the broth over medium-high heat for about 5 minutes, to thicken it slightly. (When the bubbles are uniformly small, the sauce is ready.) Taste for seasoning.

Meanwhile, pit the dates, and slice them thinly lengthwise, being careful not to let them stick together into one big date-ball.

Spoon the hot stuffing into six large, shallow bowls. Place the browned duck legs on top, and pour tablespoonfuls of broth over the meat so it pools in each bowl.

Heat a medium sauté pan over high heat, wait a minute, and swirl in the butter. When it foams, scatter the dates (making sure they don't stick together) and then the chestnuts into the pan. Sauté for 3 or 4 minutes, until the chestnuts and dates are sizzling and the butter starts to brown. Season with salt and pepper, and spoon the mixture over the duck legs. Garnish each bowl with a sprinkling of sliced parsley.

kale stuffing

NOTE If the chiles de árbol are dry and brittle you can just crush or crumble them.

Preheat the oven to 375°F.

Cut the crust off the bread, and tear the remaining loaf into 1-inch pieces. Using your hands, toss the croutons with 6 tablespoons olive oil, squeezing the bread gently to help it absorb the oil. Toast on a baking sheet for 12 to 15 minutes, tossing often, until the croutons are golden brown and crispy on the outside but still a little soft and tender inside. When the croutons have cooled, place them in a large bowl.

¾ pound country-style bread

½ cup plus 1 tablespoon extra-virgin olive oil

1 pound kale, tough rib stems removed (from about 2 large or 3 small bunches)

1 small sprig rosemary

2 chiles de árbol, sliced

1½ cups sliced onions

1 tablespoon thyme leaves

¼ cup Madeira

1½ cups chicken or duck stock

6 tablespoons (¾ stick) unsalted butter

1 cup chopped chestnuts

Kosher salt and freshly ground black pepper

Blanch the kale in rapidly boiling salted water for 2 minutes. (You may need to blanch in two batches.) Drain, and cool the greens on a baking sheet. Squeeze out the excess water with your hands, and roughly chop the kale.

Heat a large pot or Dutch oven over medium heat for 2 minutes. Pour in the remaining 3 tablespoons olive oil. Add the rosemary sprig and chiles, and let them sizzle in the oil for about 1 minute. Turn down the heat to medium-low, and add the sliced onions and the thyme. Season with ½ teaspoon salt and a few grindings of black pepper. Continue cooking for another 5 to 7 minutes, stirring occasionally, until the onions are soft and starting to color slightly.

Add the kale, and stir with a wooden spoon to coat the greens in the oil. Season with a heaping ¼ teaspoon salt, and cook the kale slowly, over low heat, for about 15 minutes, stirring often, until the kale is tender. Remove the rosemary stem and any large pieces of chile, and then pour the mixture over the croutons. Stir gently to combine.

Return the pan to high heat, and pour in the Madeira. Bring to a boil, and reduce to a glaze, about 3 minutes. Add the chicken stock, and bring to a boil. Pour the hot liquid over the croutons and kale, and toss to combine.

Wipe the pan out with paper towels, and return it to the stove over medium heat. Swirl in 4 tablespoons butter, and when it foams, add the chestnuts. Season with ½ teaspoon salt and several grinds of pepper. Sauté for 3 or 4 minutes, until the chestnuts are sizzling and the butter starts to brown.

Pour the chestnut mixture into the bowl with the croutons and kale.

Stir well, and taste for seasoning. Put the stuffing in a ceramic baking or casserole dish. Cover (you can use foil if the dish doesn't have a lid), and bake for 40 minutes. Remove the cover, and scatter small pieces of the remaining 2 tablespoons butter on top. Return to the oven, and cook uncovered for about 20 minutes, until crispy on top.

This duck recipe epitomizes fall flavors, with its leafy-green-laced stuffing, braising juices, and sweet dates—a preparation that requires something a bit full-bodied and plummy to match up to its heartiness. Taking a cue from the Madeira in the recipe, I find that dry wine from Portugal works really well as a pairing. Typically, these wines display dark, cooked-fruit flavors of prune and fig alongside touches of tobacco and cedarlike spice. Here the deep fruit notes will marry with those of the dates and Madeira, while the more savory aspects of the wine highlight the flavor of the braised duck.

beef brisket with slow-roasted romano beans and black olive aïoli

This dish is a fun twist on barbecued beef and beans. The key to the brisket's success is cooking it in advance, completely chilling it, and then slicing it and returning the slices to a hot oven until the edges are caramelized and you have achieved that much-desired juxtaposition of soft, tender braised interior and crispy, caramelized exterior.

NOTE You will probably have some brisket left over (unless your friends eat like mine!). It reheats beautifully and is also great for sandwiches and hash.

Place the brisket in a large, shallow dish, and rub the thyme, bay leaves, garlic, chiles, and cracked black pepper onto both sides of it, coating the meat well. Cover, and refrigerate overnight.

Take the brisket out of the refrigerator 1 hour before cooking, to bring it to room temperature. After 30 minutes, season the meat with 2 tablespoons salt.

Preheat the oven to 325°F.

Heat a large, heavy-bottomed sauté pan over high heat for 2 minutes. Add the olive oil, and wait for 1 minute. Place the brisket in the pan (reserving the garlic and chiles). Sear the meat on both sides, about 8 minutes per side, until it's deep golden brown. You will need to sear a portion of the meat at a time, because the entire brisket probably won't fit in the pan. To do this, leave one end of the brisket hanging off the edge of the pan, and then move that end into the pan when the other part is well seared. Once both sides are well browned, transfer the brisket to a large roasting pan that has a tight-fitting lid, or a Dutch oven.

Return the brisket searing pan to the stove over medium-high heat, and add the onion, carrot, and celery. Stir with a wooden spoon, scraping up all the crusty bits in the pan. Cook for 6 to 8 minutes, until the vegetables just begin to caramelize, then add the reserved garlic and chiles, and cook for a few more minutes.

Turn off the heat (so that the liquids won't evaporate immediately), and

6 pounds whole beef brisket, with ½-inch top layer of fat

3 tablespoons thyme leaves

2 fresh bay leaves, thinly sliced (if only dried bay leaves are available, crumble them)

10 cloves garlic, smashed

3 chiles de árbol, crumbled with your hands

1 tablespoon plus one teaspoon cracked black pepper

3 tablespoons extra-virgin olive oil

1 cup diced onion

⅓ cup diced carrot

⅓ cup diced celery

¼ cup balsamic vinegar

3 cups red wine

4 cups beef stock, or more if needed

1 recipe Slow-Roasted Romano Beans (recipe follows)

1 recipe Black Olive Aïoli (recipe follows)

Kosher salt

add the balsamic vinegar, then the wine. Turn the heat back up to medium-high, and reduce the wine by a quarter. Add the beef stock, and bring the stock to a boil over high heat. Pour the hot stock over the meat, scraping any vegetables that have fallen on the brisket back into the liquid. The stock mixture should almost cover the brisket. Cover the pan tightly with aluminum foil and a tight-fitting lid. Braise in the oven for 5 to 6 hours.

To check for doneness, carefully remove the lid and foil, watching out for the hot steam. Test the meat by inserting a paring knife into it; if the knife slides in easily, then the brisket is done.

Let the brisket cool in its juices for 30 minutes. Carefully transfer it to a baking sheet, and chill completely.

Strain the braising juices into a saucepan, pressing down on the vegetables with a ladle to extract all the liquid. Skim the fat from the braising juices, and chill.

When you are ready to serve, preheat the oven to 400°F.

Cut the cold brisket against the grain into ¼-inch-thick slices. Lay the slices in two large roasting pans (or equivalent). Heat the braising juices, and pour some over the meat, just to cover. Cook for about 20 minutes, until the meat is hot and caramelized and crispy on top.

Place the slow-roasted Romano beans at the center of six large dinner plates, and arrange the brisket on top. Drizzle some of the braising juices over the meat. Dollop a generous tablespoon of the black olive aïoli over the meat, and pass the rest at the table.

slow-roasted romano beans

2 small red onions

6 large cloves garlic, peeled

2 ½ pounds green and yellow Romano beans, stems removed, tails left on

1 tablespoon rosemary leaves

1 tablespoon sage leaves

1 tablespoon thyme leaves

¾ cup extra-virgin olive oil

Kosher salt and freshly ground black pepper

This recipe is a perfect example of the good things that come from my near-psychotic desire never to waste food! One summer, farmer James Birch had a mother lode (the official kitchen term) of Romano beans left over from the market. Now, I just can't stand to see a homeless vegetable, so I, of course, agreed to take them *all*. It was the end of the season, and some of the beans had seen better days and were a little on the tough side, so I decided to use them for staff meal, tossing them with onions, herbs, and lots of olive oil and then cooking them very slowly, with the hope of breaking down their toughness. Lo and behold, they were more delicious than the tender ones we had saved for the guests! Tender young haricots verts are best cooked al dente and served super green, but for me, this is *the* go-to method for Romano beans, tough or otherwise. The idea behind the big pieces of onion and whole peeled garlic cloves is that they will cook slowly and still be sweet, rather than burned, when the beans are done.

SERVES 6

Preheat the oven to 350°F.

Peel the onions, trim the roots, but leave the root ends intact (this will keep the onions in wedges, rather than slices). Cut the onions lengthwise into 3 or 4 thick (about ⅓-inch) wedges. Slice the garlic cloves lengthwise into three or four thick slices each.

Toss all the ingredients in a large bowl with 2 tablespoons salt and some freshly ground black pepper. Transfer the beans to a baking sheet. Roast in the oven for 40 minutes, stirring every 10 minutes or so, until the beans are completely wilted, shrunken, and concentrated in flavor, with a little caramelization around the edges. (You may need to stir more often toward the end, to keep the beans from browning too quickly.)

black olive aïoli

MAKES 1¼ CUPS

Place the egg yolk in a stainless-steel bowl. Begin whisking in the grape-seed oil drop by drop, as slowly as you can bear. Continue in this manner, following with the olive oil, as the mixture thickens. Once the mayonnaise has emulsified, add the remaining oil in a slow, steady stream, whisking all the time. If the mixture gets too thick and is difficult to whisk, add a drop or two of water.

Pound the garlic with ¼ teaspoon salt with a mortar and pestle. Add half the olives, and pound to a paste. Roughly chop the remaining olives.

Fold the garlic-olive paste and the chopped olives into the mayonnaise. Season with ¼ teaspoon salt, a squeeze of lemon juice, and the cayenne pepper. Taste for balance and seasoning. If the aïoli seems thick and gloppy, thin it with a little water; this will also make it creamier.

1 extra-large egg yolk
½ cup grape-seed oil
½ cup extra-virgin olive oil
1 small clove garlic
¼ cup pitted black oil-cured olives, such as Nyons
½ lemon, for juicing
Pinch cayenne pepper
Kosher salt and freshly ground black pepper

The combination of the tarry black olives in the aïoli with the charred meat flavor in this brisket recipe lends itself to pairing with a rich, complex wine from the Bordeaux region of France. I like the wines from the Left Bank areas, such as Graves and Margaux, whose wines tend to be dark and slightly tannic. This is also a great recipe to pair with a wine that has had time to age in the cellar, which will have even more complex, gamy qualities to work with the beef's savory braising juices.

coq au vin with bacon, potato purée, cipollini onions, and black trumpets

6 chicken legs with thighs attached

2 tablespoons thyme leaves, plus 3 sprigs thyme

¼ cup chopped flat-leaf parsley, plus 3 sprigs parsley

18 cipollini onions, or 3 dozen pearl onions

5 tablespoons extra-virgin olive oil

10-ounce slab applewood-smoked bacon

1 cup diced onion

½ cup diced carrot

½ cup diced celery

¼ cup dried porcini mushrooms

2 bay leaves (fresh or dried)

2 tablespoons tomato paste

2 cups red wine

4 cups chicken stock

1 tablespoon unsalted butter

1 pound black-trumpet mushrooms (or other delicious wild mushrooms such as chanterelles, hedgehogs, etc.), cleaned, dried, and torn into large bite-sized pieces

1 recipe Potato Purée (recipe follows)

Kosher salt and freshly ground black pepper

In the depths of winter, *coq au vin* is one of those traditional, deeply warming dishes that never fail to satisfy. It's a pretty basic recipe, actually, but the beauty, and what elevates it from a simple braise to something fantastic, is, of course, in the details. Make sure to get a really nice sear on the chicken on both sides, and cook out the tomato paste, which will thicken the broth and give it a beautiful burgundy sheen. And you just have to use a wooden spoon for this recipe. It may be one of the oldest kitchen tools, but I swear I can't understand how anyone could cook without one. I get fingernails-on-chalkboard-worthy chills down my spine when I hear the scrape of a metal spoon on a metal pot—the soft edge of a wooden spoon is perfect for scraping up the infamous crusty bits and working the tomato paste into the mirepoix.

Season the chicken with 1 tablespoon thyme leaves and 2 tablespoons chopped parsley. Cover, and refrigerate for at least 4 hours. Remove the chicken an hour before cooking, to bring it to room temperature. After 30 minutes, season the chicken on all sides with 1 tablespoon plus 1 teaspoon salt and lots of pepper.

Preheat the oven to 425°F.

Cut the unpeeled cipollini onions in quarters, and toss them in a bowl with 2 tablespoons olive oil, ½ tablespoon thyme leaves, ¾ teaspoon salt, and a pinch of pepper (if you are using pearl onions, do not cut them). Spread them on a baking sheet, and roast them for about 15 minutes, until tender. When the onions have cooled, slip off the skins with your fingers and set aside.

Turn the oven down to 325°F.

Cut two thick 2-ounce slices of bacon from the slab, and set them aside.

Heat a large sauté pan over high heat for 2 minutes. Swirl in 2 tablespoons olive oil and wait for 1 minute. Place the chicken legs, skin-side down, in the pan, and cook for 8 to 10 minutes, until golden brown and crispy. (If your pan is too small for all the legs to fit, brown them in batches, or two pans, so you don't crowd them.) Every so often, swirl the oil and rendered fat around the pan. Turn the legs over, and reduce the heat to medium. Cook for 2 or 3 minutes on the second side, until nicely caramelized. Arrange the chicken (in one layer) in a braising dish. The chicken legs should just fit in the pan.

Pour off some of the fat, and return the sauté pan to medium heat. Add the onion, carrot, celery, dried porcinis, thyme sprigs, bay leaves, and the two thick slices of bacon. Cook for 6 to 7 minutes, stirring often, until the vegetables are lightly caramelized. Add the tomato paste, and cook for another 5 minutes, scraping the pan with a wooden spoon. The tomato paste should be completely integrated into the vegetables (the vegetables will turn an orange color, and you won't see any bits of tomato paste). Add the red wine, turn the heat up to high, and reduce by half. Add the chicken stock, and bring to a boil.

Pour the broth and vegetables over the chicken, scraping any of the vegetables that have fallen on the chicken back into the liquid. The liquid should not quite cover the chicken. Tuck the parsley sprigs in and around the chicken, and cover the pan with a tight-fitting lid or aluminum foil. Braise in the oven 1½ to 2 hours.

Meanwhile, slice the remaining bacon into ⅜-inch-thick slices. Stack the slices in two piles, then cut the bacon crosswise into ⅜-inch even-sided rectangles or *lardons*.

Heat a large sauté pan over high heat for 2 minutes. Add the remaining 1 tablespoon olive oil, and allow to heat for another minute. Add the bacon, and sauté over medium-high heat for 2 to 3 minutes, until crispy, and then turn off the heat.

To check the chicken for doneness, remove the lid or foil, being careful of the steam. Pierce a piece of the chicken with a paring knife. If the meat is done, it will yield easily and be tender but not quite falling off the bone.

Turn the oven up to 400°F.

Transfer the chicken to a baking sheet, and return it to the oven to brown for about 10 minutes.

Strain the broth into a saucepan, pressing down on the vegetables with a ladle to extract all the juices. If necessary, reduce the broth over medium-high heat for about 5 minutes, to thicken it slightly.

While the chicken is browning, return the bacon pan to the stove over high heat. Wait 2 minutes, and add the butter. When it foams, toss in the black-trumpet mushrooms, the remaining ½ tablespoon thyme leaves, and ½ teaspoon salt. Cook for 2 to 3 minutes, until the mushrooms are tender. Add the onions, and cook the mixture together for another 2 to 3 minutes, until the bacon and mushrooms are a little crispy. Taste for seasoning, and turn off the heat.

Spoon the hot potato purée into six shallow bowls, and place a piece of chicken on top. Ladle the braising juices over the chicken, and let them pool in the bowl. Toss the remaining 2 tablespoons of chopped parsley into the hot bacon-mushroom mixture, and spoon it over the top.

potato purée

1½ pounds russet potatoes

1½ pounds Yukon Gold potatoes

¾ cup heavy cream

¾ cup whole milk

½ pound (2 sticks) unsalted butter, cut into chunks

Kosher salt

Place the potatoes, whole and unpeeled, in a large saucepan. Add 2 tablespoons salt, and fill the pot with cold water. Bring the potatoes to a boil over high heat, turn down the heat to low, and simmer for about 45 minutes, until tender. One type of potato may be done before the other, so check for doneness and remove one variety first, if necessary.

When the potatoes are cooked through, drain them, and set them aside to cool for 10 minutes or so. Heat the cream and milk together in a small saucepan, then turn off the heat. When the potatoes have cooled, peel them and pass them through a food mill or potato ricer. Put the riced potatoes in a heavy-bottomed pan. Heat them over medium heat a few minutes, stirring continuously with a wooden spoon, to dry them out a little. Add the butter slowly, stirring constantly. Season with 2½ teaspoons salt.

When all the butter has been incorporated, slowly stir in the warm cream mixture until you have a smooth purée. Taste for seasoning. Pass the purée through a fine-mesh *tamis* twice for an extra-smooth consistency if you like.

The red wine in the chicken's braising liquid necessitates a pairing with something that won't be either overwhelmed by the juices in the recipe, or overpowering. An overly fruity wine will battle for attention on the palate, rather than serve as a complement, whereas a wine that is too light will be lost on it. Though a tad unusual, red wines from the Jura region of France, which feature the varieties Poulsard and Trousseau Noir, would work really well here. These wines display red fruit notes and layers of smoke and gamy meat, the ideal partner for the recipe's bacon and mushrooms. For a less esoteric option, a Cru Beaujolais will work. Although darker and richer than the Jura wines, Beaujolais features a similar smoky, mineral quality.

pork cheeks with polenta, mustard cream, and horseradish gremolata

It's amazing to think how far our country has come culinarily in the last ten years. These pork cheeks were on the opening menu back in 2002, and we really had to work to convince our guests even to try them. Now the Food Network and tons of chef-driven restaurants and butcher shops around the United States are pushing ears, tongue, and even pig face. How crazy to think that the formerly awful offal is now cool! There is absolutely nothing "scary" about these super-tender nuggets braised in sherry and served over polenta with mustard cream and gremolata spiked with fresh horseradish. I especially love the gelatinous texture and toothiness of the cheeks themselves.

Season the pork cheeks with the smashed garlic, 1 tablespoon lemon zest, the thyme, and rosemary leaves. Cover, and refrigerate overnight.

Take the pork cheeks out of the refrigerator an hour before cooking, to bring them to room temperature. After 30 minutes, season the cheeks on both sides with 2 tablespoons salt and 1 teaspoon pepper. Reserve the garlic and any excess herbs.

Preheat the oven to 325°F.

Heat a large sauté pan over high heat for 2 minutes. Pour in the grape-seed oil, and wait a minute or two, until the pan is very hot and almost smoking. Place the cheeks in the pan, and sear them for about 8 minutes, until caramelized and nicely browned on both sides. Transfer the cheeks to a braising pan that has a tight-fitting lid.

Turn the heat down to medium, and add the diced onion, carrot, celery, and any reserved garlic and herbs. Stir with a wooden spoon to scrape up all the crusty bits in the pan. Cook for 6 to 8 minutes, until the vegetables just begin to caramelize. Add the sherry, turn the heat to high, and reduce the liquid by half.

Add the stock, and bring to a boil. As soon as it comes to a boil, pour the liquid over the cheeks, scraping any vegetables that fall on the meat back into the liquid. The stock mixture should almost cover the cheeks. Tuck the parsley sprigs among and around the cheeks. Cover tightly with aluminum foil and a tight-fitting lid. Braise in the oven for about 2½ hours.

3 pounds cleaned pork cheeks

6 cloves garlic, smashed, plus 1 teaspoon minced garlic

1 tablespoon plus 1 teaspoon grated lemon zest

1 tablespoon thyme leaves

1 tablespoon rosemary leaves, plus 1 small sprig rosemary

3 tablespoons grape-seed or canola oil

1 cup diced onion, plus 1 cup thinly sliced onion

½ cup diced carrot

½ cup diced celery

1 cup sherry

6 cups veal stock

6 sprigs flat-leaf parsley, plus ¼ cup chopped flat-leaf parsley

1 pound cavolo nero or other kale

¼ cup extra-virgin olive oil

1 chile de árbol, crumbled

1 tablespoon whole-grain mustard

1 tablespoon Dijon mustard

¾ cup crème fraîche

2 teaspoons finely grated fresh horseradish

1 recipe Polenta (recipe follows)

Kosher salt and freshly ground black pepper

To check the meat for doneness, carefully remove the lid and foil (watch out for the hot steam), and pierce one of the cheeks with a paring knife. When the meat is done, it will yield easily.

While the cheeks are cooking, blanch the cavolo nero in rapidly boiling water for 2 minutes. Drain, and cool the greens on a baking sheet. When they have cooled, squeeze out the excess water with your hands.

Heat a large pot or Dutch oven over medium heat for 2 minutes. Pour in the olive oil, add the rosemary sprig and crumbled chile, and let them sizzle in the oil about a minute. Turn the heat down to medium-low, and add the sliced onion. Season with ½ teaspoon salt and a few grindings of black pepper. Cook for 5 to 7 minutes, until the onion is soft and starting to color slightly.

Add the cavolo nero, stirring with a wooden spoon to coat the greens in the oil. Season with a heaping ¼ teaspoon salt, and cook the cavolo over medium-low heat for about 15 minutes, stirring often, until tender but still green.

Stir the mustards and crème fraîche together in a small bowl, and keep chilled.

Chop the minced garlic, remaining 1 teaspoon lemon zest, the chopped parsley, and the horseradish together until very fine, to make the gremolata.

When the pork cheeks are done, turn the oven up to 400°F. Transfer the cheeks to a baking sheet, and return them to the oven to brown for about 8 minutes.

Strain the broth into a saucepan, pressing down on the vegetables with a ladle to extract all the juices. If necessary, reduce the broth over medium-high heat for about 5 minutes, to thicken it slightly.

Spoon the hot polenta into six shallow bowls, arrange some cavolo nero on the polenta, and place the pork cheeks on top. Ladle the broth over the cheeks, and let it pool in the bowl. Spoon the mustard cream onto the cheeks, and sprinkle the gremolata over the whole dish.

polenta

1 cup medium-grain polenta
(I love Bob's Red Mill's
version; see Sources)

3 tablespoons unsalted butter

Kosher salt

In a heavy-bottomed pot, bring 5½ cups water and 1 tablespoon salt to a boil over high heat. Add the polenta slowly, whisking continuously. Turn the heat down to low, and continue cooking for another 20 minutes, whisking often. Add another ½ cup water and cook 1 more hour, whisking often and adding ½ cup water as needed, about every 20 minutes. The flame should be low, so that the polenta is barely simmering. As you whisk, make sure that you reach the bottom of the pan to prevent the polenta from scorching. I like to use a rubber spatula to scrape the bottom and sides of the pot.

Whisk in the butter, and taste for seasoning. Even when the polenta is finished, you might sense it thickening up a little. If so, add a little more water and whisk to get the right consistency. If you're not serving right away, cover the pan tightly with plastic wrap to keep the polenta from thickening or losing moisture. If necessary, rewarm over low heat before serving.

This is one of those dishes that can be paired with either white or red wine. The polenta and herby gremolata take this pork recipe in an Italian direction, and because of the overall brightness here, I would opt for wines from a cooler region, like Piemonte, where the morning fog allows the grapes to maintain vibrant acidity. If you opt for white, the Langhe region produces really elegant, high-toned Chardonnay that will emphasize the creaminess of the polenta and sweetness of the meat. If you prefer red, Nebbiolo is ideal: it has bright red fruit notes of cranberry and red currant that will marry with the mustard and horseradish and balance the weight of the recipe as a whole.

grilled duck breast with preserved citrus peel and sweet potato purée

In the southern-California winter, citrus comes on strong and stays for the long haul, so I am constantly challenged to come up with more and more ways to use the whole fruit as best I can. We use a lot of citrus peel, often candied, in desserts, so I thought it would be interesting to incorporate it into a savory dish as well. Worried that poaching it in a simple syrup would be too sweet, I tried to think of what to cook the strips of zest in that would give them the glossy texture of sugar but a savory and somewhat exotic note to complement the duck breast.

As inspiring as the outside world is, sometimes, because of the crazy nature of the restaurant business, it's hard to get out to get inspired at all. Therefore, some of the biggest inspirations often come from the people I work with on a day-to-day basis, and sometimes those people aren't even cooks! On the long, hot, sticky days of summer in the kitchen, we have a tradition that one of our long-standing bussers, Jesus Morales, makes *aguas frescas* in 5-gallon buckets for the staff to drink all day and night.

We call Jesus "Gee-Zus" (as in the Savior), not "Hey-Soos" (as in the traditional Mexican pronunciation), because when he first started with us, fifteen years ago, we already had two "Hey-Soos"es and, in some moment of questionable genius, I arrived at the idea of calling him "Gee-Zus." I forget how odd this is, and sometimes, when we have a new employee or someone trying out for a job, the newcomer is taken aback to hear me screaming down the hallway, "Gee-Zus, Gee-Zus, GEEEEEE-ZZZZZZUUUUSSS," like a deranged person taking the Lord's name in vain, when actually all I'm trying to do is get Jesus to run a dessert out to a table. Anyway, back to Jesus and his *aguas frescas:* One day a few summers ago, Jesus brought in some dried tamarind, soaked it, added sugar, and made Mexican *tamarindo,* which, with the addition of lemon, tastes a lot like an Arnold Palmer. Well, this became the drink of the moment for the line cooks—we immediately named it *pinche tamarindo,* just because we are smart-asses with a penchant for cursing in any language.

3 pounds Jewel or Garnet sweet potatoes

6 single, boneless Peking duck breasts, 6 to 8 ounces each

1 ounce tamarind (available at Mexican and Asian markets)

1 lemon

1 lime

1 orange

½ grapefruit

½ cinnamon stick, or ½ teaspoon ground cinnamon

½ teaspoon curry powder

1 chile de árbol, crumbled

¼ teaspoon ground cardamom

1-by-1-inch piece fresh ginger, peeled and thinly sliced

3 tablespoons honey

6 tablespoons (¾ stick) unsalted butter, cut into small cubes

2 tablespoons whole milk, plus more as needed

2 ounces dandelion greens, cleaned and dried

Kosher salt and freshly ground black pepper

I really took inspiration from seeing how Jesus had worked with the tamarind, and how it had given a nice viscosity to the drink without an overwhelming sweetness. So I used his soaking trick to make the "tamarind water," and then cooked it with citrus juice, spices, and a touch of honey.

NOTE The trick to grilling duck breasts is to cook them two-thirds of the way on the skin-side to render the fat and yield crispy skin. The rendering fat will inevitably drip into the fire, causing flare-ups, so ma ke sure to move the duck breasts around the grill as needed.

Preheat the oven to 400°F.

Prick the sweet potatoes all over with a fork, place them on a baking sheet, and bake for about 60 to 90 minutes (depending on their size), until tender when poked with a paring knife.

Light the grill 30 to 40 minutes before cooking, and remove the duck from the refrigerator. Cut away any extra fat, score the skin of the duck breasts with a sharp knife, and season both sides with salt and pepper.

Using your hands, break the tamarind apart into small pieces, and place it in a small bowl. Pour ½ cup boiling water over the tamarind, and let it sit for 5 minutes. Stir the tamarind vigorously with a small whisk or spoon, to loosen all the pulp and emulsify it with the water.

Using a peeler, make strips of zest about 1 inch wide from all the citrus. (Use a light hand when zesting to avoid the bitter white pith.) Place the zest strips in a small pot, cover with cold water, and bring to a boil. Boil for 1 minute, drain, rinse with cool water, and repeat the process two more times.

Juice all the citrus (you should have about 1 cup), and place juice with the blanched zest in a nonreactive pot that is small enough so that all the zest is submerged. Add the cinnamon stick or ground cinnamon, curry, chile, cardamom, ginger, honey, and ½ teaspoon salt. Strain 2 tablespoons "tamarind water" from the bowl of soaking tamarind, and add it to the pot.

Bring the mixture to a boil, turn down the heat to medium-low, and simmer for 12 to 15 minutes, until the sauce thickens and looks glossy. Set aside.

When the sweet potatoes have cooled just enough to handle, cut them in half. Use the knife and your fingers to peel off the skins and cut away any burnt pieces. Scoop the hot sweet-potato flesh into the bowl of a food processor fitted with a metal blade. Add the butter, 1 teaspoon salt, and a few grinds of pepper. Purée to a smooth consistency. With the blade spinning, pour in 2 tablespoons milk (plus a little more if the potatoes are too starchy to move fluidly around the bowl). Taste for balance and seasoning.

Place the duck breasts skin-side down on the cooler side of the grill. As they cook, rotate the breasts in a quarter-turn pattern every 2 minutes or so, to allow the fat to render and the skin to crisp. (This will take 6 to 8 minutes total.) Turn the breasts over, and cook a few more minutes, until the duck is medium-rare and still springy to the touch. Remove from the heat, and rest for 5 minutes on a wire rack set over a baking sheet.

Spoon the hot sweet-potato purée onto the center of six dinner plates, and place two dandelion greens, overlapping at their stems, on each one. Slice each duck breast on the diagonal, and arrange the slices on top of the purée. Spoon some of the warm preserved citrus peel and some of the juices over the duck and around the plate.

The sweet potato in this recipe has a particularly intense quality that requires pairing with a wine of similar vibrancy and weight. In this case, I recommend a full-bodied Pinot Noir from California's Santa Rita Hills. Here the climate is cool enough to maintain acidity while also providing enough exposure to the sun to develop concentration and muscularity. These wines display cherry and wild-berry notes that are ideal for the duck, as well as elements of marmaladelike citrus that accentuate the secondary flavors of the sweet potato and marry with the citrus ingredients in the recipe.

pork confit with caramelized apples
and cabbage in red wine

2½ to 3 pounds boneless pork
  shoulder, trimmed of excess
  fat

1 recipe Brine (recipe follows)

2 to 3 quarts rendered duck
  or pork fat

1 small head red cabbage
  (about 1 pound), cored
  and thinly sliced
  (about 6 cups sliced)

½ cup freshly squeezed lemon
  juice (from 2 or 3 lemons)

½ cup freshly squeezed orange
  juice (from 1 or 2 oranges)

¼ cup sugar

2 cups sliced onion
  (1 large onion)

1 tablespoon thyme leaves

1 chile de árbol, crumbled

½ teaspoon ground allspice

½ cup port

1½ cups red wine

2 teaspoons coriander seeds

1 tablespoon extra-virgin olive oil

3 apples, peeled, cored, and cut
  into 8 wedges each (choose
  a good cooking apple like
  Pink Lady, Winesap, or
  Honeycrisp)

2 tablespoons butter

½ bunch watercress, cleaned,
  tough stems removed

Kosher salt and freshly ground
  black pepper

Our sous-chef at A.O.C. is John Schlothauer. He is a deer-hunting, farm-equipment-name-dropping, nice German boy through and through. I will be honest, it took me about a year to really *get* John. He started as an extern in the kitchen, washing lettuce, prepping (but not making) the harissa, rolling bacon-wrapped dates, icing the fish, straining stocks, and cleaning the walk-in. Finally, after four or five months, we gave him a shot at the cheese bar—plating fifty or sixty cheese and charcuterie plates a night out in the dining room. Maybe because he wasn't in the actual kitchen, I somehow read his quiet, stoic-looking nature as uninterested. So, when jobs on the salad station opened up, it never really occurred to me to promote him—he just sort of seemed like the big blond grumpy guy in the corner. So he stayed, and stayed, and stayed, until at last someone encouraged me, against my better judgment, to give him a chance.

And, boy, was I wrong! When he hit that salad station, he turned it on big-time. There's a certain type of cook—big tough-guy-looking ones—whom you would never expect to have the delicate touch needed to make salads beautiful. How can this giant guy who looks like a bear, with big hands and chunky, sausagelike fingers, make the food so damned gorgeous? Well, John is the case study of that prototype. And, like all really great cooks, he makes it look effortless. I began to realize that the reason I had thought he didn't care was that I never heard any drama, any commotion, or any anything, because John always just got it done, quietly and perfectly. I remember one especially crazy Saturday night, when he was making salads, desserts, and cheese plates all at the same time, I looked down to see the most perfect-looking five-cheese plate I had ever seen. "John!" I exclaimed. "How do you make it so beautiful?" "Well," he replied sheepishly, "you did have me on the cheese bar making cheese plates for over a year, so I would hope I could get it after that." Oops.

John has another quality that is required in a truly great cook—he *loves* to eat. In all seriousness, I don't really see how you can be great at this job and have the passion that is required if you don't truly love it from both sides—as a creator and as a consumer. This dish is an ode to John's Germanic-ness—crispy, fatty brined pork shoulder with bright-ruby-red cabbage and coriander-spiked apples (at the restaurant, we actually serve it with a vinegared potato salad, too, per John's request) sums up all his true loves on one delicious plate.

NOTE Because the pork is brined, you need to start this recipe three days in advance.

Three days before serving, place the pork shoulder in the brine, completely submerged, and refrigerate for 48 hours.

After 48 hours, remove the pork from the brine. Pat it dry with paper towels, and let it sit out 1 hour, to come to room temperature.

Preheat the oven to 300°F.

Reserve ½ cup duck or pork fat, and heat the remaining fat in a large Dutch oven over low heat until just warm and melted.

Carefully lower the pork into the fat. It should be completely submerged. Cook in the oven for 5 to 6 hours, until the meat yields easily to a paring knife when pierced. If at any time the fat starts to boil, turn the oven down to 250°F.

When the pork is done, remove it from the oven and let cool in the fat for about 1 hour. Carefully take the pork out of the fat, and refrigerate it overnight. Strain the fat, cool, and store in the freezer.

In a large bowl, toss the cabbage with the lemon and orange juice and let sit for 1 hour.

Heat a large Dutch oven over high heat for 1 minute, and add 3 tablespoons sugar. After 2 to 3 minutes, when the sugar caramelizes, add ¼ cup of the reserved duck or pork fat, and stir to combine. Add the onion, 2 teaspoons thyme, the chile, allspice, 1 teaspoon salt, and ¼ teaspoon pepper. Turn the heat down to medium, and cook for about 10 minutes, stirring often, until the onion softens and begins to caramelize.

Pour in the port and red wine, and cook for another 8 minutes, until the liquid has reduced by two-thirds. Add the cabbage (with the juices) and 1 teaspoon salt, and cook for another 20 minutes, stirring often, until the cabbage is tender and the juices are nicely reduced and glazy. Taste for balance and seasoning.

While the cabbage is cooking, toast the coriander seeds in a small pan over medium-high heat for a few minutes, until the seeds release their aroma and are lightly browned. Using a mortar and pestle, pound them coarsely.

Heat a large sauté pan over high heat for 2 minutes. Swirl in the olive oil,

and wait for 1 minute. Carefully place the apples in the pan flat-side down, and add the butter, remaining 1 teaspoon thyme leaves, remaining 1 tablespoon sugar, the crushed coriander seeds, 1 teaspoon salt, and a pinch of black pepper. Turn the heat down to medium, and cook for about 5 minutes, until the apples are a beautiful deep golden brown. Turn the apples over, and continue cooking until they're golden on the second side. They should be tender and cooked through.

Place the chilled pork confit on a cutting board, and slice it against the grain into ¾-inch-thick slabs (about 5 to 6 ounces each). Taste a little piece of the pork to make sure it's seasoned correctly. If not, season with salt and pepper.

Heat a large sauté pan over high heat for 3 minutes. Swirl in 2 tablespoons of the reserved fat, wait a minute or two, and then carefully place the slices of pork confit in the pan. Let them sear for about 5 minutes without moving them, until they are crispy on the bottom. Turn the pork over, and finish cooking for 5 minutes on the second side. The meat should be very crisp, with a deep-golden crust. Carefully press down on the pork with your thumb to get a sense of whether or not it is hot and tender all the way through. If it is not, pop it in a 400°F oven for a few minutes to heat it thoroughly. (You will probably need to cook the pork in two pans or two batches.)

Spoon the hot red cabbage onto the center of six large dinner plates. Scatter a few watercress leaves around each plate, and place the pork confit on top. Arrange the apples on top of and around the pork.

brine

Crush the juniper berries coarsely in a mortar. Repeat with the allspice and then the fennel seeds.

Dissolve the sugar and salt in 2 cups hot water (just hot enough to dissolve the sugar) in a large, very clean container. Add the juniper berries, allspice berries, fennel seeds, cloves, bay leaves, chiles, onion, fennel, carrot, thyme, and parsley. Add 3 quarts very cold water, and stir to combine all the ingredients.

2 tablespoons juniper berries

2 tablespoons allspice berries

1 tablespoon fennel seeds

⅓ cup sugar

½ cup kosher salt

2 cloves

2 bay leaves (fresh or dried)

2 chiles de árbol, crumbled or broken in half

1 onion, sliced

½ bulb fennel, sliced

1 carrot, peeled and sliced

4 sprigs thyme

4 sprigs flat-leaf parsley

The cabbage and apples immediately make me think of Austria and Germany and the really versatile wines that are made there. Zweigelt from Austria is a great option. The wine comes from cool growing regions, resulting in bright red fruit notes and acidity that will balance the fattiness of the pork. Zweigelt also displays a savory and complex mineral component that will emphasize that of the cabbage and apple.

vegetables

In my world, vegetables are the true stars of the show, the leaders of the pack, the favored children. My work life is very much dictated by what is growing when—those moments of great change cause excitement, but also pressure and stress, as I work to come up with new ideas and menu items before the last season's produce is gone. When we are through the earlier part of a growing cycle, I can relax a little—always making sure the dishes are being executed properly, but more from a maintenance position than a creative one. Still, it always seems that, just as soon as I get comfortable, things change again!

The tricky thing with vegetables and fruits is that they can literally change from week to week, even though we are buying them directly from the same farmer. The first peas and favas of the season are super-sweet and tender, but almost too small at times, with a very low starch content. As the season goes on, the starch levels rise; though I love this for favas, I dread it in peas. Nevertheless, there is always a mad rush at the Santa Monica Farmers Market in late March, when the first favas show up. I actually have to remind my team to hold back—the first few weeks, the favas aren't really good yet. And they are expensive! The same goes for stone fruit. Yes, in late May it's tempting to dive full-force into peaches, nectarines, and plums, because we have grown tired of citrus, apples, and pears. But it's not really time yet. I would rather wait than try to work with a plum that I have to coax the flavor out of and manipulate to taste the way it will, naturally, if I just wait a month or so.

It's funny to me how suddenly, a few years ago, someone coined the phrase "farm to table." I would probably be considered one of its early advocates or practitioners. Of course, I love cooking from "farm to table"—especially if the alternative is "Sysco to table," "supermarket to table," or "out-of-season-produce-from-faraway-places to table"—but it just seems strange to me that that is considered a style of cooking. For me, it is a jumping-off point, or really just a description of one's philosophy or mode of procuring ingredients; it doesn't speak to what you do with that food once you get it. Truly, the goal is for everyone—consumers, restaurants, and grocery stores—to get our food locally and from well-managed sources. We should all be cooking and eating "farm to table," whether simply or intricately, using whatever modernist techniques and gadgets imaginable.

What defines a chef's style is what he or she does with the produce from the farm once it gets to the kitchen. I feel I walk the line of respecting and showing off the inner beauty and inherent deliciousness of the vegetables, while also giving them a little dressing up or a nudge of sexiness and surprise. Often it's just a matter of seasoning, adding a little olive oil, lemon, fresh herbs, nuts, or a sprinkling of cheese. The idea is to elevate and accentuate the delicious glory that is already there, without overpowering or overwhelming it.

In spring, the green power found in asparagus, peas, favas, young carrots, and pea shoots does require some prep work, but simple finishes—such as steaming, gentle sautés, and raw preparations—really show off the bright relief these treats from the garden bring us, a wonderful respite from a long winter of their darker, heavier, more brooding relatives. Summer is the easiest, quickest, most built-for-speed season when it comes to vegetable cookery. What is better than a super-ripe heirloom tomato simply cut in half, sprinkled with fleur de sel, and eaten straight off the cutting board? Green beans and corn can be blanched and on the table in less than five minutes. I love grilling summer vegetables, too, and recommend that you take advantage of the grill when it's lit and "prep" vegetables for the next day. Cold chopped grilled vegetables make a great satisfying salad for a hot day's lunch, and you can just pop your leftover grilled veggies in a hot oven, spoon over them green harissa, pistou, or tapenade, and serve with grilled toasts, farro, or couscous for a satisfying summer supper.

As we move into fall and winter, root vegetables and sturdier vegetables like squashes, kales, and members of the *Brassica* genus (cauliflower, cabbages, broccoli, and Brussels sprouts) need more manipulation and coaxing. They call out for roasting, stewing, and glazing with duck fat, balsamic vinegar, pancetta, and breadcrumbs. Some people may think root vegetables are boring, but I find the contrast of bitterness and sweetness along with the hearty

texture wonderful. Turnips, parsnips, and rutabagas are a great canvas for different flavor profiles, too. Parsnips and Turnips with Sage and Prunes taste of the Armagnac-and-foie-gras-drenched southwestern region of France, where I spent a very educational and more than mildly painful six months as a *stagiaire* in the early 1990s. Those same vegetables tossed with a spiced turmeric butter and finished with bright herbal flavors of mint are exotic and surprising in Turmeric-Spiced Root Vegetables with Kaffir Lime Yogurt and Mint Chutney.

Winter is the season of some of my most beloved ingredients—the fields are overflowing with kabocha squash, cavolo nero, Russian kale, Brussels sprouts, and all forms of carrots and broccoli. As befitting the season, these vegetables are nutrient-dense, filling, and satisfying. Many a winter day goes by when I forget to eat any meat or fish because I'm so content with my bowl of Farro and Black Rice with Mustard Greens, Currants, and Pine Nuts, topped with Long-Cooked Cavolo Nero, and Young Broccoli with Garlic and Chile. Baptized "the triple threat" by former sous-chef John Sadao, who had the misfortune of running the kitchen during my first, most torturous pregnancy, these are my perfect foods, and most days there is not anything I would rather eat.

english peas with saffron butter and pea shoots

As for many of you, when I was growing up, vegetables were nothing to get excited about. We all knew we had to eat our vegetables because they were "good for us," but no one really liked them. As was sort of the norm back then, most of the vegetables in our house were frozen. In my youth, when I saw that box of frozen Birds Eye peas, I knew they were destined for a way-too-long steaming or boiling, which rendered them, in my mind, completely inedible and high up on the most-hated-vegetable list. Then, one day, while cooking with my mom, I popped a frozen pea in my mouth, and it was a revelation! It tasted bright, perky, green—a little cold, mind you, but worlds away from the mushy brown sludge I had come to think of as peas. From then on, I always ate my peas frozen (or partially defrosted), and it became sort of a culinary trend for me as a child to prefer my food raw and cold whenever possible. The lowest moment of this new penchant for raw food was when I decided (and was allowed, for some reason!) to eat our monthly beef-liver dinner raw. Seriously, imagine a 10-year-old sitting at the table eating a plate of raw liver, rice, and frozen peas! It's funny, because I do actually have an iron stomach now, and I wonder if it was this early exposure to God knows what bacteria that trained me for the dive-iest Korean BBQ joints and late-night Thai spots on Hollywood Boulevard that I somehow survived in my twenties.

Anyway, once I discovered fresh peas out of the pod (who knew?), the love affair began and never burned out. This dish is an A.O.C. classic. But feel free to add in other spring delights, such as asparagus, thinly sliced carrots, and Swiss chard.

1/4 teaspoon saffron threads

2 tablespoons unsalted butter, softened

2 tablespoons extra-virgin olive oil

1/4 cup sliced shallots

1 teaspoon thyme leaves

1 1/2 cups English peas (from 1 1/2 pounds in the pod)

1 cup diagonally sliced sugar snap peas

3 ounces pea shoots

1/4 cup sliced spring-onion or scallion tops

Kosher salt and freshly ground black pepper

Toast the saffron in a small pan over medium heat until it just dries and becomes brittle. Pound the saffron to a fine powder, using a mortar and pestle. Stir in the butter to combine well, scraping with a rubber spatula to incorporate all of the saffron powder.

Heat a large sauté pan over medium heat for 1 minute. Add the olive oil, wait a minute, and then add the shallots and thyme. Season with 1/2 teaspoon salt and some pepper, and sauté for a few minutes, until the shallots are translucent; then add the English peas. Turn the heat down to low, and sauté the peas gently for about 3 minutes, shaking the pan a few times. Add the sugar snaps, another ½ teaspoon salt, and a little more pepper.

Stir to combine, cook for a few minutes, and then add the saffron butter and ½ cup water. Turn the heat up to medium and cook for a minute or so, until the peas are just tender. Turn off the heat, and toss in the pea shoots and spring-onion tops. Toss to combine, and taste for seasoning.

For this pairing, I look for a wine that has a degree of soft fruitiness to marry with the sweetness of the peas, and enough acidity to cut through the richness of the butter. White Rhône blends from California that use varieties like Roussanne, Marsanne, and Viognier, work well here. These wines display notes of stone fruit, like peach and apricot, that give them a richness of flavor and oily texture, alongside tart acidity and exotic spice notes of ginger and cardamom. The result on the palate is that the delicate fruit component in the wines mirrors the natural sugar in the peas themselves, while the spice notes maintain synergy with the aromas and flavors in the saffron butter.

fava bean purée with burrata and fava bean pesto

I just cannot, in good conscience, let spring go by without making fava-bean purée. It's the green, earthy, fresh, and bright answer to hummus, and never fails to garner fabulous reviews. In this version, it's served with creamy burrata and a pesto made with even more fava beans. This is another example of reinforcing the flavor of one ingredient by reiterating it a couple of ways in one dish. Thinly sliced prosciutto or coppa is a delicious addition to this dish, and if you added some grilled asparagus spears you would have a lovely spring supper.

1 baguette

1½ cups extra-virgin olive oil

2 tablespoons pine nuts

3 pounds fava beans in the pod

1 large clove garlic, minced

2 tablespoons finely chopped flat-leaf parsley

¼ cup grated Parmigiano-Reggiano

1 lemon, for juicing

1 small sprig rosemary

1 chile de árbol, crumbled

¾ pound burrata cheese

Kosher salt and freshly ground black pepper

Preheat the oven to 375°F.

Cut the baguette on the diagonal into six ½-inch-thick slices. (You may have leftover bread.) Brush both sides of each slice generously with olive oil (about 2 tablespoons in all). Arrange the slices on a baking sheet, and toast them in the oven for 10 to 12 minutes, until golden and crispy but still tender in the center.

Spread the pine nuts on a baking sheet, and toast them in the oven for 8 to 10 minutes, until they're lightly browned and smell nutty. When they have cooled slightly, coarsely chop the nuts.

Remove the beans from their pods, and bring a medium pot of salted water to a boil over high heat.

Blanch the fava beans for about 2 minutes in the boiling water. Drain the beans in a colander, cool them in ice water, and then slip them out of their pale-green shells with your fingers.

Finely chop ½ cup of the fava beans, and transfer to a medium bowl. Add half the minced garlic, the parsley, Parmigiano-Reggiano, toasted pine nuts, ½ cup plus 2 tablespoons olive oil, a heaping ¼ teaspoon salt, some pepper, and a squeeze of lemon juice. Stir well to combine, taste for seasoning, and reserve. This is the fava-bean pesto.

Heat a medium saucepan over low heat. Add the remaining ¾ cup olive oil, the rosemary sprig, and the chile. Let them sizzle in the oil for a minute or two, then stir in the remaining garlic, the remaining fava beans, ¾ teaspoon salt, and some freshly ground black pepper. Simmer the beans for 5 to 7 min-

utes, stirring occasionally, until they're tender (the exact time will depend on the starchiness of the favas). Strain the beans, reserving the oil. Discard the rosemary and chile.

Transfer the beans to a food processor, and purée them. With the motor running, pour in half the reserved oil slowly, until the purée is velvety smooth. Once the purée is smooth, pour in more of the reserved oil, to taste. Squeeze in some more lemon juice, and taste for seasoning.

Spoon the fava purée onto six plates.

Cut six nice wedges (approximately 2 ounces each) of burrata, and arrange them next to the purée. Tuck the toasts between the purée and the cheese, and spoon the fava-bean pesto over and around.

This is a really intensely flavorful recipe with complex layers of dark-green herbal notes of rosemary and thyme, hints of heat from chile de árbol, and rich, stewy garlic. Its ideal match is a wine that shares a similar depth of flavor and robust character. The Italian wine Montepulciano d'Abruzzo is a fantastic option; these wines are dark, meaty, and intense, with layers of menthol and eucalyptus reminiscent of the recipe's herbal ingredients as well as astringency, and that adds a brightening aspect on the palate. The wine's architecture is linear, giving balance to the richness of the fava purée.

morels and pea shoots with green garlic, polenta, and mascarpone

Wild mushrooms, especially morels, are a cause for celebration and always remind me of my father, whom I lost far too early on in both of our lives. He was my food soul mate and my culinary mentor without even knowing it (actually, knowing my father, *he* probably did know it!). When I think that he never lived to see me open Lucques or A.O.C., it brings tears to my eyes. It was my father who taught me to value food and time around the table, and that the simple act of cooking a meal could be so soul satisfying.

One of my favorite food memories occurred in the town of Cahors in the southwest of France when I was about twelve or thirteen. Now, my father would drive 200 miles for a good meal, and he would fly 6,000 miles for a great one. An obsessive academic, he always *studied* where and what we should eat. So I shouldn't have been surprised to learn, when he marched us into what looked like every other little bistro in France, that it was renowned throughout the region for its *morilles.* Now, that night, as a moody preteen, I wasn't so sure I wanted a big plate of mushrooms for dinner, and, as the *madame* poured my parents' wine, I said I thought the roasted chicken looked pretty good. Well, my father nearly lost it! "What do you not understand??? *These* are not *mushrooms*—they are *morels*! And one does not come to this restaurant and order the roasted goddamned chicken!" (I mentioned the part about being obsessed and passionate about food, right?) Well, of course, I had the morels, and they were insanely delicious, and once again, my crazy father was right.

In this dish, they are simply sautéed in olive oil and butter, finished with green garlic and pea shoots, and served atop soft polenta with a dollop of mascarpone.

3 tablespoons extra-virgin olive oil

½ pound morels, stems trimmed, cleaned, cut in half if they are large

2 teaspoons thyme leaves

3 tablespoons unsalted butter

½ cup diagonally sliced green garlic

¼ pound pea shoots

3 cups Polenta (page 212)

¼ pound mascarpone

Kosher salt and freshly ground black pepper

Heat a large sauté pan over high heat for 2 minutes. (If you don't have a pan that's large enough to hold all the vegetables, heat two pans and divide ingredients accordingly.) Swirl in the olive oil, and scatter the morels into the pan, being careful not to overcrowd them. Sauté the mushrooms for 3 to 4 minutes, stirring occasionally. Turn the heat down to medium, and add the thyme, ¼ teaspoon salt, and a few grindings of pepper. Let the mushrooms cook for another 6 to 8 minutes. They should be crispy on the outside, yet still tender. (The amount of cooking time really depends on the mushrooms, so watch them closely; sometimes they give off water, which will require a longer cooking time, to allow the water to evaporate and the mushrooms to crisp.)

Add the butter to the mushrooms, and when it foams, add the green garlic, toss, and cook for 1 minute. Then add the pea shoots and turn off the heat.

Spoon about ½ cup polenta onto each of six plates (or serve family-style). Give the mushroom pan a final toss, just to wilt the pea shoots, and arrange the mushrooms, green garlic, and peas shoots carefully on top of the polenta. Stir the mascarpone well to soften it and give it a runnier texture, and spoon it on top of the mushrooms.

This dish is all about earthy flavors. I like pairing it with mineral-rich, elegant whites, like those from the Puligny-Montrachet appellation of Burgundy. These wines are lean, bright, and tart with layers of slatelike saltiness and elegant acidity. Though they have a lemony citrus quality, they are not particularly sweet, keeping the pairing bright, fresh, and clean.

crushed fingerlings with crème fraîche and chives

This is one of those go-to recipes you just want to have in your repertoire. I laugh at how often people ask me how to make them or say, "Wow,
you are such a great chef. I could never make those." They are *so* easy!
The only real trick is getting the amount of water right. There should be a
lovely, starchy slurry that just coats and glazes the potatoes without their
being either too dry or too watery. You can use this technique with any
potatoes; we just like the cute little fingerlings for A.O.C.

1¼ pounds small fingerling
potatoes

4 tablespoons unsalted butter

2 tablespoons chopped flat-leaf
parsley

¼ cup crème fraîche

2 tablespoons ½-inch-snipped
chives

Kosher salt and cracked black
pepper

Place the potatoes in a large pot, cover with cold water (by at least
4 inches), and add 2 teaspoons salt. Bring to a boil, turn down the heat, and
simmer gently for about 15 minutes, until the potatoes are tender when pierced.
Reserve a cup of the water, and drain the potatoes.

Slightly smash the potatoes with the back of a large spoon, and return
them to the pot with the butter and ½ teaspoon salt. Stir to coat the potatoes
with the butter, and add a few tablespoons of the reserved cooking water to
moisten the potatoes and create a little buttery sauce to coat them. Taste for
seasoning, and stir in the parsley.

Spoon the potatoes into a large bowl, and top with the crème fraîche,
chives, and cracked black pepper.

Like the morel recipe before it, this fingerling preparation speaks of earthy
elegance with a touch of bright-green herbaceous flavor. This is another
recipe that works well with bright, high-acid white wines that have a strong mineral
component. Pouilly-Fuissé, Chablis, and wine from the Mâcon appellations in Burgundy all offer lovely pairing opportunities. They all display elegant citrus fruit notes,
depth of minerality, and bright acidity that will marry with the tart flavor of the crème
fraîche and highlight the savory quality of the chives.

corn pudding with poblanos and queso fresco

2 medium poblano chiles

3 tablespoons unsalted butter, softened

½ cup finely diced yellow onion

1 teaspoon thyme leaves

1 cup fresh corn (from about 1½ ears)

¾ cup whole milk

1 extra-large egg

2 extra-large egg yolks

1¾ cups heavy cream

Pinch cayenne pepper

1 cup grated Gallego cheese (or Asiago, Jack, or other melty cheese)

¼ recipe Cornbread (page 169)

½ teaspoon thinly sliced chile de árbol

⅓ cup crumbled Mexican queso fresco

2 tablespoons cilantro leaves

1 tablespoon extra-virgin olive oil

½ lime, for juicing

Kosher salt and freshly ground black pepper

Most dishes don't just come out of thin air. They are inspired by something new, something at the market, and sometimes by other dishes I'm already making. This one is a stepchild of one of my all-time favorite recipes, Caramelized Bread Pudding with Chocolate and Cinnamon from *Sunday Suppers at Lucques.* What started out as my go-to dessert recipe has been the basis for so many other sweet and savory puddings. I keep the proportion of liquid, eggs, and bread the same, because I love the way it yields a really custardy result with a nice crispy bread topping. To play up the corn flavor, I puréed some corn into the milk, creating a "corn milk" to make the custard base, added sautéed corn, and used cornbread as the bread element. It's wonderful by itself, with a salad and heirloom tomatoes or sautéed chanterelles, or as a side dish for grilled steak, pork, chicken, or even barbecue. I have taken it to more than one summer cook-out with much success.

NOTE If the chile de árbol is dry and brittle you can crush or crumble it.

Char the poblanos on a medium-hot grill, on the burner of a gas stove, or in the broiler. Place the peppers in a small paper bag, close the bag tightly, and set it on a plate to steam for 15 minutes.

Peel the charred poblanos carefully over a strainer. Do not run the peppers under water or you will lose some of the delicious juices. Remove and discard the stem, seeds, and membranes, and cut the remaining roasted peppers into ½-inch dice.

Preheat the oven to 350°F.

Heat a small sauté pan over medium-high heat for 1 minute. Add 2 tablespoons butter, and when it foams, add the onion and ½ teaspoon thyme. Cook for 2 to 3 minutes, stirring with a wooden spoon, until the onion is softened and slightly golden. Add the diced poblanos, ¼ cup corn, ¼ teaspoon salt, and a pinch of pepper, and cook for another 2 to 3 minutes, until the corn is tender. Set aside, and cool to room temperature.

In a food processor, purée the remaining ¾ cup corn with the milk, and transfer to a large bowl. Whisk in the egg and yolks, cream, puréed corn, 1¼ teaspoons salt, the cayenne, and a pinch of black pepper. Add the grated cheese and cooled onion-poblano mixture, and stir well.

Cut the cornbread into ¾-inch-thick slices, and spread it with the remaining 1 tablespoon butter. Break up the cornbread into smaller pieces, and arrange it in an even layer on the bottom of an 8-by-8-inch baking dish. Pour the custard over the cornbread, pressing down with your fingers to make sure the bread soaks up the custard. Scatter the remaining ½ teaspoon thyme and the sliced chile over the top.

Place the baking dish in a roasting pan, and pour warm water into the pan to come halfway up the sides of the pudding dish. Bake for 50 minutes to 1 hour, until the custard is set and the cornbread puffs up slightly. The pudding will be springy to the touch. Let it cool for at least 10 minutes.

Just before serving, toss the queso fresco and the cilantro leaves with the olive oil, a pinch of salt, pinch of pepper, and a squeeze of lime, and arrange over the top of the pudding.

This pudding is deeply rich and packed with a good dose of heat from the poblano chiles, and therefore, it needs to be paired with a wine that can stand up to the powerful flavor and spice. The Southwestern influence in this dish immediately takes me to the Baja Peninsula, where some amazing wine is being made from varieties like Cabernet Sauvignon, Merlot, and Syrah. These wines feature dark, concentrated fruit and grippy tannins that make them ideal partners for this recipe. They are a little more difficult to find, though, so, for an option that is more readily accessible, I would choose a Syrah from California's Paso Robles area. The region's soils and hot climate are ideal for growing hearty, full-bodied Rhône varieties whose black-fruit and cedar notes will balance the heartiness and spice in the pudding.

string and shell bean ragout
with tapenade

Approximately ½ cup extra-virgin olive oil (depending on number of varieties of beans)

¼ cup finely diced onion

2 teaspoons minced garlic

1 tablespoon thyme leaves

2½ cups fresh shell beans, such as flageolets, cranberry beans, lima beans, and black-eyed peas

½ pound green beans, stems removed, cut on the diagonal into 1½-inch pieces

½ pound yellow wax beans, stems removed, cut on the diagonal into 1½-inch pieces

2 tablespoons finely diced shallot

2 tablespoons sliced opal basil

2 tablespoons chopped flat-leaf parsley

1 recipe Tapenade (recipe follows)

Kosher salt and freshly ground black pepper

Fresh shelling beans are one of those things that you might not even know exist if you shop only at the supermarket. They are, indeed, the fresh version of many of the beans we commonly think of as dried—cannellini beans, flageolet beans, borlotti or cranberry beans, and more.

I actually can't imagine summer without a kitchen full of everyone from the dishwasher to the servers to the chef de cuisine shucking beans. This dish is a great way to show off all the available varieties alongside their string-bean brethren, moistened with a little of their cooking juices until just glazed and saucy. Tapenade, that olive icon of southern France, gives a sharp, savory, salty note (olives, anchovies, capers, oh my!) to the very vegetal ragout.

For each type of shell bean, heat a small or medium saucepan over medium heat for 2 minutes. Swirl 2 tablespoons olive oil into each pan, and divide the onion, garlic, and 2 teaspoons thyme between them. Sauté over medium heat for about 5 minutes, until the onion is translucent. Add the shell beans (again, cooking each variety separately), and cook a few minutes, stirring to coat them in the oil. Add a pinch of salt and water to cover by 2 inches. Simmer for 10 to 15 minutes, until the beans are just tender. (The cooking time will really depend on the beans. Taste one to see if it's done.) Remove from the heat, and cool the beans separately in their cooking liquids.

While the shell beans are cooking, blanch the green and yellow string beans together in a large pot of boiling salted water 2 to 3 minutes, until tender but still al dente. Transfer the string beans to a baking sheet to cool.

Drain the shell beans, reserving their cooking liquids.

Heat a large sauté pan over high heat for 1 minute. Swirl in 3 tablespoons olive oil, and add the string beans, diced shallot, and remaining 1 teaspoon thyme to the pan. Season with ½ teaspoon salt and some pepper. Cook for 3 to 4 minutes, tossing to coat the string beans in the shallot mixture. Add the shell beans, and stir gently, being careful not to crush them. Add about ½ cup (or a little more if you like) shell-bean liquid to moisten the ragout. Taste for seasoning, toss in the basil and parsley, and transfer the ragout to a large, shallow bowl. Spoon some tapenade over and around the dish and pass the rest at the table.

tapenade

Chop two-thirds of the olives coarsely, and chop the remaining third finely.

Using a mortar and pestle, pound the garlic, anchovy, and half the capers to a paste. Stir in the olives, remaining capers, parsley, and olive oil. Season with a squeeze of lemon juice, to taste.

¾ cup pitted Niçoise olives

1 small clove garlic

1 salt-packed anchovy, rinsed, bones removed

2 teaspoons salt-packed capers, rinsed, drained, and coarsely chopped

1 tablespoon chopped flat-leaf parsley

¼ cup extra-virgin olive oil

½ lemon, for juicing

The beauty of this shell-bean ragout is that it is earthy, warm, and comforting while still being light and summery. It has a dark, briny punch from the tapenade that works really well with a red wine that is bright and earthy and offers a similar contrast of deep, dark fruit. Wines from the south of France, like Costières de Nîmes and the many Vin de Pays regions are great options, because they are made from blends of dark, meaty varieties like Syrah, Mourvèdre, and often Grenache that brings a bright red fruit tone into the mix. These wines offer structure and tannin that will highlight the black olives in the tapenade, as well as a fruitiness that will pick up on the sweet notes in the string beans.

haricots verts niçoise with summer squash and opal basil

Sautéing haricots verts, summer squash, and cherry tomatoes in an anchovy-spiked butter with caramelized shallots and basil sends me into a tailspin of daydreams, fantasies, and memories of Nice and the French Riviera. The smell of *panisses,* the gorgeous buildings, beach, and people, the *joie de vivre* that just permeates the city and its surroundings are almost too much. It's amazing, the power of smell and taste, and how easy it is to be transported to another world and another feeling with food. Dig in and dream!

NOTE Make sure to use a large, wide sauté pan (my 14-inch All-Clad is my favorite) for this and other vegetable preparations that need lots of surface area to achieve a nice sear. The sear gives texture that will make the vegetables more delicious than if you piled them up too high in a smaller pan. If the pan is too full, the vegetables steam and stew rather than sear, and the texture is monochromatic and not as interesting on the palate.

¾ pound haricots verts, stems removed, tails left on

½ pound summer squash

24 cherry tomatoes (about ½ pint)

3 tablespoons extra-virgin olive oil

3 medium shallots, peeled and thinly sliced

1 teaspoon thyme leaves

1 heaping teaspoon minced anchovy

2 tablespoons unsalted butter

½ lemon, for juicing

2 tablespoons sliced basil, ideally opal and green

2 tablespoons chopped flat-leaf parsley

Kosher salt and freshly ground black pepper

Blanch the haricots verts in a large pot of salted boiling water for 2 minutes, until tender but still al dente. Remove to a baking sheet or platter to cool.

Cut the squash into ⅛-inch-thick slices. If you're using long zucchini-type summer squash, slice them on the diagonal. Cut round or pattypan squashes in half lengthwise, then into half-moons.

Slice the tomatoes in half, and sprinkle evenly with ¼ teaspoon salt and a few grinds of pepper.

Heat a large, wide sauté pan over medium heat for about 1 minute. Swirl in the olive oil, heat for 1 minute, and then add the sliced shallots and thyme. Season with ½ teaspoon salt and several grinds of black pepper. Cook for about 4 minutes, using a wooden spoon to stir the shallots around the pan continuously. (If they begin to burn, turn the heat down to low.)

When the shallots start to caramelize, add the anchovy and 1 tablespoon butter. (Use the wooden spoon to break up any anchovy clumps.) As soon as the butter foams and bubbles, add the squash, and toss to combine. Increase the heat to high, add the blanched haricots verts with ½ teaspoon salt and a few grinds of pepper, and toss again to combine. Cook for 3 to 4 minutes, then push the mixture to one side of the sauté pan. Add the remaining 1 tablespoon butter to the empty side, tip the pan so that the butter pools as it melts, and cook for a minute. When the butter starts to brown and smell nutty, add the cherry tomatoes to it. They will sizzle and pop for a minute; then toss all the vegetables together.

Cook for 1 minute more, tossing often so all the flavors meld and everything is coated in the butter. Finish the dish with a squeeze of lemon juice, the sliced basil, and the chopped parsley. Taste for seasoning, and transfer to a platter.

The mere mention of anything "Niçoise" takes my mind to the south of France and the wide array of rosés available in the summer months. There is just something about the combination of olives, haricots, and tomatoes that works so well with wine from areas like Bandol, Côtes de Provence, Cassis, and Corbières. These wines balance elements of melon and citrus, with a floral-based perfume and a good degree of muscularity, making them the perfect counter to the sweet and salty character of the cherry tomato and anchovy in the recipe.

stuffed squash blossoms with green romesco

There is truly just one moment in the heart of summer when decadent stuffed and fried squash blossoms make so much sense. I have never understood chefs' ordering cases of them from produce companies, only to find themselves sifting through the sad and wilted flowers looking for something decent—what is appealing about that? But when you see them growing in the garden, in that moment in summer when you feel your garden, your home, and possibly your whole block might be taken over by summer squash, that moment when they are so prolific, suddenly it makes sense that the French and Italians came up with so many ways to *use up* these gorgeous blossoms.

Experiment with the stuffing and make it your own, depending on your taste and what you have available. The cheeses listed here are really just a guideline. Ricotta makes a nice tender base and "holds" the other cheeses best. Parmigiano gives wonderful animal-rich flavor, and the Manchego melts into the ricotta, so you have the combination of a pillowy light cheese and the stringy pull of a melty cheese. You can serve the squash blossoms as a side dish or a first course, but I probably love them best as an hors d'oeuvre set out on a platter for guests to munch on with cocktails or a glass of rosé. The green romesco is a little involved, so, if you are short on time, feel free to substitute Pistou (page 104) or Fava Bean Pesto (page 227).

1½ cups fresh ricotta

½ cup grated Parmigiano-Reggiano

½ cup grated Manchego, Asiago, or other melty cheese

½ cup crème fraîche

½ cup finely diced sopressata or other dry salami

2 tablespoons diced shallots

¼ cup chopped flat-leaf parsley

18 large squash blossoms, ideally with small squash attached

2 to 3 quarts vegetable oil, for frying

1 recipe Tempura Batter (page 133)

½ lemon, for juicing

½ recipe Green Romesco (recipe follows)

½ cup Marcona almonds, crushed

Kosher salt and freshly ground black pepper

In a large mixing bowl, fold together the ricotta, Parmigiano, Manchego, crème fraîche, sopressata, shallots, parsley, 2 teaspoons salt, and lots of freshly ground black pepper. Taste for seasoning.

Carefully open each blossom by tearing down one of the natural seams. Fill with 1 to 2 tablespoons cheese mixture (the blossom should be as full as possible while still being able to close completely), reshape the flower around the filling tightly, and set aside.

Heat the oil to 350°F on a deep-frying thermometer, over medium heat, in a heavy, wide-bottomed pan.

One by one, dip the squash blossoms into the tempura batter, shake off the excess, and gently drop them into the hot oil. Cook the blossoms until they're

golden brown, about 2 minutes on each side, drain on paper towels, squeeze a little lemon juice over the top, and season lightly with salt and pepper.

Arrange three blossoms on each of six dinner plates, or pile them all up on a platter to serve family-style. Spoon the green romesco and scatter the crushed Marcona almonds over the top.

green romesco

Once I played around with making a green version of harissa (see Green Harissa, page 75), I became obsessed with making green versions of some of my other favorite sauces and condiments. In this recipe, jalapeños step in for dried ancho chiles, and green tomatoes and tomatillos play the role of the traditional red tomato. The fried bread, hazelnuts, almonds, garlic, and olive oil remain the same, and I added in lots of cilantro and parsley for body and bright flavor. This recipe makes 2 cups, so you will have some left over, which, in my mind, is a good thing—spoon it over grilled fish or chicken, or roasted and grilled summer vegetables with burrata or ricotta.

MAKES 2 CUPS

2 tablespoons hazelnuts

2 medium-sized green tomatoes

3 small tomatillos

2 jalapeños

¾ cup plus 2 tablespoons extra-virgin olive oil

1 slice country bread, about 1 inch thick

2 tablespoons Marcona almonds

1 clove garlic, chopped

1½ cups cilantro leaves (from about 1½ bunches)

¾ cup chopped flat-leaf parsley

Kosher salt and freshly ground black pepper

Preheat the oven to 375°F.

Spread the hazelnuts on a baking sheet, and toast for 8 to 10 minutes, until they smell nutty and are golden brown.

Char the green tomatoes, tomatillos, and jalapeños on all sides on a medium-hot grill, or on the burners of a gas stove, or in the broiler, until all sides are just blackened (you want to char the skin without burning the flesh). Place the tomatoes and peppers in a large paper bag, close it tightly, and let them steam for at least 10 minutes. (They sometimes leak, so put the closed bag on a plate.)

Open the bag, and let the tomatoes and peppers cool slightly. Peel each one carefully. Do not run them under water or you will lose all their delicious juices. Work over a strainer set in a bowl to catch their juices. Tear the jalapeños in half lengthwise, along their natural seam, and remove (and reserve) the seeds and membranes.

Meanwhile, heat a medium sauté pan over high heat for 2 minutes. Add 2 tablespoons olive oil, and wait 1 minute. Fry the slice of bread on both sides

until golden brown. Remove the bread from the pan, and cool. Cut it into 1-inch cubes, and set aside.

In a food processor, pulse together the hazelnuts, almonds, garlic, and fried bread until the bread and nuts are coarsely ground. Add the tomatoes, tomatillos, jalapeños, cilantro, parsley, 1 tablespoon salt, and some freshly ground pepper, and process for 1 minute more.

With the machine running, slowly pour in the remaining ¾ cup olive oil, and process until you have a smooth purée. Taste for balance and seasoning. If you would like the romesco to be spicier, you can add some of the jalapeño seeds and membrane and puree again.

The beauty of stuffed blossoms is the contrast of rich, cheesy ingredients with the sweet, green, delicate flavor inherent in the squash. This versatile flavor combination allows for a variety of white, rosé, and red pairing options. Because of the inclusion of green romesco in this recipe, I like to stick with Spanish wines, specifically wines from the Rioja region, to keep the coupling regionally and thematically pure. For white, I find that wines made from the Viura variety work really well. These wines show notes of ripe stone fruit and delicate acidity, much like a soft California Chardonnay, which will provide an extension of the sweet vegetal flavor of the squash while also providing an acidic break from the richness of the cheeses. For red, Riojas made predominantly from Garnacha work equally well, since the bright raspberry fruitiness and herby qualities in these wines work in much the same way.

young broccoli with garlic and chile

Broccoli, broccoli, how do I love thee? Let me count the ways. I don't know where it came from, or how it started, but broccoli truly is my favorite thing to eat. I know, I know, it's weird and strange that, with all the variety of foods available to me at any time, broccoli is the one I most often choose. Though we do get "special" broccoli—a few different Italian varieties grown by some of our local farmers, picked young, and served soon thereafter—I actually think the cooking technique is the most important part of this recipe. In fact, I have prepared delicious broccolini from the supermarket using this method in a pinch. It's all about having your pan hot enough and using enough olive oil to give the broccoli a nice sear and glaze, so it tastes sumptuous rather than steamed and mild-mannered. Bathed in olive oil and with bits of sweet shallot, toasted garlic, and spicy chile entwined with it, broccoli is sexy!

1½ pounds heirloom Italian-style broccoli, ends trimmed (you can also substitute broccolini or other small varieties of broccoli)

6 tablespoons extra-virgin olive oil

3 cloves garlic, thinly sliced

2 shallots, thinly sliced

1 chile de árbol, thinly sliced on the diagonal

Kosher salt and freshly ground black pepper

NOTE If the chile de árbol is dry and brittle you can just crush or crumble it.

Bring a large pot of heavily salted water to a boil.

Blanch the broccoli for a couple of minutes in the rapidly boiling water, until just tender and al dente. Drain, and cool on a platter or baking sheet.

Heat a large sauté pan over high heat for 2 minutes. Pour in ¼ cup olive oil, and add the garlic, shallots, and chile. Cook a few minutes, until the shallots are translucent. Add the broccoli and 1 teaspoon salt. Stir well, coating the broccoli with the other ingredients and bathing it in the oil. Drizzle the remaining 2 tablespoons oil over the broccoli, and sauté for 3 minutes, tossing often. Sprinkle another teaspoon salt and a pinch of black pepper over the broccoli, toss, and taste for seasoning.

The garlic and chile in this recipe take the broccoli from being bright and vegetal to rich and deeply hearty. I like to pair a Syrah-based wine with this, but one that is on the bright and gamy side, which expresses the lighter aspects of the variety, rather than the dark and jammy. Good examples of this are wines from Crozes-Hermitage and Hermitage, where the vines are grown in a relatively cooler climate and are therefore more elegant and restrained than most New World incarnations.

balsamic-glazed brussels sprouts with pancetta

I have made this recipe perhaps a thousand times, literally. We offer it on our Thanksgiving to-go (and in-house) menu at Tavern, and the first year, I single-handedly cooked more than 300 pounds of the little buggers. Since we're in Los Angeles, about 30 percent of the orders request a vegan preparation. At first I was concerned, but this recipe actually works well if you use all olive oil, leaving out the pancetta, and substituting for the veal stock about half the amount of water, if you feel so inclined. I, of course, like the pancetta and veal stock! It wouldn't be Thanksgiving at our house without these Brussels sprouts, and Sweet Potatoes with Bacon, Spinach, and Romesco (page 253) on the table.

1 pound small Brussels sprouts, washed and trimmed

2 tablespoons extra-virgin olive oil

2 tablespoons unsalted butter

¼ pound pancetta, finely diced

2 tablespoons finely diced shallots

1 tablespoon minced garlic

¼ cup balsamic vinegar

1 cup veal or chicken stock

Kosher salt and freshly ground black pepper

If the Brussels sprouts are larger than 1 inch in diameter, cut them in half lengthwise.

Heat a large sauté pan over high heat for 2 minutes. Swirl in the olive oil and butter, and wait another minute. Add the Brussels sprouts, and season them with 1 teaspoon salt and some pepper. Shake the pan, rolling the Brussels sprouts around, to help them brown evenly. After a few minutes, turn the

heat to medium, and cook for another 3 to 4 minutes, until the sprouts soften slightly.

Add the diced pancetta to the pan, stir, and cook for a minute or two, until the pancetta starts to crisp. Stir in the shallots and garlic, and cook for another minute or so, until they're translucent. Pour in the balsamic vinegar, and reduce by half. Add the veal stock, and reduce to about ¼ cup, stirring and shaking the pan often to glaze the Brussels sprouts. If you start to run low on liquid before the sprouts are cooked, add a little water to the pan.

This is a super-full-flavored vegetable recipe that has an intensity and depth of flavor from the concentrated balsamic and meaty veal stock in the glaze. The preparation works really well with Cabernet Sauvignon, Old and New World in style, because the iron and pine notes of the variety highlight the meatier aspect of the recipe. In a New World Cabernet interpretation, the oak element works well with the sweetness in the balsamic; in an Old World version, the wine's typical leather and gamy character plays off of the high-toned saltiness of the pancetta.

turmeric-spiced root vegetables with kaffir lime yogurt and mint chutney

Turmeric is a rhizome or rootstock of a South Asian member of the ginger family. As the major ingredient in curry and a cheaper alternative to saffron, it is commonly used in Indian, South Asian, and Middle Eastern cooking as much, it seems, for its color as for its flavor. In fact, in the past turmeric was used for dyeing textiles and fabrics, for making cosmetics, and even for religious and cultural ceremonies, Hindu and other, especially in India. Turmeric is considered to have medicinal uses and is even being studied currently for its potential cancer-fighting properties.

In this dish, the turmeric pairs up with cumin, coriander, and paprika to spice up roasted root vegetables and give them an unexpected and exotic twist. First the vegetables are roasted in a very hot oven, an unorthodox method we first came up with at Lucques. We were having problems when working with baby vegetables, unable to get the sear and caramelization we wanted without overcooking the vegetables. Even with our deck oven cranked to 550°F, the results were either tender and pale or nicely browned and mushy. My longest-running kitchen employee, Rodolfo Aguado, who started working for me as a surly fifteen-year-old dishwasher at Campanile and now runs our very busy catering department (and has three kids of his own), came up with the brilliant idea of preheating the sheet pans before placing the vegetables on them. It really works wonders: you get a great roasted sear and can control the tenderness-versus-mushiness issue as well.

9 small or 3 medium carrots, peeled, stems attached if possible

9 small or 3 medium parsnips, peeled, stems attached if possible

6 small or 2 medium turnips

6 small or 2 medium rutabagas, peeled

6 tablespoons extra-virgin olive oil

1 tablespoon thyme leaves

½ teaspoon cumin seeds

¼ teaspoon coriander seeds

3 tablespoons unsalted butter, softened

¼ teaspoon smoked paprika

½ teaspoon ground turmeric

1 cup Greek-style yogurt

1 tablespoon kaffir lime juice, plus ½ teaspoon finely grated zest

2 ounces turnip or mustard greens, cleaned and sliced

1 recipe Mint Chutney (recipe follows)

Kosher salt and freshly ground black pepper

Preheat the oven to 425°F.

Slice the carrots and parsnips in half lengthwise. If they are on the bigger side, then slice each half lengthwise again, into long quarters.

Clean the turnips and rutabagas, cut off the tails, and trim the stems, leaving ¼ inch of the stems. Cut small turnips and rutabagas in halves or quarters; if they're larger, cut them in half and then into ½-inch wedges.

Toss the vegetables with the olive oil, thyme, 1 teaspoon salt, and some freshly ground pepper.

Preheat two heavy-duty baking sheets in the oven for 3 to 4 minutes. Carefully remove the baking sheets from the oven, place the vegetables on

them, and roast them, tossing a few times, for about 25 minutes, until they are tender and a little caramelized.

While the vegetables are roasting, toast the cumin seeds in a small pan over medium-high heat about 2 minutes, until the seeds release their aroma. Using a mortar and pestle, pound the cumin, and transfer it to a small bowl. Repeat with the coriander, and add it, with the softened butter, paprika, and turmeric, to the bowl. Stir to combine well.

Stir the yogurt, lime juice, lime zest, and a heaping ¼ teaspoon salt together in a small bowl. Taste for seasoning.

When the vegetables are done, combine them in one pan and toss in the turnip greens and the turmeric butter. The heat of the roasted vegetables will melt the butter and wilt the greens. Taste for seasoning.

Arrange the vegetables on a platter, and top with the kaffir lime yogurt. Spoon the mint chutney over and around the yogurt and vegetables (or pass the yogurt and chutney at the table).

mint chutney

Using a mortar and pestle, pound the garlic and a pinch of salt to a paste, and transfer to a small bowl. Pound the mint and parsley, and add it to the garlic. Add the olive oil, lemon juice, ¼ teaspoon salt, and ⅛ teaspoon ground pepper, and stir well to combine. Taste for balance and seasoning.

1 small clove garlic

1 cup coarsely chopped mint

¼ cup coarsely chopped flat-leaf parsley

½ cup extra-virgin olive oil

2 tablespoons freshly squeezed lemon juice

Kosher salt and freshly ground black pepper

Whenever I see root vegetables in a recipe, I think of Cabernet Franc, which, at its core, has a vegetal flavor profile that is much like that of the vegetables themselves. Since this is a fairly delicate and herby preparation, I would stay with a wine that is lighter in body, to keep things in balance. For Cabernet Franc, wine from the Bourgueil appellation of the Loire Valley is ideal. Here the wine is lighter in body and shows more bright red fruit and acidity than in other areas. The wine's elegance and delicacy will be in balance with the overall weight of the dish, while its greener elements will mesh with the mint in the chutney.

parsnips and turnips with sage and prunes

1 pound turnips (about 2 large), peeled

¾ pound parsnips (about 3 large), peeled

½ cup rendered duck fat, or more to taste

2 sprigs thyme

10 fresh sage leaves

½ cup sliced prunes

2 tablespoons chopped flat-leaf parsley

Kosher salt and freshly ground black pepper

This recipe was inspired by one of my favorite chefs and mentors, David Tanis, who is now well-known to the world for his fabulous cookbooks (*A Platter of Figs* and *Heart of the Artichoke)* and his column in the *New York Times.* Before all that, he was a secret treasure, beloved by all of us lucky enough ever to work at Chez Panisse. Now, David is not your typical chef with a big belly, loud yell, and white toque; he is a Berkeley chef and a particularly unusual one at that. Let's just say he puts the "arts" into "food arts." With his big, puffy plume of thick gray hair, his rough-and-tumble beard, and his faraway-looking eyes, it was pretty hard to get a handle on him, and what he wanted, back in my early days on the salad station at Chez Panisse. The menu changed daily, and 30 minutes before service started, we had "testers" or "tasters" (I actually still, to this day, don't know which it really was—it sort of felt like both). I started on the lunch salad station, coming in at 8 a.m. to hear what my dishes for the day would be and to start setting up. Well, in those days, it would often be 10 or 10:30 a.m. before David would walk through the door. In the meantime, my good friend Russell Moore (who had already been there for years and now owns the fabulous Camino Restaurant in Oakland) would help me guess what David might want to put on the menu. "Hmmm, well, there was spit-roasted lamb on the menu downstairs last night, so he might want a sandwich . . . or maybe a salad. . . . Hmmm, we did a salad with chicken yesterday, so he might decide on more of a composed plate. . . . Hmmm, he's been feeling very Moroccan these days, and he does like eggs. . . . Hmmm, maybe we should put some eggs on to soft-boil." "Seriously?" I thought to myself. "We are going to guess what he's going to want?" And as my anxiety level rose and my heart raced faster, David would finally walk through the door. "Phew," I thought to myself, "he's finally here, and we can work this out." David shuffled in, his hair all disheveled and crazy; he looked around a little, and then headed straight to the espresso machine. Finally, he made his way to my station. "Hellllooooo," he said, "*ça va*?" "*No,*" I thought to myself, "it most certainly does not *va*! I'm in the weeds, I have no idea what I'm making except, I hope, something with eggs, and we open in one hour! . . ." "*Oui, ça va,*" I sheepishly replied.

Then, with visions of hillsides and vineyards in his eyes, David would start to ramble on and on about Spain, and bullfighting, and some dish he had at a tapas place, and chicken, and chickpeas, and cinnamon. "OK! You got it, right?" "Oh yes, thank you so much," I replied, my heart sinking. Thank God for Russ and my other pals Joe Guth and Tony Brush, who would then fill me in on what all that meant in David-speak; an hour later, by some miracle, I would have the completed dish. David would come back at 11:20 a.m., another espresso in hand, taste the dish, make some genius suggestion or critique which would change the whole thing from good to great, and then shake the plate—literally take the plate between two fingers and shake it, sometimes almost knocking it over and across the cutting board. "Just plate it more like that," he would say, and I would look down, and suddenly what had been a perfectly nice-looking plate of food was stunning. Oh, the wacky magic of David Tanis.

A year or so later, when I had moved up to the hot line, David taught me to make this delicious slow-cooked sauté of parsnips and turnips. My favorite part of the dish was the contrast of some crispy sweet bits and some just barely tender, fresh-tasting pieces. I have added the sage and the prunes, because they make so much sense to me. It's funny: When you cook at a restaurant, even though you are cooking for many people over the course of the evening, generally you are cooking fewer portions at a time, and you have more burners and more pans to use (there is a human dishwasher there, too). Because of this, I am used to cooking two or three orders of parsnips and turnips in a large pan rather than six, so, when I went to test this recipe at home, for six portions, the results inherently changed. There is less surface area, and the vegetables actually get a little more broken up, but as I was cooking it, it reminded me so much of the "German fried potatoes" (or "GFPs," as they were called at our house) that my mom used to make. As I smelled the duck fat permeating the turnips, sage, and prunes sizzling in the pan, I realized this dish has turned into a sort of French hash-browns, with equal parts sophistication and comfort. You can substitute olive oil and butter for the duck fat, but I highly recommend searching out the duck fat and trying it this way at least once (duck fat keeps beautifully in the freezer, so you can just have it on hand for when those southwestern-French moments hit you). *C'est délicieux!*

Use a mandoline to slice the turnips and parsnips into ⅛-inch-thick rounds.

Heat a very large, wide sauté pan over high heat for 1 minute. Add ¼ cup duck fat, the thyme, the sage, half the turnip slices, and half the parsnip slices. Without stirring, sprinkle ¾ teaspoon salt evenly across the top. After 1 minute, give the pan a good shake to loosen the vegetables. Use a metal spoon or spatula to flip them and to dislodge any that are stuck. Grind a bit of pepper over the top, and cook for another minute without stirring. Transfer these cooked turnips and parsnips to a baking sheet or platter.

Swirl the remaining ¼ cup duck fat in the pan and repeat the process with the remaining vegetables.

When the undersides of the vegetables start to get crispy, add the first batch back to the pan. Continue cooking for about 10 minutes, using tongs or a large spoon to flip the vegetables occasionally. Scatter the sliced prunes on top, and cook for another 6 minutes—without stirring, but flipping every minute or so. (Stirring will break up the vegetables. You want the root vegetables to stew in the duck fat and get crispy on some sides.)

Turn the heat off, transfer to a platter, and sprinkle the parsley across the top. Drizzle on another tablespoon of melted duck fat if you're a piggy like me, and serve.

This recipe speaks of autumn, and the ideal wine echoes that quality, with a soft fruitiness and hints of exotic spices. Pinot Noir from various areas of the Central Coast of California, like the Santa Rita Hills, works well for this. I particularly look for those that are made with a good dose of new French oak in the aging process. These wines display bright red plum notes that become softened with cedarlike back notes when made in an oakier style. This dusty, aromatic element is vital in this pairing, because it highlights the perfume and softness of the sage and herbs.

sweet potatoes with bacon, spinach, and romesco

Sometimes you come up with a certain way of preparing a vegetable that is so good there is really no reason ever to try to cook it any other way. This sweet-potato recipe is one of those dishes. As if roasting them with brown butter, brown sugar, sherry, and sage until crispy and caramelized on the outside and tender on the inside isn't enough, the potatoes are finally tossed with bacon *lardons* and spinach (greens!), and drizzled with spicy chile-based romesco. I think if I stopped bringing this to my mom's for Thanksgiving dinner I might not be invited back!

4 pounds sweet potatoes, Jewel or Garnet

⅓ cup brown sugar

1 cup sherry, reduced to ½ cup

8 ounces (2 sticks) unsalted butter

1 tablespoon sliced sage leaves

2 teaspoons thyme leaves

¾ pound slab bacon

½ pound young spinach, cleaned

½ cup Romesco (page 24)

Kosher salt and freshly ground black pepper

Preheat the oven to 400°F.

Peel the sweet potatoes, and cut them into 1½-inch cubes. Place them in a large bowl, and toss with the sugar and reduced sherry.

In a medium sauté pan, cook the butter over medium heat for 6 to 8 minutes, until it's brown and smells nutty. Remove from the heat, and let cool a few minutes. Add the sage and thyme to the butter, and pour it over the sweet potatoes, scraping the pan with a rubber spatula to get all the brown bits. Toss with a large spoon, being careful of the hot butter. Season with 1 tablespoon salt and ¼ teaspoon pepper. Transfer the sweet potatoes to a large roasting pan, and bake in the oven for 50 minutes to 1 hour, until they are caramelized and tender. Stir with a metal spatula every so often, to coat the potatoes evenly with the butter and sugar.

While the potatoes are cooking, slice the bacon lengthwise into ⅜-inch-thick slices. Stack them in two piles, then cut the strips crosswise into ⅜-inch-thick even-sided rectangles, or *lardons*. Heat a large sauté pan over medium heat for 1 minute. Add the bacon, and cook for about 5 minutes, until it's tender and lightly crisped. Using a slotted spoon, transfer it to a plate.

When the sweet potatoes are done, remove the pan from the oven and toss in the bacon and spinach. Taste for seasoning, and arrange in a shallow bowl or large platter. Spoon the romesco over and around the sweet potatoes.

The combination of sweet potatoes, romesco, and bacon makes for the ultimate contrast of flavors on the palate: spicy, sweet, and salt. It has heartiness, density, and texture that really need to be paired with a wine that is full-bodied and equally complex. To pay homage to the Spanish roots of the romesco, I look to the deep, rich wines of the Priorat. This region, where the climate is hot and the soils are poor, creates wines that are fruity, fleshy, and concentrated. The plummy, figlike notes in the wine will marry in flavor and texture with the sweet potatoes, while the wine's earthy aspects work with the bacon and spice.

long-cooked cavolo nero

Another recipe on the "Suzanne likes to have this constantly available to eat so we can't take it off the menu" list, this cavolo-nero preparation has become a house standard at all of my restaurants. The key to it, and maybe to life and eternal happiness, now that I think of it, is lots of olive oil, rosemary, and chile. Oh, and patience. And paying attention. I guess the key is getting more complicated the more I think about it.

Take your time, letting the greens break down, get super-soft, and then a little crispy. Stir with a wooden spoon and watch the kale cook, making sure each leaf is coated and gets a chance to sizzle in the rosemary-infused oil. You can use this technique with other kales and hearty greens, but, no matter how many times I try to branch out, I always come back to cavolo nero—something about the way the deep-green leaves turn almost black, the way they hold up to the long cooking but get so sweet and crispy without burning. Cavolo nero will always be the kale of my dreams!

4 bunches cavolo nero, cleaned, center ribs removed

¼ cup plus 2 tablespoons extra-virgin olive oil

1 small sprig rosemary

2 chiles de árbol, crumbled

1 cup sliced onion

2 cloves garlic, thinly sliced

Kosher salt and freshly ground black pepper

Bring a large pot of heavily salted water to a boil over high heat.

Blanch the cavolo nero in the rapidly boiling water for 2 minutes. Drain, let cool, and squeeze out the excess water with your hands.

Heat a large pot or Dutch oven over medium heat for 2 minutes. Pour in ¼ cup olive oil, and add the rosemary sprig and one of the crumbled chiles. Let them sizzle in the oil for about a minute. Turn the heat down to medium-low, and add the sliced onion. Season with ½ teaspoon salt and a pinch of freshly ground black pepper. Cook for 2 minutes, and stir in the sliced garlic. Continue cooking for another 5 to 7 minutes, stirring often with a wooden spoon, until the onion is soft and starting to color.

Add the cavolo nero and remaining 2 tablespoons olive oil, stirring to coat the greens with the oil and onion. Season with a heaping ¼ teaspoon salt, and cook the greens slowly over low heat for about 30 minutes, stirring often, until they turn a dark, almost black color and get slightly crispy on the edges. Remove the rosemary and chile before serving.

This cavolo-nero preparation has a flavor all its own, with a deep yet sweet earthiness, dark-green herbal element, and chewy texture. It has meatiness to it that works well with rich, intense wines. Malbec is a great option, because it is typically dark-fruited and almost inky black in color, like the cavolo itself. When made in an Old World style, like those from the French region of Cahors, Malbec can be dense and decidedly unfruity. New World Malbec, from areas like South America, are softer and more approachable, displaying concentrated blackberry and blueberry notes that will merge with the sweet flavors in the caramelized onion and garlic, and smoky, herbal qualities that will bring out the recipe's rosemary and spice components.

wild mushrooms persillade

This is actually more of a technique lesson than a recipe. Cooking mushrooms is so easy when you do it right; then, once you get the hang of it, you will find yourself cooking mushrooms all the time, adding them to salads or pastas, baking them on tarts, or just eating them as is. Make sure you use a big enough pan (again, the goal is to sear and create caramelization, not to stew), get the pan hot enough, and really pay attention when you are cooking. If the pan is smoking and the mushrooms are getting too dark, turn the heat down; if they give out a lot of water, leave the heat on high and let them cook without stirring—that liquid will evaporate, and then you can carry on, adding a little more butter if needed.

Persillade is a fancy French way of saying that something is cooked with garlic and parsley. Simple, but I think you will agree that sizzling the parsley and garlic together in the butter really brings out their flavors and permeates the whole dish with a deep, woodsy, very French flavor.

¼ cup olive oil

2 tablespoons unsalted butter

2 pounds wild mushrooms, such as chanterelles, black trumpets, or hedgehogs, cleaned

2 teaspoons thyme leaves

2 teaspoons minced garlic

3 tablespoons finely chopped flat-leaf parsley

Kosher salt and freshly ground black pepper

NOTE If the mushrooms are large, tear them into approximately 2-inch pieces. (They will shrink when you cook them, so don't make them too small.)

Heat two large sauté pans over high heat for 2 minutes. Add 2 tablespoons olive oil to each pan, and heat for another minute. Swirl 1 tablespoon butter into each pan, and when it foams, scatter the mushrooms in the pans. Season each with 1 teaspoon thyme, ¾ teaspoon salt, and a healthy pinch of freshly ground black pepper.

Sauté the mushrooms for about 5 minutes, stirring occasionally, until they're tender and a little crispy. (The cooking time will depend on the particular mushrooms you use.)

Move the mushrooms to make a little empty spot in each pan. Place the garlic in that empty spot; cook for a minute or two, until it sizzles and turns translucent but before it browns. Add the parsley and toss well, stirring with a wooden spoon, to combine quickly and integrate the garlic and parsley with the mushrooms. Taste for seasoning.

When pairing with mushrooms, I like to find a wine that has a little bit of funk to it. I want to play off of the mushrooms' forest-floor-like aromas and pleasantly dirty taste. Red wine from France's Bandol region, made predominantly from Mourvèdre, fits this bill. These Provençal wines are hearty and dark in fruit, with an earthy, barnyardlike background and wild gaminess. They often have an herbal component and meatiness to them that will not only reflect the darker flavors in the mix of mushrooms, but will also bring out the bright green flavor in the combination of parsley and garlic.

farro and black rice with mustard greens, currants, and pine nuts

This dish started out as a sauté of farro and black rice to serve as an accompaniment to pan-roasted bass. The recipe Wild Striped Bass with Farro, Black Rice, Green Garlic, and Tangerine is in *Sunday Suppers at Lucques.* I can't remember where and when I first came across farro all those years back, but it was a life-changing moment for me. I remember being immediately hooked on its chewy, nutty texture and deep, earthy flavor. You just *feel* good when you eat it. Now, I have served it in more ways than I could ever remember, but the day I combined it with black rice was chapter two in my farro love story. As much as I adore farro, it can be a little heavy when served on its own; it needs something else to sneak between its kernels and break things up. Black rice is perfect, because it's a similar size, so you get both grains in the same bite, but it's softer, more aromatic and exotic in flavor, and crisps up in the pan in an equally great but different way. The two together are so much better than either on its own. And this is my absolute favorite preparation of the two—the combination of the greens, the pine nuts, and the unexpected sweetness of the currants (which *look* very much like the rice, so you can't tell what you are about to take a bite of) just can't be beat. I could and often do eat this daily.

6 tablespoons extra-virgin olive oil

1 cup diced onion

2 bay leaves, preferably fresh

2 dried chiles de árbol

¾ cup black rice (forbidden rice)

¼ cup white wine

1 tablespoon thyme leaves

1½ cups farro

3 ounces cleaned mustard greens, torn into 2-inch pieces

⅓ cup Currants and Pine Nuts (recipe follows)

2 tablespoons chopped flat-leaf parsley

Kosher salt and freshly ground black pepper

Heat a medium saucepan over medium heat for 1 minute. Swirl in 2 tablespoons olive oil, and add ½ cup diced onion, 1 bay leaf, and 1 chile, crumbled. Cook, stirring often, until the onion is translucent, about 3 or 4 minutes. Add the rice, stirring to coat it with the oil, and toast it slightly. Pour the white wine into the pan, and reduce by half. Add 4½ cups water and 1 teaspoon salt, and bring to a boil. Turn the heat to low, and simmer for about 40 minutes, stirring occasionally, until the rice is tender but slightly "al dente." When the rice is almost done, stir continuously for about 5 more minutes, until all the liquid has evaporated. Season with a few grindings of black pepper, and transfer the rice to a baking sheet to cool. Discard bay leaf.

While the black rice is cooking, heat a second medium saucepan over medium heat for 1 minute. Swirl in 2 tablespoons olive oil, the remaining

½ cup diced onion, the thyme, and the remaining bay leaf. Cook, stirring often, until the onion is translucent, about 3 or 4 minutes. Add the farro, stirring to coat it with the oil, and toast it slightly. Add 8 cups water and 2 teaspoons salt, and bring to a boil. Turn the heat to low, and simmer for about 30 minutes, until the farro is tender and just cooked through. Strain the farro, and transfer it to a baking sheet to cool. Discard the bay leaf.

Heat a large sauté pan over high heat for 1 minute. Slice the remaining chile thinly on the diagonal (or crumble it if it's very dry). Swirl in the remaining 2 tablespoons olive oil, and add the farro, ¼ teaspoon salt, and a few grindings of black pepper. Cook for 5 minutes, stirring constantly with a wooden spoon, scraping the bottom of the pan, and letting the grains "stir-fry." Add the rice, stir to combine, and cook for another 2 or 3 minutes, until heated through. Add the mustard greens, toss to wilt, and then stir in the currants and pine nuts and the parsley. Taste for seasoning.

currants and pine nuts

I originally came up with this little salsa to serve over a Sicilian-inspired swordfish dish. The combination is classic, but I wanted a way to be able to spoon it over the fish to sauce it, rather than just scattering the currants and pine nuts on top. I wanted something to bind the two ingredients and integrate them into a whole. When I stirred it all together, I loved the result, and started spooning it over salads, antipasto, fish, and quail.

MAKES 1 CUP

⅓ cup extra-virgin olive oil

1 small sprig rosemary

1 chile de árbol, crumbled

¾ cup finely diced red onion

⅓ cup dried currants

½ cup pine nuts

¼ cup balsamic vinegar

2 tablespoons chopped flat-leaf parsley

Kosher salt and freshly ground black pepper

Preheat the oven to 375°F.

Place the olive oil, rosemary, and chile in a small pot over medium heat. After about 2 minutes, when the rosemary and chile start to sizzle, add the onion and ½ teaspoon salt. Turn the heat down to low, and let the onion stew very gently until tender (about 8 to 10 minutes). Transfer the mixture to a bowl, and discard the chile and rosemary. Set aside.

Meanwhile, place the currants in a small bowl, and cover with hot water. Let the currants soak for 10 minutes, and then drain them.

Toast the pine nuts on a baking sheet in the oven, stirring frequently, for about 8 minutes, until golden brown.

Add the balsamic to the pot you used to cook the onion, and reduce it by two-thirds. Use a rubber spatula to scrape the vinegar into the bowl with the onions.

Stir the pine nuts, currants, and parsley into the onion mixture. Taste for seasoning.

Suzanne and I have shared countless plates of this grainy, chewy deliciousness. I enjoy it the most with crisp white wines that show delicate fruit and a degree of nuttiness to marry with the character of the farro itself. Taking my cue from the currants and pine nuts, I look to the island of Sicily for a wine pairing. The white wines made with Grillo grapes are a great example. They show spicy stone-fruit flavors, bright acidity, and clean, salty mineral notes that bring out the fruitiness in the currant–pine-nut relish and highlight the nuttiness and texture of the grains and greens.

from the wood-burning

oven

Caroline and I had been looking, quietly, all over town for a space to execute our sophomore restaurant. When I heard that Antica Pizzeria might be available, I knew instantly that it was perfect. I loved the high ceilings, and the way the space was broken into different areas. I loved the patio, the great storefront, but most of all, what sealed the deal for me was the wood-burning oven.

I am inherently a tactile, manual, low-tech, wood-and-brick-loving person at heart. I know intellectually that you can work wonders with plastic bags and vacuum packing; I have tasted sublime creations made with liquid nitrogen, meat glue, and other such things; but personally I want to get my hands in the food, I want to feel and smell the wood burning, I want smoke in my eyes and a true charred crust. So my soul belongs to cooking over a wood-burning grill or in a wood-burning oven.

All the things that people complain about in the wood-burning oven are the things I love the most. Yes, it's dirty! Yes, it's hot! Yes, you get smoke in your eyes, and sometimes tiny coals actually fly out and hit you! Yes, it's alive and constantly changing, never the same from day to day! As someone who has been cooking in restaurants night after night for so many years, I find the dance with the wood and the fire to be exciting and fun. I love that it's always unpredictable and super-interactive.

When I started writing this book, I really struggled with what to do if you don't happen to have a wood-burning oven at home, because some of these dishes are much-beloved A.O.C. classics, and I know people want the recipes. I was pleasantly surprised with the great results I had using a very hot conventional oven when I tested these recipes at home. You may not get quite the smokiness and intense heat (or the burns!), but I think you will be pleased with the way these come out, wood oven or not.

Except for the Clams with Sherry, Green Garlic, Favas, and Almond Aïoli, these dishes are on the menu at A.O.C. year-round, so I have not categorized them by season.

clams with sherry, green garlic, favas, and almond aïoli

The combination of clams, sherry, and fava beans feels very Spanish to me, and I love the way the elements all roast together in the oven, creating an intensely sherry-y, briny, clam-y broth. The key here is really to watch the clams as they are cooking, and to baste the clamshells with the broth halfway through the cooking process. This prevents the shells from exploding, but also helps the broth reduce more quickly, and gets the stonelike, beachy flavor of the shells themselves into the broth. We mix this dish up, depending on the season—it works beautifully with the addition of artichokes in spring, or by substituting lima beans or other fresh shelling beans in the summer, and dried beans in winter. The almond aïoli, another nod to the Spanish flavor profile, is delicious spread on the toasts before using them to soak up the rich and intensely flavored broth.

NOTE If the chiles de árbol are dry and brittle you can just crush or crumble them.

Preheat the oven to 350°F.

Bring a medium pot of salted water to a boil over high heat.

Remove the beans from their pods. Blanch the beans for about 2 minutes in the boiling water. Drain the beans in a colander, cool them in ice water, and then slip them out of their pale-green shells with your fingers.

Scatter the shelled fava beans, green garlic, chiles, thyme, and ¼ cup olive oil in a large (12-inch round or equivalent) oven-to-table baking dish. Season with ¼ teaspoon salt and several grinds of pepper. Bake for 5 minutes, until everything sizzles.

Arrange the clams on top, and cook for another 5 minutes. Pour the sherry over the clams. Cook 7 to 8 minutes, basting the shells once halfway through, so they don't dry out and burn or crack.

Turn up the oven to broil, scatter the cubed butter evenly across the clams, and broil for 5 minutes, basting the juices over the shells once more, until the clams open completely. Remove the baking dish from the oven, scatter the scallions and chopped parsley, and taste for seasoning.

1½ pounds fava beans in the pod

1 cup thinly sliced green garlic

2 chiles de árbol, sliced

2 teaspoons thyme leaves

½ cup extra-virgin olive oil

3 pounds Manila clams, well scrubbed

1 cup dry sherry

8 tablespoons (1 stick) unsalted butter, cut into small cubes

½ cup diagonally sliced scallions

2 tablespoons chopped flat-leaf parsley

½ loaf ciabatta or other rustic country bread

1 clove garlic

1 recipe Almond Aïoli (recipe follows)

Kosher salt and freshly ground black pepper

Meanwhile, cut the bread into ½-inch-thick slices. Brush both sides of each slice generously with the remaining ¼ cup olive oil. Toast the slices until golden and crispy but still tender in the center. While the toasts are warm, rub them with the garlic clove.

Serve clams with the toasts and a bowl of almond aïoli to pass at the table.

almond aïoli

Place the yolk in a stainless-steel bowl. Begin whisking in the grape-seed oil drop by drop. Once the mixture has thickened and emulsified, you can whisk in the remaining grape-seed and almond oils in a slow, steady stream. If the mixture gets too thick, add a drop or two of water.

Pound the garlic with ¼ teaspoon salt with a mortar and pestle. Whisk the garlic paste into the aïoli. Season with ¼ teaspoon salt, a squeeze of lemon juice, and the cayenne. Taste for balance and seasoning. If the aïoli seems thick and gloppy, thin it with a little water. In addition to thinning the aïoli, this will make it creamier.

1 extra-large egg yolk

¾ cup grape-seed oil

¼ cup pure, unfiltered almond oil

1 small clove garlic

½ lemon, for juicing

Pinch cayenne pepper

Kosher salt

Since sherry is an ingredient in this recipe, I focus on it as the driving force behind my wine pairing. I want to find a wine that will work with the sherry, reflecting its general flavors, rather than opting for one that clashes or battles with it. The sherry used here is light and lean in quality, with an intense tartness and hints of toasted hazelnut. To marry with this, I like to stick with wines made from Pedro Ximenez, a Spanish white variety used in sweet sherry and other dessert wine. When off-dry, Pedro Ximenez shows all the nutty richness found in sherry, but when vinified dry, it becomes incredibly elegant and lean with very delicate peachiness, bright green savory notes, and glycerine-like minerality. It is clean and tart, keeping the pairing vibrant and fresh, and is light enough to be in balance with the dish as a whole.

arroz negro with squid and saffron aïoli

¾ pound small squid, cleaned

1 teaspoon finely grated lemon zest, plus ½ lemon for juicing

2 teaspoons minced garlic

2 chiles de árbol, sliced

3 tablespoons chopped flat-leaf parsley leaves

¼ cup extra-virgin olive oil

1 small sprig rosemary

½ cup finely diced red onion

½ cup finely diced red bell (or other sweet) pepper

1 recipe Fish Stock (recipe follows)

1¼ cups Bomba, Valencia rice, or, in a pinch, Arborio

¼ cup canned tomatoes, preferably San Marzano or Muir Glen, lightly crushed by hand

1 tablespoon squid ink

1 cup white wine

¼ cup diagonally sliced scallions

1 recipe Saffron Aïoli (recipe follows)

Kosher salt and freshly ground black pepper

Arroz negro is basically a paella-style rice dish made black by the addition of squid ink. Our A.O.C. version is flavored with the aromatic Spanish sauce *sofrito*, rosemary, and chile, and topped with small squid cooked on top at the last second. A dollop of saffron aïoli at the end melts into the blackened rice for a creamy and exotic finish. I love these festive one-pot meals that encourage friends and family (and even strangers) to gather around the table, engage, and interact.

NOTE If the chiles de árbol are dry and brittle you can just crush or crumble them.

Cut the squid bodies crosswise into ¼-inch rings, and leave the tentacles whole. (If you're using larger squid, cut the tentacles into quarters.) Season the tentacles and rings with the lemon zest, 1 teaspoon minced garlic, one sliced chile de árbol, and 1 tablespoon chopped parsley for a few hours.

Preheat the oven to 375°F.

Heat a 12-inch cast-iron, paella, or other good-looking oven-to-table pan, over high heat for 2 minutes. Swirl in the olive oil and rosemary. When the rosemary starts to sizzle, add the onion, red pepper, the remaining 1 teaspoon garlic, remaining chile, ¼ teaspoon kosher salt, and a pinch of black pepper. Turn down the heat to medium-low, and cook, stirring often, about 10 minutes, until the vegetables are completely stewed and tender.

Meanwhile, bring the fish stock to a boil in a saucepan, and then turn off the heat.

Turn up the heat under the peppers to high, add the rice, stirring to coat it in the oil and vegetables, and toast for about 2 minutes, until the grains are golden brown and crispy. Add the tomatoes and 1 teaspoon salt. Cook for 2 or 3 minutes, stirring vigorously with a wooden spoon to break up and cook the tomatoes. Add the squid ink, and stir very well to combine. Pour in the wine, and let it reduce by three-quarters, without stirring, about 4 minutes.

Add 3½ cups hot fish stock to the pan, and place it in the oven, uncovered. Bake for 15 minutes, until the liquid is almost completely absorbed and the rice is nearly tender. Season the squid with ¼ teaspoon salt and a few grinds of pepper, and scatter it across the rice, arranging the tentacles in an open and beautiful way. Bake for another 2 to 3 minutes, until the squid is just cooked and slightly crispy in some places. Squeeze a little lemon juice over the whole dish, and sprinkle the scallions and remaining 2 tablespoons parsley over the top. Dollop some of the saffron aïoli in the middle, and pass the rest at the table.

fish stock

MAKES ABOUT 1 QUART

Toast the saffron threads in a small pan over medium heat, just until they dry and become brittle. Pound the saffron in a mortar to a fine powder.

Toast the fennel seeds in the small pan for a few minutes, until the seeds release their aroma and darken slightly. Add them to the mortar, and pound the seeds coarsely with the pestle. Pour the vermouth into the mortar, and use a rubber spatula to scrape up every last bit of the saffron from the sides.

In a large bowl, combine the fish bones, the saffron-vermouth mixture, the leek, fennel, tomato, orange, and parsley. Cover, and refrigerate overnight.

Transfer the marinated fish bones and vegetables to a large stockpot, and add 2 quarts water. Bring to a boil, then turn down the heat to a low simmer, and cook 2 to 3 hours, until reduced to approximately 1 quart. Strain and chill.

⅛ teaspoon saffron threads

¼ teaspoon fennel seeds

¼ cup dry vermouth

½ pound fish bones, rinsed

½ small leek, roughly chopped

¼ small fennel bulb, roughly chopped

½ small tomato, roughly chopped

One ¼-inch-thick slice orange

2 sprigs flat-leaf parsley

saffron aïoli

½ teaspoon saffron threads
1 extra-large egg yolk
½ cup grape-seed oil
½ cup extra-virgin olive oil
1 small clove garlic
½ lemon, for juicing
Pinch cayenne pepper
Kosher salt

Toast the saffron in a small pan over medium heat just until it dries and becomes brittle. Be careful not to burn it.

Place the egg yolk in a stainless-steel bowl. Begin whisking in the grape-seed oil drop by drop. Once the mixture has thickened and emulsified, you can whisk in the remaining grape-seed and olive oils in a slow, steady stream. If the mixture gets too thick, add a drop or two of water.

Using a mortar and pestle, pound the saffron, garlic, and ½ teaspoon salt. Scrape every little bit of the mixture into the mayonnaise with a rubber spatula, and whisk to combine. Season with a squeeze of lemon juice and the cayenne. Taste for balance and seasoning. If the aïoli still seems thick and gloppy, thin it with a little water. In addition to thinning the aïoli, this will make it creamier.

This black-colored, deeply savory rice preparation has been on the A.O.C. menu from day one. Everybody seems to love how the intense brininess of the squid ink melds with the garlic-infused aïoli. We used to get a kick out of the guests who left the restaurant raving about the black-rice dish and happily grinning with ink-stained teeth. For wine pairing, I really focus on the oceanic flavor that the squid brings to the table. I want to find a wine that will reflect that quality while also bringing out the herb and spice elements of the rice. I find the boldly flavored Spanish reds from coastal Catalan regions, like Penedès, make the most appropriate choice, because they are made to drink with this type of food. These wines tend to be dark and full-bodied, made from varieties like Garnacha, Cariñena, and Monastrell, and show the coastal aromas of salty sea air. On the palate, they feature black fruit notes of cassis and plum, as well as a dark-green rosemary-and-thyme herbal quality that is a virtual continuation of the flavor profiles found in this recipe. Other hearty reds from Spain, like those from Priorat and Toro, will work as well.

brioche with prosciutto, gruyère, and a sunny-side-up egg

For me, this dish is the perfect decadent single-diner meal. When I'm really hungry and need to feel comforted and that I'm really treating myself, this brioche is the way to go. It's the combination of the melty cheese on top of buttery brioche, the generous amount of lemony frisée salad spiked with parsley, the ribbons of prosciutto, and, of course, that crowning glory of a sunny-side-up egg that seals the deal.

NOTE Home broilers really vary. Make sure to keep your eyes glued to your brioche, so it doesn't go up in flames if yours is particularly powerful.

Place the frisée in a large bowl with the whole parsley leaves, chopped parsley, and scallions. Cover with a kitchen or paper towel, and refrigerate.

Preheat the broiler to high.

Arrange the oven rack at the top position, closest to the broiler.

Lightly spread ½ tablespoon butter on one side of each brioche slice. Arrange the slices butter-side up on a baking sheet, and toast them under the broiler for about 1 to 2 minutes, until golden brown. (If necessary, rotate the brioche slices halfway through, so that they brown evenly.) Turn the slices over, and toast the unbuttered side until just golden.

Cut the sliced Gruyère, if necessary, and arrange it to fit exactly on top of the toasted brioche; any exposed brioche will burn. Set aside.

Heat two large sauté pans over high heat for 1 minute, and then add 1 tablespoon of butter to each pan. When the butter foams, gently crack three eggs into each pan, being careful not to break the yolks. Season the eggs with salt and pepper, cook 1 minute, and then turn off the heat.

Meanwhile, toss the frisée with the olive oil, lemon juice, ½ teaspoon salt, and a pinch of black pepper. Gently mix with your hands, and taste for balance and seasoning.

Place the brioche slices under the broiler for 3 minutes or so, until the cheese melts. Transfer one brioche slice to each of six dinner plates. Mound the frisée salad atop the brioche, and weave 1 ounce of sliced prosciutto through

6 ounces cleaned frisée (from 2 large or 4 small heads)

¼ cup whole flat-leaf parsley leaves, plus 2 tablespoons chopped

2 tablespoons diagonally sliced scallions

5 tablespoons unsalted butter, softened

Six 1-inch-thick slices brioche

1 pound Gruyère cheese, sliced about ⅛ inch thick

6 extra-large eggs

2 tablespoons extra-virgin olive oil

2 tablespoons freshly squeezed lemon juice

6 ounces prosciutto di Parma or San Daniele, thinly sliced

Kosher salt and freshly ground black pepper

each salad. Using a metal spatula, carefully place the eggs on top of the salads, making sure that some of the herbs and frisée peek out from underneath the egg and prosciutto.

I'm so envious of the diners at A.O.C. when I see them diving into this melty, open-faced, egg-topped sandwich. I always imagine that it would be the perfect thing to eat after a night of too much drinking. But when I am actually looking for a wine pairing, rather than a wine antidote, I think, for inspiration, of the Gruyère and its dominating flavor in this recipe. This Swiss cow's milk cheese has an intense, concentrated sweetness and density that become even more powerful and savory when it's melted. The flavors are akin to those of raclette, and for this reason, I find that white wines from Savoie, an Alpine area in eastern France, adjacent to Switzerland, work well with it. Wines here are made from varieties like Roussanne, Roussette, Jacquère, and Gringet and display soft floral and spice notes that mirror the sweetness and honeyed flavor of the Gruyère. The wines also show brightening acidity to work with the recipe's other savory ingredients, as well as to cut through the overall richness of the dish.

roasted cauliflower with curry and red vinegar

¼ teaspoon coriander seeds

¼ teaspoon cumin seeds

1 teaspoon curry powder

1½ teaspoons bittersweet paprika

1 medium head cauliflower, cored and cut into florets

1 small yellow onion, peeled, cored, and cut into sixths

2 tablespoons extra-virgin olive oil

2 tablespoons unsalted butter, melted

1½ tablespoons red-wine vinegar

1 tablespoon chopped cilantro

Kosher salt and freshly ground black pepper

It's funny how certain dishes that become so beloved actually found their way onto the menu. When we were setting up A.O.C., we did all of our training down the street, at Lucques. One night, my Lucques sous-chef at the time, Rob Chalmers, cooked whole cauliflower heads with a mess of spices, curry, and vinegar for staff meal. We all went crazy—it was so so good! The second I tasted it, I knew: some things are just too delicious to keep in the kitchen, and this one had to go on the opening menu at A.O.C.

A few months in, our otherwise stellar *Los Angeles Times* review called the cauliflower the one "clinker" on the menu. Now, something you have to realize about chefs is that you can give us 999 compliments but if there is one criticism *that* is what we focus on. So, while everyone else was drinking champagne and celebrating, I was at the grill, stewing about the cauliflower comment! Pretty silly, I know, but I had faith in that dish, and I loved it, as did many customers, so I held my head high and told myself that I was not going to see my beloved cauliflower bullied off the menu. And there it stayed, loved by many, and most certainly not a "clinker."

Preheat the oven to 450°F.

Toast the coriander seeds in a small pan for a few minutes, until the seeds release their aroma and are lightly browned. Using a mortar and pestle, pound them coarsely. Repeat with the cumin seeds.

Combine the coriander, cumin, curry, paprika, ½ teaspoon salt, and a few grindings of black pepper in a small bowl. Stir together to combine.

Place the cauliflower and onion in a large mixing bowl, and pour the olive oil and melted butter over the top. Sprinkle the spice mixture over the cauliflower, and toss well, to coat the vegetables completely in the oil, butter, and spices. Add the vinegar, and toss again to combine well.

Place the cauliflower in a single layer on a baking sheet. Roast for about 30 minutes, stirring every 8 minutes or so, until the cauliflower is tender and nicely caramelized. Scatter the cilantro over the cauliflower, toss with a large spoon, and taste for seasoning.

Everyone loves this preparation's exotic layer upon layer of flavor, a blend of aromatic spiced notes, savory caramelized onion, brightening acidity, and back notes of smoke. I always like pairing it with Cabernet Franc, either a light-bodied version from the Napa Valley, or in the form of Chinon from the Loire. Cabernet Franc is fresh and bright, with brambly fruit and dark savory elements that partner nicely with the curry and spice, as well as an inherent pleasant green vegetal quality that works really well with cruciferous vegetables. The key is to choose a wine that is not overly concentrated or high in alcohol, so as to avoid overpowering the cauliflower, as well as to keep the spiciness of the recipe in check.

lamb meatballs with spiced tomato sauce, mint, and feta

The cumin-and-cinnamon-spiked tomato sauce and meatballs in this dish send my mind to exotic places. This is a great party dish, or actually great for any time you want to prep ahead and just pop one dish into the oven when you are ready to serve. It works wonderfully with grilled toasts or flatbreads, or spooned over pasta cooked simply with olive oil, garlic, and parsley. You could also add grilled eggplant and peppers to the dish in summer, or roasted squash and carrots in the winter months, if you want to bring vegetables to the party.

In a large bowl, mix together the onion, cream, egg yolks, cinnamon, cumin, Aleppo pepper, and cayenne. Place the lamb in the bowl, and season evenly with 2½ teaspoons kosher salt and lots of black pepper. Add the breadcrumbs and parsley, and use your hands to combine the mixture well. Shape the meat into 1½-ounce balls.

Preheat the oven to 400°F.

Pour the tomato sauce into a large (12-inch-diameter or 9-by-11-inch) oven-to-table baking dish.

Heat two large sauté pans over high heat for 2 minutes. Swirl 2 tablespoons oil in each pan, and wait a minute. Place the meatballs carefully in the pans, and cook for a few minutes, until nicely browned. Turn the meatballs over, and continue cooking on all sides until they are evenly colored. Transfer the meatballs to the baking dish, placing them about ½ inch from each other.

Bake for 15 to 20 minutes, until the sauce is bubbling and the meatballs are just cooked through.

Top each meatball with crumbled feta, and scatter the mint over the whole dish.

¾ cup finely diced onion

¼ cup heavy cream

2 extra-large egg yolks

½ teaspoon ground cinnamon

1 teaspoon freshly ground cumin

1 teaspoon crushed Aleppo pepper

Pinch cayenne pepper

2 pounds ground lamb

1 cup fresh breadcrumbs

¼ cup chopped flat-leaf parsley

1 recipe Spiced Tomato Sauce (recipe follows)

¼ cup extra-virgin olive oil

¼ pound feta cheese

2 tablespoons sliced mint leaves

Kosher salt and freshly ground black pepper

spiced tomato sauce

3 cups canned tomatoes,
    preferably San Marzano
    or Muir Glen

½ teaspoon cumin seeds

3 tablespoons extra-virgin
    olive oil

1 small sprig rosemary

1 chile de árbol, crumbled

1 cup diced onion

1 teaspoon thyme leaves

Pinch ground cinnamon

Pinch cayenne pepper

1 bay leaf, preferably fresh

½ teaspoon sugar

¼ cup freshly squeezed orange
    juice, plus 3-inch strip of
    orange zest

Kosher salt and freshly ground
    black pepper

Pass the tomatoes through a food mill.

Toast the cumin seeds for a few minutes in a small pan over medium heat, until they release their aroma and are lightly browned. Pound them finely in a mortar.

Heat a medium saucepan over medium-high heat for 1 minute. Swirl in the olive oil, add the rosemary and chile, and heat another minute. Add the onion, thyme, cumin, cinnamon, cayenne, and bay leaf, and sauté for 5 to 6 minutes, until the onion is translucent. Add the tomatoes, sugar, orange juice and zest, heaping ½ teaspoon salt, and some freshly ground pepper. Cook for 8 to 10 minutes over medium-low heat, until reduced by one-third. Taste for seasoning.

It seems only appropriate to pair this recipe with a wine that will pay homage to the Italian roots of the tomato-sauce-and-meatball combination. To work with the richness of the sauce and the gamy lamb, I opt for a Sangiovese-based wine, like Chianti Classico or the more esoteric Montefalco Rosso from Umbria. Sangiovese displays bright red cherry fruit notes and lean spiciness that I find to be really complementary to tomato-based sauces such as this. These wines highlight the high-toned sweetness of the stewed tomatoes while also marrying with the tartness and acidity in the feta.

salt cod—potato gratin with piquillo peppers, currants, and mahón

OK, this is one of those recipes with a few more steps, but I know there are devoted cooks out there who want to make this sort of thing. This recipe is sort of a deconstructed Spanish version of the Provençal brandade. To make brandade, potatoes and salt cod are cooked together with garlic and herbs in milk, then strained out and blended with cream and lots of olive oil into a rustic purée. In this version, I cook the salt cod in the traditional garlic milk but simply shred it instead of puréeing it. The potato purée is cooked separately and then layered with the salt cod and Mahón cheese into a gratin dish. I, for one, am not a proponent of the Italian culinary rule of never cooking cheese and fish together in one dish. I love the way the cheese melts into the smooth potatoes and chunky, salty shreds of cod. The salad of Spanish piquillo peppers, parsley, mint, and currants gives a bright and sweet finish to this decadent gratin.

Place the salt cod in a large nonreactive container, cover with cool water by 6 inches, and refrigerate. Soak the cod this way for 48 hours, changing the water every 12 hours. After 48 hours, strain the salt cod and place it on a roasting rack to drain, in the refrigerator, for at least 4 hours.

Preheat the oven to 400°F.

Toss the potatoes with 1 tablespoon olive oil, the 3 cloves unpeeled garlic, 3 thyme sprigs, and 1 teaspoon salt. Place them in a roasting pan, cover with aluminum foil, and cook for about 45 minutes, until tender when pierced. (Cooking time will vary with the size, age, and variety of potatoes.)

When the potatoes have cooled, peel them. Turn the potatoes on their sides and cut them into ¼-inch-thick slices. Season with salt and pepper.

Meanwhile, place the salt cod in a large saucepan with the milk and peeled garlic. Make a cheesecloth sachet with the bay leaves, parsley, peppercorns, and the remaining 7 sprigs thyme. Peel the onion, stick it with the cloves, and add it, and the sachet, to the pot.

Bring the salt cod to a boil over medium-high heat, and then turn down to a simmer and cook for about 30 minutes, until the salt cod is tender and

Ingredients

2 pounds salt cod

1½ pounds Yukon Gold potatoes

2 tablespoons extra-virgin olive oil

3 cloves garlic, unpeeled, smashed, plus ⅓ cup peeled cloves garlic

10 sprigs thyme

½ gallon whole milk

2 bay leaves, preferably fresh

6 sprigs flat-leaf parsley

1 tablespoon black peppercorns

1 onion

3 cloves

3 cups Potato Purée (page 208)

2½ cups Béchamel (recipe follows)

¼ pound Mahón (or Asiago or aged Jack) cheese, grated

¼ cup currants

¾ cup julienned piquillo peppers

¼ cup small flat-leaf parsley leaves or sliced larger leaves

¼ cup small mint leaves or sliced larger leaves

1 teaspoon freshly squeezed lemon juice, or to taste

Kosher salt and freshly ground black pepper

flakes easily. (Again, depending on the age, nature, and provenance of the cod, cooking time will vary.)

Strain the cod and garlic. Discard the milk, sachet, and the clove-studded onion. When the cod has cooled, flake it with your hands, mash the cooked garlic with a fork, and gently stir together the cod and garlic.

Preheat the oven to 425°F.

Spoon 1 cup of potato purée in uneven dollops in a 12-by-12-inch (or equivalent) gratin or baking dish. Scatter one-third of the cod and garlic over the potato purée, and arrange one-third of the potato slices in between and around the fish. Spoon 1 cup of béchamel over the cod and potatoes. Season with salt and pepper, and sprinkle one-third of the Mahón over the top. Continue layering with the potato purée, cod, potatoes, béchamel, and cheese (seasoning as you go along) until the gratin dish is almost full.

Bake the gratin for about 25 minutes, until it is bubbly and golden brown on top.

While the gratin is baking, place the currants in a small bowl, and cover with hot water. Let the currants soak for 10 minutes, and then drain well.

Place the piquillo peppers in a small bowl with the currants, parsley leaves, mint, ⅛ teaspoon salt, and a few grindings of pepper. Toss with the remaining tablespoon olive oil and a teaspoon of lemon juice. Taste for balance and seasoning and place the piquillo salad at the center of the gratin.

béchamel

MAKES 2½ CUPS

Bring the milk and cream to a boil in a medium saucepan and turn off the heat.

Place the butter in a second medium saucepan over medium heat. When it foams, add the flour, and whisk to combine completely. Turn the heat down to medium-low, and cook a few minutes, whisking all the time, until the flour is a light-sandy color.

Pour in one-third of the milk-cream mixture, and whisk vigorously to incorporate. Add another third of the milk-cream, and continue whisking. When the milk is fully incorporated, add the last third, turn the heat up to medium, and bring to a simmer, whisking all the time, until very smooth. Cook for 10 minutes, whisking often, and then remove from the heat. Season with salt, pepper, and a few gratings of nutmeg.

2¼ cups whole milk
¾ cup heavy cream
2 tablespoons unsalted butter
3 tablespoons all-purpose flour
Small piece fresh nutmeg
Kosher salt and freshly ground
   black pepper

Most recipes that feature salt cod need to have a fruity element, like the currants in this recipe, to balance out the fish's intense, salty flavor. Likewise, when selecting a wine to pair with the salt cod, the goal is to find a wine that has a good dose of fruit in it as well. Choosing a wine that is too lean and acidic will cause the entire combination to become too salty and acrid for the palate to bear. Since this recipe shows a Spanish slant with its use of peppers and Mahón, I recommend sticking with a wine from the northwestern regions of Spain, like Galicia, and the neighboring Portugal, where salt cod is an iconic ingredient. Varieties grown in the region include Albariño, Godello, Torrontés, and Treixadura, all of which have high degrees of bright fruitiness and mineral complexity that would make them capable partners for the recipe's blend of salty, sweet, spicy, and tart.

torchio with kabocha squash, radicchio, walnuts, and taleggio

I always say that restaurants are like people, and it's amazing how certain people (and restaurants) in your life can have such a big effect on your path and your final landing point. Al Forno in Providence, Rhode Island, was such a place for me.

I cringe now when I remember how I knocked on the door, my freshman year at Brown, all pleased with myself after a summer in the pastry kitchen at Ma Maison here in Los Angeles. I had a great plan: "I could make desserts and sell them to you," I told Johanne Killeen (oh, dear Jesus, did I really say that?). She sweetly but sternly replied that at Al Forno they make everything to order and from scratch. I must have had a funny look on my face, so she said, "Yes, we even make the desserts to order."

Well, something in my naïve but curious nature must have touched her because Johanne asked me if I was looking for a job. I wasn't supposed to be, of course—I was supposed to be studying early-twentieth-century diplomatic relations between the United States and the Soviet Union—but, unable to resist, I replied, "Yes!" Well, she didn't have any positions in the kitchen, so I happily went to work at Al Forno as a server. I just knew in whatever capacity I wanted to be there, in that gorgeous little space with all the delicious foods they put out. I remember walking down College Hill to get to work in the afternoon, and smelling the wood grill about five blocks away, before I could even see the small storefront restaurant at 3 Steeple Street.

A year or so later, I finally got a coveted (and much-less-well-paying) position in the kitchen. From my perch at the salad-and-dessert station, making apple tarts and cranberry gratins to order, while trying also to keep up with an incredibly busy pantry station, I would stare longingly at the wood-grill and deck-oven stations just next to me. One of Al Forno's signature dishes was their baked pastas—various seasonal ingredients tossed with cheese, herbs, and cream and then baked to crispy perfection in the pizza oven. This is my ode to those fabulous pasta dishes.

1 small kabocha squash (about 2½ pounds) (to yield 1½ pounds after peeling and seeding)

7 tablespoons extra-virgin olive oil

2 teaspoons thyme leaves

½ head radicchio

½ teaspoon minced rosemary

¾ pound Taleggio cheese

¾ cup walnut halves or pieces

1 pound torchio (or rigatoni) pasta

1 recipe Three-Cheese Sauce (recipe follows)

½ cup freshly grated Parmigiano-Reggiano

Kosher salt and freshly ground black pepper

Preheat the oven to 425°F.

Cut the squash in half lengthwise, and remove the seeds. Place the squash cut-side down on a cutting board, and use a sharp knife to remove the peel. Cut the squash into 1½-inch chunks.

Toss the squash with ¼ cup olive oil, 1 teaspoon salt, some pepper, and the thyme. Place the squash on a baking sheet, and roast in the oven about 15 minutes, until tender when pierced.

While the squash is roasting, make the three-cheese sauce.

Place the half-head of radicchio cut-side down on a cutting board, and slice it into 1-inch-thick ribbons. Toss the radicchio with 2 tablespoons olive oil, the rosemary, ½ teaspoon salt, and some pepper.

Remove the Taleggio rind, and cut the cheese into 1-inch chunks.

Toss the walnuts with remaining 1 tablespoon olive oil and ¼ teaspoon salt.

Preheat the oven to 450°F.

Blanch the pasta in boiling salted water for exactly 3 minutes, drain, and rinse with cold water until cooled. Transfer the pasta to a large mixing bowl. Spoon the warm three-cheese sauce over the pasta, add the radicchio and some pepper, and toss well to combine. Place half the pasta in a large (12-inch round or 9-by-12-inch rectangle) oven-to-table baking dish. Tuck half the squash, half the Taleggio, and half the walnuts into the pasta. Top with the remaining pasta, and tuck in the remaining squash, Taleggio, and walnuts. Sprinkle the grated Parmigiano on top, and bake for about 20 minutes, until bubbling and crispy on the top.

three-cheese sauce

Bring the milk to a boil in a medium saucepan, and turn off the heat.

Place the butter in a medium saucepan over medium heat. When it foams, add the flour, and whisk to combine completely. Turn the heat down to medium-low, and cook a few minutes, whisking all the time, until the flour is a light-sandy color.

Pour in one-third of the milk, and whisk vigorously to incorporate. Add another third of the milk, and continue whisking. When the milk is fully incorporated, add the last third, turn the heat up to medium, and bring to a simmer, whisking all the time, until very smooth. Cook for 10 minutes, whisking often, and then remove from the heat.

Stir in the cream, Fontina, Gruyère, Parmigiano, ¾ teaspoon salt, some pepper, and a few gratings of nutmeg. Taste for seasoning.

2½ cups whole milk

2 tablespoons unsalted butter

2 tablespoons all-purpose flour

½ cup heavy cream

1¼ cups (5 ounces) grated Italian Fontina

¾ cup (3 ounces) grated Gruyère

¼ cup (1 ounce) grated Parmigiano-Reggiano

Small piece fresh nutmeg

Kosher salt and freshly ground black pepper

Nothing is more fragrant or wonderfully aggressive than melted Taleggio cheese. Anytime there is any form of warm Taleggio in the restaurant's dining room, heads turn and noses raise. It's the kind of stinky sweetness that is hard to compare and that is insanely wine-friendly. For this pairing, I seek out wines from the Lombardy region of Italy, where Taleggio itself is made. This region makes stunningly beautiful whites and reds, both of which are appropriate partners for this recipe. For white, I like wines made from Trebbiano, which have a touch of honeyed sweetness and delicate acidity, because their fruitiness brings out the pleasantly sweet quality in the cheese while keeping it bright. Red wines from the region include varieties such as Nebbiolo and Barbera, which are less acidic and slightly fruitier than those from the more northern regions of Italy. Both red and white work well with this recipe; their softness and fleshy fruit notes will highlight the sweetness of the cheese, while bringing a silkiness of texture to the entire pairing.

desserts

I actually started my culinary career in the pastry kitchen. My high school had a wonderful program back then called Senior Projects, in which all seniors were given two weeks off from school to pursue something they had always been passionate about or interested in. It was completely obvious to me that I should go work in a restaurant. Now, I don't know if at that time I had any inkling that this might lead to a career path, or if it was just that I loved cooking, food, and restaurants and wanted to get a look behind the scenes. Whatever it was, it led me marching down Melrose Avenue (where fifteen years later I would open my own restaurant) to Ma Maison, the most acclaimed and fabulous L.A. restaurant of the time.

Ma Maison was such a wonderful and unique place. And talk about groundbreaking: the phone number was unlisted, the setting was a small bungalow with fake grass and pink flamingos for patio décor, the Rolls-Royces and vintage Porsches were lined up out front, and Orson Welles had a table inside where he lunched every day. Owned by Patrick Terrail, whose family's famed Michelin-starred restaurant Tour d'Argent in Paris is one of the world's most famous and beloved restaurants, Ma Maison served amazing French food in a "California Casual" setting long before anyone had ever thought to come up with a name for such a thing.

It was Monsieur Terrail who came to the gate at 3 p.m. on a Tuesday when I timidly knocked all those years ago. I explained that I was a senior in high school, that Ma Maison was my favorite restaurant (the one I always chose for my birthday dinner), that I really wanted to learn to cook from the best, and that I wanted to come work for free for two weeks. "*Oui, oui, oui, mais bien sûr!* Of course, you come back and work with us. *C'est magnifique!*" And then he closed the gate and presumably went back to Zsa Zsa Gabor or whatever supermodel he was dating at the time. "Great," I thought, "that was easy."

Of course, two months later, when I showed up for my first day, no one had any idea what on earth I was talking about! But no matter, I had gotten my foot in the door and I was not taking it out. Being a seventeen-year-old girl, I was taken immediately to the pastry kitchen. And I was thrilled. I had always wondered how tarts, galettes, *tuiles,* custards, cakes, and *île flottante* were made. And, lucky for me, the pastry chef was quite understaffed, so she took to showing me how to make something once and then having me make it over and over again. I was in heaven! I used to come home night after night and set up shop in my home kitchen and do it all over again. I would load my parents up with desserts to take to work, give to the neighbors, and, of course, eat. "Don't you think you could work on some savory food?" my father would ask. It's crazy to think that even he, the king of the sweet tooth, was over it.

I did eventually move into the savory kitchen when I got to Providence, Rhode Island, but my pastry roots have always stayed with me, and I feel so lucky to have had that training all those years ago. In fact, after leaving Al Forno to open another restaurant in Providence, called Angels, Chef Jaime D'Oliveira put me in charge of the salads *and* the dessert menu. It was there I started to hone my own style of desserts, and it was the first time (but not the last) that my penchant for making "slutty" desserts was recognized. Not to be vulgar, but I do think that desserts should have a little something-something going on. They should be decadent, a little over-the-top, crave-able, something really to long for, and to gasp at when you eat them. With desserts (and, actually, most of my food), I try to walk a very fine line of showing off the beauty of the product and "letting it speak," as they say, but also amplifying its voice or dressing it up for the occasion a little. I do feel that, if you're going to have dessert, you should just go for it. Enjoy it, indulge, and be satisfied and excited with your decision to splurge.

Now that I think about it, the pastry bug has been hard for me to shake. In the early nineties, I spent a year cooking in France, much of it at Alain Passard's then two-star but now three-star Paris restaurant, Arpège. Nine months into my time there, I realized that, although I was living in the City of Lights, I might as well have been in Cleveland, because I worked such long hours that all I ever saw was during the morning rush to work and the long late-night bike ride back to my tiny (but charming) apartment. So I decided to spend my last three months in Paris at a pâtisserie, so that I could learn more about pastry but also have the evenings off to enjoy a little of what the city had to offer. I was back to knocking on doors again.

Before I started knocking, I decided to try to figure out which pâtisseries made the most delicious pastries in Paris, so that I could plan my attack. I embarked on an obsessive-compulsive, calorie-rich exploration of every pâtisserie of note in all twenty *arrondissements*. Ten days and ten pounds later, I found it, the pâtisserie I most wanted to work at, and it had been right there on Rue de Rivoli, right down the street from my mini-apartment, the whole time. Continuing my lucky streak, when I made my move, Christian Pottier himself was at the shop and was happy to take me for a three-month *stage* at his gorgeous shop, Pâtisserie Christian Pottier.

Monsieur Pottier was a Parisian through and through. He had literally never been out of the Île-de France, never mind to the United States or other countries abroad. And as we chatted over laminated doughs, fondants, and ganaches, I came to realize that he thought the rest of the world was pretty much like Paris. He asked me what the croissants were like at my neighborhood pâtisserie in Los Angeles. I told him how, at least back then, every neighborhood didn't have a pâtisserie, and instead Americans mostly ate cereal and eggs for breakfast. *"On mange quoi?"* he asked. Cereal is for horses, he told me. This led to long conversations about chocolate chip cookies, brownies, peanut butter, carrot cake (again, he had the horse question), pumpkin pie, and so on. Monsieur Pottier and I made a deal: he would teach me his mother's recipes for pot au feu and pork rillettes, and I would teach him all the American standards of which he was so skeptical. What fun we had, baking, laughing, and sharing our cultural heritages and traditions that winter. The chocolate chip cookies and brownies were such a hit that he actually sold them in the shop! Oatmeal cookies were, as expected, not understood (better for animal feed, he told me), and pumpkin pie—well, that was just *dégueulasse.*

What I took from those months with Monsieur Pottier and my time at Ma Maison, Al Forno, and Angels was a passion for baking and desserts, and a love of the tradition and classic methods of pastry. When it comes to creating desserts for my own restaurants, I approach them very much the way I approach the savory food. The season and the market are the starting point, and from there I love to use classic and not-so-classic influences and ideas. Obviously, what we are striving for in the sweet kitchen is the same as our goals in the savory kitchen. We are working toward deep, clean, and powerful flavors, combinations that sing and complement without overpowering, and, most important, an integration that unites the various components and makes them one delicious whole.

Just as with savory food, balance and seasoning play a crucial role in the success of a dessert. Though I don't like desserts to be too sweet, they need enough sugar to make them feel and taste finished. As with a savory recipe that needs salt, sometimes if you skimp a bit on the sugar a dish can fall flat. And salt, yes, desserts absolutely need salt. As always, we are working to play off sweet, salty, acidic, bitter, and umami flavors, and orchestrate them into a final product that is cohesive and just works when it hits the palate.

I often quote one of my mentors and good friends, Catherine Brandel, who was my first chef at Chez Panisse: "Sometimes you just need to lighten things up with a little heavy cream." It sounds crazy, but I actually feel that whipped cream or whipped crème fraîche plays the same role that a few leaves of dandelion, arugula, or other greens play for me in a savory dish. It provides a nice break, and clears the palate for another bite of what is to come. My pastry chef, Christina Olufson, and I often try to plate desserts without that beloved dollop, and time and time again, as I'm tasting, I want to reach my spoon into some pillowy and clean-tasting whipped cream if it's not there. Somehow it helps balance desserts and unify their flavors at the same time.

I have worked with some great pastry chefs over the past fifteen years of owning my own restaurants. And it's not an easy job. Though I try to give them free rein—and mostly do, especially after they have been with me a few years—I still taste every new dessert. I work with them to make sure that the desserts are the best they can be, and that they fit with the rest of the menu and the restaurant.

I feel so lucky to have had Christina Olufson as my pastry chef for the last three years. We do monthly tastings together, where Christina presents her latest ideas for desserts and we taste and talk about them together. Even if I usually feel like heading to the vomitorium after these tastings (a person should never eat more than five desserts in one seating), I love those times with Christina, really thinking, considering, and adjusting the dishes together.

We have worked very hard to adjust these restaurant recipes for the home kitchen. I have noted the more involved and time-consuming recipes, because I know there are those of you who want to prepare something more involved, and those of you who would rather not. As with any recipe, but especially with pastry, read the recipes thoroughly before you start, and make sure to follow the directions very closely. Pastry and dessert recipes are a little more temperamental and particular, just like the lovely cooks and chefs who prepare them, so be precise and pay close attention. As we say in the savory kitchen, "It's pastry's world, we just live in it!"

frozen meyer lemon meringue tart with gingersnap crust and blueberry compote

4 extra-large eggs

6 extra-large egg yolks

2¾ cups sugar

2 cups freshly squeezed
    Meyer-lemon juice
    (from about 10 lemons)

12 tablespoons (1½ sticks)
    unsalted butter, cold,
    cut into ½-inch cubes,
    plus 6 tablespoons melted
    butter for crust

2 cups Gingersnap
    (recipe follows) cookie
    crumbs

4 extra-large egg whites,
    at room temperature

1 recipe Blueberry Compote
    (recipe follows)

A few years back, my husband, David, and I were invited by our good friend Marc Vetri to participate in his Great Chefs Event in Philadelphia. Now, not to sound jaded, but we do a lot of charity events, and though they are all for wonderful causes, sometimes they all sort of start to blend together. Marc's event had a great reputation for bringing together an incredible number of talented chefs from around the country for a great party—there's always much eating, drinking, and madness to be had when chefs get together.

So there we were, at our booth, handing out little plates of ceviche, when we were asked please to stop serving and listen to the speaker. The next few minutes changed my life. Liz Scott, a beautiful, slight, elegant-looking woman, took the microphone and told us the story of her daughter Alex, who as a four-year-old cancer patient decided that she wanted to have a lemonade stand on her front lawn to raise money for other kids with cancer. As she told the story of what she and her family and poor Alex had gone through, and how her daughter had risen up and looked beyond her own self to help others, and had eventually died, at age eight, having just reached her goal of raising one million dollars, I looked over at David, through my own tear-soaked eyes, and saw him equally distraught and practically bawling. It was then that we decided we wanted to join this fight against childhood cancer, and that we would come back to Los Angeles and, with Caroline, put on our own event to raise money for Alex's Lemonade Stand Foundation.

So every year, in the fall, we gather our closest chef and winemaking friends and put on a big event attended by more than a thousand people, called L.A. Loves Alex's Lemonade. To date, we have raised over one and a half million dollars for children's cancer research. Every year, when Meyer lemons are in season, we like to create a dessert in Alex's memory, to give us a chance to tell her story and spread the word of her incredible spirit and efforts. This Meyer-lemon meringue pie was one of our favorite Alex's desserts over the years.

You can help, too! No donation or effort is too small—just this year, some children from our preschool had a stand and mailed in eighteen dollars. Check it out at www.alexslemonade.org and www.lalovesalexs lemonade.com.

NOTE You will need a blowtorch, kitchen or otherwise, to toast the meringue.

Whisk the eggs, egg yolks, and 1¾ cups sugar together in a bowl. Whisk in the lemon juice, and transfer to a medium saucepan. Cook over medium heat for 6 to 8 minutes, stirring frequently with a rubber spatula, scraping the bottom and sides of the pan. The custard will thicken, and when it's done it will coat the back of the spatula. Whisk in the cold cubed butter, a little at a time, until completely incorporated. Strain the mixture, and chill for at least 2 hours in the refrigerator.

Stir 2 cups of gingersnap cookie crumbs with 6 tablespoons melted butter until completely incorporated. Line a 10-inch tart shell with plastic wrap (this will make it easier to get the tart out of the shell), and, using your fingers, press the gingersnap mixture into the shell, pressing the sides first and then the bottom to form an even crust. Refrigerate until you are ready to assemble the pie.

Process the lemon custard in an ice-cream maker according to the manufacturer's instructions, and pour into the prepared tart shell, using an offset spatula or a dinner knife to smooth the top. Freeze for at least 5 hours or overnight.

Next, make the meringue. Place the egg whites and remaining 1 cup sugar in the bowl of a stand mixer. Whisk to combine, and then place the bowl over a pot of boiling water and whisk until the mixture is warm and the sugar has completely dissolved. Return the bowl to the mixer, and, using the whisk attachment, whip the whites at high speed until they are glossy and have doubled in volume.

Spread a 1½-inch layer of meringue over the top of the frozen lemon custard. Using an offset spatula or a dinner knife, make a swirling design with the meringue. You can keep the tart in the freezer at this point (up to a day in advance), until you are ready to serve.

When you are ready to serve, use a kitchen blowtorch to "toast" the meringue.

Cut six wedges from the tart, making sure the plastic is not still attached, and place them on six dessert plates. Spoon a couple of tablespoons of the blueberry compote next to the wedges.

gingersnaps

1½ cups all-purpose flour

1¼ teaspoons baking soda

1¼ teaspoons ground cinnamon

1½ teaspoons ground ginger

¼ teaspoon kosher salt

8 tablespoons (1 stick) unsalted butter

⅔ cup plus 2 tablespoons sugar

¼ teaspoon pure vanilla extract

3 tablespoons molasses

1 extra-large egg

If you are baking the gingersnaps for the crust of the Frozen Meyer Lemon Meringue Tart, you will need only half the recipe, so you can enjoy the other half as gingersnap cookies.

MAKES 4 DOZEN COOKIES, OR 3½ CUPS CRUMBS

Sift the flour, baking soda, 1 teaspoon cinnamon, and the ginger together. Stir in the salt.

In a stand mixer fitted with the paddle attachment, cream the butter and ⅔ cup sugar at medium-high speed for 3 to 4 minutes, until the mixture is light and fluffy. Add the vanilla, molasses, and egg, and beat until fluffy again. Add the dry ingredients slowly, and mix at low speed until combined.

Form the dough into a 1-inch-thick flat disk, wrap in plastic, and place in the fridge. Chill for 1 hour, until firm.

Preheat the oven to 350°F.

To make gingersnap crumbs for crust, roll the dough to ⅛-inch thickness on a generously floured surface. Use a fork to poke holes all around the dough, and place it on a parchment-lined baking sheet. Bake for about 20 minutes, until golden brown and crisp. When the gingersnaps have cooled completely, purée them to crumbs in a food processor.

To make cookies, combine remaining 2 tablespoons sugar and ¼ teaspoon cinnamon in a small bowl, and set aside. Shape the dough into logs about 1½ inches in diameter, and refrigerate a few hours (to make them easier to slice). Slice the dough into ¼-inch-thick rounds, and place them ½ inch apart on a parchment-lined baking sheet. Sprinkle with cinnamon sugar, and bake for 12 to 15 minutes, until golden and crispy around the edges.

blueberry compote

Place the sugar in a medium saucepan. Split the half vanilla bean in half lengthwise, and use a paring knife to scrape out the seeds and pulp into the sugar. Add ⅓ cup water, and bring to a boil over medium heat, without stirring. Cook for about 10 minutes, swirling the pan occasionally, until the mixture is an amber caramel color.

Meanwhile, stir 1 tablespoon water into the cornstarch (this is called a "slurry" and will help thicken the fruit juices).

When the sugar has reached an amber caramel color, add half the fresh blueberries and the brandy to the pot. The sugar will harden. Cook for a minute or two over low heat, stirring gently, until the berries release their juices and the sugar dissolves.

Strain the mixture over a bowl, then return the liquid to the pan, whisk in the cornstarch slurry, and cook for another minute, stirring often, until it comes to a boil. Transfer the cooked berries to the bowl, and stir in the remaining fresh and the dried blueberries. Pour the thickened juices over the berries, and stir to combine. After the compote has cooked down, remove the vanilla bean.

½ cup sugar

½ vanilla bean

2 teaspoons cornstarch

2 cups fresh blueberries

2 tablespoons good-quality brandy

¼ cup dried blueberries

Meyer lemon has a richness and intensity all its own that, when concentrated for this pie and then frozen, becomes even more flavorful. The gingersnap crust gives the recipe a softening, spicy aspect that balances out the fruit element. I look to my wine pairing to do much the same as the crust, softening the intensity of the fruit and rounding it out with complexity. I like Coteaux du Layon, a Loire Valley dessert wine made from Chenin Blanc, for this. The Chenin Blanc, when in this more concentrated, off-dry form, becomes intensely spicy, with notes of cardamom, ginger, and clove that mirror the gingersnap flavor of the crust. And because it is made in a region with relatively cool climate, the wine, though definitely sweet, retains a good amount of acidity, keeping it from being cloying and allowing it to mesh elegantly with the frozen citrus.

chocolate mascarpone tart with pistachios in olive oil

When Christina Olufson took over a few years back as head pastry chef, this was the first recipe she developed on her own, and it's a big winner. A rich, creamy mascarpone mousse is sandwiched between a cocoa crust on the bottom and a shimmering milk-chocolate layer on top.

We do a lot of special events at A.O.C., from Paella Night, to our La Tomatina celebration, to a release party for *olio nuovo*—the first pressing of fresh extra-virgin olive oils of the season, which are meant to be used quickly and abundantly. Christina and I struggled with what to serve for dessert at that dinner. I knew I wanted to do an olive-oil cake, but wanted something very olive-oil-y to serve with it. "I wish," I said to Christina, "we could make a sweet version of the pistachio aillade we use in the savory kitchen." Well, as is so often the case with Christina, I didn't need to wish for long before it magically appeared. She left out the garlic (thank God) and added in a little sugar, and our beloved savory sauce (see page 119) was magically transformed to the perfect pastry sauce. As a matter of fact, it's so good that I use it to sauce two desserts in this book, this chocolate tart and the Crème Fraîche Cake with Santa Rosa Plums as well. Chocolate is such an interesting ingredient—we all know it pairs well with salt, but it works beautifully with many savory ingredients, including, and especially, olive oil. Just what I need, a reason to have more olive oil!

MAKES ONE 11-INCH TART

1 extra-large egg yolk

1½ cups heavy cream

1½ cups all-purpose flour

2 tablespoons cocoa powder

¼ cup granulated sugar

¼ teaspoon kosher salt

8 tablespoons (1 stick) cold unsalted butter, cut into small pieces

1 cup (6 ounces) finely chopped 36% milk chocolate

⅔ cup (3⅓ ounces) finely chopped unsweetened or baking chocolate

½ cup whole milk

2 cups very cold Mascarpone Mousse (recipe follows), or more if needed

2 tablespoons crème fraîche

1 recipe Sweet Pistachios in Olive Oil (recipe follows)

NOTE This is one of the more involved and "restauranty" recipes. You can make the tart dough and the mousse the day before serving if you like—in fact, making the mascarpone mousse in advance so it can chill is a very good idea. The only tricky part of this recipe is making sure the mascarpone mousse is cold enough and the ganache is cool enough that they don't melt each other when you put the tart together.

Preheat the oven to 350°F.

Whisk the egg yolk and ¼ cup cream together in a small bowl.

Sift the flour and cocoa powder together in the bowl of a stand mixer fitted with the paddle attachment. Stir in the sugar and salt. Add the butter to the bowl all at once and paddle on medium speed for about 2 minutes, until you have a coarse meal. (Do not overmix or the butter and flour will turn into one big lump.)

Gradually add the cream-and-yolk mixture, and mix on low speed until the dough just comes together. Transfer the dough to a large work surface and bring it together with your hands to incorporate completely. Shape the dough into a 1-inch-thick disk. Sprinkle a little flour over the dough, and roll it out to a ¼-inch-thick circle, flouring as necessary. Starting at one side, roll and wrap the dough around the rolling pin to pick it up.

Unroll the dough over an 11-inch tart pan. Gently fit the dough loosely into the pan, lifting the edges and pressing the dough into the corners with your fingers. To remove the excess dough, roll the rolling pin lightly over the top of the tart pan for a nice clean edge, or work your way around the edge pinching off any excess dough with your fingers.

Prick the bottom of the tart dough with a fork, and line it with a few opened and fanned-out coffee filters or a piece of parchment paper. Fill the lined tart shell with beans or pie weights, and bake 15 minutes, until set. Take the tart out of the oven, and carefully lift out the paper and beans. Return the tart to the oven and bake another 15 to 20 minutes, until the crust is firm to the touch. Allow crust to cool to room temperature.

While the tart shell is cooling, combine the finely chopped chocolates in a medium bowl. Heat ½ cup cream and the milk in a heavy-bottomed saucepan over high heat to scald it; it will just begin to bubble around the edges but don't bring to a full boil. Immediately pour the hot cream mixture over the chocolate and let sit for 1 minute without touching it so that the chocolate melts. Whisk to combine completely and set aside to cool. This is the ganache.

When the tart shell has cooled completely, spread the chilled mascarpone mousse evenly across the bottom of the tart crust. (It should fill it to about two-thirds; add more mousse if necessary.) Freeze the tart for 30 minutes.

Pour the room-temperature chocolate ganache over the very cold mascarpone mousse, filling the remaining third of space. Chill the tart 1 hour, until the chocolate is set enough to cut.

Just before serving, place the remaining ¾ cup cream and the crème fraîche in a mixing bowl. Whip at medium-high speed with the whisk attachment until you have very soft peaks. (You could also whip by hand.)

Cut six slices from the tart and place them on six dessert plates. Stir the pistachios in olive oil before spooning 2 heaping tablespoons over and around each tart slice, allowing some pistachios to fall down the sides. Dollop with whipped crème fraîche.

mascarpone mousse

MAKES ABOUT 3 CUPS

Sprinkle the gelatin over ¼ cup cool water in a small saucepan and set aside.

Fasten a candy thermometer to a small stainless-steel saucepan, and add the sugar and ¼ cup water. Cook the sugar over medium heat, without stirring, for about 5 minutes, or until the thermometer reaches 115°C / 240°F. Remove the pan from the heat.

Meanwhile, whip the eggs at high speed in the bowl of a stand mixer fitted with a whisk attachment until they are pale and frothy, about 10 minutes. Scrape down the sides of the bowl with a rubber spatula as needed for thorough whipping.

Very slowly pour the hot sugar into the whipped eggs and continue whisking until the mixture is cool. (You can test the temperature by putting your hand on the bottom of the bowl.)

Add 2 tablespoons of cream to the bloomed gelatin and warm over medium-low heat, stirring constantly, for about 30 seconds, or until the gelatin dissolves completely. Turn off the heat and let the cream mixture cool to room temperature.

Meanwhile, whip the remaining ½ cup cream to soft peaks in the bowl of a stand mixer fitted with the whisk attachment (or whip by hand).

In a large bowl, stir together the mascarpone and the lemon juice. Using a rubber spatula, gently fold in the cooled gelatin mixture, the egg mixture, and finally the whipped cream. Cover and chill the mousse.

¼-ounce package
(heaping 2¼ teaspoons)
Knox powdered gelatin

¾ cup sugar

2 extra-large eggs

½ cup plus 2 tablespoons heavy cream

½ pound mascarpone

1½ teaspoons freshly squeezed lemon juice

sweet pistachios in olive oil

3 ounces shelled pistachios
(about ¾ cup)

½ cup good, finishing-quality
extra-virgin olive oil

1½ teaspoons sugar

½ teaspoon freshly squeezed
lemon juice

½ teaspoon finely grated
orange zest

¼ teaspoon kosher salt

Preheat the oven to 350°F.

Spread the pistachios on a baking sheet, and warm them in the oven for 3 to 5 minutes. This will help bring out their bright-green color. Do not toast them or brown them at all; if you do so, they will turn the sauce brown. Remove the pistachios from the oven, and set aside until they are cool enough to touch. Roughly chop them, so the largest piece is no bigger than a pea. Discard any skins that have fallen loose.

Meanwhile, stir the olive oil, sugar, lemon juice, orange zest, and salt together in a medium bowl to dissolve the sugar. When the pistachios have cooled to room temperature, add them to the bowl, and stir to combine.

I love that there is slightly savory bent to this chocolate dessert, with the addition of pistachios in olive oil, bringing an earthiness and complexity not found in many dessert preparations. I find that red dessert wines from Italy show a similar complexity, much like the dry wines made there. With this particular dessert, I recommend pairing a Recioto della Valpolicella, a sweet wine made in the Verona region of Italy, and related to Amarone. These wines are made from a blend of varieties such as Corvina, Rondinella, and Molinara and have a deep, dark, figlike fruitiness. They have a silkiness and spiciness to them that echo the dark-chocolate aspect of the tart while also cutting through its rich texture.

sticky toffee pudding with blood orange, tangerine, and whipped crème fraîche

I am generally not a sticky-toffee-pudding person. The classic British steamed pudding always seems too sweet, and a little reminiscent of a dreaded Christmas fruit cake. So, when Christina Olufson came to me with this dish, my heart sank. It's funny, but Christina and I probably have a more honest relationship than many people have with their spouses. And the key to that successful relationship is my total honesty with her, which sometimes involves a strange stream of consciousness about memories, flavors, textures, and so on, in my attempt to explain what I do and don't like in a dessert.

Christina is awesome, and she works really hard, and 95 percent of the time her desserts are spot-on and don't need any of my meddling. Those are the tastings I love. No matter what people may think of us, we chefs generally just want everything to be great and not to have to correct anyone on anything. I hate having to tell Christina, who is constantly trying new things and pushing herself, that I don't like something she has created. So, when she told me she was making something that I inherently don't like anyway, I was dreading the tasting. And then she put it in front of me, the lightest, most subtle yet flavorful and rich creation! Spiked with dates and bathed in a delicious toffee sauce, the cake itself is divine, but pairing it with the bright, tart citrus and the sour note of crème fraîche was genius. Every element plays off all the others for a delicious and incredibly well-balanced dessert.

SERVES 12

½ pound whole Medjool dates, pitted and chopped

1 teaspoon baking soda

8 tablespoons (1 stick) unsalted butter, softened, plus more for the pan

1¾ cups all-purpose flour

1½ teaspoons baking powder

¼ teaspoon kosher salt

1 cup dark-brown sugar

¼ cup granulated sugar

2 extra-large eggs

1 recipe Toffee Sauce (recipe follows)

3 blood oranges

2 tangerines

6 kumquats

1 cup heavy cream

2 tablespoons crème fraîche

Place the dates and baking soda in a bowl, and pour 1 cup boiling water over them. Let them sit for 1 hour, and then strain the dates (reserve the water). Purée them in a food processor, pour the liquid in, and pulse to combine.

Preheat the oven to 350°F.

Prepare a 9-inch springform pan by spreading butter on the inside surfaces, lining the bottom with parchment paper, and buttering the parchment.

Sift the flour and baking powder together. Stir in the salt.

In a stand mixer fitted with the paddle attachment, cream the butter and sugars at medium-high speed for 4 to 5 minutes, until light and fluffy. Add the eggs, and beat until fluffy again. Add the date purée and the flour mixture, alternating, to the butter mixture, and combine well.

Pour the batter into the prepared pan. Bake for 35 minutes, until the pudding is dark brown. Immediately after removing the pudding from the oven, pour ½ cup of toffee sauce over the top. Let the pudding rest for 15 minutes before serving.

While the pudding is baking, cut the stem and blossom ends from the blood oranges. Place the oranges cut-side down on a cutting board. Following the contour of the fruit with your knife, remove the peel and cottony white pith, working from top to bottom, and rotating the fruit as you go. Slice each orange into 8 to 10 pinwheels.

Peel the tangerines, separate them into segments, and remove all the white veins, or pith. Slice the kumquats into pinwheels. Chill the fruit until you are ready to serve.

Using a stand mixer fitted with the whisk attachment (or by hand), whip the cream and crème fraîche together to soft peaks.

Slice six pieces of warm pudding (the pudding serves twelve) and place them on six dessert plates. Spoon the rest of the warm toffee sauce over the slices. On each plate, dollop a heaping tablespoon of the whipped crème fraîche next to each piece and arrange the citrus evenly over and around the pudding. Scatter the kumquats in a beautiful natural style.

toffee sauce

2 tablespoons unsalted butter

½ cup lightly packed dark-brown sugar

Generous pinch kosher salt

6 tablespoons heavy cream

NOTE You can make the toffee sauce ahead of time and warm it up when you are ready to use it.

Place the butter, sugar, and salt in a medium saucepan. Over medium-high heat, cook, stirring constantly, until the butter has melted and the sugar has dissolved. Stir in the cream, and cook for another 3 or 4 minutes, until the mixture boils.

The toffee-cake itself is soft and mellow in flavor, with a delicate gingerlike spiciness. This makes for the ideal foundation from which the citrus ingredients can shine, and sets up the inspiration for my wine pairing. I want the wine to reflect the citrus notes in the dessert, so I opt for Muscat, like the elegant Muscat du Cap Corse from the island of Corsica. This wine has a bright marmaladelike quality of preserved orange and mandarin that mimics the fruit flavors in the recipe, allowing them to flow seamlessly from one to another on the palate.

bing cherries with walnut-chocolate tart and vanilla ice cream

Think of this dessert as a deconstructed waffle-cone sundae. Yes, I know that sounds odd, but the walnut tart plays the role of the waffle cone, all crispy, crunchy, and caramelized. Make sure to serve a big, generous scoop of vanilla ice cream on top, and when you spoon over the cherries and they blend with the chocolate chunks buried in the tart shell, I think you will know you have given Ben & Jerry's a run for their money.

The walnut-chocolate tart actually started out as a riff on pecan pie that I turned into a tart and added chocolate to—I mean, why not? It's amazing and wonderful to me how switching out one key ingredient can really change a dish. I had worried that your palate would sense the pecan-pie-ness in the corn-syrup-and-brown-butter base, but in reality, with the walnuts and the addition of the cherries, this tart really just became its own new creation. I love when that happens.

MAKES ONE 11-INCH TART

½ recipe Pâte Sucrée (recipe follows)

1½ cups chopped raw walnuts, plus 1½ to 2 cups raw walnut halves

4 tablespoons (½ stick) unsalted butter

½ vanilla bean

1 cup sugar

½ cup light corn syrup

½ cup dark corn syrup

¼ teaspoon kosher salt

3 extra-large eggs

¾ cup chopped bittersweet chocolate

1 recipe Vanilla Ice Cream (recipe follows)

1 recipe Cherry Compote (recipe follows)

¾ cup heavy cream

¼ cup crème fraîche

On a lightly floured work surface, roll the chilled tart dough out to a 12-inch circle about ¼ inch thick. Starting at one side, roll and wrap the dough around the rolling pin to pick it up. Unroll the dough over an 11-inch fluted tart pan. Gently fit the dough loosely into the pan, lifting the edges and pressing the dough into the corners with your fingers. To remove the excess dough, roll the rolling pin lightly over the top of the tart pan for a nice clean edge, or work your way around the edge, pinching off any excess dough, with your fingers. Chill for 1 hour.

Preheat the oven to 350°F.

Spread the chopped walnuts on a baking sheet, and toast 8 to 10 minutes, until they appear lightly browned and smell toasted.

Place the butter in a small sauté pan. Split the half vanilla bean lengthwise, and use a paring knife to scrape out the pulp and seeds into the butter. Add the vanilla pod to the pan, and cook the butter and vanilla over medium heat, swirling the pan a few times, until the butter browns and smells nutty. Strain the vanilla bean from the brown butter, discarding the pod.

In a large mixing bowl, whisk together the sugar, corn syrups, and salt. Add the warm brown butter, and then the eggs.

Spread the toasted chopped walnuts in an even layer over the prepared tart shell. Scatter the chocolate over the chopped walnuts. Place the walnut halves in concentric circles over the chopped walnuts and chocolate. Pour the filling evenly over the nuts, and bake about 40 minutes, until the filling is set.

Let the tart cool for at least 15 minutes. Remove from the pan, cut six wedges from the tart (it will serve ten to twelve), and top with big scoops of vanilla ice cream. Spoon the cherry compote over the ice cream and around the plate. Finish each plate with a dollop of whipped crème fraîche.

pâte sucrée

MAKES ENOUGH FOR 2 TARTS

¼ cup heavy cream

2 extra-large egg yolks

2¾ cups plus 2 tablespoons all-purpose flour

¼ cup plus 3 tablespoons sugar

¼ teaspoon kosher salt

½ pound (2 sticks) unsalted butter, cold, cut into small cubes

Whisk the cream and egg yolks together in a small bowl.

In a stand mixer fitted with the dough hook, combine the flour, sugar, salt, and butter at medium speed until you have a coarse meal. Gradually add the cream and yolks, and mix until just combined. Do not overwork the dough. Transfer the dough to a large work surface, and bring it together with your hands to incorporate completely. Divide the dough in half, shape into

1-inch-thick disks, and wrap the disks in plastic. Chill for at least 1 hour. You can freeze the extra dough for another tart another day.

vanilla ice cream

Split the vanilla bean in half lengthwise, and, using a paring knife, scrape the seeds and pulp into a medium saucepan. Add the vanilla pod, milk, and cream, and bring to a boil over medium heat. Turn off the heat, cover, and allow the flavors to infuse for about 30 minutes.

Return the mixture to the stove, and bring it back to a boil over medium heat, stirring occasionally. When it boils, turn off the heat.

Whisk the egg yolks and sugar together in a bowl. Whisk a few tablespoons of the warm cream mixture into the yolks to temper them. Slowly, add another ¼ cup or so of the warm cream, whisking constantly. At this point, you can add the rest of the cream mixture in a slow, steady stream, whisking all the time. Pour the mixture back into the pot, and return it to the stove.

Cook the custard over medium heat for 6 to 8 minutes, stirring frequently with a rubber spatula, scraping the bottom and sides of the pan. The custard will thicken, and when it's done it will coat the back of the spatula. Strain the mixture, and chill for at least 2 hours in the refrigerator. Process in an ice-cream maker according to the manufacturer's instructions.

1 vanilla bean
2 cups whole milk
2 cups heavy cream
4 extra-large egg yolks
½ cup sugar

cherry compote

Split the half vanilla bean lengthwise, and use a paring knife to scrape out the seeds and pulp. Place the vanilla seeds, pulp, and pod in a medium pot. Add the sugar and 2 tablespoons water, and bring to a boil over medium heat, without stirring. Cook for about 10 minutes, swirling occasionally, until the mixture is a dark amber caramel color.

Add half the cherries, the brandy, port, and orange zest to the pot. The sugar will harden. Reduce heat to low, and cook for 4 to 5 minutes longer, until the sugar dissolves and the cherries release their juices. (The fruit should be cooked but not mushy.)

½ vanilla bean
⅓ cup sugar
¾ pound cherries, washed, stemmed, and pitted
1½ tablespoons good-quality brandy
1½ tablespoons port or red wine
1-inch-wide strip of orange zest
1½ tablespoons cornstarch

Strain cooked cherries from the juice, reserving the juice. Add cooked fruit to the remaining uncooked cherries, and mix well to combine. Combine the cornstarch with 2 tablespoons of reserved juice in a small bowl. (This "slurry" will help thicken the compote.) Return remaining juice to the pot on the stove. Whisk in the cornstarch slurry, and cook over medium heat another minute or two, until it comes to a boil.

Pour the thickened juices over the cherries, and stir well to combine.

When pairing wine with this dessert, I really focus on the walnuts in the recipe. The combination of the nuts with bright red cherry brings my wine-pairing mind to Italy and the country's nutty Vin Santo. This wine can be made from a variety of grapes including Malvasia, Trebbiano, and even Sangiovese, and always has a deliciously toasted walnut-and-caramel quality. Vin Santo can vary in style from very dry to very sweet, but with this dessert, I prefer a Vin Santo with a touch of sweetness to add emphasis to the cherries while complementing the vanilla in the ice cream.

watermelon and strawberry coupe
with torn mint

When I was a kid, I was lucky enough to get to travel to France with my parents on a few occasions. Since I was a young girl, whether I was abroad or not, my focus was mainly on small furry animals and ice cream. I remember my father going crazy on my sister and me one day in Paris, as he marched us up the steep hills of Montmartre to see the Sacré-Coeur Basilica. As we were walking, my sister Jessica was looking down the alley and said, "Look, Suzannie, look at those cute white kittens." *"What?"* my father roared. "Do you think I brought you all the way here, six thousand miles, to the most beautiful city in the world, to look at a goddamned cat?"

Though he may have found our fascination with domesticated animals incomprehensible, he was completely on board with our ice-cream obsession. I have such strong memories of my lactose-intolerant father sitting at the breakfast-room table after dinner with a pint of Häagen-Dazs, a spoon, and a stack of *Wall Street Journal*s, never looking up once until he had hit the bottom of that container of Vanilla Swiss Almond. Anyway, in France, our sugar teeth were suddenly considered culturally appropriate. Whereas my mother would never stop at a Baskin-Robbins just because I asked, if we saw a *couperie* in our travels, as long as it was after 10 a.m., we could pretty much always convince my parents to stop in. And you don't just drop by a *couperie* for a cone or a scoop—no, no, no, a *couperie* takes its ice-cream-sundae making very seriously, often listing thirty or more concoctions, with pictures and everything!

I do think there is a very particular art and skill to building the perfect coupe, and Christina Olufson is a master. In this refreshing and light summer sundae, she layers an intense strawberry sorbet and an icy watermelon granita with a small dice of strawberries and watermelon, mint, and whipped crème fraîche. Each layer keeps its own integrity and personality, but when you dig your spoon down deep and get a little bit of each layer, it's summer perfection in a glass.

1 cup ¾-inch-diced strawberries (from ½ pint)

¼ cup sugar

1 cup ¾-inch-diced watermelon (from ½ pound)

20 fresh mint leaves, torn into small pieces

¾ cup heavy cream

¼ cup crème fraîche

1 recipe Watermelon Granita (recipe follows)

1 recipe Strawberry Sorbet (recipe follows)

Toss the diced strawberries in a bowl with sugar, and let sit for 15 minutes. Add the diced watermelon and three-quarters of the mint, and gently combine with a large spoon.

Meanwhile, whip the cream and crème fraîche to soft peaks in the bowl of a stand mixer fitted with the whisk attachment (or by hand).

Set out six short 8-ounce glasses. Use a fork or metal spoon to scrape the watermelon granita. Then put one ice cream scoop of granita into the bottom of each glass. Add one scoop of strawberry sorbet atop the granita. Dollop 2 tablespoons of whipped cream, and arrange 2 heaping tablespoons of the fruit mixture on top.

Add another scoop each of watermelon granita and strawberry sorbet, followed by another dollop of whipped cream. Make a last beautiful layer of fruit, and sprinkle on the remaining torn mint leaves. Serve immediately.

watermelon granita

Traditionally, granita is not processed in an ice-cream machine but, rather, set to freeze and then scraped. I actually started out trying to make a sorbet, but had trouble with its being icy because of the high water content of watermelon. But when I tasted it all together, I actually liked the icy texture of the watermelon as a contrast to the rich and dense strawberry sorbet and the creamy whipped crème-fraîche-spiked cream. It's funny when it works out like that!

MAKES 1 QUART

5 cups diced watermelon, seeds removed (from about 3 pounds watermelon with rind)

½ cup sugar

2 tablespoons organic agave syrup

1 tablespoon tequila or vodka

3 tablespoons lemon juice

NOTE Homemade ice creams tend to get hard and icy, because they don't have as much air whipped into them as commercial ice creams and don't have any of the stabilizers often used. Alcohol doesn't freeze, and therefore keeps the granita less icy. You can leave it out if you like, but if so, make sure to take the granita out of the freezer at least 15 minutes before serving, because it will be very hard. The agave syrup yields a creamier granita or ice cream than granulated sugar.

Set the watermelon in a strainer over a large bowl for about 15 minutes, to remove any excess water. Then toss the watermelon in a large bowl with the sugar and agave syrup, and let sit 30 minutes. Transfer the fruit to a blender with the tequila and lemon juice. Purée until very smooth, and taste for balance.

Process the purée in an ice-cream maker according to the manufacturer's instructions. Leave mixture in the freezer for several hours to freeze completely.

strawberry sorbet

MAKES 1 QUART

5 cups sliced strawberries
(from 2 pounds fruit)

½ cup sugar

3 tablespoons organic agave
syrup

1 tablespoon gin or vodka

2 tablespoons freshly squeezed
lemon juice

NOTE Homemade ice creams tend to get hard and icy, because they don't have as much air whipped into them as commercial ice creams and don't have any of the stabilizers often used. Alcohol doesn't freeze, and therefore keeps the sorbet less icy. You can leave it out if you like, but if so, make sure to take the sorbet out of the freezer at least 15 minutes before serving, because it will be very hard. The agave syrup yields a creamier sorbet or ice cream than granulated sugar.

Slice the strawberries in half, and remove the stems. Toss the berries with the sugar and agave syrup, and let sit 30 minutes. Transfer the fruit to a blender with the gin and lemon juice. Purée until very smooth, and taste for balance and seasoning.

Process the purée in an ice-cream maker according to the manufacturer's instructions.

When choosing wine to pair with dessert, I often look to wines that are not sweet themselves, so as to keep the whole combination from becoming cloying. In other words, there can be too much of a good thing, particularly when we're talking about sugar. This dessert, with its candied strawberry and watermelon flavors, is a good example. I like to pair this recipe with a rosé, one that shows a good dose of melon and red berry fruit. California rosés, such as those made from Syrah, tend to be softer and fruitier, with more delicate acidity, which allows them to echo the softness of fruit in the dessert.

nectarine and blackberry galette
with buttermilk ice cream

In reality, for all the great dessert recipes in the universe, an open-faced fruit galette with a super-crumbly, buttery crust is my favorite way to enjoy summer fruit. The creamy almond filling that lies just below the fruit is based on a classic *crème d'amande* recipe I learned working in the pastry kitchen of a two-star restaurant in France way back in the day. This nut-based "cream" is made by puréeing nuts with butter, powdered sugar, brandy, a little flour, eggs, and egg yolks. I love using it as a layer of extra flavor and to give texture to crêpes and tarts. This is another one of those "feel free to experiment" recipes—if you prefer pistachios, hazelnuts, or pine nuts, substitute them for the almonds. And, any array of stone fruit and berries in the summer, or thinly sliced apples or pears in the fall and winter, works beautifully in this preparation.

SERVES 10 TO 12

4 ounces blanched almonds

½ cup confectioners' sugar

6 tablespoons unsalted butter, softened

2 tablespoons all-purpose flour

1 tablespoon good-quality brandy or rum

1 extra-large egg

1 extra-large egg yolk

3 yellow nectarines (about 1 pound)

4 tablespoons granulated sugar

2 tablespoons freshly squeezed orange juice

1 tablespoon freshly squeezed lemon juice

1 recipe Cornmeal Galette/ Crostata Dough (recipe follows), chilled

½ pint blackberries

2 tablespoons heavy cream

1 recipe Buttermilk Ice Cream (recipe follows)

In the bowl of a food processor fitted with a metal blade, combine the almonds and confectioners' sugar, and pulse four or five times, for about 2-second intervals, until the mixture resembles a coarse meal. Add the butter, flour, brandy, egg, and egg yolk, and blend until completely combined. This is the "almond cream."

Cut the nectarines in half, remove the pits, and then cut into ½-inch-thick slices. Toss the nectarine slices in a bowl with 3 tablespoons granulated sugar and the orange and lemon juices.

Preheat the oven to 400°F.

Line a baking sheet with parchment paper. Roll the chilled dough out to a 14-inch circle about ⅛ inch thick, and place on the prepared baking sheet.

Spread the almond cream in an even layer from the center outward, leaving a 3-inch border of dough. Arrange half the nectarines on top, followed by half the blackberries, and then continue with the remaining nectarines and berries. Using your hands, carefully fold the 3-inch border of dough over the fruit in circular, overlapping folds. Freeze the galette for 15 minutes (this buttery crust is best when cooked from very cold).

Brush the dough with heavy cream, and sprinkle with the remaining tablespoon granulated sugar.

Bake for 35 minutes, rotating the pan halfway through baking. Reduce the oven temperature to 350°F, and bake for another 10 minutes, until crust is golden and the fruits are cooked.

Cut six wedges from the galette (the galette will yield twelve portions), and place them on six dessert plates. Serve with scoops of buttermilk ice cream.

galette/crostata dough

Place the flour, salt, and sugar in the bowl of a food processor fitted with a metal blade, and pulse to combine. Scatter cubed butter evenly over the flour mixture, and pulse four or five times, for about 2-second intervals, until the mixture resembles a coarse meal with visible chunks of butter.

With the blade spinning, pour 4 tablespoons ice water into the bowl, and stop processing as soon as the dough clumps. (There is a moment when the coarse meal begins to look like ricotta, and then it quickly comes together as a ball of dough.)

Shape the dough into a 1-inch-thick flat disk, wrap in plastic, and chill for at least 1 hour.

VARIATION For Cornmeal Galette/Crostata Dough, add 3 tablespoons finely ground cornmeal to the flour mixture.

2¼ cups all-purpose flour

1 teaspoon kosher salt

¼ cup sugar

½ pound (2 sticks) unsalted butter, cold, cubed

buttermilk ice cream

2 cups heavy cream

1 cup whole milk

6 extra-large egg yolks

½ cup sugar

1 cup buttermilk

Combine the cream and milk in a medium saucepan over high heat. Warm the mixture until it scalds; as soon as tiny bubbles appear around the edges of the pan, remove from the heat.

Whisk the egg yolks and sugar together in a large bowl. Whisk a tablespoon of the warm cream mixture into the yolks to temper them. Slowly, add another few tablespoons or so of the warm cream, whisking constantly. At this point, you can add the rest of the cream mixture in a slow, steady stream, whisking all the time. Pour the mixture back into the pot, and return it to the stove.

Cook over medium-low heat for 5 to 7 minutes, stirring frequently with a rubber spatula, scraping the bottom and side of the pan. When the custard thickens and you feel some resistance as you stir, remove from the heat. Strain the custard into a bowl placed over an ice bath.

Stir in the buttermilk. Chill for at least 2 hours in the refrigerator. Process in an ice-cream maker according to the manufacturer's instructions.

I'm a sucker for this galette, with its buttery, crispy crust and vibrant fruit elements. It has just the right amount of decadence and sugar to be sweet without being overbearing or heavy. It also makes for a great wine-pairing opportunity. The fruit retains a bright, fresh quality even through baking, which allows it to pair well with a dry wine. I like to focus on the tartness of the nectarines in the recipe and look to a wine that reflects the same quality. I really like it with Chardonnay from California's Central Coast. These wines show ripe stone-fruit flavors, softening touches of oak, and vibrant, tart acidity. They have a delicate sweetness that allows them to work with desserts like this one that are bright and slightly savory.

crème fraîche cake with santa rosa plums and pistachios in olive oil

This is the perfect go-to summer dessert recipe. The light, fluffy cake batter has a lovely sour note from the crème fraîche, and it is layered with plum caramel and lots of ripe, juicy plums before being baked into crusty-topped deliciousness. Depending on what is available, we have added blackberries, or nectarines, and even made the whole recipe with figs instead of plums. In the heat of summer, when the market and my countertops are overflowing with super-ripe fruit, this cake is the perfect vehicle for the season's juicy, luscious delights. Although it's delicious without them, the pistachios in olive oil really push this cake into the stratosphere of wow factor—not necessary by any means, but oh so good.

MAKES ONE 9-INCH CAKE

18 tablespoons (2¼ sticks) unsalted butter, softened at room temperature, plus a little for the pan

2¾ cups all-purpose flour

1 cup sugar, plus 1 tablespoon for sprinkling

¼ cup semolina flour

1½ teaspoons baking powder

½ teaspoon baking soda

½ teaspoon kosher salt

1¼ cups crème fraîche

6 extra-large egg yolks

8 Santa Rosa or other ripe plums (about ¾ pound)

1 recipe Plum Caramel (recipe follows)

¾ cup heavy cream

1 recipe Sweet Pistachios in Olive Oil (page 300)

Prepare a 9-inch round springform pan by spreading butter on the inside surfaces, lining the bottom with parchment paper, and buttering the parchment.

Combine the flour, 1 cup sugar, the semolina, the baking powder, the baking soda, and the salt in the bowl of a stand mixer fitted with a paddle attachment, and paddle just to combine. Add the butter and ½ cup crème fraîche, and continue to paddle until the mixture starts to come together but is still crumbly. Add another ½ cup crème fraîche and the egg yolks, and then increase the speed to medium-high, paddling until the color lightens to a uniformly pale yellow.

Preheat the oven to 375°F.

Cut four of the plums in half, remove the pits, and then cut into ¾-inch wedges.

Spread half of the batter into the prepared cake pan. Drizzle ⅓ cup plum caramel over the batter, and arrange half the plum wedges on top. Dot the remaining half of the batter on top of the arranged plums and caramel, and gently spread to cover the plums. Arrange the rest of the plum wedges on top, and sprinkle with the remaining 1 tablespoon of sugar.

Bake for 30 minutes, then reduce oven temperature to 350°F and bake for another 30 minutes, until the cake begins to pull away from the sides of the pan and a toothpick inserted into the center comes out clean. The cake should be golden brown and spring back slightly when you touch the center. Cool the cake on a rack for at least 15 minutes.

Using a stand mixer fitted with the whisk attachment, whip the cream and the remaining ¼ cup crème fraîche together to soft peaks. (You can also do this by hand.) Cut the remaining three plums in half, remove the pits, and then cut into ¾-inch wedges.

Spoon 1½ tablespoons plum caramel onto each of six dessert plates. Cut six slices from the cake (which gives 10 to 12 slices total), and place them at the center of the plates. Dollop the whipped crème fraîche next to the cake, arrange three to four plum wedges around them, and spoon the pistachios over and around the cake.

plum caramel

NOTE This sauce can be a little tricky, especially depending on the water content of the particular plums you use. Make sure that the sugar has really caramelized and is a deep amber brown before adding the plum purée. The plum purée may cause the caramel to seize up at first, but just keep whisking and it will dissolve again and become a smooth sauce. Turn off the heat once it's dissolved, because if you reduce it too much it will become too sweet.

Slice the plums into small wedges, discarding the pits. Place the fruit in the blender with the brandy and lemon juice, and purée until very smooth.

Split the half vanilla bean in half lengthwise, and use a paring knife to scrape out the seeds and pulp into a medium saucepan. Add the vanilla pod, the sugar, and ½ cup water. Bring to a boil over medium heat, without stirring, and cook for about 10 minutes, swirling the pan occasionally, until the mixture is a deep amber color. Slowly add the plum-purée mixture, whisking constantly. (If the plum-purée mixture is added too quickly, the caramel can seize; keep whisking over medium heat and it will all come together again.) Continue cooking, until any sugar that has seized has dissolved. Turn off the heat and cool.

¾ pound plums (about 8 to 10, depending on the fruit size)

2 tablespoons good-quality brandy

1 tablespoon freshly squeezed lemon juice

½ vanilla bean

¾ cup sugar

The stars of this recipe are the luscious baked plums that are interlaced in the body of this creamy cake. I find that a great match for this is Late Harvest Viognier, a dessert wine that is produced in areas of central and nothern California as well as France's Rhône Valley. When made in an off-dry style, Viognier is taken to a new level of concentration, with intensified stone-fruit notes, aromatic baking spices, and tart acidity. It works well in this pairing, because its own plummy fruit flavors and spiciness blend in with those in the cake, while its acidity gives the combination a lift on the palate.

grilled fig leaf panna cotta with figs and melon sorbet

The restaurant business is an incestuous one, and we have seen more than a few couples result from our staffing choices. It's getting to a point where Caroline and I are considering taking a matchmaking fee from our more amorous employees. Seriously, we have God knows how many couples, three marriages, and two children under our belt as a result of love in the workplace at our restaurants, so it shouldn't really be a surprise that our pastry chef and A.O.C. chef de cuisine are a couple.

Sometimes when a cook dates a noncook or non-restaurant person (we call them "normal people"), those civilians are appalled by how much restaurant people want to go out, eat, and drink. So, when you get two restaurant people together, the eating-and-drinking plan can get a little crazy. Last summer, Christina Olufson and Lauren Herman planned a trip to northern California, and when I saw their dining itinerary, even I was impressed—back-to-back lunches and dinners, with even some midafternoon meals and stops at bars and pastry shops squeezed in. And it was a week long, a virtual marathon of wining and dining! Even knowing how much they love eating and drinking, I didn't honestly think they would really be able to complete this maniacal *tour de NoCal*. So, when they asked me to make them a reservation at my friends Russell Moore and Allison Hopelain's fantastic wood-burning mecca, Camino Restaurant, I actually told Allison I didn't think they would really make it.

But Lauren and Christina are like Lance Armstrongs of eating: they cannot be stopped, they start strong and finish strong, without the steroids. They were not going to miss Camino, and in the end it was their favorite meal and experience of the whole trip. While they were there, Allison served them a grilled fig-leaf ice cream, and Christina loved it so much that she came right back home and came up with this Grilled Fig Leaf Panna Cotta.

We actually use fig leaves quite a bit in the savory kitchen—wrapping fish in them to grill, baking goat cheese on them, and roasting pork with them—but this was the first time we used them in a dessert. The flavor is so hard to describe, the closest I can get is that they smell like coconut

¼-ounce package (2½ teaspoons) Knox powdered gelatin

5 or 6 fresh fig leaves, washed and dried

2 cups heavy cream

1 cup whole milk

½ cup sugar

Vegetable oil, for molds

2 tablespoons crème fraîche or yogurt

1 recipe Walnut Pain de Gênes (recipe follows)

1 recipe Walnut Lace Cookies (recipe follows)

9 ripe figs

½ ripe cavaillon, honeydew, or other melon

1 recipe Melon Sorbet (recipe follows)

milk and something else unique and exotic that I can't quite put my finger on. It only made sense to serve this fig-leaf panna cotta with fresh figs, summer melons, and melon sorbet. I love the way the rich, creamy panna cotta plays against the icy-cold and refreshing sorbet. In true restaurant form, we have taken it up a notch with a crispy walnut *tuile* and soft walnut *pain de Gênes* to augment the panna cotta. Honestly, it's delicious without those components, too, so if it seems like too much work, just skip those steps. But for a special occasion, or if you just love to bake, all the elements together are something very special.

Place ¼ cup cold water in a large bowl, sprinkle the gelatin over it, and gently swirl the bowl to combine.

Using tongs, gently grill 2 or 3 fig leaves for about 2 minutes, rotating frequently and being careful not to burn them. Or, alternatively, fan each leaf over a gas stove, without directly touching the flame, until the leaf begins to smell toasted. It is important that the leaves get toasted and have slightly golden-brown spots and edges but are not burned.

Combine the cream, milk, and fig leaves in a medium saucepan, and bring to a boil over high heat. Turn off the heat, cover, and let sit for 30 minutes, allowing the fig leaves to steep in the hot liquid.

Strain the leaves from cream mixture, discard them, and return the liquid to the saucepan. Heat this cream mixture over medium heat to a scald, add the sugar, and stir until it dissolves. Slowly whisk the cream mixture into the bloomed gelatin until completely incorporated.

Chill the cream mixture over an ice bath, stirring occasionally, until it's at room temperature or slightly cool.

Prepare six 3-inch ring molds (or individual ramekins) by lightly brushing vegetable oil on the inside surfaces.

Pour a small amount of the cream mixture into a bowl, and whisk in the crème fraîche or yogurt. Then whisk that thickened cream–crème-fraîche mixture back into the cream. (Tempering the cream this way creates a very smooth and silky panna cotta.)

Pour the panna-cotta cream into the prepared molds, and chill in the refrigerator for 2 to 3 hours, until set.

When ready to serve, cut the remaining three fig leaves in half and place them on each of six dessert plates. Cut six 3-inch circles of walnut *pain de Gênes* and place one in the middle of each fig leaf. Center one walnut lace cookie atop each cake. Carefully unmold the panna cottas on top of each cake-cookie stack. (To unmold, gently press your finger down on the panna cotta close to the edge, pulling lightly inward, to the center, and then moving your finger along the perimeter of the panna cotta. When flipped upside down, it should pop right out.)

Trim the stems of the figs, and cut each one in half. Place one fig half on top and one fig half on either side of each panna cotta. Thinly shave the melon with a vegetable peeler; weave the slices around the plates, and place scoops of melon sorbet nestled among the fruit.

walnut pain de gênes

MAKES ONE 13-BY-9½-INCH CAKE

Preheat oven to 350°F. Toast walnuts for 12 to 15 minutes, stirring every 3 minutes to be sure they don't burn. Cool to room temperature.

Prepare a 13-by-9½-inch cake pan by lightly buttering the inside surface, placing a piece of parchment on the bottom, and then lightly buttering the parchment.

Sift the cake flour, baking powder, and salt together, and set aside.

Combine the walnuts and sugars in the bowl of a food processor fitted with a metal blade. Pulse four or five times, until the mixture resembles a fine meal.

Measure out half of the mixture (1¼ cups) and set aside. With the blade spinning, drizzle the walnut oil over the remaining ground-nut mixture, and process for 30 seconds. (There will still be small walnut pieces, and the mixture won't be completely smooth.)

In the bowl of a stand mixer fitted with a paddle attachment, paddle the butter at medium-high speed for 2 minutes, until the mixture is light and fluffy. Add the dry walnut mixture, and continue to paddle for 2 minutes, until the butter is light and fluffy again.

Add the eggs, one at a time, and paddle at low speed until incorporated, scraping down the bowl as needed. Add the nut paste and paddle to combine, and then add the sifted dry ingredients, mixing just until there are no lumps.

Spread the batter evenly in the prepared pan. Bake for about 30 minutes, rotating the pan halfway through baking, until light golden brown and baked through. The cake should be spongy to the touch; if your finger leaves an indentation, the cake needs to cook a little longer.

Cool to room temperature.

2 cups raw walnut halves or pieces

8 tablespoons (1 stick) unsalted butter, at room temperature, plus more for the cake pan

6 tablespoons cake flour

¼ teaspoon baking powder

¼ teaspoon kosher salt

6 tablespoons granulated sugar

½ cup plus 2 tablespoons confectioners' sugar

2 tablespoons walnut oil or olive oil

2 extra-large eggs, at room temperature

walnut lace cookies

¾ cup raw walnut halves
   or pieces

2 tablespoons all-purpose flour

¼ teaspoon kosher salt

½ cup granulated sugar

2½ tablespoons unsalted butter

2 tablespoons firmly packed
   dark-brown sugar

2 teaspoons light corn syrup

¼ teaspoon pure vanilla extract

Combine the walnuts, flour, and salt in the bowl of a food processor fitted with a metal blade. Pulse four or five times, until the mixture resembles a medium-coarse meal. Remove the blade, and transfer the mixture to a large bowl.

Combine the granulated sugar, butter, brown sugar, and corn syrup in a medium saucepan, and bring to a boil over high heat. Turn off the heat, and stir in the vanilla extract. Pour into the bowl with the walnuts, and gently fold together with a rubber spatula.

Chill the dough in refrigerator for 2 hours.

Preheat the oven to 350°F.

Line a baking sheet with parchment paper. Scoop dough into roughly 2-teaspoon balls, then, using your hands, roll into perfectly round spheres, and place on prepared baking sheet, several inches apart. Bake for 10 to 12 minutes, until cookies are a deep amber color in the middle. (When cookies cool, they should be crispy; if soft in the middle, bake for 1 to 2 minutes more.)

melon sorbet

1 small ripe green- or orange-
   fleshed melon,
   about 2 pounds

¼ cup sugar

2 tablespoons honey

½ lemon, for juicing

Remove the rind and seeds, and cut the melon into 1½-inch chunks. Toss the melon with sugar and honey, and let sit for 30 minutes. Transfer the fruit to a blender, and purée until very smooth. Season with lemon juice to taste.

Process the purée in an ice-cream maker according to the manufacturer's instructions.

This super-aromatic and light-bodied dessert really needs to be paired with a delicate wine. Malvasia, vinified dry, from various regions in Italy and Portugal, is a great match for this. This variety is loaded with sweet melon and delicate white flower notes and tends to be light in body and only slightly acidic. It makes for a lovely apéritif, and its delicate freshness and aromatic qualities allow it to reflect the flavors that are present in this plating without overwhelming or clashing with them.

vanilla pot de crème with dulce de leche, marcona almonds, and a layer of chocolate

When I was a kid, I hated swimming lessons. We used to go once a week to the Glendale YMCA for the dreaded class. I think it was something about that locker-room–chlorine smell, or the way I always felt the old ladies with the bathing caps were looking at me funny, or maybe it was just having to get changed in public. I don't know what it was, but I used to get literally sick to my stomach just at the thought of going there. In fact, I used to use that sick-to-my-stomach line as much as I could, so that I could sit on the sidelines with my mom while my sister swam (it only worked about half the time).

What I did love about swim lessons, however, was that our route to Glendale drove us right by a Foster's Freeze. Most of the time, if I could balance complaining about my stomach and asking for an ice cream, I could usually sweet-talk my mom into a cone of soft-serve vanilla "ice cream" dipped in chocolate. Foster's Freeze is a classic southern-California soft-serve ice-cream stand that started in Inglewood in 1946, and those cones were the first time I ever experienced a Magic Shell—you know, that chocolate coating that magically hardens when it hits ice cream and hence creates a shell.

Years later, in the A.O.C. pastry kitchen, we were playing around with a Spanish-inspired pot de crème. (I know, it's hard for me to get away from the French thing, and, by the way, how much better is pot de crème than flan?) I envisioned our classic vanilla custard with a secret surprise of dulce de leche at the bottom, but I also wanted a chocolate element that would complement but not overwhelm the vanilla. I said to Christina, in a flashback to Foster's Freeze circa 1979, "What if we made a 'magic shell'?" so that the lucky diner would crack through a thin layer of hard chocolate, through the rich vanilla custard, to the dulce de leche at the bottom. After much research and testing, Christina figured out that just adding a little cocoa butter or grape-seed oil to the chocolate would create that shell. This dessert never fails to *wow*.

One 14-ounce can sweetened condensed milk

1½ cups whole milk

1½ cups heavy cream

2 vanilla beans

6 extra-large egg yolks

½ cup sugar

3½ ounces 68% dark chocolate

½ ounce cocoa butter, or 1½ teaspoons grape-seed oil

½ cup Marcona almonds

Place the can of condensed milk in a medium saucepan, cover with water by at least 2 inches, and bring to a simmer over medium heat. Cook for 4 hours, replenishing the water as needed. Let the can cool to room temperature before opening it to find the dulce de leche inside.

Combine the milk and 1 cup cream in a medium pot. Split the vanilla beans in half lengthwise, scrape out the seeds and pulp with a paring knife, and add them to the pot. Add the vanilla pods. Bring to a boil over high heat. Turn off the heat, cover, and let infuse for 30 minutes.

Preheat the oven to 325°F.

Using a stand mixer fitted with the whisk attachment, beat the egg yolks and sugar at high speed for about 3 minutes, until the mixture is thick and pale yellow. When you lift the whisk attachment, the mixture should form ribbons as it falls from the whisk. With the mixer at low speed, add the warm cream slowly, ¼ cup at a time, to temper the eggs. When half the cream has been incorporated, you can add the rest more quickly. Strain the mixture, and let sit for 20 minutes. Skim all traces of foam from the cream.

Spoon 2 tablespoons dulce de leche into the bottom of each of six coffee cups or ramekins. Pour the cream mixture on top, and place the cups in a roasting pan. Pour hot water into the pan to come halfway up the outsides of the cups, cover completely with foil, and bake in the oven for about 30 minutes, until the custard is just set.

Cool to warm and then chill in the refrigerator at least 4 hours.

Melt the chocolate and cocoa butter in a double boiler. One by one, spoon 1 tablespoon of the chocolate mixture onto each pot de crème, and immediately tip the cups to swirl the chocolate around the top of the custard, forming an even layer of chocolate. Chill until ready to serve.

Whip the remaining ½ cup cream to soft peaks, and chop the almonds coarsely. Spoon a dollop of whipped cream onto each pot de crème, and sprinkle the chopped Marconas over the top. Serve the pots de crème on pretty napkins set on dessert plates.

The dulce-de-leche element, with its nutty, caramel, sweet, and salty character, is the driving force behind my wine pairing. I find that Pedro Ximenez, made into sweet sherry and off-dry wine, is a great match. It is rich and unctuous with fruit flavors of prune and orange rind that highlight the vanilla element in the recipe. It is dark in both color and flavor, with notes of molasses, chocolate, and toasted hazelnut that form the perfect marriage with the toffeelike flavor and chocolate in this recipe.

ricotta cheesecake with dried fruit compote and walnut biscotti

The ricotta adds a nice lightness to this Italian-inspired cheesecake. In the fall, we love it with dried fruit compote, but it's also great with strawberries in spring, and figs, berries, and stone fruit in summer.

MAKES ONE 9-INCH CHEESECAKE

Preheat the oven to 325°F.

Brush the bottom and sides of an 8- or 9-inch springform pan with the oil, and line the bottom with parchment paper. Brush the parchment paper with oil, too.

Using a stand mixer fitted with the paddle attachment, beat the cream cheese and ricotta together for 3 to 4 minutes, until smooth. Split the half vanilla bean lengthwise, scrape out the seeds, and add them to the cheese. Add the sugar, and continue to run the mixer a few more minutes, until the mixture is smooth and slightly fluffy. With the machine running, add the eggs, one by one, and paddle to combine. Stir in the lemon juice, and transfer the mixture to the prepared pan.

Bake for about 45 minutes, until the cheesecake is just barely set and when you gently shake the pan the filling moves together as one—sort of like Jell-O. Cool in the pan, and then chill (still in the springform pan) for at least 4 hours or overnight.

Cut six slices (the cheesecake yields ten to twelve slices), making sure the paper on the bottom of the cheesecake is not still attached, and place the slices on six dessert plates. Spoon 2 tablespoons of the dried fruit compote over and around each slice. Serve the walnut biscotti on the side of each plate.

2 teaspoons vegetable oil

¾ pound good-quality cream cheese

2 cups fresh whole-milk ricotta cheese, drained if wet

½ vanilla bean

1½ cups sugar

6 extra-large eggs

1½ tablespoons freshly squeezed lemon juice

¾ cup Dried Fruit Compote (recipe follows)

1 recipe Walnut Biscotti (recipe follows)

dried fruit compote

½ vanilla bean

2 cups sugar

¼ cup dried apricots,
cut in quarters

¼ cup dried blueberries

¼ cup dried cherries

¼ cup golden raisins

¼ cup Thompson raisins

¼ cup dried plums, cut in half

2 strips of orange zest,
using a vegetable peeler

1 cinnamon stick

2 tablespoons freshly squeezed
orange juice

4 tablespoons freshly squeezed
lemon juice

NOTE This recipe calls for 1½ cups of dried fruit. I have listed the combination that we usually use, but feel free to mix it up however you like, as long as you have 1½ cups total fruit. At Tavern and The Larder we serve this compote over Scottish oatmeal with a little butter and salt swirled in—one of my favorite breakfasts. It will last for months in the refrigerator.

Split the half vanilla bean lengthwise, scrape out the seeds, and add the seeds, pulp, and pod to a medium saucepan with the sugar and 2 cups water. Bring to a boil over medium heat, swirling the pan until the sugar has dissolved completely.

Add the dried fruits, orange zest, and cinnamon stick to the pan. Bring it all just to a boil over high heat, then turn off the heat. Add the orange juice and lemon juice to cut the sweetness. Cool to room temperature.

walnut biscotti

Line a baking sheet with parchment paper.

Sift together the flour and baking powder. Stir in the salt.

In a stand mixer fitted with a whisk attachment, cream the butter and ¼ cup plus 2 tablespoons sugar at medium-high speed for 2 to 3 minutes, until the mixture is light and fluffy. Add the egg and orange zest, and beat until fluffy again. Add the dry ingredients slowly, and combine at low speed. Right before the dough comes together, add the walnuts, and mix for a couple of seconds, just to incorporate.

Turn the dough out onto a lightly floured work surface, and shape it into a log about 2 inches in diameter. Sprinkle with remaining 2 tablespoons sugar, and transfer to the prepared baking sheet.

Chill in freezer for 20 minutes. Preheat the oven to 350°F.

Bake for 30 to 35 minutes, rotating the baking sheet from front to back midway through the baking time, until the log is very light golden brown and firm to the touch; a toothpick inserted in the center will come out clean.

When the log has cooled completely (this works best if the log is cooked the day before), again preheat the oven to 350°F.

Slice the log on the diagonal into ¼-inch-thick biscotti. Place them cut-side up on a parchment-lined baking sheet, and bake for 12 to 15 minutes, flipping after about 7 minutes, until they are light golden brown.

1⅓ cups all-purpose flour

¾ teaspoon baking powder

¼ teaspoon kosher salt

4 tablespoons (½ stick) unsalted butter, softened at room temperature

½ cup sugar

1 extra-large egg

1 teaspoon finely grated orange zest

½ cup walnut halves or pieces

This cheesecake has a delicately nutty flavor and light texture, coming from the sheep's milk in the ricotta, that balances with the intensity and weight of the dried fruit in this plating. I find that Sauternes, with its sharp, intense alcohol-driven aromas and high-toned fruit notes, plays really well off of the tart milkiness of the cake. The wine's golden-raisin-like flavor meshes with the fruit in the recipe, while its spicier aspects connect with those of the biscotti.

s'mores with caramel popcorn and chocolate sorbet

Inspiration and favorite recipes can come from the strangest places. A few years ago, we were asked to cater a very famous and outspoken reality star's wedding. She had all kinds of crazy requests, including a mashed-potato bar where we would serve mashed potatoes in martini glasses with "assorted toppings." Don't worry, we talked her out of that one, but she was obsessed with having s'mores as a passed dessert after the wedding cake. We all grumbled and groaned, complaining about what a silly idea that was, until Breanne Varela, my pastry chef at the time, came up with this version of the fireside childhood treat that changed all of our minds. It was *so* good that I have served it at many a party, including my good friend Marc Vetri's Great Chefs Event for Alex's Lemonade Stand Foundation, not two but three years in a row, just because the guests keep requesting it.

As with so many things in life, what appears to be simple is really a lot of work! This recipe has five subrecipes, which, try as I might to combine them into one, just make more sense to keep separate, restaurant-style. The good news is, you can prep everything days in advance and assemble when you are ready to serve.

These s'mores make a great passed dessert (yes, our reality star was right) on their own, but I'm also giving instructions for how we serve them at the restaurant, with chocolate sorbet and candied caramel corn.

1 recipe Graham Crackers (recipe follows)

1 recipe Bittersweet Chocolate Ganache (recipe follows)

1 recipe Marshmallows (recipe follows)

1 recipe Caramel Popcorn (recipe follows)

1 recipe Chocolate Sorbet (recipe follows)

Arrange the oven rack at the highest position, and preheat the broiler to high.

Place the graham crackers on a baking sheet, and top each one with a square of chocolate ganache. Arrange a marshmallow cube centered on each chocolate.

Broil the s'mores for about 30 seconds to 1 minute, until the marshmallow is charred and bubbly. (You can also use a blowtorch to char the marshmallows quickly.)

Arrange the s'mores on a large platter, and serve with bowls of caramel corn and scoops of chocolate sorbet alongside; or make individual servings by placing two s'mores on each plate, setting a scoop of sorbet next to them, and scattering the caramel corn over the top and around the plate.

graham crackers

MAKES ABOUT TWENTY-FOUR
2-BY-2-INCH GRAHAM CRACKERS

3 heaping tablespoons
    mild-flavored honey,
    such as orange blossom

3 tablespoons whole milk

1½ teaspoons pure vanilla extract

1 cup all-purpose flour,
    plus more for dusting

⅓ cup whole-wheat flour

⅓ cup packed dark-brown sugar

½ teaspoon baking soda

Scant ½ teaspoon kosher salt

3½ tablespoons unsalted butter,
    cold, cut into small pieces

3 tablespoons granulated sugar

¾ teaspoon ground cinnamon

Combine the honey, milk, and vanilla in a small bowl, and set aside.

Combine both the flours, brown sugar, baking soda, and salt in the bowl of a food processor fitted with a metal blade. Pulse to combine. Add the butter, and pulse for about fifteen 1-second pulses, or until the mixture resembles fine meal. Add the honey-milk mixture, and pulse for about seven 2-second pulses, or until the dough just comes together.

Turn the dough out onto a piece of plastic, and pat it into a disk. (It will be quite sticky.) Wrap the disk tightly in the plastic, and put it in the refrigerator for at least 2 hours to chill, or for up to 3 days.

Preheat the oven to 350°F.

Stir the granulated sugar, cinnamon, and a pinch of salt together to make the cinnamon sugar.

Roll the dough out on a work surface generously dusted with flour (or between two sheets of plastic, if it's especially sticky) to an ⅛-inch-thick rectangle. Using a straight-edge as a guide, cut the rectangle into 2-inch squares (a pizza cutter works well, if you have one). Reroll the scraps to cut out more squares. You can shape any leftover dough into what my friend Mike Chessler (see page 158) calls the "chef's cookie"—for the chef to eat herself, or use to placate a needy child or mate.

Dust the squares liberally with cinnamon sugar, and carefully transfer them to a baking sheet. Bake the graham crackers for 16 to 18 minutes, until they are deep golden brown and crispy all the way through.

bittersweet chocolate ganache

Place the chocolate in a mixing bowl, and line a 13-by-9-inch baking dish with plastic.

Pour the cream into a small, heavy-bottomed saucepan. Cook over high heat until it scalds. As soon as tiny bubbles form around the edges of the pot, begin counting. After 30 seconds, pour the hot cream mixture over the chocolate and let it sit for 1 minute to melt the chocolate. Whisk together, working quickly and vigorously from the center toward the edges of the pan to prevent the mixture from "breaking," until they form a homogenous mixture.

While it is still hot, pour the ganache into the prepared pan and use an offset spatula to spread it as evenly as possible. It will be about ¼ inch deep. Chill in the refrigerator for about 1 hour, or until the ganache is set.

Lift the ganache out onto a clean cutting board. Using a straight-edge and a rolling cutter or knife, cut the chocolate into 1¾-inch-by-1¾-inch squares. Remember to peel away any plastic.

½ pound chopped bittersweet chocolate

1 cup heavy cream

marshmallows

MAKES ABOUT 50 1-BY-1-INCH MARSHMALLOWS

Line an 8-by-8-inch baking dish with a sheet of plastic wrap. Brush the plastic wrap with the grape-seed oil, or spray it with nonstick cooking spray.

Pour ¼ cup cool water into the bowl of a stand mixer fitted with the whisk attachment, and sprinkle the gelatin over the water. Set aside to bloom.

Meanwhile, combine the sugar, corn syrup, and ¼ cup water in a medium saucepan. Fasten a candy thermometer to the pan, bring the mixture to a boil over medium heat, and boil, without stirring, for about 5 minutes, until the temperature reaches 240°F.

Slowly pour the mixture into the bowl with the gelatin, and whip at medium speed for 2 to 3 minutes. Use a paring knife to cut the ½ vanilla bean lengthwise, and scrape all the tiny seeds into the bowl, discarding the pod. (Or add the vanilla extract.) Mix at high speed for 5 more minutes, or until it's white, fluffy, and glossy; the mixture will double in volume.

Spread the marshmallow into the prepared pan. (No surprise that it will

1 tablespoon grape-seed oil or unflavored nonstick cooking spray, for the pan

¼ ounce package (heaping 2¼ teaspoons) Knox powdered gelatin

1 cup granulated sugar

¼ cup light corn syrup

½ vanilla bean, or 1 teaspoon pure vanilla extract

be sticky, but do your best to smooth the top into as even a layer as possible.) Set aside for about 5 minutes, to cool to room temperature.

Spray the top with pan spray, or brush gently with grape-seed oil. (This prevents the marshmallow from sticking when you cut it into pieces.) Use scissors to cut the marshmallow into 1½-by-1½-inch cubes. Store in an airtight container for up to several days.

caramel popcorn

MAKES 6 CUPS

1 tablespoon grape-seed or canola oil

¼ cup popcorn kernels

¾ cup packed dark-brown sugar

½ cup light corn syrup

8 tablespoons (1 stick) unsalted butter

½ teaspoon pure vanilla extract

½ teaspoon baking soda

1¼ teaspoons kosher salt

Preheat the oven to 300°F.

Line a baking sheet with parchment paper.

Combine the oil and popcorn kernels in a large, wide skillet. Cover the pan, and pop over high heat, shaking the pan constantly to prevent burning, for about 5 minutes, or until nearly all of the kernels have popped. Transfer just the popped kernels into a large mixing bowl.

Wipe out the pan, discarding any unpopped kernels, and return it to the stove. Add the brown sugar, corn syrup, and butter. Cook over high heat, and bring the mixture to a boil, stirring occasionally. Turn off the heat, and stir in vanilla, baking soda, and 1 teaspoon salt.

Drizzle the caramel over the popcorn, and quickly toss to coat as evenly and thoroughly as possible. Spread the caramel corn on the prepared baking sheet in a single layer.

Bake for about 20 minutes, stirring the caramel corn and rotating the pan after 10 minutes for even cooking. To test for doneness, remove a piece or two from the oven and let it cool for 2 or 3 minutes before tasting it; when you taste it, it should be crispy and the sugar shouldn't stick to your teeth. If it does, let the popcorn cook for a few minutes longer, then test it again. You don't want to cook it too long, or it will get the bitter taste of burnt sugar.

Remove the caramel corn from the oven, and sprinkle it with the remaining ¼ teaspoon salt.

chocolate sorbet

Place the chocolate in a large bowl.

Bring the water and corn syrup to a boil, and carefully pour one-quarter of the syrup over the chocolate. Let sit for 1 minute, and then whisk the mixture until emulsified. Pour in another quarter of the syrup, whisk again until re-emulsified, and then add the remaining half of the syrup and whisk until well combined.

Chill for at least 1 hour in the refrigerator.

Process in an ice-cream maker according to the manufacturer's instructions.

5½ ounces 70% bittersweet chocolate

1¾ cups water

⅓ cup corn syrup

Every adult reverts to memories of childhood at the mere mention of s'mores. This more grown-up, refined version provides that same graham-cracker-and-chocolate flavor in a bite-sized, elegant package. They pair really well with Banyuls, a fortified wine from the Languedoc-Roussillon region of France. Made predominantly from Grenache Noir, this wine is similar to vintage port, but with far less concentration and more acidity, making it slightly lighter and far less cloying. It has a dark, figgy fruit quality that mirrors the dark sweetness of the chocolate, as well as a cinnamon spiciness that works well with the flavor of the graham cracker.

roasted pear crisp with cranberries and yogurt sherbet

Yes, yes, yes. I know it would be easier just to toss the raw pears with the cranberries. Trust me, I tried it. But it was just not as delicious as this version, where the pears are pan-roasted before being layered with the cranberry compote and topped with a crisp, crumbly mixture. Use this crisp topping all year long with apples, berries, and stone fruit as well.

MAKES ONE 8-BY-10-INCH PAN, OR EQUIVALENT

1¼ cups all-purpose flour

½ cup plus 2 tablespoons granulated sugar, plus 4 teaspoons or as needed for skillet and baking dish

¼ cup dark-brown sugar, plus 2 tablespoons for the pan

½ teaspoon kosher salt

¼ teaspoon ground cinnamon

Pinch freshly grated nutmeg

12 tablespoons (1½ sticks) unsalted butter, cold, cut into small pieces, plus more for the pan

12 ripe but firm pears, preferably Comice or D'Anjou, peeled, cut into 1-inch wedges (about 5 pounds)

1 recipe Cranberry Compote (recipe follows)

1 recipe Yogurt Sherbet (recipe follows)

Preheat the oven to 375°F.

Combine the flour, ½ cup plus 2 tablespoons granulated sugar, ¼ cup dark-brown sugar, salt, cinnamon, and nutmeg in the bowl of a food processor fitted with a metal blade. Pulse a few times, just to combine the ingredients. Add 8 tablespoons cold butter, and pulse just until the butter and dry ingredients come together and resemble a coarse meal. Turn the meal out into a bowl and use your fingers to squeeze it into clumps. Transfer the topping to an airtight container, and refrigerate it until you are ready to use it.

Heat a cast-iron skillet over high heat for 1 minute. Add 1 tablespoon butter, and sprinkle 1 teaspoon of the granulated sugar evenly over the bottom of the skillet. Add half the pears cut-side down in a single layer. (You will need to cook the pears in batches.) Cook the pears for about 6 minutes without moving them, until the undersides are golden brown. Use tongs or a spoon to turn the pears to caramelize the other cut sides in the same way; turn each pear as it is done, because some will brown faster than others; be careful not to overcook them, because they will turn mushy. The second side will brown much faster–about 2 minutes. Remove the pears from the skillet to a sheet pan in a single layer, and let cool to room temperature.

Wipe out the pan with paper towels, and cook the remaining pears in the same way, adding butter and granulated sugar to the pan before adding the pears, as before.

To assemble the crisp, rub a little butter on the inside surfaces of an 8-by-10-inch baking dish, and sprinkle remaining 2 tablespoons brown sugar over the butter. Arrange half of the roasted pears in the pan and spoon half of the cranberry compote over them. Top with the remaining pears, generously dollop the rest of the compote over the fruit, and sprinkle the crisp topping on the top.

Place the dish on a baking sheet to catch any juices that bubble over, and bake for 30 to 40 minutes, until the crisp topping is golden brown and the fruit is bubbling up around the edges. Remove the crisp from the oven, and let it cool slightly before serving. Serve with yogurt sherbet.

cranberry compote

2 cups fresh or frozen cranberries
2 ounces dried cranberries
¼ cup sugar
1 cinnamon stick
Grated zest of ½ orange
½ vanilla bean

I love the textural difference between the dried and fresh cranberries. We do this with our blueberry compote as well; it's not necessary, but it's lovely to have that little chewy texture in with the luscious cooked fruit.

MAKES ABOUT 1 CUP

Combine the fresh or frozen cranberries, dried cranberries, sugar, and cinnamon stick in a medium saucepan. Add 1 cup water. Sprinkle the orange zest over the pan. Scrape the vanilla seeds out of the ½ vanilla bean, and drop the seeds and bean pod into the pan. Bring to a boil over high heat. Reduce the heat, and simmer the compote, stirring occasionally, until the cranberries are tender and the compote is thickened, 15 to 25 minutes.

Cool to room temperature. Remove and discard the cinnamon stick and vanilla pod. Use, or transfer to an airtight container and refrigerate for up to 2 weeks.

yogurt sherbet

Vanilla ice cream better look out! A few months back, I finally broke down and got a home ice-cream maker. Our family (basically, my kids) went nuts, churning everything they could into ice cream. And the winner? The house favorite with the 6-and-under set? Not peanut butter, not strawberry, but this tangy and brightly flavored yogurt sherbet!

MAKES 1 QUART

1 pound plain whole milk yogurt (my favorite is Straus Family Creamery)

1 tablespoon vodka

½ teaspoon pure vanilla extract

¼ cup organic agave syrup

1½ cups whole milk

½ cup sugar

NOTE Homemade ice creams tend to get hard and icy, because they don't have as much air whipped into them as commercial ice creams and don't have any of the stabilizers often used. Alcohol doesn't freeze, and therefore helps the sherbet to be less icy. You can leave it out if you like, but if so, make sure to take the sherbet out of the freezer at least 15 minutes before serving, since it will be very hard. The agave syrup yields a creamier sherbet or ice cream than granulated sugar.

Stir the yogurt, vodka, vanilla, and agave syrup together in a medium bowl, and set aside.

Combine 1 cup of the milk with the sugar in a large saucepan, and bring it to a boil over high heat. Turn off the heat, and stir in the remaining ½ cup of milk. Ladle out about ½ cup of the warm milk, and gradually add it to the bowl with the yogurt, whisking constantly. Continue to add the warm milk in this way until you have added all of it.

Transfer the mixture to an airtight container, and refrigerate for several hours, until chilled completely.

Process the cold yogurt mixture in an ice-cream maker according to the manufacturer's instructions.

Pairing wine with this crisp is a matter of balance. Too much sugar makes for a cloying experience, but not enough sweetness makes the pairing fall flat. With this recipe, I've had matchmaking success with Moscatel Dulce, a dessert wine from southern Spain. This wine tends to be fairly sweet, displaying notes of white flowers, high-toned white fruit notes, gingerlike spice, and a hint of acidity. Depending on the age of the vines and style of winemaking, this wine can have an element of caramel that blends with the spice and toast of the roasted pears in the recipe. The addition of yogurt sherbet brings a tartness and textural contrast that brightens the pairing and balances it all on the palate.

pink lady apple crostata with whipped mascarpone and armagnac prunes

2¾ pounds Pink Lady apples, peeled, cored, and cut into 1-inch slices

¼ cup plus 1 tablespoon granulated sugar

4 tablespoons (½ stick) unsalted butter, cold, cubed

1 recipe Galette/Crostata Dough (page 315), chilled

2 tablespoons heavy cream

½ pound mascarpone

1 recipe Armagnac Prunes (recipe follows)

Kosher salt

My cravings for this dish convince me that I must have been a grandmother in the southwestern region of France at some point in my cosmic journey. When I lived in France for a year, back in the early 1990s, I worked for a time in the Landes region, and I used to love riding my *bicyclette* around the low-lying hills and seeing small foie-gras farms and Armagnac distillers that really just looked like tiny farmhouses. Prunes are, oddly enough, a treasured treat in our house. I love them, my kids love them, my husband thinks we are nuts!

It makes complete sense, in the "what grows together goes together" school of thought, that prunes and Armagnac pair so beautifully, because the most coveted prunes in France are from Agen, less than 85 miles from the town of Armagnac. Cooked into a silky, boozy, luscious sauce flecked with chewy pieces of sweet, dense fruit, the Armagnac prunes are far more than the sum of their parts. When they're spooned over a buttery-crusted apple galette—man, I can feel the wind blowing through my hair as I ride through those hillsides on a crispy winter day in Les Landes.

SERVES 10 TO 12

Preheat the oven to 350°F.

Place 1¼ pounds of apple slices in a shallow baking dish. Add ¼ cup water, and sprinkle 1 tablespoon granulated sugar over the fruit. Cover the pan with aluminum foil, and bake the apples for 1½ to 2 hours, until they are tender and soft. Remove the apples from the oven, and set them aside to cool to room temperature. Purée the apples, along with any juices, in a blender, until smooth.

Place the butter in a small saucepan over medium-high heat. Cook for a few minutes, swirling the pan often, until the butter browns and smells nutty.

Pour the browned butter into a large bowl with the remaining apple slices (1½ pounds), 3 tablespoons sugar, and a healthy pinch of salt. Toss to coat the fruit evenly.

Line a baking sheet with parchment paper. On a lightly floured work surface, roll the chilled dough out to a 14-inch circle about ⅛ inch thick, and place on the prepared baking sheet.

Preheat the oven to 400°F.

Spread the apple purée in the center of the dough with an offset spatula, leaving a 3-to-4-inch border for the edge of the crust. Mound the apple slices on top of the apple purée. Fold the crust over apples, creating a rustic, free-form tart. Chill the tart in the freezer for 15 minutes.

Brush the crust with the cream, and sprinkle with remaining tablespoon sugar.

Bake for 35 minutes, rotating the pan halfway through baking. Reduce the oven temperature to 350°F, and bake for about another 10 minutes, until the crust is golden and apples are cooked.

Mix the mascarpone in a medium bowl until smooth and the consistency of softly whipped cream.

To serve, heat the prunes until the caramel is fluid enough to drizzle. Cut six slices from the crostata (the crostata serves ten to twelve), and place them on six dessert plates. Arrange about five prune halves over and around each slice, drizzle additional caramel on the plates, and dollop with generous spoonfuls of whipped mascarpone.

armagnac prunes

MAKES 2 CUPS

Place the prunes in a small bowl, and soak in Armagnac overnight (or longer).

In a small saucepan, melt the butter with the cream.

Combine the sugar, corn syrup, and 1 tablespoon water in a medium saucepan, and bring to a boil over medium heat without stirring. Cook for about 10 minutes, swirling the pan occasionally, until the mixture is a deep-amber color.

Slowly add the melted-butter mixture, whisking constantly. Continue cooking for another minute longer, then remove caramel from the heat, stir in the salt, and let cool.

Stir in the Armagnac-soaked prunes. Refrigerate until ready to use.

5 ounces prunes (about 15), pitted and cut in half

1 cup Armagnac

3 tablespoons unsalted butter

1 cup heavy cream

½ cup sugar

2 tablespoons light corn syrup

½ teaspoon kosher salt

I love this crostata and the way it balances the bright, tart flavors in the apples with the dark and concentrated quality of the Armagnac-soaked prunes. It's a little bit like the story of Goldilocks: it's not too heavy, not too light, it's just right. For pairing, I like to work off of this same idea and use a wine that has a good amount of sweet fruitiness as well as high-toned acidity. I find that Late Harvest Chardonnay fits this bill, because it has a naturally applelike character that is on the brighter side of the flavor spectrum, allowing the wine to complement the flavors in the apples themselves. Of course, being a dessert wine, the Chardonnay has a concentration of texture and syrupy richness that works well with the alcohol in the prunes.

spiced "pumpkin" fritters with chocolate sauce and candied pepitas

Think of these as pumpkin-pie doughnuts. Do I need to say more? Oh, with chocolate sauce and candied, spiced pepitas. I actually find fried desserts to be great for dinner parties. You can do the prep ahead and still get that *wow* factor at the table—I mean, who doesn't like pumpkin pie *and* doughnuts?!

You will notice that these "pumpkin" fritters are actually made using winter squash. I find real pumpkin to often be very watery and lacking in flavor so I prefer the richness and sweetness of squash such as kabocha or butternut.

MAKES ABOUT 20 FRITTERS

½ kabocha or butternut squash, about 1 pound

¼ cup whole milk

2 teaspoons dry yeast

3 cups all-purpose flour

1 teaspoon kosher salt

1½ teaspoons ground cinnamon

½ teaspoon ground ginger

¼ teaspoon ground cardamom

⅛ teaspoon freshly grated nutmeg

⅛ teaspoon ground cloves

4 tablespoons (½ stick) unsalted butter, melted, plus a little for the bowl

1 extra-large egg

⅔ cup dark-brown sugar

½ teaspoon pure vanilla extract

1 cup granulated sugar

2 to 3 quarts vegetable oil, for frying

1 recipe Chocolate Sauce (recipe follows)

1 recipe Candied Pepitas (recipe follows)

NOTE While the fritter batter rises, prepare the chocolate sauce and fried pepitas.

Preheat the oven to 400°F.

Cut the squash in half lengthwise, and place on a baking sheet cut-side up. (Don't remove the seeds yet; they give extra flavor.) Cover with foil, and roast for about 1 hour, until very tender. Let cool for 10 minutes, and then scoop out the seeds and discard them. Purée the warm squash through a ricer or food mill, and measure out ½ cup. (You can reheat any leftover purée, season it with salt, pepper, and butter, and eat it for dinner!)

In a large bowl, heat ¼ cup water and the milk to body temperature. Sprinkle yeast evenly across the surface, and allow the yeast to bloom for 10 to 15 minutes.

Whisk the flour, salt, ½ teaspoon cinnamon, and the other spices together, and then sprinkle across bloomed yeast. Make a well in the center, and set aside.

Combine the squash purée, butter, egg, brown sugar, and vanilla, and pour into the well of the dry ingredients. Fold together with a rubber spatula until incorporated; be careful not to overmix the batter, or the fritters will be tough. (Some specks of flour are OK.)

Lightly brush a large bowl with melted butter. Scrape batter into the bowl, and flip the batter upside down, so that all sides are covered with a little of

the melted butter. Cover with plastic, and allow the batter to rise in a warm, draft-free place for about 1 hour, until doubled in size.

Let the batter rest for at least 1 hour in the refrigerator, and then bring it to room temperature when you are ready to fry. (Chilling the batter in the fridge develops the flavor and creates more tender fritters.)

Combine 1 cup granulated sugar with the remaining 1 teaspoon cinnamon in a large bowl, and set aside.

Heat the oil to 350°F on a deep-frying thermometer, over medium heat, in a heavy, wide-bottomed pan.

Scoop heaping tablespoons of batter, and use a second spoon to push rounded spoonfuls into the hot oil. Don't overcrowd the pan; the fritters shouldn't be touching. Fry for 2 to 3 minutes, until deep golden brown on all sides.

Drain the fritters on paper towels, and pat to remove any excess oil. While they're still hot, toss fritters in the bowl with cinnamon-sugar mixture. Pile the fritters up on a platter, or divide among six dessert plates. Drizzle with ¾ cup chocolate sauce, sprinkle with candied pepitas, and serve remaining chocolate sauce on the side for dipping.

chocolate sauce

MAKES ABOUT 1 CUP

Chop the chocolate into small chunks, and place in a large bowl.

In a saucepan, combine the sugar with ⅔ cup water, and bring to a boil. Add the cocoa powder to the boiling water, and whisk to combine. Bring to a boil again, whisking constantly, and then immediately pour the water over the chopped chocolate, and let sit for 1 minute to melt the chocolate. Whisk together until combined, working from the inside out, to emulsify the mixture. Cool to room temperature.

3 ounces 68% dark chocolate

3 tablespoons sugar

¼ cup good-quality unsweetened cocoa powder

candied pepitas

¼ teaspoon cumin seeds

2 teaspoons unsalted butter

½ cup raw pumpkin seeds

1 tablespoon sugar

Generous pinch each of kosher
    salt, ground cinnamon,
    freshly grated nutmeg,
    and ground cloves

1 teaspoon honey

Toast the cumin seeds in a small pan over medium heat for 2 to 3 minutes, until the seeds release their aroma and are lightly browned. Pound them coarsely in a mortar.

Melt the butter in the cumin pan over medium heat. Add the pumpkin seeds and sugar, then sprinkle the salt and spices over them. Toss the pumpkin seeds to coat them well with the butter, and cook a few minutes, until just after they begin to pop and color slightly.

Turn off the heat, and wait for 30 seconds. Add the honey, tossing well to coat the pumpkin seeds. Spread on a plate, and let them cool.

This dessert needs to be paired with a wine that will accentuate the exotic spice elements of the fritters while also complementing the chocolate in the sauce. I find that Monastrell Dulce from the Jumilla region of Spain works really well. Monastrell when vinified dry is a dark, ripe, and fruit-laden wine. When it's off-dry, its flavors are intensified into a seductively soft and rich potion with plum and fig fruit notes and elements of chocolate, espresso, and spicy smoke. It has the right amount of cocoa to work with, and not be overpowered by, the chocolate sauce, and a spiciness and softness of texture to marry with the fritters.

butterscotch pot de crème with salted cashew cookies

Some recipes just torture us chefs, in a way. We love that people love them, but it's funny that sometimes we end up almost resenting those dishes that are most beloved by our guests, because it seems that, no matter what we do, everyone still just wants short ribs and butterscotch pot de crème. Now, don't get me wrong: this dessert is amazing, maybe just too good for its own, or, should I say, Christina's good. I just tell her it's her own fault and she shouldn't have made it so delicious!

NOTE This is another great make-ahead dessert that never fails to please the crowd, but make sure to chill the pots de crème completely before serving.

6 tablespoons unsalted butter

1 cup brown sugar, tightly packed

½ teaspoon kosher salt

1 cup whole milk

2 cups heavy cream

6 extra-large egg yolks

¼ teaspoon fleur de sel

1 recipe Salted Cashew Cookies (recipe follows)

Preheat the oven to 325°F.

Melt the butter in a medium saucepan over medium heat. Stir in the sugar and salt, and stir. When the sugar has dissolved, add the milk and 1½ cups cream, and bring to a boil over medium heat. Turn off the heat.

Whisk the egg yolks in a bowl, and then whisk a few tablespoons of the hot cream mixture into the yolks to temper them. Slowly, add another ⅓ cup or so of warm cream, whisking constantly. At this point, you can add the rest of the cream mixture in a slow, steady stream, whisking all the time. Pour the mixture back into the pot, and return it to the stove.

Cook the custard over medium heat for 6 to 8 minutes, stirring frequently with a rubber spatula, scraping the bottom and sides of the pan. The custard will thicken, and when it's done it will coat the back of the spatula. Strain the mixture, and pour it into six coffee cups or ramekins. Place them in a roasting pan, and pour hot water into the pan to come halfway up the outsides of the cups. Cover completely with foil, and bake for 30 to 40 minutes, until the custard is just set.

Let cool in the water bath for 15 minutes, and then chill for at least 4 hours before serving.

Just before serving, place the remaining ½ cup heavy cream in the bowl of a stand mixer fitted with the whisk attachment. Whip at medium-high speed until you have very soft peaks (you can also do this by hand).

Top each pot de crème with a generous dollop of whipped cream and a sprinkling of fleur de sel. Serve the pots de crème on pretty napkins set on dessert plates, with the cookies next to them.

salted cashew cookies

½ pound (1⅔ cups) cashews

8 ounces (2 cups) all-purpose flour

1 teaspoon baking soda

8 tablespoons (1 stick) unsalted butter, softened

1½ cups (½ pound) dark-brown sugar

1 extra-large egg

1 teaspoon pure vanilla extract

½ teaspoon fleur de sel

Kosher salt

Preheat the oven to 350°F.

Spread the cashews on a baking sheet, and toast for 8 to 10 minutes, until they're lightly browned and smell nutty. When the nuts have cooled, chop them coarsely.

Sift the flour and baking soda together. Add ¼ teaspoon kosher salt.

In a stand mixer fitted with the paddle attachment, cream the butter and sugar at medium-high speed for 3 to 4 minutes, until the mixture is light and fluffy. Add the egg and vanilla extract, and beat until fluffy again. Add the dry ingredients slowly, and mix at low speed. Stir in the fleur de sel and the cashews.

Scoop 1-tablespoon balls of dough, and place them 1 inch apart on a parchment-lined baking sheet. Bake for 18 to 20 minutes, until the cookies are crispy on the edges but still a little soft in the center.

On its own, this is a pretty rich and weighty dessert, so, rather than just marrying flavors, I want to pair it with something that will provide a sense of lightness and lift on the palate. And although this is supposed to be a wine pairing, I recommend sipping on a small batch, long-aged bourbon when digging into this pudding. Bourbons that are made in an artisanal vein become dark and syrupy, with heady caramel and molasses notes. They make lovely companions to rich desserts, because they have a definite sweetness and candied quality, but they are, of course, highly alcoholic, and must be consumed slowly and carefully. The alcoholic heat in the finish on the palate works in much the same way as the acidity does in a wine. It provides a break to the buttery aspect of both the pot de crème and the bourbon itself and, like the fleur de sel in the recipe, brings a brightening contrast on the palate.

persimmon cake with crème fraîche and maple pecans

Crisp, crunchy varieties of persimmons, like Fuyus, are great eaten out of hand, sliced into salads, and diced into salsas, but this cake is the perfect way to show off the softer Hachiya types, which need to be completely soft before they are eaten. My palate has strange textural issues—mostly that I like some oddball ones that other people generally don't appreciate. Bring on the chewy, the stringy, the slimy, and even snotty textures! The strange gelatinous interior of a super-ripe persimmon reminds me of an aloe plant in a way, and I think it's that very dense and wet texture that makes this cake so ethereal. This recipe was inspired by farmer James Birch of Flora Bella Farm, who is, shall we say, a little spacey, in the most charming and lovely way—meaning that sometimes he forgets to let anyone know what he's growing and what he would like to sell. When he comes for lunch, for example, I'll ask him, "Hey, James, how's it going?" Then he'll just happen to mention, "Well, I do have four cases of very ripe chocolate persimmons on my truck." Thank goodness, Christina and the gang are used to this type of kooky farmer behavior, so she responded, "Great! Let's bake a cake or two." I love that these persimmons actually taste of fall and winter—as if they have been grown in fields of cinnamon, nutmeg, and clove. It's very strange but so magical to have those flavors reinforced by the fruit itself. This is a great one for the Thanksgiving or Christmas buffet.

MAKES ONE 10-INCH CAKE

1¾ cups (approximately 3½ sticks) unsalted butter, at room temperature, plus a little for the pan

About 3 ripe Hachiya persimmons (to yield 1 cup puréed flesh)

2½ cups all-purpose flour

1 teaspoon baking soda

1½ teaspoons baking powder

½ teaspoon ground cardamom

¼ teaspoon freshly grated nutmeg

½ teaspoon ground cinnamon

Pinch ground cloves

¼ teaspoon kosher salt

1 cup heavy cream

½ teaspoon pure vanilla extract

1½ cups sugar

2 extra-large eggs

¼ cup crème fraîche

1 recipe Maple Pecans (recipe follows)

Preheat the oven to 350° F.

Prepare a 10-inch round cake pan by lightly buttering the inside surfaces, lining the bottom with parchment paper, and buttering the parchment.

Cook 4 tablespoons butter (½ stick) in a small saucepan over high heat for a few minutes, swirling the pan, until the butter browns and smells nutty. Set aside to cool.

Scoop the ripe flesh from the persimmons, and purée in a blender until smooth. Measure out 1 cup purée.

Whisk together flour, baking soda, baking powder, the spices, and salt in a small bowl, and set aside.

In another bowl, combine the purée, ¼ cup cream, vanilla, and cooled browned butter.

Paddle the remaining 1½ cups butter and the sugar in the bowl of a stand mixer at medium-high for 3 minutes, until light and fluffy. Add eggs one at a time, scraping down the sides of the bowl after each egg.

Decrease the paddle speed to low. Alternately add the flour mixture and persimmon-purée mixture to the bowl, in three additions, beginning and ending with the flour mixture.

Evenly spread the batter into the prepared pan. Bake for about 1 hour, until cake feels springy to the touch.

Whip the remaining ¾ cup cream and the crème fraîche to soft peaks.

Cut six slices from the cake (the cake will yield ten to twelve servings), and place on six dessert plates. Dollop with whipped crème fraîche, and scatter the candied pecans over the cake and around the plate.

maple pecans

NOTE Maple sugar can be found at Trader Joe's, Whole Foods, specialty stores, and, of course, online. Although you can substitute turbinado or even brown sugar, the maple sugar makes it extra maple-y and special.

1½ cups pecans
2 tablespoons maple sugar
1 tablespoon maple syrup
½ teaspoon kosher salt

Preheat the oven to 350°F.

Line a baking sheet with parchment paper.

Combine all the ingredients in a large bowl. Spread evenly across the prepared baking sheet. Bake, stirring every few minutes, for about 10 minutes, or until nuts are toasted.

This cake epitomizes winter with its weighty texture and dense fruitiness. I love how the crème fraîche brings a lightness of body and brightening flavor to the composition, and look for a wine to continue in that mode. Madeira is perfect for this, because, along with its overall nut-laden flavor, it brings a degree of texture and tart acidity to the palate. In this pairing, I opt for one that is in the mid-range of sweetness, made from the Bual or Verdelho grape varieties, which possesses back notes of stone fruits and caramel that will marry with the sweetness of the persimmons and pecans, while its tart acidity works in sync with the crème fraîche.

I am, at my core, a list maker, a collector, an obsessive-compulsive who loves the feeling of accomplishment the way other people love the feeling of cashmere, chocolate, drugs, and alcohol. So it makes total sense that, when we opened A.O.C. in 2002, what started out as notes for the staff about the cheeses we were currently serving turned into a marathon opus collection of cheese information. Doing the research, learning the stories, tasting the cheeses, and making notes became part of the ritual of inducting a cheese into our restaurant family. It feels pretty joyful to be able to print it all in one place, for the whole world of cheese lovers to see. Bear in mind these are our in-house notes, in which grammar, capitalization, and polite language often go out the window. Quirky as it is, I hope the list provides a guide to send you on your cheesy path to taste-bud happiness.

Learning about cheese is sort of like learning about wine. You can study and memorize names and places, methods and techniques, but ultimately you really learn by tasting. I'm lucky to work in a place that orders hundreds of pounds of cheese a month, so I get to try a lot of different things, but I have also had some wonderful guidance on what to buy and what to try along the way.

There are several books and websites that have been indispensable to my cheese self-education. Probably the most important and influential is Steven Jenkins's *Cheese Primer*. I have pored over Max McCalman's *Cheese: A Connoisseur's Guide* and I love the Eyewitness Handbooks' *French Cheese*, with a foreword by Joël Robuchon, as well as their more recent *The World Cheese Book*. For domestic bliss, *The New American Cheese* by Laura Werlin is unbeatable.

This brings me to the European idea of an *affineur*. An *affineur* is someone who seeks out very special examples of particular cheeses, then brings them back to their own caves (they often also have cheese shops) and ages those cheeses. Sometimes they even play an active role in affecting the development of those cheeses by choosing to bathe them in certain brines and wines, adding herbs or leaves, and controlling the temperature and humidity of the environment.

The great thing about knowing who these *affineurs* are is that you know that any cheese that bears their names will be amazing. Michele Buster at Forever Cheese (www.forevercheese.com) took me under her Spanish and Portuguese cheese wing back in 2002 when we were just dreaming up A.O.C. Her website is a wonderful resource as well. Peggy Smith and the gang at Cowgirl Creamery always inspire me with their own cheeses as well as their perfect picks of the best cheese from around the world. So when you see Pascal Beillevaire, Jean d'Alos, Chantal Plasse, Hervé Mons, Neal's Yard Dairy, Cowgirl Creamery, or Forever Cheese on the label of a particular cheese, buy it and enjoy!

goat

CANADA

tournevent chèvre noir (Quebec) Semi-hard, with waxed natural rind. Can be raw or pasteurized. The Fromagerie Tournevent goat dairy is located in Chesterville, Quebec, in the heartland of French Canada's mountainous dairy country. Since 1979, they have offered a variety of goat cheeses, but this aged goat cheddar is the most interesting.

The pâte (the "paste"—or interior of the cheese as opposed to the rind. Why does everything sound better in French?) is white and dense with an exquisite, fine, and generous flavor with nutty, caramel, and buttery accents. It is aged for a minimum of 1 year at low temperatures to preserve the deeper original milk flavors. The aging process often develops "flavor crystals" (converted lactose sugars) that literally "pop" in your mouth to enhance the flavor and pleasure.

FRANCE

ailine-vignes (Savoie) Raw goat's milk. Named after a school near Paris where the cheese is aged, Tomme Ailine-Vignes is washed with white wine and aged for 6 months. *Affineur* Roland Barthélemy created this cheese. He is the first cheese specialist to have earned the "Meilleur Ouvrier de France" title (Best Craftsman in France), usually reserved for chefs and artisans.

barbeillon (Loire Valley) Raw goat's milk, in little tetilla shapes, with bloomy ashed rind. Made by Madame Barbeillon of course! *Affineur* Pascal Beillevaire.

besace du berger (Rhônes-Alpes region) Small pasteurized goat's milk cheeses in the shape of—how do I say?—pointed breasts? nipples? baby bottles? Help! Anyway, they are ashed and perfect examples of classic goat cheese.

blanc bleu du rizet (Auvergne) Raw goat's milk. Farmstead, cylindrical cheese, sometimes with blue-and-white molding. *Affineur* Pascal Beillevaire. The mold is naturally formed and very subtle. The texture of this goat's milk cheese is firm, smooth, and chalky. The flavor is subtle and gently acidic, with a long finish of green apples. Rizet is the name of the family that makes the cheese.

bonde de gâtine (Poitou-Charente) Raw goat's milk semi-soft crottin. Mild, uncooked, unpressed cheese from the marshy *gâtine* area of Poitou. *Bonde* means the plug of a wine barrel (the shape), and *gâtine* (*terre gâte*) means

"spoiled earth" (in a good way, spoiled by the lush quality of the flora). The cheese is dense, slightly acidic, with a slightly salty pâte that melts in the mouth, leaving a rich flavor, like fresh almonds or apricot seeds. Each small cheese is made from no less than 2 liters of raw goat's milk and is made immediately after milking, completely by hand. From our new *affineur* friend Pascal Beillevaire, who originally started as a raw-butter producer in Nantes (northern France), then expanded by starting to buy and age cheeses. He now has 5 shops in Gay Paris.

la buche des causses (Quercy) Pasteurized goat. These 6-ounce ingot-shaped logs are the classic French goat cheese. Made by the small cooperative Les Fermiers de Rocamadour (who also make Gariotin, Lingot, etc.), it has a wrinkly, bloomy rind, which encases a creamy-to-molten texture just under the rind, and slightly-firmer-to-chalky middle. It is goaty and can be slightly barnyardy and has just enough salt and tang to make you want to take another bite!

bûcherondin or bucheron (Loire Valley) Pasteurized goat cheese. Semi-aged, ripening for 5 to 10 weeks. Ivory-colored pâte surrounded by a bloomy white rind. Soft, but semi-firm in texture, this cheese when young has a somewhat mild flavor, which becomes sharper as it matures. As it ages, its texture becomes drier: the mouthfeel of the center is dense and claylike, with the crumb dissolving on the tongue, while the section near the rind is almost creamy and can be gooey at room temperature.

cabécou du périgord Small, flat disk, pasteurized, rindless. The goat cheese of the southwest! White, soft, and creamy.

le cabri-ariégeois Raw Vacherin-style goat's milk cheese. It is so rare that I when I discovered it I couldn't find any info online or in any books! It is from the Ariège region of France, which is in the Pyrénées and borders Spain and Andorra. Rich and a little stinky, it comes in a round wooden box like a Vacherin and has a washed rind top. Outrageous cheese I am thrilled to have!

cabriflore (Deux-Sèvres) From the small town of Celles-Sur-Belle (just south of the Loire), famed for its plethora of extraordinary dairy products. This elegant pasteurized goat's milk cheese has a wrinkled, natural rind covered in vegetable ash. This layer of ash serves to cut its bright, acidic tang and bring a pleasant balance to the cheese. Quite smooth and evanescent texture, with notes of sweet cream and almond.

cabrioulet (Pyrénées) Washed-rind, semi-soft, raw goat's milk cheese, pungent, rich and milky, creamy and supple. This cheese is made by the Cabri-Ariégeois people, but then finished by Jean d'Alos.

carre chèvre du poitou (Poitou-Charentes) Pasteurized goat. Large, square-format bloomy-rind cheese. Runny, gooey, mushroomy, earthy.

cathare (Languedoc) Raw goat. The Cathare proudly carries the crest of its region, the Languedoc. The Occitane cross is inscribed on the face of the cheese. The cheese's form is a flat disk covered in charcoal powder. Otherwise, after *affinage* (maturing) the pâte hardens and develops a smooth, fine texture, with a subtle goat's milk taste typical of the goat's cheeses found in this region of France. The taste is distinctly of goat's milk, enriched by the aging process. *Affineur* Pascal Beillevaire.

cendré de niort (Provence) Handmade raw-milk goat cheese. Chantal Plasse *affineuse*. Small rounds on chestnut leaves, great dense goaty flavor, moldy and delicious.

chabrin (Pyrénées) Made by Onetik. Firm cheese made from pasteurized goat's milk. The rind is thick and yellowish-gray; the pâte is ivory-colored and has a smooth, slightly oily texture. The flavor is sweet and refined, with hints of olive, hazelnut, and fig. Aged for 3 months, it is creamy and smooth. Pairs well with rustic Jura reds.

charollais (Burgundy) Pasteurized goat's milk. A classic 4-inch-tall cylinder of chèvre that really shows off the flavors of the milk. Salty, acid, and sweet.

p. jacquin chèvre (Loire Valley) Can be raw or pasteurized, aged, ashed disk of goat cheese. Jacquin is a very well-respected producer. If the cheese is labeled "*berceau*," this means it is his aged version of the cheese. Flinty, classic goat. Some of these have been very runny, too.

chèvrefeuille "fleur verte" (Périgord) Pasteurized *gâteau*-style fresh goat cheese. Light, delicate, coated on the outside with herbs—thyme, rosemary, pink peppercorns. Has the sweet tanginess of fresh milk.

le chevrot (Poitou-Charentes) Made by Sèvre et Belle. Semi-soft pasteurized cheese made from goat's milk, with an edible natural rind and a stronger goat flavor and aroma. The rind is pale with gold streaks. Each weighs about 6 or 7 ounces. The cheese itself has a fresh, buttery, faintly winey taste and an inviting aroma of ripe figs. It is also known for having a distinct freshness of flavor and a supple, lush quality, which contrasts nicely with a slightly nutty, almost fermented taste.

clisson (Loire-Atlantique, on the Atlantic Coast) Semi-soft, washed-rind pasteurized goat cheese. More proof (as if we needed it) that Jean d'Alos is *God*! This 10-pound wheel is aged 4 months—when it is first made, it is washed in Muscadet (local wine from the region), but then our hero Jean washes it in Sauternes in his caves. The orange rind is slightly sandy but amazingly delicious. The cheese itself is a pale, almost white, color.

clisson, also known as **tome d'aquitaine au sauternes** (Bordeaux) These 12-pound pasteurized goat's milk tomes (this is the correct regional spelling, not a typo!) are actually made by a cheesemaking co-op in the Loire Valley. While still young, the wheels are sent to Jean d'Alos's famous caves in the town of Bordeaux. It's quite a sign of the prestige and importance of the *affineur* that Clisson is considered a cheese of the Bordeaux region rather than a Loire Valley creation. Once in M. d'Alos's capable hands the tomes are washed with a brine solution flavored with Muscadet and Sauternes, which speeds up the growth of good bacteria and gives layers of deep complex flavor and a beautifully stinky aroma. The texture of this semi-soft wonder is supple and almost chewy (in a great way)! One of my favorites.

clochette (La Chapelle Saint-Laurent) Pasteurized goat's milk cheese from the Poitou region, made by Chèvrechard. This cheese is made by very gently hand-ladling curd into a bell-shaped mold. It is aged for 30 days.

coeur du berry (Berry, in the Loire Valley) Pasteurized goat's milk, soft, ashed, with 45 percent fat content. *Coeur* means "heart." Soft, creamy, with a delicate tang typical of fresh goat cheeses. From famous maker Jacquin.

correzon (Limousin region, France) Raw semi-soft ashed farmstead goat's milk cheese. Cheesemaker Xavier Cornet is both a traditionalist and an innovator. He raises 100 Alpine chamois goats, and though he makes the local specialty, he has also played around with this cheese by using very fresh milk, tying it in cloth (like a *gaperon*), and letting it drain. Aged under ash. Very rare. Pascal Beillevaire *affineur*.

couronne lochoise (Touraine, Loire Valley) Raw goat's milk. This unique cheese is made in very small quantity by the Fréval family, on the rich pastures of their farm. Recognizable by its doughnut shape, semi-soft, ashed, with 45 percent fat. The name "Couronne Lochoise" means "the Crown of Loches"—the Loches being the name of the town. Pascal Beillevaire *affineur*.

crottin du périgord Raw, sweet, semi-soft little barrel-shaped cheeses from mountain milk. From the foie-gras-and-truffle region of France. Wrinkled natural rind, earthy flavor. Soft in the center and starting to get runny on the outside.

dalle charentaise (Loire Valley) Raw goat's milk, Pascal Beillevaire *affineur*. Complex and sweet, with a slightly mineral, stonelike taste.

dome de saint-estephe See Taupinière (page 361).

le fleuret (Dordogne, southwestern France) Pasteurized creamy, small rounds of soft goat cheese.

gour noir (Auvergne) Semi-soft raw goat's milk. In the village of Lapleau Corrèze, the Arnaud family possess a herd of white Saanen goats. The goat's milk produces this delicate little cheese. The taste is full of subtle flavors, with an accent on the savor of goat's milk.

grand gousier (the Vendée, a department in west-central France, on the Atlantic's Bay of Biscay) This cheese is from La Fromagerie de la Venise Verte, situated near the Abbaye de Maillezais, the abbey where Rabelais and Pantagruel hung out. It takes 50 liters of goat's milk to make one tomme. After the cheese is pressed, it is washed regularly with a brine that will eventually give the rind an orange color. Halfway through the *affinage*, Pascal Beillevaire takes the cheese and adds his touch. He dips it in a *saumure* and then covers it with fresh chive, ending up with a tomme that has a fresh acidity thanks to the chive and yet a long mouth from the aging process.

herbillette, also known as tome de bordeaux (Bordeaux) Pasteurized goat. *Affineur* Jean d'Alos. An aged goat cheese inspired by the Corsican cheese Brin d'Amour, this 3-month-old cheese is crusted over with aromatic layers of herbs. The thyme, savory, juniper, coriander, fennel, and cayenne seep into the tangy, pure white goat pâte and punch up the flavor with an aromatic herbiness.

herbiette (Provence) Raw goat's milk disk coated in *herbes de provence* (thyme, rosemary, savory, etc.), starting to ooze around the edges. Rare, small-production cheese; our friend Chantal Plasse is the *affineuse*.

herbiette (Nantes) Semi-soft raw goat cheese from northern France, coated in herbs similar to those on Brin d'Amour (thyme, savory, juniper, coriander, fennel, and cayenne). From the genius that is Jean d'Alos!

jean faup tomme de chèvre (Pyrénées) Raw goat tomme—classic Pyrénées-style handmade artisanal cheese. Great semi-soft texture, almost taffylike chew.

le lingot (Quercy) Pasteurized goat cheese from southwestern France (Quercy is between Périgord and Languedoc-Roussillon). Small brick-shaped bar (like a gold brick), perfect classic French goat cheese. Slightly aged on the outside, but still chalky at the center. Produced by a group of artisanal cheesemakers called Les Fermiers de Rocamadour.

lingot dauphinois (Rhône Valley) Raw-milk goat cheese from Chantal Plasse (our new fave *affineuse*). Flat brick shape.

marcilly sur maulne (Sainte-Maure-de-Touraine, France) This raw goat's milk log dates back to the Middle Ages. It was named after the Moors, who occupied the region during the eighth and ninth centuries. The curd is hand-ladled, and then a straw is inserted to give stability to the cheese when it is salted or ashed. It is then ripened 2 to 4 weeks. When fully matured, it has a balanced, round flavor with slightly salty sourness and an aroma of walnut, though the flavor can vary with the season: in spring it tastes of hay, and in fall more of hazelnut. *Affineur* Pascal Beillevaire ages the cheeses further.

maxi-dôme (Auvergne) Soft-ripened pasteurized goat cheese. Its name is derived from its dome shape. This cheese is made in the summer for fall or winter consumption.

montrachet (Burgundy) Semi-firm raw goat cheese, weighs about 7 ounces. Squat barrel wrapped in chestnut leaf with a strip of raffia. Crinkly almond rind. Some blue mold on a fluffy field of white. A little heady at first, then sweet, tangy, a little salty, milky. This one is relatively gentle. Rind is mild.

mothais sur feuille (Poitou-Charentes) Raw goat's milk, small disk of farmer's cheese wrapped in a chestnut or plane leaf. Ours is slightly aged.

pavé blésois (Loire Valley) Semi-soft raw goat's milk. Natural silver mold. An elegant cheese with fine, dense, smooth texture and slightly piquant taste.

le pavé de jadis (Berry, France) Brick-shaped (*pavé* is "paving stone" in French), ash-covered pasteurized goat cheese from a great maker, Jacquin. It is a classic white-white, chalky goat cheese, also slightly acidic.

pélardon (Languedoc) Raw goat's milk, from a rural area. Young goat cheese has almost no rind and a compact, nutty pâte. The balance of acidity and salt is just right, and there is a full, rich, milky flavor with a lingering aftertaste. Very small *affinage* production from Chantal Plasse. This cheese is a candidate for AOC status.

pentu de l'étang (Loire Valley) Triangular-shaped raw goat cheese, dusted with ash, semi-firm, with full tangy flavor. *Affineur* my man Pascal Beillevaire! The dense white pâte flakes like slate.

le petit bichon (Loire Valley) Pasteurized goat's milk. Bloomy rind with runny, milky center. Made by Jacquin—fine maker of artisanal goat cheeses in the region.

le petit fiancé des pyrénées Washed-rind disk of runny, smelly, amazing raw goat cheese. Highly allocated from a small producer in the Pyrénées. A gourmand's fantasy!

picandou frais (Midi-Pyrénées) Soft pasteurized goat cheese, fresh and milky. This cheese has a light sourness that balances the direct milkiness beautifully.

la pointe de bique Non-AOC (just out of the area) Pouligny-Saint-Pierre made by Jacquin (famous *affineur*). Pasteurized, truncated, tallish four-sided pyramid. Beige exterior. Fragile, moist, creamy interior with piquant flavor and goaty aroma. The name means "nanny goat's horn."

poivre d'âne (Provence) Raw goat's milk. Name means "pepper of the donkey"—nice!! Natural-rind cheese of rectangular shape, flavored with summer savory, a Southern European herb similar to thyme and mint with a peppery bite that gives the cheese its characteristic flavor. The natural rind is blue. Poivre d'Âne is very similar to Banon cheese. The period of ripening is about 1 month, the fat content is 45 percent. Medium hard and dry, great flavor.

pouligny-saint-pierre (Loire Valley) Raw, truncated, tallish four-sided pyramid. This AOC cheese is very rare outside of the area. Beige exterior. Fragile, moist, creamy interior with piquant flavor and goaty aroma. Closely related to other traditional Loire Valley chèvre, such as Selles-sur-Cher, Sainte-Maure, Valençay.

pyramide colombier (Loire Valley) Pascal Beillevaire *affinage* selection. This raw goat's milk cheese is in a unique high-pyramid format. It cuts an imposing figure on the cheese counter or cheese board. Has an aroma of goat and straw, with a beautiful blend of tartness, sweetness, and saltiness.

roves des garrigues (Provence) Soft, fresh cheese made with raw goat's milk by the local herders of the Cévennes. The taste is determined by the variety of herbs that the goats find during their treks through the mountains. The milk is very dense, imparting to cheese the aromas typical of Mediterranean shores: thyme and rosemary. The rind is merely a thin crust, and the pâte is white. The cheese itself has a slight thyme flavor and is typically eaten while just barely mature.

sainte-maure (Poitou-Charentes) Pasteurized goat's milk. Same as Sainte-Maure-de-Touraine, but can't be AOC since it's not from the region of Touraine.

sainte-maure caprifeuille (Loire Valley) Sainte-Maure Caprifeuille is a log-shaped, aged raw goat cheese that has a sweet and delicate taste with undertones of acid and salt. It has a bloomy rind with a pâte that is semi-soft but hardens as the cheese ages. The wrinkled appearance of the rind provides a rustic flavor component to the cheese. The pâte is dense and white and has a chalky texture when young, with a fresh and tangy flavor. After the cheese matures, the pâte will become less moist and crumbly, with a sharper and nuttier flavor.

sainte-maure-de-touraine (Touraine, Loire Valley) AOC raw goat's milk, traditional French log-shaped chèvre with rind of natural mold and a long straw going through its center to help hold it together and ventilate the cheese from the interior. Balanced, fine-textured with salty and sour tones. Some say it has the aroma of walnuts. Oozing around the outside. Available plain or with ash.

saint-germain (Charolais region, Burgundy) Raw goat's milk, in the shape of a small tower. Semi-soft, natural rind. The region is best known for the prestigious local cattle known as the Charolais, so when this local goat's milk cheese achieved AOC status it was a big pat on the back! This cheese is produced mostly by women who have followed in their mothers' footsteps. It takes 2 to 2.5 liters of milk to make just one cheese. These cheeses have the aroma of almonds and hazelnuts and the taste of mushrooms and the cellar.

saint-nicolas-de-la-dalmerie (Languedoc-Roussillon) Raw goat's milk, made by a tiny group of fewer than 10 orthodox monks. Farmstead semi-soft cheese in the shape of a small ingot, with smooth angles made from stainless-steel molds. Unique flavor perfumed by the scrubland of the region—thyme, savory, and other local herbs. *Affineur* Pascal Beillevaire.

la sancerre (Loire Valley) Raw goat's milk, twice as big as its cousin Crottin de Chavignol. Perfect balance of acidity and saltiness. Pascal Beillevaire *affineur*.

le sarlet (Périgord) Made by Le Chèvrefeuille. Semi-soft to soft cheese made from goat's milk. It is a soft-ripened cheese that embodies a true goaty flavor. Slightly salty with a creamy texture.

selles-sur-cher (Touraine) This AOC pasteurized-milk goat cheese is an old cheese, handmade for many generations. It has maintained its integrity as an artisanal product. It was one of the first cheeses to receive AOC status, in 1975. A thick disk with beveled sides coated in a thin layer of fine wood charcoal that is subtly tinted blue. Its pâte, by contrast, is snowy white, with a downy rind that shows superficial molding at the edges. Ours are pretty aged, with a nutty flavor. They are starting to get runny around the edges—they melt in your mouth! Locals are adamant about eating the rind.

taupinière de saint-estèphe (Saint-Estèphe region, Bordeaux) Raw goat's milk cheese made by a man named M. Jousseaume at his farm. The name means "molehill" and refers to the domelike shape. During its 2-week aging process, the cheese absorbs the natural mold in the cellar, which gives it a nutty flavor and a lemony tang. M. Jousseaume won the cheese awards for this cheese every year from 1980 to 2000!!

tetoun de sainte-agathe (Alpes-de-Haute-Provence) Small raw soft goat's milk cheese with tangy goat's milk flavor, has pepper and savory notes on the bottom, giving it a typical Provençal flavor. Lightly spicy, supple, and unctuous. Of course there is a story. On every February 15, in the Alpes-de-Hautes-Provence, Sainte-Agathe's day is celebrated. In the third century, Agathe—a beautiful and holy virgin—was selected by the Sicilian prefect as a concubine. Agathe refused, and the prefect forced her to cut off her own breast and eat it. Since then, Christian women all along Provence have honored Agathe by making and eating edible confections in the shape of a breast. *Tetoun* means "nipple" in the local dialect.

thym tamarre (Provence) Raw goat's milk cheese, semi-soft, with bloomy rind. An original and distinctive farmstead cheese—sort of a pointed oval shape with an elegant branch of thyme across the center. The particularly rich milk used to make this cheese comes from a special breed of goat from Provence—this results in an especially delicious and savory flavor.

tomme de chèvre au chardonnay (Pays de la Loire) Pascal Beillevaire *affineur*. This unique French Tomme de Chèvre is washed weekly with a mixture of salt brine and Chardonnay made from California vines. The result is a Tomme de Chèvre that has a supple pâte and a unique flavor.

tommette du tarn (Pyrénées) From *affineur* Hervé Mons. Through 3 generations, this dairy has been dedicated to the production of special cheeses. Father started the company and has since retired. Son took over with a mind for making very high-quality artisan cheeses. Grandson produces some of the milk that is used, along with 4 other local farms in the area. They must all respect strict quality rules, such as no GMO (genetically modified) food for the goats, and goats must be grazing outdoors for at least 200 days per year. When the cheeses arrive at the Maison Mons caves, they are aged on wood planks, and flipped and washed every week, to develop their beautiful light-red color.

tonnelet Semi-soft raw goat cheese aged from 60 to 90 days, by Pascal Beillevaire. Tonnelet is shaped like a drum, has a geotrichum rind with natural grayish-blue mold. The flavor is lactic, a bit acidic, rich, and grassy-herbaceous. It comes from Normandy, which is much better known for dairy cows than herds of Alpine chamois and Saanen goats.

trois cornes (Vendée) Raw goat's milk. This pretty, semi-soft cheese with a natural, bloomy rind had completely disappeared from the cheese landscape. Luckily, several works had been written with information about Trois Cornes. The cheese originated in Sableaux et Chaillé les Marais. Based on this, *affineur* Pascal Beillevaire approached a goat herder with the precise specifications that he had researched. The result, after 10 years, is pure happiness for all partners. Trois Cornes is once again a staple in the Vendée region. Its inimitable taste touts the indigenous summer flavors that are part of a true *fromage de terroir.*

truffe de valensole (Provence) Raw goat's milk, semi-firm, with an ashed natural rind. Farmstead AOC cheese. The village of Valensole is famous for the excellent truffles that are found there. This cheese is shaped by hand to resemble these highly prized truffles. To mimic the color, they are dusted with a fine coat of black ash. The white pâte (inside part) has a slight tang and smells of the scrubland of Provence, where the goats graze—munching on herbs such as rosemary, thyme, lavender, and savory.

valençay (Berry, Loire Valley) Pasteurized goat from a famous cheesemaking region. It was recently granted AOC status. Valençay was originally shaped like a perfect pyramid. But Napoleon stopped at the Castle of Valençay on his return from the disastrous campaign in Egypt, and was so offended by the pyramid shape that he drew his sword and chopped off the top! To make this cheese, the raw curd is cast in a mold, then removed, covered in salted charcoal ashes, and ripened for at least 3 weeks. Ours is from the famous producer Jacquin. Beautiful pure white interior. Try with Loire Valley wines or other Sauvignon Blanc!

vallée d'aspe (Pyrénées) Raw semi-hard goat's milk cheese from what is really sheep's milk country; this cheese is made in the style of Ossau-Iraty but with goat's milk. Natural rind. White pâte is supple and creamy, becomes firm as it ages. Nutty, robust flavor.

ENGLAND

ticklemore (Coventry) Semi-hard pasteurized goat cheese from master cheesemaker Neal's Yard Dairy in the beautiful English countryside. Each cheese is pressed, dry-salted, hand-molded, and aged 10 weeks in baskets, creating a thick, natural rind with the imprint of the basket. The 5-pound wheels are then aged 2 to 3 months at Neal's Yard Dairy, turned twice a week. Dry and chalky in the center but softer toward the edges. With 48 percent fat. Medium-flavored, slightly acidic.

ITALY

brunet (Alta Langhe) Soft cheese made from raw goat's milk. This cheese has a paper-thin rind and light, velvety texture. The flavor is very delicate with just a hint of tanginess. Even those who don't like goat's milk cheese are going to LOVE this one!

caciotta capra foglie noce (Veneto) Made by Latteria Perenzin. Firm cheese made from pasteurized goat's milk and wrapped in walnut leaves. Beneath the leaves, this cheese has a slightly coarse rind and ivory-colored pâte; the texture is compact. The cheese itself has a very floral, tangy flavor and is complemented well by the nutty, earthy notes imparted by the leaves. Pairs well with dessert wines, especially Venetian Raboso Passito.

cappello del mago (Piemonte) This is an artisan goat version of Toma Brusca (or Castelrosso) produced by Caseificio La Giuncal in the town of Fobello. Each cheese that the family makes is a handmade work of art. This cheese is slightly crumbly, creamy, and full-flavored. The drum-shaped wheels have a natural-mold rind with plenty of healthy yellow mold. The wheel is lovingly wrapped in straw and brown paper and finished off with sealing wax. It won top prizes for goat cheese in the Valsesia and Piemonte regions in 2008.

capra valtellina (Lombardy) Pasteurized. From high in the mountains that divide Italy from Switzerland, where goatherds have been herding and making cheese for centuries. This is a flavorful and complex 6-month-aged goat cheese.

capretta (Piemonte) Pasteurized goat cheese aged in natural caves for 45 to 90 days. The texture changes from moist and open to dense and rich. The sweet flavor is accented by the bracing flavor of the laurel leaf on top.

caprino cremoso (Piemonte) Pasteurized goat's milk cheese produced by Caseificio La Bottera, a third-generation farm and creamery in northeastern Italy, between the hills of the Langhe and the steeper mountains of Bisalta. Although the dairy traditionally specialized in cow's milk cheeses, in recent times they have expanded their range by buying additional milk from selected local farmers in the region. Several wafer-thin shavings of black truffle, from nearby Alba, are placed on the top rind. The cheeses mature for only a few days before release, and Caprino Cremoso is best consumed young. The texture is soft and bone-white in color, topped with the delicate truffle shavings. Caprino Cremoso pairs very well with sparkling or fruity white wines as well as gently flavored breads such as walnut.

ciabra di capra (Piemonte) Made by Caseificio La Bottera. Soft-ripened cheese made from pasteurized goat's milk. Under a thin, bloomy rind is an intensely creamy cheese that becomes softer and more melting with age. Its layered flavor has notes of fresh cream, hay, and herbs. Though it is an assertive goat cheese, its pungency is tempered by the lush, full texture.

crutin con tartufo Pasteurized cheese from the hilly Langhe region of Piemonte. This cheese has pieces of truffle in it, and is also stored in caves with truffles that perfume the cheese.

fiorito in cherry leaves (Puglia) This wonderful Italian cheese is made with pasteurized goat's milk. It is aged for 25 days, which allows it to develop a supple texture while retaining a great deal of creaminess. With age, the interior becomes softer, eventually becoming runny and smooth. The exterior is wrapped in cherry leaves, lending a slight earthiness and bitterness to the cheese.

montes (Sardinia) Raw goat cheese made by Cooperativa Dorgali Pastori. Firm, made from whole goat's milk. The interior is white, with small, sparse eyes. Tangy and goaty.

nocetto di capra (Lombardy) Soft-ripened, pasteurized goat cheese produced with milk from Orobica goats, which are indigenous to Bergamo. The cheese is sweet, well balanced, and like velvet on your tongue.

palareto (Tuscany) Raw goat's milk cheese from a special small cheese producer called Caseificio Bertagni, in the Garfagnana area of Tuscany. The 2-pound wheels are aged on pine boards.

pantaleo (Sardinia) Semi-hard pasteurized goat cheese. There are not many aged goat cheeses in Italy, so I am always happy to find one. This Pantaleo is ivory colored with a pale rind. Made with milk from the Capra Sarda goat, it is aged at least 100 days, resulting in a full-flavored, sweet cheese with a clean, floral finish. It certainly does not taste like what you expect from a goat cheese.

pizzetto di capra (Lombardy) Washed-rind pasteurized goat cheese from Lombardy, a goat's milk Robiola. Made by Ambrogio Arnoldi, who makes our Taleggio Gusto Antico and Strachitunt. This is the first time he has exported this cheese to the U.S. The flavor is sweet with a touch of earthiness.

plin di capra (Piemonte) Pasteurized goat cheese made by Caseificio Reale. Soft-ripened cheese made from goat's milk. In the local Piemontese dialect, *plin* means "pinch," which is what these small goat cheeses look like. Beautiful, clean goat's milk flavor with a dense but creamy texture.

stracapra (Lombardy) Raw goat. Made by Ambrogio, who makes our Taleggio. StraCapra is a washed-rind soft goat cheese, essentially a goat's milk Taleggio. Creamy and sweet, it is rich and full-bodied with a mellow tanginess.

tronchetto di capra affinato al miele (Piemonte) Semi-soft pasteurized goat cheese made by La Casera. This cheese has a dense but creamy texture. It's aged in natural cellars, coated with locally made honey. It has a delicate, tangy flavor with sweet honey notes.

PORTUGAL

cabra pimentão (northern Portugal) Semi-hard pasteurized goat cheese rubbed with olive oil and paprika. Slightly spicy and full-flavored.

gardunha (Serra da Estrela) Washed-rind raw goat cheese produced at the base of Mount Serra da Estrela, in the Beira Baixa region. Typical of the region, since goats are found more in the valleys and sheep in the mountains. Atypical, because it is 100 percent goat, as opposed to mixed-milk, as are most Portuguese cheeses.

palhais (central Torres Vedras region) Semi-soft pasteurized Portuguese button (small round) cheese—flavorful and salty in a good way. This is a typical table cheese in Portugal. We marinate them in ultra-virgin olive oil, thyme, rosemary, and sliced chile de árbol.

ribafria (Torres Vedras) Semi-hard pasteurized goat's milk cheese, covered with black peppercorns. It is quite full and spicy. Tell customers not to eat all the peppercorns—they are there to flavor the cheese.

SPAIN

abrigo (Valencia) Pasteurized goat cheese, made since 1970 in the town of Catí. The cheese is aged for 5 months and is indigenous to the region. Once upon a time, the goats milked were the Celti Iberica breed, but now Murciana goats are used. The cheese is complex, multilayered, and sweet, with wonderful milk proteins that explode in your mouth.

autor (Valencia) A farmhouse raw goat cheese from Quatretonda, 60 kilometers outside of Valencia, produced at the estate Heretat de Pere (father's inheritance). Simona, the cheesemaker, uses thistle rennet to coagulate the curd, and ages the cheese 60 days in the underground cavern. Some of my favorite Spanish and Portuguese cheeses are made with thistle rather than animal rennet, I love the deep, robust, earthy flavor the thistle imparts. The family started as goat herders and moved into cheesemaking a few years ago. All the milk comes from 100 Murciana goats bred and raised on the farm. The cheese is at times creamy, other times drier—depending on the seasons. Herbs, grass, and citrus all play in the finish.

cabra romero (La Mancha) Pasteurized goat's milk semi-hard cheese, bathed in extra-virgin olive oil and rosemary like Romao (but goat, not sheep).

caña de cabra (Murcia) Soft-ripened pasteurized goat's milk log in the style of French goat Bûcheron.

caña capricho de cabra (Murcia) Pasteurized soft log, coated in black pepper. Not as intense as the Portuguese Ribafria!

celestine (Montalbán) Pasteurized goat Camembert. Yeasty, bloomy rind, runny interior.

clara (León) Raw goat's milk. Murciana milk is used to make this artisan cheese with a natural mold rind. It is rich and sweet, with hints of lemon.

de cal bardines (Catalonia) Soft pasteurized goat cheese mixed with garlic and parsley and hand-rolled into little balls. Marinated in olive oil, chile, and rosemary. Made by the same cheesemaker as Nevat.

garrotxa (Catalonia) Semi-hard pasteurized goat's milk cheese. Pâte is firm, almost flaky, yet moist and smooth. It melts on the tongue, revealing mild herbal flavors to go along with its wonderfully tangy mouthfeel and a hint of hazelnuts in the aftertaste.

ibores (Extremadura) Semi-firm pasteurized goat cheese rubbed with paprika. It has a silky texture and a clean finish—some hints of grass from its native homeland.

leonora (León) Pasteurized goat's milk cheese from a small producer. Brick-shaped, with natural mold, compact white pâte. Layered, complex flavor, with long, lingering finish. Smooth, full-bodied, with a nice balance of acidity and tanginess. Great with white wines.

majorero (Fuerteventura Island, Canary Islands) DO (Designation of Origin) raw goat from just 100 kilometers from Africa! The island has farming traditions that go back centuries. The milk comes from a special breed of goats that exist only on the island—they produce thick, aromatic, high-fat milk. Large, aged wheels with "eyes" in interior, slightly gummy texture; acidic, piquant, buttery.

montcabrer (Catalonia) Semi-firm pasteurized goat's milk cheese, aged in charcoal. From the same producer as Nevat! Creamy texture—you can taste the sweetness of the milk from the Murciana goats. Earthy, full-flavored, slightly tangy at the finish.

monte enebro (Avila) Pasteurized. From La Mancha, west of Madrid. The name means "Juniper Hill." This is a very limited-production, labor-intensive cheese. It is hand-shaped, lightly covered with ash, and cured for 1 to 2 months. It is assertive, creamy, tangy, salty, with a compact pâte.

murcia curado (Murcia) Artisan DO raw cheese from southeastern Spain. Murcia is the birthplace of the Murciano-Granadina breed of goat, the best milk-producing goat breed in all of Spain. They are well acclimatized to the heat and aridness of the Mediterranean region, with great migrating abilities to take advantage of good grazing lands, and a perfect milk-producing shape, consisting of large, well-implanted udders. Now you know about the goat, but this cheese is the aged (curado) version made with pressed pâte, washed but not cooked. It has an intense white interior color and a creamy, elastic texture. Bathed in red wine, which gives a red exterior and imparts a strong floral bouquet, then aged at least 45 days.

murcia al vino (Murcia) Artisan pasteurized cheese from southern Spain. Semi-soft goat cheese with a smooth violet rind that has been soaked in wine for 48 to 72 hours, then aged about 75 days. It has a sweet, smooth flavor.

nevat (Catalonia) Soft-ripened pasteurized goat cheese invented and produced by Josep Cuixart of Can Pujol. From the heart of the Barcelones Mountains, he makes the cheese using only his own and neighboring herders' fresh, same-day milk. Nevat's rind is treated with a *Penicillium* mold, enabling a beautiful bloomy white rind that transforms the curd. As it matures, it softens from a semi-soft texture. Delicate, sweet, with a slight tang. *Nevat* means "snowed" in Catalan.

oz (Castilla y León) Pasteurized goat cheese. From the same producer as Leonora. Similar to Leonora, but the pâte is more compact and creamy, and less flaky. The name comes from *hoz* (pronounced "oz"), which in local dialect means "canyon."

patacabra (Aragón) This pasteurized goat cheese is from central Spain, east of Madrid. It is a washed-rind cheese—full-flavored, with a buttery finish, earthy, and creamy. It comes in a 5-pound brick.

pau sant mateu (Catalonia) Washed-rind 2-pound pasteurized goat's milk cheese from the mountains just north of Barcelona. Semi-soft, smooth, with pale-orange rind. Becomes creamy and pungent as it ages.

san mauricio (Zaragoza, Aragón) Farmhouse pasteurized goat cheese. Slightly salty, spicy, with silky texture. A little like Monte Enebro. Same maker as Patacabra. Julian is completely passionate about his cheesemaking and recently won an award for this complex goat cheese. San Mauricio is a true farmhouse cheese, produced only with the milk from Julian's goats. Aged at least 45 days, it has a semi-firm texture and a balanced sweet-and-sour flavor, with a distinguished finish.

santa gadea (Valle de Manzenado) Pasteurized goat's milk. Santa Gadea Farm is located in San Cristóbal de Rioseco, a little town overlooking the Ebro River. This farmstead organic goat cheese has a wonderful intensity of flavor, most likely due to the wild grasses and herbs that the free-range goats enjoy at will at any time of the day. Soft and crumbly, Santa Gadea has an edible rind, with the pâte turning creamy and runny around the edges as the cheeses age. Great with quince paste, honey, and dates, or Serrano ham and black-olive tapenade.

sant gil d'albio (Tarragona) This is a special, artisanally produced version of the famous Spanish cheese Garrotxa. Semi-hard pasteurized cheese, made by a family just outside of Tarragona. Usually Garrotxa has mold growth on its rind, but this version is clean and rubbed with olive oil. Luscious depth and great acidic balance. Full-bodied and flavorful, with a long, smooth finish that hints of nuts and herbs.

sierra cabra (Sierra del Segura, Murcia) Pasteurized organic goat's milk cheese. The goats roam free, grazing in the fields. Cured in olive oil, giving the cheese a flavor of ripe olives, apples, and vegetables. Aged 8 months. Hints of herbs and grass.

vare (Asturias) Farmhouse raw goat cheese, named for a tiny town in northern Spain. Six years ago, a young couple decided to make goat cheese because there are so many cow's milk cheeses in the area. They have over 450 goats, which produce all the milk. They also grow all the feed for the goats. The pâte of the cheese is off-white to ivory, with a smooth, dense, firm texture. The aroma suggests cooked milk, with a little caramel. The taste is fruity, herbaceous, and sweet, with very well-balanced salt and acidity.

veigadarte (Castilla y León) Pasteurized goat's milk log, aged 1 month. A sumptuous cheese encased in a thin layer of oak ash under its white, bloomy rind. This log-shaped cheese ages from the outside in; often a slice of Veigadarte will be a creamy beige color near the edge and a pure-white color in the middle. It has a very smooth texture because of the high butterfat content of the Verata and Avila goats' milk; the flavor is slightly earthy, with a pronounced goaty tang. Pairs well with Albariño, Vinho Verde, or Cava wine.

la yerbera (Murcia) Pasteurized goat's milk semi-hard cheese. This cheese is cured with ground almonds and almond and olive oils.

dallenwiler geisschäse (Dallenwil) Raw goat's milk made by the Odermatt family. A lovely, traditionally made cheese with a washed rind that gives it a lightly funky aroma. The texture is semi-firm and smooth; it has a fresh milky flavor mingling with flavors of nuts and herbs.

dallenwiler wychäs (Dallenwil) Made by the Odermatt family. A lovely goat cheese manufactured in the traditional way, the red-wine-washed cheese gains a deeply barnyardy aroma but has a semi-firm, smooth texture. It has a fresh milky flavor mingling with flavors of nuts and herbs with fruity overtones.

U.S.A.

alpine shepherd (Lakeport, California) Raw aged goat cheese from Yerba Santa Dairy in northern California. The curds are tied in nylon bags and air-dried for up to 14 months. The cheese becomes earthy and hard, with a grana-style texture and robust butterscotch flavor.

andante dairy (Petaluma, California) Cheesemaker Soyoung Scanlan studied biochemistry and then, in 1999, decided to make cheese. She is also an avid musician, and names all her cheeses after musical terms. **acapella** Soft-ripened pasteurized goat's-milk cheese. **cavatina** Cavatina is a soft-ripened small log-shaped cheese made from pasteurized goat's milk. It has a mild, buttery flavor with a slightly tart finish. **contralto** Pasteurized goat, washed rind. Soyoung made a washed-rind cheese in the format of French Reblochon. This cheese is made from milk collected on the ranch where Andante Dairy is located. The flavors are intensely rich, with grass and earth and dominating goatiness. Texture is soft and oozing. **etude** Hard cheese made from pasteurized goat's milk. The texture of this cheese is slightly grainy; it crumbles easily. It is aged for 6 months. It has a mildly piquant, somewhat sweet flavor with goaty aromas and a clean, hay-filled finish. **tomme dolce** Pasteurized goat. This is semi-firm, in the style of goat's milk cheeses of the Pyrénées. Soyoung washes it with a friend's plum conserve and plum brandy, which imparts a little sweetness to the cheese.

aspen ash (Niwot, Colorado) Haystack Mountain Goat Dairy's pasteurized goat's milk cheese has a soft-ripened bloomy rind with vegetable ash. Texture is light and creamy. Great mouthfeel and outstanding flavor.

bermuda triangle (Cypress Grove, Arcata, California) Handmade with the chef in mind, Bermuda Triangle is made from pasteurized goat's milk. Soft-ripened and double-rinded, with ash and surface ripening, has earthy yet mild flavor; the texture becomes creamier with age.

bittersweet plantation evangeline (Gonzales, Louisiana) Pasteurized triple-crème goat cheese, aged 3 to 4 weeks. Started by chef John Folse, Bittersweet Plantation Dairy is actually one of the best-respected artisanal American cheesemakers—this cheese won the gold medal at the World Cheese Awards. The dairy works to create products that represent the 7 nations that came together to create the Cajun and Creole heritage. This 4-ounce wheel has tangy, soft, almost runny pâte. Named after the heroine of Longfellow's epic poem about the exile of the Acadians from Nova Scotia (but you knew that).

bonne bouche (Websterville, Vermont) Pasteurized goat cheese with soft ash rind, from Vermont Butter & Cheese Creamery proprietors Allison Hooper and Bob Reese. Considered their flagship cheese, Bonne Bouche made its first appearance in 2001. Its name translates from the French to "Good Mouthful," and it certainly lives up to that. Smooth, creamy, and luxurious, these rounds of ashed cheese are mild, but acidic enough to remind you of fresh chèvre.

capricious (Eureka, California) Pasteurized washed-rind goat's milk cheese, won Best in Show at the American Cheese Society awards. It is a hard-aged nutty, fruity, crumbly cheese, similar to Parmesan. But a farmstead cheese made from a small single herd of goats in NoCal!

capriole goat cheeses (Greenville, Indiana) Take a ride through the lush and rolling hills of southern Indiana, where the winters are hard and the accents grow soft, and you'll stumble upon Capriole Goat Cheeses and their wonderful world of cheese. They were among the first of the new American artisanal cheesemakers. From Cowgirl Creamery Web site: "In a bit of serendipity, when Judith Schad and her husband, Larry, bought their current property in 1976, they discovered that in the nineteenth century the property had belonged to Larry's great-great-grandfather. To honor family tradition, they decided to build their new log cabin right over the foundation of the old house. First populating their family farm with all manner of animals, they soon fell in love with how affectionate, independent, and mischievous their goats were." These goats give the milk for the fabulous Capriole goat cheeses. **crocodile tears** Pasteurized goat cheese with traditional rennet, bloomy rind. Soft in texture. It has a deep and tangy flavor in a petite cone of dense, aged goat cheese. In imitation of similar cheese found all over French markets, the wrinkled rind has been flecked with a russet douse of paprika. **mont st. francis** Raw goat cheese. Mont St. Francis has a glowing ruby-red washed rind and is named for a local monastery. Rich, beefy, and deliciously aromatic, this cheese was one of the first great washed-rinds in America. **old kentucky tomme** Raw goat's milk, semi-hard farmstead cheese. Modeled after Tomme de Savoie, from eastern France. Mellow, buttery, and mild, with mushroomy overtones. Aged 8 months; natural rind; 4-pound wheels. A note from Judith on raw milk: "It's truly in the raw-milk cheeses that everything contributing to the character of the milk comes through—the limestone that affects the soil & water here, the natural browse growing in our woodlands, years of selective breeding for flavor, and the molds and flora that flourish seasonally. For years we produced these cheeses from pasteurized milk & the difference with raw milk is so distinctive, we've become true believers." **sofia** Semi-soft pasteurized cheese made with goat's milk. This dense and tangy chèvre is beautifully marbled with soft gray whorls and undulations of vegetable ash. Its texture is fine and silky in the mouth, becoming denser and more velvety with age. It ripens under a light, wrinkly geotrichum rind, delicate and slightly sweet, and so is never mushroomy, overpowering, or soapy. Pairs well with crisp white wines. wabash cannonball Pasteurized handmade farmstead goat cheese. This 3-ounce ashed ball is similar to the chèvres found in French farmers' markets. After being shaped, the fresh curd is dried slightly and then enters the cave, where it forms a wrinkly rind like its European cousins. Paper-wrapped and packaged in wooden crates, so that the cheese can breathe and develop. Beautiful little cheese!

classico (Tumalo Farms, Bend, Oregon) Firm, pressed, cooked cheese made from pasteurized goat's milk. Aged for 8 to 12 weeks, the wheels are carefully turned and wiped daily. This boldly flavored farmstead cheese has a tangy and pleasantly sharp flavor with hints of toffee. Pairs well with a domestic Pinot Gris.

coach farms triple cream (Pine Plains, New York) Pasteurized goats' milk cheese, decadently rich; it has smooth dense texture with buttery, earthy flavors and clean finish. After selling their Coach Leather Company, the Cahn family started a goat dairy over 20 years ago. At the time there was no market for the cheese, but they persevered, and now make some of this country's best artisan cheese.

coupole (Vermont Butter & Cheese Creamery) Pasteurized goat's milk, ripe and runny. Hand-shaped, sprinkled with ash. Strong ripe rind and creamy pâte. Notes of flowers, citrus, hazelnuts.

cypress grove pee wee pyramid (Humboldt County, California) Pasteurized small pyramid-shaped goat cheese from the Redwood Coastal Region of northern California.

fenacho (Tumalo Farms, Bend, Oregon) Pasteurized farmstead goat cheese. This tomme is semi-hard and flavored with fenugreek. Tumalo Farms is surrounded by views of the Cascade Mountains, 3,600 feet above sea level in the high desert. The DeCastilhos family used to work in Silicon Valley, in the tech industry. On vacation in Brazil, they discovered the delicious local artisanal cheeses and

became obsessed. They researched for 2 years—running a farm, making cheese—and their interest grew in traditional Dutch and Italian cheeses.

goat's leap (Napa Valley, California) Barbara and Rex Backus moved from L.A. to Napa Valley in 1972. They bought a herd of lamancha goats (really cool Spanish breed, with tiny ears) and started making cheese. If you go to their Web site, at goatsleap.com, you can see that they have traced the lineage of each goat and have names for all of them. They even name the cheeses after particularly favorite goats! carmela Raw goat's milk cheese. Firm 6-pound wheel dusted in paprika. eclipse Pasteurized barrel-shaped goat cheese, with bloomy ashed rind and a layer of ash in the center. Crowned with a star anise that flavors the whole cheese. hyku Pasteurized goat cheese with bloomy rind. Very creamy, elegant, and subtle. kiku Pasteurized soft young goat cheese wrapped in fig leaves that have been doused in Sauvignon Blanc. Aged 3 weeks. sumi Pasteurized, ashed, flat-topped pyramid, created by adding the milk in layers. Firm, with a long finish, yet creamy. sybil Pasteurized goat cheese with bloomy rind, about 1 pound each.

harvest cheese Raw goat's milk from the Berkshire Hills in Massachusetts. Made by Joe and Carolyn Hillman; they have been farming in the area on a small scale for a number of years, but the cheese thing is new to them. The Harvest Cheese is produced only from spring until autumn, when their herd of 40 Alpine goats are able to graze on organic pasture, consisting of native grasses and herbs, as well as the local hillsides and woodlands. This cheese is made by hand in small batches, using traditional methods, then aged on the farm in the "cave," and washed, turned and brushed like a Pyrénées tomme. Sweet, almost buttery tone, with floral, nutty taste, also grass, mushrooms, and earthiness; 6-to-7-pound semi-hard wheels with natural rind.

haystack mountain goat dairy (Longmont, Colorado) Located on 7 acres of rich agricultural plains that skirt the foothills of the Rocky Mountains near Boulder, this is one of 50 true farmstead cheesemakers in the country. They raise Saanen and Nubian goats on a mixture of alfalfa and grain, milking the goats twice a day and then just letting them hang out and relax the rest of the time! Haystack has won quite a few awards from the American Cheese Society over the last 12 years. haystack peak Creamy pyramid-shaped pasteurized goat cheese, with a bloomy rind that gives character and complexity. There is a layer of vegetable ash under the rind. queso de mano The first raw goat cheese from Haystack Mountain. Made entirely by hand (hence the name), has white interior and robust nutty flavor with herbal hints. Texture like Spanish Garrotxa. Aged at least 4 months. red cloud Raw goat's milk. A smooth, soft, washed rind with a powerful flavor that is balanced and complex. Aged for 60 days. The rind has a reddish hue. snowdrop Small white disk of pasteurized goat cheese. Firm and silky with a dense, creamy interior.

hubbardston blue (Hubbardston, Massachusetts) Soft-ripened blue goat cheese from Westfield Farm. Bright-blue rind covered in powdery gray bloom. Complex taste reminiscent of truffles and mushrooms. Like Camembert, this cheese ripens from the outside in. Inoculated with *Penicillium roqueforti*. Won Best in Show from the American Cheese Society.

humboldt fog (Humboldt County, California) Pasteurized signature cheese for Cypress Grove Chevre. This ripened goat's milk cheese is made in the Redwood Coastal Region of northern California, which is second only to London for foggy days. The cheese was fashioned after and named for the northern-California coastal weather, with a layer of ash in the center and, under the exterior, white mold. It is reminiscent of a perfect foggy day. Won first place in American Cheese Society awards. This creamy cheese has a nice acidic tang in the finish.

juniper grove farm (Redmond, Oregon) Pierre Kolisch, a former corporate lawyer in dreaded southern California, apprenticed in Normandy for a few years before buying his orchard-studded land in the high-desert cowboy country of Oregon. He started with 4 goats! pyramids A rich, mold-ripened raw-milk cheese modeled on the French Valençay. tumalo tomme A raw-milk aged goat cheese, this is a firm washed-rind cheese. The flavor is deep and reflects the pastures, forages, and high-desert environment.

mayor of nye beach (Logsden, Oregon) Pasteurized, traditional rennet, washed in beer, semi-firm, aged 2 months or more. Cheesemaker Patricia Morford fulfilled a long-held dream when she started making cheese with the milk from her small herd of goats. Pat grew up with goats and brought knowledge and experience as she established the milking herd. The quality of the herd's milk comes through in all of her cheeses. Patricia uses veal rennet to produce her cheeses, giving her the precise results that she desires. Reminiscent of French farmhouse cheese and made in 1-pound squares, the Mayor of Nye Beach is washed with local ale before aging for a minimum of 2 months. It has a big, pungent flavor with a bit of sweetness.

monocacy ash (Boyds, Maryland) This soft-ripened, white-mold pasteurized goat cheese is coated in vegetable ash and has a layer of ash running through the center. All of the milk used comes from Toggenburg and Alpine goats born and raised on Cherry Glen Farm.

pugs leap farm (Healdsburg, Sonoma County) Started by a gay couple who moved from San Francisco. The land belonged to Eric Smith's grandparents; his partner is the French cheesemaker Pascal Destandau. This small dairy started with just 2 goats, Edith and Eudora. Now the gang is up to 30 happy gals. pavé New Farmstead pasteurized goat's milk cheese. Bloomy rind, made by cutting the curd into very fine pieces to allow for maximum drainage, which results in a very creamy texture. petit marcel Farmstead pasteurized goat's milk cheese. The Petit Marcel is a small disk aged just 2 weeks!

redwood hill farm (Sonoma County, California) A certified organic farm that has been family-owned since 1968. bucheret Pasteurized goat's milk. Bucheret has a white, bloomy *Penicillium candidum* rind and a dense, buttery interior. The flavors evolve from mild when young, to tangy and slightly sharp as the cheese ages. Bucheret will soften under the rind as it ripens, and the flavors will become more rich and complex. camellia Pasteurized, Camembert-style, soft, bloomy-rind, small disk of goat cheese handmade in Sebastopol. cameo Pasteurized goat cheese, the slightly more rambunctious sister of Redwood Hill's famous soft-ripened Camellia. Larger in size, and adorned with fresh peppercorns and local herbs, Cameo makes its presence known on a cheese plate. Rich, with whispers of the classic pungency goat's milk is so well known for; the pâte is incredibly luxurious and melts lovingly on your tongue. The fresh peppercorns add a bright floral note, which is a delightful contrast to the darker flavor profile it accompanies. crottin Pasteurized goat's milk from Sebastopol. Small French-style handmade aged goat.

taupinière (Sonoma County, California) Laura Chenel was one of the first "new" artisanal American cheesemakers. Her first big break was when Alice Waters put her goat cheese on the menu at Chez Panisse when it first opened (almost 35 years ago!). This is a newish cheese for Laura Chenel—it's aged, pasteurized, "molehill" (*taupinière*)–shaped, with a bloomy rind, flaky and crumbly.

twig farm goat tomme (West Cornwall, Vermont) Semi-hard, farmstead raw goat's milk tomme, with natural rind. Twig Farm is a small husband-and-wife dairy and cheesemaking operation 10 miles south of Middlebury. They have a small herd of their own goats (17 does and 14 kids at this point!) and use milk from their neighbors' organically raised cows for their cow's milk and mixed-milk cheeses—all cheeses handmade and aged in their cave.

valsetz (Logsden, Oregon) Pasteurized goat's milk, with bloomy rind, soft. From Rivers Edge Chèvre. The cheesemaker Patricia Morford grew up with goats and brought knowledge and experience as she established the milking herd. She uses rennet to produce her cheeses, giving her the precise results that she desires. Valsetz is a surface-ripened cheese that is smooth and dense when young and develops creaminess as it ages.

zingerman's lincoln log (Ann Arbor, Michigan) Pasteurized goat's milk "Bûcheron-style" log made at Zingerman's Creamery. Artisanally made, mold-ripened, aged 2 weeks. Creamy mouthfeel with hints of citrus. Zingerman's is an amazing specialty-foods emporium. Check out their Web site—zingermans.com. Anyway, after selling cheese for years, they decided to start making their own. And you will never guess who works there—sous chef Aliza Miner's brother—how's that for a small world?

mixed milk

GOAT/COW

andante dairy minuet (Petaluma, California) Pasteurized goat's milk enriched with cow's milk crème fraîche thin mold rind) from a one-woman dairy. This small cheese combines the richness of triple crème with the bright taste and fine texture of goat cheese. Cheesemaker Soyoung Scanlan studied a biochemistry and then, in 1999, decided to make cheese. She is also an avid musician, and names all her cheeses after musical terms. This one is dedicated to Soyoung's mentor, Sadie Kendall, who makes Kendall Farms' Crème Fraîche. trio Pasteurized cow's and goat's milk, plus crème fraîche, in this triple cream created especially for A.O.C. by artisan cheesemaker Soyoung Scanlan.

blanco sottobosco (Cuneo, Italy) made by Caseificio La Bottera. Handmade from a blend of pasteurized cow's and goat's milk. The cheese is studded with black truffles from Alba. It has a slightly dry texture and a fresh, earthy flavor. Aged for 6 weeks in a dedicated mountain cave whose walls are made of *tufo* (porous rock).

caldwell crik chevrette (Montesano, Washington) Raw goat's and cow's milk make this semi-firm cheese from the Estrella Family Creamery. "Chevrette" is a term used in parts of France to describe a cow-goat blend. Washed rind, soft pâte, bright-orange-and-gold skin. Named for the creek that runs through the farm. This small family grass-based dairy is on 164 acres in a region that once supported 500 dairies (there are now only 10).

condio alle spezie (Veneto, Italy) Raw goat and cow. Large wheel. The rind is coated with parsley, sesame, oregano, and marjoram. Semi-soft, with great texture, creamy and smooth finish. *Condio* means "seasoned" in local dialect. Made by Sergio, the same cheesemaker as the Sottocenere.

gamoneú (Asturias, Spain) This expensive cheese is also known as Gamonedo. Asturias Province, in northern Spain, is best known for great cheeses. Gamoneú is sometimes made with cow's, goat's, and sheep's milk, although ours doesn't have any sheep's milk. It is made in a manner similar to Cabrales but not wrapped in leaves. It is lightly smoked for 10 days in a sauna, and then lightly pressed and aged in natural caves for at least 2 months. It is sometimes blue and sometimes not—ours is not. Actually, it is starting to mold a little around the rind, which is typical. It has a great dense chewy texture, with stunningly complex, earthy, sharp flavor. There are hints of pepper and smokiness on the finish. Very little is exported to the U.S.

kunik (Thurman, New York) Pasteurized. It is a unique and voluptuous triple-crème cheese made only in the Warrensburg area at this small family farm. It is a white mold-ripened wheel made from goat's milk and Jersey-cow cream. The use of goat's milk gives tanginess and flavor while the cow's milk makes Kunik more flavorful than a Brie-type cheese, yet more subtle and sumptuous than similarly ripened goat cheeses.

seascape (Paso Robles, California) Made by Central Coast Creamery. An original, hand-crafted artisan cheese made from blended pasteurized goat and cow milk. Seascape is a hard cheese with a slightly crumbly texture and a complex tanginess, a true American original.

tome de rocollets (Loire Valley, France) Pasteurized goat-cow-blend semi-hard cheese painstakingly washed with Sauternes and topped with a sprinkling of cayenne pepper, juniper, savory, and white and black peppercorns.

twig farm soft wheel (West Cornwall, Vermont) Made by Michael Lee and Emily Sunderman, owners of Twig Farm. Semi-soft washed-rind cheese made from raw cow and goat's milk. It is cave-aged for 80 days and has a rich, creamy texture and pleasant flavors of hay and earth.

SHEEP/GOAT

amarelo da beira baixa (Alentejo, Portugal) Raw sheep's and goat's milk DO cheese. Artisanal production. Cheese is slightly buttery, with a strong but pleasant aroma and a slightly acidic, winelike finish. Thistle is used as the coagulant, which I love!

mobay Pasteurized play on the classic French cheese Morbier. From Carr Valley Cheese Company in Wisconsin. Artisan cheese, half goat and half sheep, separated by a layer of vegetable ash. Won second place 2005 and 2006 at American Cheese Society.

sola val casotto (Piemonte, Italy) Flash-pasteurized (ideally, this will have less effect on flavor of the milk than traditional pasteurization) sheep-goat cheese. Semi-firm, with sweet, milky flavor.

tomme du berger (Provence, France) Aged by Hervé Mons. A truly artisanal raw sheep's and goat's milk cheese. *"Tomme du berger"* means "tomme of the shepherd"; in this case, the mixing of raw goat and sheep milk is determined by the cheesemakers' supply. The beautiful orange rind is washed with brine. Its pungent flavor develops with several daily washings and, typically, a 2-to-3-month aging period. As it ripens, it gets wonderfully soft and sticky, with a supple interior, hazelnut and animal aromas, and meaty, salty flavor.

tomme brebis chevre (Pyrénées, France) Pasteurized sheep and goat milk. Andante Dairy selection—cheesemaker Soyoung Scanlan spent part of 2009 scouting for the best French cheeses. In the Pyrénées, she was able to meet and make cheese with the shepherds responsible for this tomme. The rind is thick and reddish-orange; the pâte is ivory-colored and has a smooth, slightly oily texture. The flavor is sweet and refined with hints of olive, hazelnut, and butter.

tomme corse u taravu (Corsica, France) Raw sheep and goat, made of 80 percent sheep's and 20 percent goat's milk. Aged 3 to 7 months, this is a fantastic and rare cheese; crumbly texture; nutty accents, a touch of saltiness, and a spicy finish. Produced only during the milking season of local Corsican herds. Orange and ocher natural molds give a colorful and rustic rind. These molds originate from tree barks (oak, chestnut, and eucalyptus). Made by a cooperative of 6 shepherds and a master cheesemaker.

COW/SHEEP

adelle (Scio, Oregon) Pasteurized, soft-ripened sheep-cow cheese. Made by Ancient Heritage Dairy, a small sheep dairy that lies between the Cascade Mountains and the Willamette Valley. The sheep and cows are raised without hormones on sustainable land. They graze on wild rye, mint, clover, and other herbs and grasses. The makers believe that this is the foundation for their cheese.

caciotta al tartufo (Umbria, Italy) Semi-soft pasteurized cow-sheep cheese flavored generously with black truffles. Creamy, sumptuous, and made for the holidays!

caciotta rossosini (Lazio, Italy) Pasteurized semi-soft Caciotta. *Caciotta,* a term of endearment meaning "big little cheese," is a name used for small-format semi-soft sheep's milk cheese sometimes mixed with cow's and goat's that is more of a table or eating cheese than the more fancy DO pecorinos. Pecorino snobs may look down on the fact that cow or goat milk is sometimes blended into the sheep's milk—the only milk in the eyes of pecorino pros! This one is named for its red wax covering; it has a light, sweet flavor. Michele from Forever Cheese recommends it for breakfast!

gabietou (Pyrénées, France) *Affineur* Jean d'Alos. Raw cow and sheep, traditional rennet, natural rind, semi-soft. Aged for 3 months. Gabietou hails from the steep pastures of the Western Pyrénées, where cows and sheep alike graze on alpine grass, wild herbs, and flowers. Gabietou is an original creation from Gabriel Bachelet, a renowned cheesemaker in the Pyrenean town of Pau. Bachelet swirls cow and sheep milk together to make this supple, rich cheese. He gently washes the cheese's exterior with a brine made of rock salt from local warm springs, which gives the rind a copper glow. Gabietou covers your tongue with undertones of tropical fruit that are underscored by a deep earthiness.

hudson valley camembert (Old Chatham, New York) Pasteurized sheep's and cow's milk Camembert-style square, soft-ripened cheese from Old Chatham Sheepherding Company. This is the largest sheep dairy in the U.S., but the 1,200 East Friesian crossbreed of sheep are raised on organic fields and pastures with care and attention. Silky texture, with mellow, buttery flavor and a nice hint of tanginess. This cheese has won numerous awards over the years.

formaggio al tartufo (Tuscany, Italy) Made by Caseificio Bertagni, a very small cheesemaker. Pasteurized cow-sheep cheese with flecks of black truffle. The staff loves this cheese!

mona (Catawba, Wisconsin) Wisconsin Sheep Dairy Cooperative. Pasteurized cow and sheep. The Midwestern sheep-dairy industry dates back to the 1980s, and the WSDC is currently composed of 12 farms. Each of these farms boasts fluffy flocks of between 100 and 400 ewes. Mona is nutty and sweet on the tongue, with a moist but sometimes crumbly texture.

patte d'ours (Béarn, France) Raw cow's and sheep's milk from the Pyrénées, in the southwest of France. This cheese is very similar to Gabietou. *Affineur* Pascal Beillevaire. Patte d'Ours is an uncooked, pressed cheese with a smooth, soft, sticky pâte. The mixing of the softer, more subtle-tasting cow's milk with the pronounced acidity of the sheep's milk is a delight to the palate. The name means "bear's foot."

pilota (Basque Country, France) This pasteurized cow-sheep cheese comes from the Pyrénées. It is full-flavored, meaty, musty, fairly salty, with a hint of nutty sweetness. The texture of Pilota becomes very dense and creamy in the mouth.

robiola bosina (Piemonte, Italy) Pasteurized cow's and sheep's milk cheese. Robiola is a very general and overarching term that can sometimes be confusing. Straightforward Robiolo is made with all cow's milk but Robiola Bosina is a mixture of cow and sheep. These small bloomy-rind square slabs of unctuous, milky deliciousness are always a hit. When young they are pillowy, mild, and silky, but as they age they get really runny and slutty while still never being too overpowering in flavor.

robiola due latti (Piemonte, Italy) Soft cheese made from cow's and sheep's milk by Luigi Guffanti. The paper-thin white rind covers a straw-colored pâte. It has a creamy, velvety texture and a rich flavor with savory notes and a herbaceous finish.

rosso di langa (Piemonte, Italy) Made by Caseificio dell'Alta Langa. Soft pasteurized cheese made from cow's and sheep's milk with an annatto-wash rind. The paper-thin yet surprisingly resilent white rind covers a straw-colored, richly fragrant pâte. At maturity, this cheese has a delicate, velvety texture; the flavors are sweet and slightly reminiscent of cherries.

bica de queijo Raw mixed-milk cheese from Portugal with washed rind and sprinkling of paprika. Tied up like a package with string! Super-cute! Semi-soft, with great earthy, animal flavor. Very Portuguese!

campo de montalban (La Manga, Spain) This cheese was called a Manchego until 1985, when Manchego got its DO. It has a similar texture and appearance but exhibits characteristics of all three milks. Rich, buttery, with a nice balanced finish.

gran canaria (La Valle, Wisconsin) Pasteurized mixed milk from Carr Valley Cheese Company. This cheese is

marinated for a minimum of 2 years in extra-virgin olive oil. Robust, pungent cheese with a crumbly body, like Parmesan. Won Best of Show at the American Cheese Society awards.

la tur (Alta Lange, Italy) Semi-soft-to-soft pasteurized cheese with a straw-colored soft, wrinkled natural rind. It has light and fluffy texture, becoming creamy toward the rind, and a delicate, harmonious flavor that suggests crème fraîche, with hints of mushroom and a sour-cream tang.

robiola langhe (Piemonte, Italy) Raw mixed-milk cheese. Delicious, fresh cheese that becomes soft and more homogenous as it forms a bloomy white rind. Langhe is the region, and also refers to the style of cheese. Different from the Bosino, which is a washed-rind.

sitio da perdiz (Abrantes, Portugal) Semi-firm, fruity, balanced mixed-milk cheese. "New style," full-flavored, with interesting full finish.

trois laits (Ariège, France) Raw mixed-milk cheese from the Pyrénées, semi-hard, with washed rind. Created in the 1990s by cheesemaker Sylvie Domenc, who added sheep and goat milks to the famous local cheese called Bethmale. Matured slowly in humid cellars in order to keep the pâte smooth and supple. Flavor is slightly fruity.

toma della rocca (Piemonte, Italy) Pasteurized mixed-milk from Caseificio Alta Langa. Wrinkled, with natural geotrichum rind. Creamy, tangy, fluffy, has a nice balance of the 3 milks.

sheep

mount emu creek (Victoria) Cloth-wrapped cheddar-style pasteurized sheep's milk cheese. Made by sheep farmers who realized 10 years ago that their sheep would be great for milk as well as for wool.

mount emu creek romney fresca Another great cheese from this now defunct (boohoo) Australian cheese-maker. Romney refers to an old English breed of sheep that were brought to Australia for their wool and meat. The Mount Emu folks bred them to become good milkers, too. It is a semi-hard, open-textured cheese that is surprisingly moist because it has been wrapped in wax. It is also smoked, to create Mount Emu Creek Smoked Romney.

CROATIA

paski sir (Pag Island) A 1-year-aged pasteurized sheep's milk cheese. Crosswinds gently salt what little vegetation the island has. As a result, the indigenous sheep produce very little milk. The cheesemaker, Nenad, who has been making cheese for 15 years, owns just a fraction of the 40,000 sheep on the island. His cheese is rich and flavorful, with a beautiful crystallinity and gentle sweetness. The importer Forever Cheese worked nearly 5 years to import it.

ENGLAND

berkswell (Coventry) Raw sheep's milk from Neal's Yard Dairy. This is one of the most coveted cheeses from the British Isles. The raw milk is drained in colanders, which gives the cheese its distinctive appearance. It is dense, rich, nutty, earthy. Handmade at sixteenth-century Ram Hall, at the edge of Berkswell Village, in the heart of England.

spenwood (Coventry) Raw sheep, from Neal's Yard Dairy. Made by Anne Wigmore in Berkshire. Anne was inspired by the pecorinos she discovered in Sardinia. Spenwood is a hard, pressed cheese. In common with pecorino, it is brined after pressing, rather than having dry salt added into the curd. The result is close-textured with rich, nutty, sheepy, and long-lasting flavors.

FRANCE

l'abbaye de bel loc (Pyrénées) Raw sheep's milk. The Pyrénées is major sheep-milk-cheese country. This AOC cheese is similar to Ossau-Iraty but made at an abbey by Benedictine monks. These cheeses are made by pressing the finely cut curd into molds and then stacking them to press the curd and expel the whey. They are bathed with a brine and then placed in caves to age, where they are turned and hand-rubbed with salt. The resulting cheese is oily with butterfat, yet firm and supple. Taffylike mouthfeel. Classic, delicious cheese!

ardi gasna (Basque country) From affineur Gabriel Bachelet. For centuries this cheese was made in various sizes and shapes. Now this raw sheep's milk cheese is made in 3-kilogram wheels with a natural brushed rind and notes of hay and toast.

bastelicaccia (Corsica, France) Farmstead raw sheep's milk cheese, family-made. Semi-soft, with natural rind. Evening and morning milk are mixed with a small amount of rennet, which lengthens the time of curdling and limits the level of draining of whey. The cheese is made in a traditional irregularly shaped cylindrical mold, salted, and allowed to drain. Then it develops a light mold and is ready to eat! From affineur Pascal Beillevaire. Such a cool cheese!

le berger de rocastin (Loire Valley) Pasteurized Brie-style sheep's milk cheese. Fromage d'Affinois de Brebis (other name) is soft-ripened, with a creamy texture, sweet taste, and a bloomy rind. Produced by the renowned Fromagerie Guilloteau, it is very similar to the other sheep-milk bloomy-rind cheeses made by the same company. The cheese is produced in a rectangular shape. The pâte is mild and rich, and the rind provides a savory flavor and texture and builds complexity.

brebicet (Rhône-Alpes region) Made by Fromagerie Guilloteau. Pasteurized sheep's milk, semi-soft. The rind is bloomy, white with small stripes, beneath which lies an unctuous ivory pâte. Aged for a mere 14 days, this cheese is spreadable and luscious, with a mild, milky flavor and a hint of salt.

brebichon (Corsica, France) Soft-ripened cheese made from sheep's milk. This cheese is made in the shape of a thick, small disk with an edible, white bloomy rind. It has a creamy white pâte with a rich and somewhat nutty flavor. Unlike other soft-ripened cheeses, Brebichon does not become runny in the center as it ages.

brebiou (Béarn) Pasteurized, soft, pillowy sheep's milk cheese from southwestern France (as in béarnaise!). Mound-shaped wheel with tall sides creating a fluffy, thick interior and a layer just under the rind that will become runny with age. The flavor is mild and delicate—sweet, milky, and slightly savory.

brebirousse d'argental (Lyon) Soft, pasteurized sheep's milk cheese. Its thin, delicate, washed rind shelters a fresh, mild-tasting cheese with notes of fresh hay and a slight tang. Its texture is smooth and velvety, like very thick cream.

le brebis "clos du bardy" (Aquitaine) Pasteurized soft bloomy-rind cheese from southwestern France.

brebis corse (Corsica, France) *Affineur* Pascal Beillevaire. Raw sheep's milk cheese made in the style of a Venaco cheese, one of the most typical Corsican cheeses. The name was originally derived from the place of production, Venaco, a town in the center of Corsica, but it is no longer made there.

brebis du lavort (Puy-de-Dôme, Auvergne) Raw sheep's milk cheese recently created by Patrick Beaumont, who found the mold in Spain. This special mold gives the cheese its unique crater form. The milk comes from Lacaune sheep (a popular breed in the Auvergne). Aged 100 days.

Crazy rind due to natural mold, with an interior pâte that becomes tender and rich, with a subtle delicate and fruity flavor. *Affineur* Pascal Beillevaire.

brebis du lochois (Touraine) Raw sheep's milk cheese from a classically goat's milk territory. Small cheese with a bluish-gray mold covering a velvety interior and soft taste of the grasslands. Pascal Beillevaire *affineur*.

brebis fougère (Corsica, France) Hervé Mons *affineur*. Washed-rind raw sheep's milk farmhouse cheese. During the aging process, the wheels are washed with a local Corsican alcohol, allowing the finished cheese to keep for several months. The rind is orange and decorated with a large fern leaf, in reference to a time when the cheeses were fully wrapped in leaves. The pâte is smooth and ivory in color; the aroma is surprisingly light for a washed-rind cheese, and is lightly barnyardy and herbaceous in nature. The flavor is sweet and aromatic.

caruchon papillon (Roquefort-sur-Soulzon) Semi-soft pasteurized cheese made by Fromagerie Papillon, famous Roquefort producers, in the quiet *département* of Aveyron, France. This cheese is the spitting image of Pont l'Évêque, with a similar soft texture in the pâte, but much more pungency from the pasteurized sheep's milk. It is washed with brine for 10 weeks, and then allowed another growth of pale bloomy mold, so its aroma is not nearly as pungent as that of other washed-rind cheeses.

cazelle de saint affrique (Midi-Pyrénées) Pasteurized sheep's milk. It is flipped twice a week during its 3-week *affinage*, resulting in a surprisingly well-balanced cheese with a yeasty, fruity aroma while young; as it ages, the aroma becomes more animal and nutty. The rind is natural and is very thin and white. The pâte is slightly chalky at the center and very creamy just under the rind. The flavor of this cheese is herbaceous and sweet, with some acidity and a hint of salt. From another amazing *affineur*, Hervé Mons.

fleur du maquis (Corsica, France) Raw sheep's milk cheese. Pillow-shaped squares weighing about 1.5 pounds, coated in dried rosemary, thyme, savory, coriander seeds, juniper berries, and chiles. Creamy soft pâte, which, when well aged, starts to run! Great flavor from the herbs. You probably don't want to eat all the herbs. Flavors of hazelnuts, and even olives.

fumaison (Auvergne) Semi-hard lightly smoked raw sheep's milk cheese. Pressed uncooked from *affineur* Pascal Beillevaire. Made to look like a fat sausage or salami—sort of a play on the fact that it is smoked—it has deep and complex flavors of hickory and ashes. A unique cheese that may win over folks who think they don't like smoked cheese (like me!).

grands causses (Aveyron) Semi-hard raw sheep's milk cheese from *affineur* Pascal Beillevaire. This cheese is made by the Seguin family with milk from Lacaune sheep (the same variety used to make Roquefort). The cheeses are patiently matured on wooden shelves and brushed regularly. The rind is smooth, fine, and almost silky.

mouflon (Touraine) Raw sheep's milk cheese. The Touraine region is mostly known for its goat's milk cheeses. The name Mouflon comes from a breed of wild mountain sheep who roam the European Alps. Under its thin ashy rind is a fabulous, appealing, and savory cheese. Wow. From *affineur* Pascal Beillevaire.

ossau-iraty (Basque and Béarn regions) AOC raw sheep's milk. Large farmer's wheel made with the milk from Manech ewes, in the Pyrénées in France. Pressed cheese with natural brushed rind. Firm, oily texture, nutty, olivey, fruity flavor. This cheese has been made for 4,000 years!!

panache d'aramitz (Western Pyrénées) Another French sheep's milk stroke of genius from *affineur* Pascal Beillevaire: this is an Ossau-Iraty from a special producer—aged 5 months, 9-pound wheel, traditional rennet, natural rind.

pérail de brebis (Rouergue, France) Soft, bloomy-rind raw sheep's milk cheese from the Midi-Pyrénées. This cheese is from the same region as Roquefort and actually was first made from the leftover milk curd from Roquefort production. This cheese smells of ewe's milk, with a mild flavor and smooth, velvety texture, like that of rich, thick cream.

petit agour (Basque Country) Raw sheep's milk cheese—pressed, not cooked; 50 percent fat content. Small-format traditional Basque Country cheese. Same makers as famous AOC Ossau-Iraty. This cheese won the gold medal in French cheese awards in 2002.

petit basque (Pyrénées) Made by Istara. Firm cheese made from pasteurized sheep's milk. It has a smooth, slightly oily texture and a wonderfully sweet flavor with hints of olive, hazelnut, and fig. It is aged for 90 days.

pitchounet (Midi-Pyrénées) Raw sheep's milk semi-soft cheese, natural-rind, made by a farmer in the limestone plateaux of the Parc des Grands-Causses.

le puits d'astier (Auvergne) Made by Laiterie Antoine Garmy. This big, rustic, doughnut-shaped cheese is made from pasteurized sheep's milk. "*Puits*" in name, and the hole, reflect the open wells found in this part of Auvergne. Beautiful yellow molds and wonderful vegetal and earthy flavors.

pyrénées de brebis (Western Pyrénées) Raw sheep's milk wheel. This is a little confusing, but both Pascal Beillevaire and Jean d'Alos purchase this same cheese from an artisanal cheesemaker, Fromagerie du Pays d'Aramits. Jean d'Alos calls his version Panache d'Aramitz (see facing column). This is Beillevaire's. A special-production Ossau-Iraty.

tomme brûlée (Midi-Pyrénées) Raw sheep's milk cheese, born at the foot of the Baigura Mountain, in the heart of the "humped" and verdant Basque Country. After milking the sheep, which are only from local breeds (Basco Béarnaise, Manech Tête Noire, Manech Tête Rousse), they add rennet, and the molding takes place. Over time and with much care, the rind asserts itself, and the pâte changes in character, becoming more refined and flavorful. At this moment, they burn the surface, which will give some subtle and delicate smoked marks. Has 45–50 percent fat content. From *affineur* Pascal Beillevaire.

tome de josé Raw sheep's milk tome from José Bové, a Roquefort cheesemaker and anti-globalization activist who is best known for his assault on the McDonald's being built in his hometown. He is also active against GMOs, junk food, and U.S. trade tariffs. He's a cool-looking, mustachioed, pipe-smoking 49-year-old. The cheese is aged 3 months. Similar to a Basque-style sheep's milk cheese—pale-yellow pâte, rich, beefy, salty, sweet, nutty flavor. Large 8-pound wheels covered with a brown rind.

tome de villetritouls (Languedoc) Raw sheep's milk tome, complex but mild, with slightly cheddarlike flavor. From *affineur* Jean d'Alos.

tomette d'hélette (Basque Country) Raw sheep's milk cheese, courtesy of Jean d'Alos. Small cylinder of semi-soft cheese with aromatic, floral notes and herbaceous flavor. Uncooked, pressed; traditional rennet; aged 4 months.

tomme du lévézou (Pyrénées) Raw sheep's milk. These sheep's milk cheeses from the Pyrénées are some of the oldest cheeses on earth. This large semi-hard tomme has a creamy beige interior and a nutty, fruity, olivey flavor. With 50 percent fat content.

tommette de brebis (Pyrénées) Produced on a small farm by only one family, and then aged by the Schmidhauser family in the natural cellars of the Annecy Castle in the Savoie region. The family says, "In the silence of our cellars, time and the human hand work together to develop flavor. The whole process involves continual handling, and at regular intervals, the cheese, stored on racks, is felt, turned over according to a very precise schedule, and probed to ascertain the authenticity of the desired taste."

tommette de corbières (Languedoc) Raw, small hexagonal-shaped cheese made by a kooky cheesemaker in southwestern France, near the Spanish border, who just wanted to make something different. The firm pâte is pale yellow and almost translucent. Aged about 2 months, the cheese develops a mild, nutty, slightly honeylike flavor.

tommette de lucciana (Corsica, France) Raw sheep's milk, aged bloomy-rind small wheel. A selection of *affineur* Hervé Mons. Semi-firm, deep, earthy almost briny (olives?) nutty flavor. Very small production—an unusual and delicious cheese.

u pecurinu (Corsica, France) Corsica has been passed back and forth between Italy and France for centuries, so it's sort of a morph of the two cultures, languages, etc. Hence the funny "Pecurinu" name. This is a 50-percent-fat raw milk tomme made in the traditional style.

ITALY

bianco sardo (Sardinia) Pasteurized sheep's milk cheese with a gorgeous, pronounced basket rind. Aged a minimum of 6 months, it is sharp and full-flavored, not salty. Sometimes referred to as Moliterno or Canestrato.

brinata pecorino fresco (Florence) Pasteurized sheep's milk. Soft, white, nice holes, fresh milky flavor.

cacio fiore (Lazio). Raw sheep's milk. This small-format square cheese with a white mold rind is semi-firm, full-flavored, slightly tart and floral at the same time. Made with thistle flower.

cinerino di fossa Made by Casa Madaio. June 13 has always marked the arrival of summer for the inhabitants of Castelcività, a small village on the slopes of the Alburni Mountains, where the Feast of Saint Anthony is celebrated with bonfires. Casa Madaio has tried to interpret the feelings and richness of this area. The burning of aromatic branches of myrtle on the bonfires in honor of the saint produces a very fine ash, which is the precious ingredient for Cinerino di Fossa. During the weeks after June 13, the ash is collected and used to treat the cheese. This will then mature in the natural caves and hollows. *Fossa* means "ditch."

fiore sardo (Sardinia) Pasteurized sheep's milk. Cheese has cylindrical or wheel shape. The rind is natural, golden-yellow to black, and has a sour, damp smell. The cheese is hard and grainy and has a wonderfully rich flavor, with caramel sweetness, salty tang, and a hint of fruit. Rennet from lamb is used to coagulate the milk. When drained, the curds are scalded in hot water to seal the rind. Then they are stored on a woven reed shelf, where they absorb the sweet smoke as they dry. Ripening continues in another room or the attic, and the cheeses are periodically rubbed with olive oil and sheep fat to keep them moist. This cheese ripens in 3 to 6 months.

moliterno bianco sardo (Sardinia) Pasteurized sheep's milk—i.e., pecorino. Moliterno is the type of cheese. It is moist, salty, with nice crystallization. This one is made in Sardinia, bathed in extra-virgin olive oil, and aged 4 to 6 months.

moliterno with truffles (Sardinia) Pasteurized sheep's milk. Rich, nutty flavor with veins of black truffle.

nuvola di pecora (Emilia-Romagna) Translates as "Sheep Clouds." Saucer-shaped Nuvola is a semi-soft pasteurized sheep's milk cheese, aged 30 days, with a bone-white interior. Mild and creamy cheese with a velvety sweetness and a great tang of sheepy-ness. It won gold at the 2010 World Cheese Championship.

il pastore (Lazio) Pasteurized sheep's milk cheese, semi-hard, aged about 3 months, with a nutty, full flavor.

pecorino crotonese sfizio (Lazio) Firm cheese made from pasteurized sheep's milk. The pâte is a luminous flaxen color, and the rind is often orange, which comes from the wicker baskets used in the aging process. Pecorino Croton-ese is meaty and robust and has a flavor that falls somewhere between Parmigiano-Reggiano and Pecorino Romano. This pecorino is aged about 4 months and has a nutty richness with just a touch of sharpness.

pecorino di fossa Pasteurized sheep's milk. The tradition of making this cheese dates from the 12th century. Farmers hid their cheese in caves during the Saracen pirate raids. Now the cheese is wrapped in cloth and buried in caves in mid-August, and then dug up November 25, during the Festival of Santa Caterina. The cheese becomes deformed and acquires exceptional flavor and fragrance. As you can imagine, it's a very rare cheese.

pecorino di grotta (Romagna) Pasteurized sheep's milk. This traditional cheese dates from ancient times, when impoverished housewives would hide cheese in the basement (*grotta*) to sell for spending money. To this day, it is still aged in caves, for 80 to 90 days, during which it forms a beautiful rind and pronounced, deep flavor. Firm in texture, with sweet buttery finish.

pecorino foglie di noce (Emilia-Romagna) Pasteurized farmhouse sheep's milk cheese, aged in walnut leaves in ventilated caves to give it a particular perfume and flavor. Wonderful paired with artichokes and raw vegetables. Walnut leaves ripen only twice a year, so both production and availability are limited.

pecorino ginepro (Emilia-Romagna) This pasteurized sheep's milk cheese is bathed in balsamic vinegar and juniper (*ginepro*) and aged. Nuanced flavors, with a hint of sweetness.

pecorino lucano stagionato (Puglia) Made by Masseria Rosa d'Alvano. Farmstead cheese made with sheep's milk. Smoother, sweeter, and less salty than many pecorinos, the Stagionato is aged a minimum of 1 year, during which it develops a hard, granalike texture and a strong, slightly sharp flavor with notes of grass and chocolate.

pecorino nocino (Basilicata) Firm pasteurized sheep's milk cheese. It is a fairly young pecorino wrapped in walnut leaves, with a nice, settled flavor, some nuttiness, and a certain herbaceousness on the finish from the leaves.

pecorino toscano stagionato DOC pasteurized sheep's milk cheese made from milk from Tuscany, Umbria, or Lazio under the strict guidelines of the consortium. Aged 5 months. Firm texture, with nutty, refined butterscotchy finish.

robiola murazzano (Piemonte) Raw milk, DOP. Fat, fresh cheese produced from sheep's milk, pure or in a percentage not inferior to 60 percent. The sheep's milk comes mainly from the native breed Pecora delle Langhe (Langhe Sheep), which, having been in danger of extinction, has experienced a significant revival thanks to the production of this cheese, although it is still classified as being in danger of extinction. Murazzano DOP comes in a cylindrical form with flat faces, 10 to 15 centimeters in diameter and circumference height from 3 to 4 centimeters, weight ranging from 300 to 400 grams. It is a milky-white cheese, its texture slightly thick, soft, sometimes with some holes. The outer part has no rind, is milky-white in the fresh, whole cheeses and straw-yellow in the aged cheeses. Its taste, fine and delicately fragrant, recalls the sheep's milk with which it is made. Today every whole cheese is still made by hand.

sfizio pecorino crotonese (Lazio) Artisanal pasteurized cheese aged in wicker baskets. Sold both fresh and aged. Made January to June, when sheep's milk is more abundant.

toma reale (Piemonte) Pasteurized sheep's milk cheese, soft-ripened. Made in the typical Piedmontese Robiola style but using only sheep's milk. It stays a bit firmer than the mixed-milk varieties and is mild, sweet, and buttery, with a very slight grassiness.

tuada (Tuscany) Pasteurized sheep's milk from local Garfanina sheep. Aged 8 to 9 months. *Tuada* means "aging cellar" in the local dialect. Matured with a coating of ash

and olive oil on beech boards. Also, winner of gold medal at European Mountain Cheese Olympics 2004 (anyone heard of these Olympics?).

tuala (Tuscany) Pasteurized sheep's milk, from local Garfanina sheep. Minimum of 3 months aging on beech boards. This yellow pecorino has a very rich, full flavor, and is very fragrant.

THE NETHERLANDS

ewephoria (North Holland) Semi-hard cheese made from pasteurized sheep's milk. Made in the style of the great Dutch Goudas, and aged for a minimum of 12 months, this cheese has some crystalline structure that provides a pleasant textural contrast. The aroma is bold and nutty, with the faint traces of meatiness. The flavor is truly reminiscent of caramel, with soaring hazelnut notes and a hint of salt in the finish. Pairs well with dry and full-bodied whites, or light and aromatic reds.

PORTUGAL

azeitao (Setúbal) Handmade raw sheep's milk cheese. Soft, aged 90 days. DOP (AOC of Portugal). Setúbal is in central Portugal, to the east of Lisbon. In 9-ounce rounds; thistle flower used as rennet. Strong, earthy flavor. Very Portuguese. If not a DO, it's called Ovelha Amanteigado.

estribeiro (Alentejo) Raw sheep's milk cheese, chewy, spongy small disk, rustic, earthy, and delicious—stronger as it ages!

ovelha amanteigado (Setúbal) Pasteurized sheep's milk artisanal cheese, very similar to Azeitao. In fact, there is a huge political war going on in the region, because the major Azeitao producers are fighting these people over being able to call *their* cheese Azeitao; they want them to be required to share some co-op responsibilities or something. Anyway, our cheese lady is into supporting these folks, because she thinks they are being screwed over! She also sells us the Azeitao. Thistle rennet, small 1-inch-tall round of cheese, soft texture, tons of earthy, robust flavor.

serpa (Alentejo) DOP raw sheep's milk cheese produced according to traditional methods for another DOP cheese called Serra da Estrela (see below). This cheese is made only with the milk of Merino sheep, the predominant breed in the region. It is straw-yellow in color, with strong aroma and flavor. It has a creamy texture with thistle rennet.

serra da estrela (Beiras) Pasteurized sheep milk. This DO cheese dates back to the twelfth century. It's famous throughout the world for its unique character and intense flavor. The Bordaleira ewes produce some of the finest milk in all of Portugal. The cheese is handmade; it takes an average of 3 hours to make 1 cheese, and only 2 or 3 are made per day, per person. The cheese is made from November through February using milk collected from a single milking. Thistle is used as rennet and is evident in the flavor profile of the cheese. Serra da Estrela is eaten in two styles—buttery and rich, when it oozes once you cut into it, and more mature, when it is more cohesive and firm and a bit more pungent.

tintus (Setúbal) Raw-milk semi-soft cured sheep's milk cheese. Silky-smooth, with hints of fruit and herbs on the finish—maybe from the thistle rennet. Also has a certain cheddary flavor to me.

SPAIN

caña de oveja (Murcia) Soft-ripened pasteurized sheep's milk log in the style of French goat Bûcheron. From the southern coast of Spain.

caprichos de la pastora torta de oveja (Castilla y León) Made by Quesería La Antigua de Fuentesaúco. A raw-milk sheep cheese using thistle rennet and known as a torta because of its cakelike appearance. In Spain, the cheese is cut in half horizontally, and both halves are then wrapped in cloth, to be served by scooping out the unctuous pâte.

idiazábal (Basque Country) Smoked raw sheep's milk cheese from Navarra. Smoked with hawthorn and cherrywood and aged 6 months. You can really taste the animal qualities of the raw milk.

la leyenda (La Mancha) Raw 1-year-aged sheep's milk cheese, rubbed with oil and fine herbs and then soaked in Solera brandy for 4 or 5 days. It is beautifully balanced, with a nutty finish.

malvarosa (Valencia) Beautiful pasteurized sheep's milk cheese made from the milk of a recently revived breed of sheep called Guirra, which almost went extinct!! It is shaped and aged in cheesecloth and has an almost butterscotchy flavor.

manchego el trigal (La Mancha) Raw-milk (rare) artisanal version of the DO cheese, which is often imitated—kind of like Brie, in that the many bad ones out there don't mean that the great ones aren't still great. From the central plains of Spain, it is firm, pressed, and aged. Mild, slightly briny, nutty flavor.

ombra (Catalonia) Pasteurized sheep's milk cheese that tastes unlike any other Spanish sheep's milk cheese. Full-flavored, with a sweet, lingering finish. Often there are crystallized proteins as well—tastes sort of like a sheep's milk Parmigiano.

pata de mulo (León) Raw-milk artisanal cheese made from the milk of Churra and Castellana sheep. The cheese is left out (don't tell the health department!) on wooden boards to flatten slightly and take on its characteristic shape, then aged to develop its natural gray rind. Has buttery, full flavor, very special.

romao (La Mancha) Artisanal raw sheep's milk cheese made by one family. This semi-hard cheese is hand-rubbed in olive oil and fresh rosemary, and then aged in caves for 8 months. It is chewy and complex, with a long finish.

roncal (Navarra) Raw DO hard, pressed, aged cheese, rare and hard to find. They have been making this cheese in this region for over 3,000 years!!! It is rich with olivey, nutty flavors, similar to a Manchego or pecorino. Roncal is the first Spanish cheese to obtain DO status!

torta del casar (Extremadura) DO raw Merino sheep's milk with wild thistle rennet. It ripens like a Vacherin. Buttery, nutty. The bone-white interior is enclosed in a rough, washed rind, which is wrapped in cloth. The top is cut off, and the oozy, glistening, puddinglike cheese is scooped out with a spoon.

torta de la serena (Extremadura) Raw DO sheep's milk cheese. You cut the top off this round disk of cheese and scoop out the creamy, runny, soft cheese. Only the milk of Merino sheep is used. The sheep produce very little milk, with a strong flavor. Food lovers' dream.

zamorano (Castilla y León) Raw-milk DO cheese. Milk from Churra sheep. Semi-hard, very flavorful, and with a slight tartness at the finish.

U.S.A.

andante dairy (Petaluma, California) Artisan cheese-maker Soyoung Scanlan brings her background in science and classical music to her craft. Each cheese is named after a musical term. **musette** Raw sheep's milk cheese from Andante Dairy. This is Andante's first attempt at an aged sheep's milk cheese. Similar to a pecorino, except it is washed with organic molasses. Musette has notes of caramel, butter, and burnt sugar. **partita** Partita is a soft-ripened cheese made from pasteurized sheep's milk. It has a rich, buttery flavor with a long, lingering finish. This is the first of many sheep's milk cheeses to come from Andante Dairy.

bad axe (Westby, Wisconsin) Pasteurized sheep's milk cheese from Hidden Springs Creamery. This cheese is made by Brenda and Dean Jensen (with help from their Amish neighbors) from their Lacaune and Friesian sheep. Aged for 2 months and sealed in a wax rind, it is semi-soft and has a little tartness and lots of flavor. It's named for the Bad Axe River, which runs through Westby.

baserri (Marshall, California) From Barinaga Ranch. Raw, firm, with natural rind. The sheep graze on pasture all year long. Marcia Barinaga has been crossbreeding their East Friesian sheep, which are known for their prolific milk production, with the hardy Katahdin, descendants of North African sheep. Marcia's first cheese is called Baserri, named for the ancient tile-roofed cheesemaking huts in the Pyrénées, where Basque herders continue to make cheese in traditional ways. Barinaga Ranch's Baserri is an exquisite raw-milk cheese with a rich, nutty flavor. It is aged for 60 days. Available only from June through September.

bellwether farms pepato (Petaluma, California) Semi-soft raw sheep's milk cheese with whole peppercorns throughout. Vegetarian rennet, natural rind. san andreas (Petaluma, California) Raw sheep's milk. From Sonoma County. Aged 3 or 4 months. Creamy and smooth, with just a hint of a sour finish. Won second place at the American Cheese Society, 2005. Natural rind, vegetarian rennet. The famous San Andreas Fault runs right through Bellwether Farm.

ben nevis (South Albany, Vermont) Farmstead raw sheep's milk cheese from Bonnieview Farm. Neil Urie is the cheesemaker; his family came from Scotland 4 generations ago and settled on this 470-acre farm as cow dairy farmers. It is said that the land reminded Neil's great-grandfather of the family farm in Scotland (called Moss End). In the 1990s, Neil was bored and dismayed by the day-to-day of being a milk farmer, so he decided to make sheep's milk cheese! It took him 3 years of careful planning to switch the farm over. He now has 200 sheep on 200 acres, along with lambs, pigs, and turkeys; llamas guard the gang from coyotes and stray dogs! Neil admired the Major Farm in

Putney (about 3 hours away) and spent years studying with David Major. Eventually, Neil made some cheeses that were sold under the Vermont Shepherd name. Now he has finally made his own cheeses under his own label. Ben Nevis is the highest mountain in Scotland. The cheese is a medium-small shaped square with natural rind that tastes of almonds, grass, and the earth.

bingham hill sweet clover Semi-soft raw 3-month-aged sheep's milk table cheese from Colorado, creamy, with nutty, mildly sheepy flavor. Bronze medal at the 2005 World Cheese Awards. Bingham Hill is a beautiful landmark northwest of Fort Collins, outside of the town of La Porte, Colorado. Over 150 years ago farmers and trappers migrating to the unexplored Western frontier settled this area, creating one of the first communities in northern Colorado. Their triumphs and hardships are still remembered and celebrated today by historians and local history buffs. Bingham Hill Cheese Company chose their name to express their love of exploring and celebrating the Old World way of doing things.

dante (Stum, Wisconsin) Raw sheep's milk cheese from the Wisconsin Sheep Dairy Cooperative. Buttery, nutty flavor also reminiscent of the green grass of Wisconsin—Wisconsin cheese expert says it's "a cheese for the adventurous." My favorite of the 120 cheeses we carry. This cooperative of Wisconsin and Minnesota sheep producers started in the 1980s.

friesago reserva (Carver County, Minnesota) Semi-hard raw sheep's milk cheese from a family farm called Shepherd's Way (the same people who make Big Woods Blue). Aged a minimum of 4 months. Taste is rich, mellow, and deliciously sheepy! The farm is run by a couple and their 4 sons; they have 400 East Friesian sheep on 80 acres. Some say this cheese is similar to a Manchego or Parmigiano in style.

hope farm tomme de brebis (East Charleston, Vermont) Semi-firm raw sheep's milk—buttery and rich with a smooth texture. Dense and subtle, with a lemony finish. Only available seasonally.

kinderhook creek (Old Chatham, New York) Made by Chatham Sheepherding Company. Soft cheese made from 100 percent pasteurized sheep's milk. This 14-ounce soft-ripened cheese is an American original. The East Friesian ewe's milk brings out the *terroir* of New York's Hudson Valley, from which they graze. It has a delightfully creamy, even spreadable texture, developing a natural rind and creamy, firm pâte with mushroom overtones; oozes at its peak.

major farms vermont shepherd Semi-hard raw sheep's milk cheese made seasonally at Major Farms in, you guessed it, Vermont. It is made from mid-April to October, when the fields are abundant with wild herbs and grasses. Aged in the farms' underground caves in 6-pound wheels with natural pale rind and a sweet flavor reminiscent of herbs. This was, unbelievably, our first American sheep cheese ever at A.O.C.—shame on me!

marisa, cave-aged (La Valle, Wisconsin) Made by Carr Valley Cheese Company. Firm seasonal cheese made with milk from pastured Wisconsin sheep. It is a pasteurized cheese, white in color, with a mellow flavor, complex and sweet—qualities that reminded Master Cheesemaker Sid Cook of his daughter Marisa, whom he named the cheese after. Won 3rd Runner Up in 2008 American Cheese Society's Best in Show!

ocooch mountain (Westby, Wisconsin) Raw sheep's milk cheese from Hidden Springs Creamery. This is a cave-aged mountain-style cheese aged in the Jensens' own cellar, built under their house. They are surrounded by Amish farmers, who help them work the land. This is a delicious, nutty, almost Gruyère-like cheese that has occasional crystallization. This cheese was a huge hit with the staff.

oldwick shepherd (Tewksbury Township, New Jersey) Raw sheep's milk cheese from Farmersville Cheeses.

Cave-aged for a minimum of 3 months. Hard, natural rind—smooth texture and light earthy flavors—hints of truffles and nuts.

la panza gold (Santa Margarita, California) This award-winning raw sheep's milk cheese draws its name from the gold-mining region in California's La Panza Mountains, near the Rinconada Dairy. The La Panza Gold rind is washed with sheep-milk whey, developing a rich golden color as it ages. Evocative of farmstead Corsican cheeses, La Panza Gold has rustic, earthy flavors with fruity undertones. In 2006, the American Cheese Society awarded first place to La Panza Gold in the farmstead sheep-milk-cheese category.

piedmont everona (Rapidan, Virginia) Semi-hard farmstead raw sheep's milk cheese made by Dr. Patricia Elliott (a family physician). Traditional rennet, natural rind, rich buttery, floral flavor. Sweet and nutty, with a lovely aftertaste. Dr. Elliott originally got a few sheep to entertain her border collie, and then had to find something to do with the milk! Now she has 100 sheep, whom she loves for their sweet good nature! Won best farmstead sheep's milk cheese at the 2005 American Cheese awards!

sally jackson sheep's milk cheese (Oroville, Washington) Semi-firm cheese made from sheep's milk and wrapped in chestnut leaves. It opens in the mouth with ripe, full, and brackish flavors of damp leaves and chestnuts, and develops rich, oaky and bourbonlike flavors, with notes of dried porcini and aged apricots. Pairs well with Pinot Noir or red Burgundy.

simply sheep (Warrensburg, New York) A decadent, bloomy-rind raw sheep's milk cheese that appears every March. Beneath the snow-white rind is a fluffy yet dense, butterfat-laden interior that tastes of citrus and nutty, sheepy goodness. Melts in your mouth. From the talented cheesemakers up at Nettle Meadow Farm in the Adirondacks.

valentine (Madras, Oregon) A pasteurized, bloomy-rind, soft-ripened, sheep's milk cheese from Ancient Heritage Dairy. This is one of our favorite cheeses, and definitely a popular choice. It is named after the dairy's first and most endearing ewe, Val. The folks at Ancient Heritage say it best: "Valentine can be buttery, herby, with an elegant rich finish. When aged just right, it can be drippy and full of sheep milk round and soft deliciousness."

vermont dandy (Townshend, Vermont) Semi-hard raw sheep's milk cheese from Peaked Mountain Farm. Smooth, creamy texture. Rich, earthy flavor with hints of sweetness and nuttiness. The Works family has been farming the Connecticut River Valley since 1731! The current generation converted an old horse farm to a state-of-the-art sheep dairy and cheesemaking facility. The farm is home to 100 milking ewes and lambs, who are pampered and enjoy rotational grazing with fresh fields twice daily. They are milked only 2 times a day, from May to October—the philosophy is "better pastures mean richer milk and better milk means better cheese." This farm actually produces Vermont Shepherd as well as its own cheeses. They also make maple syrup and have 250 blueberry bushes.

willow hill alderbrook (Milton, Vermont) Soft-ripened raw sheep's milk cheese from a small certified organic dairy in Vermont—the new hit at Cowgirl Creamery! **summertomme** Raw sheep's milk cheese from Vermont. This is not really a tomme, but, rather, a small round modeled on Brin d'Amour. Bloomy rind with lots of hearty herbs (rosemary, thyme—very Provençal in flavor profile), rich buttery notes, floral finish. Runny and delicious. This cheese has won a medal at the World Cheese Awards every year since it was introduced in 2001.

COW

AUSTRALIA AND NEW ZEALAND

jindi triple cream (Gippsland, Victoria) Bloomy-rind pasteurized triple crème. The milk comes from their own herd of Jersey cows. Incredibly rich, creamy, buttery, and flavorful.

mount dumet double cream Pasteurized cow's milk double crème from Whitestone Dairy in New Zealand, who also make Whitestone Blue. Brie-style, creamy, bloomy-rind cheese.

seal bay triple cream Pasteurized triple cream from King Island Dairy in Tasmania, who also make Roaring Forties. Silky, buttery texture with Australian spunk and balls!

AUSTRIA

hubaner (Doren) Raw cow's milk. Hubaner has some taste characteristics of a number of cheeses (Comté, Swiss, Gruyère). The wheels are consistently washed for 8 months to produce an Austrian cheese with a nutty, slightly salty taste. Serve with a rich red wine and charcuterie.

BELGIUM

le poteaupré (Hainaut) Pasteurized cow's milk Trappist cheese. As the story goes, in 1696, a young technician from the Auberge de Poteaupré softened up a starving wolf by offering it this creamy cheese. Today, Chimay's master cheesemaker has rediscovered the ancient recipe and has re-created the true Poteaupré. Semi-soft pâte; washed rind with a lightly bloomy white flourish. It has an unctuous texture and is straightforward and clean on the palate, with a delicious perfume of hazelnuts. The crème de la crème of Trappist cheeses.

wavreumont (Werbomont) This washed-rind raw-milk Trappist cheese from the south of Belgium is one of the only true remaining monastic cheeses in the country. The abbey agreed to let cheesemaker Mark Rosen use their ancient recipe, and the results have been superb. This brine-brushed rarity has an extremely thick and dense pâte that is bursting with grassy sweetness and a pleasant lingering, musky aftertaste. Wavreumont is a perfect marriage with the wheat beers of southern Belgium and Germany.

wynendale (Flanders) Pasteurized cow. Difficult to find in the U.S., this spicy jewel of West Flanders is crafted with full-cream cow's milk following an ancient tradition of Burgundy. The name "Wynendale" is undeniably linked to medieval Burgundian history. Wijnendale Castle, amid the mysterious woods and the green pastures of Flanders, was referred to as the "castle of delight" by Burgundian dukes.

BRITISH ISLES AND IRELAND

appleby's cheshire (Cheshire, England) Raw cow's milk. This is the world's last cloth-bound Cheshire. It is thought to be England's oldest cheese—it is referenced in the Domesday Book and possibly dates back as far as Roman times. The distinctive orange color comes from annatto seed. It is made at Abbey Farm in Cheshire with the milk from Friesian-Holstein cows, and aged by Neal's Yard Dairy.

ardrahan (Kanturk, County Cork, Ireland) Semi-soft washed-rind pasteurized cow's milk cheese with pungent aromas, buttery texture, and complex, delicate flavor. Farmhouse cheese first produced in 1983 by the Burns family, this cheese has won many awards and is a cheese-head favorite. Handmade with Friesian cow's milk, turned every day.

coolea (County Cork, Ireland) This pasteurized Friesian cow's milk Gouda-style cheese is made by the Williams family, who brought their recipe from Holland. It has won many awards. Aged 6 months to 1 year, sometimes even 2 years. A rich, nutty cheese with a fruity tang on the finish; texture is firm and smooth with occasional "eyes."

doddington (Northumberland, England) Farmstead raw cow's milk from North Doddington Farm. Around 1990, the Maxwells spent time in the Netherlands, France, and around the U.K., learning about cheesemaking. After 3 years of experimentation and tweaking, their first cheese came out in 1993. The recipe can be defined as a British territorial-style cheese—it lies somewhere between a cheddar and a Leicester variation. Aged on pine shelves in the cool Northumbrian air for 10 to 15 months. It is waxed and sealed and turned regularly. Complex aroma and deep flavor.

durrus (County Cork, Ireland) Washed-rind raw cow's milk cheese. Similar in concept to the region's other washed cow's milk cheeses, Gubbeen and Ardrahan, but raw milk and aged a little longer. This is the favorite of the 3 of Lenny from Cowgirl Creamery. Earthy, musty, and deeply flavored. The cheesemaker is Jeffa Gill on Sheep's Head Island, and the *affineur* is Neal's Yard Dairy.

gorwydd caerphilly (Ceredigion, Wales) Raw cow's milk, traditional Welsh cheese. Developed in the 1830s by farmers to use up excess milk. By 1910, making Caerphilly became difficult, because there was a lot of competition from cheaper English cheese. During World War II, it was illegal to make any cheese except cheddar for anything but personal consumption. Caerphilly practically disappeared—until cheesemaker Chris Duckett revived it. He was the only farmhouse Caerphilly maker in the U.K. until he taught Martin Todd Trethowan of Gorwydd how to make it. Uses vegetarian rennet, aged on the farm for 2 months. The cheese exhibits a lemony taste with a creamy texture on the outside and a firmer but moist interior. As it ages, the cheese develops a natural-mold rind. The moist, earthy pâte is pale yellow and has a unique stripe of white at its center. The flavor is fresh and fruity with a pleasant acidity. Neal's Yard Dairy is the *affineur*.

gubbeen (County Cork, Ireland) Washed-rind pasteurized cheese from the southwest of Ireland. Semi-soft texture with fruity notes, clean acidity, and a pungent rind. Aged by Neal's Yard Dairy. In the same family as Durrus and Ardrahan.

hawes double gloucester (Yorkshire, England) Pasteurized cow's milk cheese colored with annatto from our friends at Neal's Yard Dairy, so you know it's fantastic. This is made by Wensleydale Creamery in central England. Gloucesters have been made since the sixteenth century. Traditionally, a Single Gloucester was made on days when butter was produced, and a Double was made on non-butter-producing days by using the overnight milk added to the afternoon milk. This one is cloth-wrapped. Typically aged 6 to 9 months before sale. Rich and smooth, almost cheddarlike.

isle of mull cheddar (Isle of Mull, Scotland) Raw Scottish cheddar from a tiny island called the Isle of Mull, famous for its beautiful town (Tobermory) and Scotch whisky (Ledaig). The Friesan and Holstein cows graze on the spent grain left over from making Scotch!!! They are drunk and happy and make delicious milk. This bandage-wrapped cheddar is a little softer than most British cheddars and a little more strongly flavored. Amazing finish—a little tingly, and I swear you can taste the booze! Too cool! Aged by Neal's Yard Dairy.

keen's cheddar (Somerset, England) Raw farmstead cheese, one of the 4 "classic cheddars." Made in large cylindrical wheels, aged for about 2 years. What makes a cheddar a cheddar is the recipe. The curd is scalded twice and then "cheddared," or milled, by repeatedly cutting and piling the curd in order to remove the whey and break the curd into fine particles that are smooth and silky. This process, along with the aging, gives cheddar its distinct taut texture and unique flavor. The cheddaring process was invented in Somerset (southwestern England), and that is still where most farmhouse cheddars are made. At A.O.C. we choose Keen's from Neal's Yard Dairy—the famous cheese shop and *affineur* in England. The Neal's Yard folks go to the Keens and pick out what they think are the best wheels of their cheese, and then they age them perfectly—the best of the best!

lincolnshire poacher (Lincolnshire, England) Raw milk cheese. Simon Jones is a fourth-generation family farmer on the edge of the beautiful Lincolnshire wolds, about 5 miles from the coast. The lush pastures sit on chalky land in an area where dairy farms and cheesemaking are virtually unknown. This is a handmade, traditional cheese made from a herd of 170 Holstein cows between the months of October and May—most of the cows are calving in the fall, so they don't have too much milk in the summer. The cheese is matured 18 to 24 months. Since Simon began making this cheese, he has won numerous awards, including three consecutive gold medals at the British Cheese Awards. Lincolnshire Poacher is meaty and sharp and at times can bear a surprising hint of pineapple.

montgomery's cheddar (Somerset, England) Farmhouse raw cheddar from one of the few producers left who make it the traditional way. For well over a century, they have made their cheese at Manor Farm in Somerset. The 56-pound cheeses are cloth-wrapped and typically aged between 14 months and 2 years. They develop full-bodied richness, lingering nutty flavor, and a wonderful balance.

mrs. kirkham's lancashire (Lancashire, England) Raw cow's milk cheese from one of the last Lancashire makers to mix curd for 3 days to make cheese. It is affectionately known as "buttery crumble"—it is just that buttery and crumbly, with a clean, sharp, acidic tang. Cloth-bound, with a natural rind that is buttered during aging! Aged by Neal's Yard Dairy!

quickes traditional cheddar (Devon, England) Farmhouse raw cheddar matured in muslin cloth, made in traditional style from Quickes' own herd of cows. The Quicke family name derives from the Anglo-Saxon tribe called Hwicki, which has a history going back 14 centuries! For the last 400 years, this family has been farming in the Devon countryside and using their profits to buy land. Devon is famous for its dairy products, such as Devonshire cream. The lush grass is perfect for rich, creamy milk!

stinking bishop (Gloucestershire County, England) Made by Charles Martell. Semi-soft washed-rind cheese made from raw cow's milk. It is washed with pear brandy that is made from the Stinking Bishop variety of pear. The washing encourages a pungent and spirited aroma. However, the pâte of the cheese is soft, creamy, full-flavored, but decidedly mild.

FRANCE

l'abbaye de timadeuc (Brittany) Pasteurized cow's milk, actually the only cheese from Brittany. It is produced by monks and related to Port du Salut. The pâte is delicately salty and soft with a tender taste. Pressed but not cooked, with a washed rind. As it ages, the rind turns an orange-yellowish color.

affidelice au chablis Raw cow's milk cheese in the Époisses style, made by Berthaut. The rind is washed once a week with Chablis, which gives it a distinctive winey taste and smell. It has a creamy orange color that ages to a deep copper. Similar to Ami du Chambertin.

ami du chambertin Artisanal raw cow's milk cheese in the style of Époisses but made a few villages over, in the famous wine village of Gevrey-Chambertin (this is why it is not allowed to be called Époisses under AOC rules). Rind is washed with Marc de Bourgogne (local brandy from Burgundy). Small disk in wooden box. Shh! This cheese is illegal as it's a raw milk cheese aged less than 60 days. Smooth, moist reddish-brown rind. Rich, huge flavor. Deliciously smelly, barnyard aroma. Steven Jenkins (cheese stud) calles L'Ami "staggeringly delicious" and says "absolutely my favorite French cheese. Everything you know about eating will be redefined with your first taste."

banon de chalais (Banon) Semi-soft pasteurized small disk of cow's milk cheese bathed in eau-de-vie, wrapped in chestnut leaves (to allow the rindless cheese to ripen), and then tied with raffia or straw. Banon develops a fruity, winey, nutty, woodsy flavor. This cheese was historically made with goat's milk near the town of Banon, on the border of the Rhône Valley and Provence.

beaufort alpage (Savoie) Aged by Joseph Paccard. Semi-hard cheese made strictly from raw cow's milk. This venerable cheese was already known in the time of the Romans and is named after a small rural town in the French Alps; it is made from the milk of Tarentaise cows, which live in the mountains and graze exclusively on natural pastures. Each wheel is aged for a minimum of 4 to 6 months in mountain cellars, resulting in a cheese that is generally richer and creamier than other mountain cheeses, such as Gruyère or Comté. It has a pleasant aroma of milk, butter, and honey. The rind is rubbed, clean, and robust, with a uniform yellow-to-brown color. The pâte is smooth and very firm, but supple, with few eyes; some crystalline structures may be present. The flavor profile is flowery and herbal, with a hint of caramel in the finish.

bourboule (Auvergne region) Semi-hard raw cow's milk cheese. Small, with natural rind brushed during aging in humid cellars. The pâte is supple and has the pronounced accents of the *terroir,* with 45 percent fat. Great country table cheese from *affineur* Pascal Beillevaire.

brie de meaux (Champagne and Île-de-France region) From *affineur* Jean d'Alos. Pasteurized cow's milk, with traditional bloomy rind. Traditional Brie de Meaux is made from raw cow's milk. Many of the best cheesemakers out there—Robert Rouzaire among them—make 2 nearly identical cheeses, but the one shipped to the U.S. is made with pasteurized milk. Milky and luxurious, this "king of cheeses" rolls on your tongue and down your throat, leaving behind faint flavors of garlic and delicate white mushrooms. Brie de Meaux is the most famous of the Bries. An AOC, it must come from the town of Meaux.

brie de melun (Île-de-France) White bloomy rind with beige mottling. Buttery, golden pâte, with beefy, nutty, garlicky, mushroomy flavor. Brie de Melun is also an AOC and comes from the town of Melun (duh!). It is smaller-format and slightly more rustic than Brie de Meaux, and unlike Meaux, is always made with raw milk.

brillat-savarin (Normandy) Pasteurized cow's milk triple crème from Normandy. Amazing buttery, creamy texture, with great cheese taste. Bloomy rind, which smells mushroomy and rich. Especially great when from our friend fabulous *affineuse* Chantal Plasse.

brique des flandres (Boulonnais area) Traditional soft washed-rind raw cow's milk cheese from the north of France. This cheese would have disappeared if not for the Bernard family, who embraced it and brought it back. The rind is bright-orange-colored (like Mimolette), with roucou seed. Mild but interesting taste, with nuances of almond, hazelnut, mushrooms, and a little spicy tang. Very unusual! From *affineur* Pascal Beillevaire.

camembert (Normandy) Made by Le Pommier. Pasteurized cow's milk, soft cheese. This is a classic Camembert sourced by the *affineur* Hervé Mons. The aroma is pleasantly rich, and the flavor is full-bodied and slightly salty, with hints of truffle, mushrooms, and garlic. Pairs well with light reds from the Loire Valley.

cap gris nez (Nord-Pas-de-Calais) Semi-soft washed-rind raw cow's milk, from the northern coastal region of France. Family cheesemakers, each of whom plays a role, whether looking after the herd, cheesemaking, or marketing. Similar to Maroilles and other cheeses of the north of France. Creamy and full-flavored. Cap Gris Nez is a famous peak on the seaside cliffs of the French channel coast, only 30 kilometers from England, known for bird-watching. The name means "Gray Nose Peak"! Beillevaire started as a raw-butter producer in Nantes (northern France), then expanded by starting to buy and age cheeses. He now has 5 shops in Gay Paris.

carré du pierre Antoine (Moselle region, in Lorraine) Pasteurized cow's milk. From northeastern France, near Alsace. Washed with Mirabelle (plum eau-de-vie).

chaource (Chaource) Pasteurized cow's milk. Semi-soft to soft triple-crème cheese. This soft-ripened bloomy-rind cheese is good to eat at any stage of maturation and is covered by a velvety soft-ripened, bloomy rind that smells of the white mushrooms that grow plentifully in the region. Once opened, the fully aged version is buttery and thick. A young version will be flaky inside and mild in the mouth; slightly older ones will ooze and have nutty characteristics.

chaumes (Périgord) Pasteurized cow's milk cheese from the southwest of France, made by traditional cheese-making processes. Translated literally, *chaumes* is French for "stubble." Based upon traditional Trappist-style cheeses, it is a rather popular cheese among modern French varieties, in particular with children. A soft, pale cheese with a rich, full-bodied flavor and smooth, creamy, quite rubbery texture.

comté (Jura) Raw cow's milk cheese aged by Marcel Petite. A milder and creamier version of a Gruyère, this cheese has been produced in France since the reign of Charlemagne. Although Swiss Gruyère may be better known, the French variety is no less special. Created by local villagers in Alpine dairies called *fruiteries*. Its milk comes only from Montbéliard and Teachete de L'est cows. Marcel Petite is one of the great *affineurs* of Comté; using their relationship with the *fruiteries,* these *affineurs* select the best wheels and continuously care for and test them throughout the aging process. The wheels are then released, at their peak of perfection. It has an ivory-to-yellow-colored pâte with hazelnut-sized eyes scattered throughout. The aroma is reminiscent of citrus fruits and roasted butter. It has an exceedingly complex, nutty, and caramelized flavor.

coulommiers (Île-de-France) Raw cow's milk. Soft-ripened, bloomy rind. This thick, flat disk comes in a wooden box and is considered a "rougher" Brie, with soft, uneven interior; at its center, it has the sourness of a fresh cheese. Pâte of pale yellow that has a sweet, melting taste. Full, rich, buttery flavor, with notes of mushroom, truffle, and garlic.

couserans (Pyrénées) Semi-soft farmstead raw cow's milk cheese. Washed rind. Uncooked, pressed. Made by a woman, Sylvie Domenc, in a region made well known by bicycle enthusiasts—the Tour passes right through it. Refined, soft, and fruity in flavor. Its origin dates back to the nineteenth century. Produced in the high mountains. Natural rind, beautiful elastic pâte strewn with tiny eyes. From *affineur* Pascal Beillevaire.

cremeux des citeaux (Burgundy) This unctuous triple crème is ripened to perfection by *affineur* Rodolphe Le Meunier (from Tours, France). The initial cheese is made by Fromagerie Delin, which makes some of the best soft-ripened cheese in France. This pasteurized cow's milk cheese develops rich, buttery flavors with just a hint of earth and nuts.

délice d'argental (Burgundy) Pasteurized cow's milk. Made by hand on a vineyard, crème fraîche is added to the curds, which gives it extra richness and a soft lactic tang. The thin bloomy rind gives an earthy note but the creamy center is luscious, rich, and velvety.

délice de bourgogne (Burgundy) Soft, pillowy pasteurized cow's milk triple crème from famous maker Didier Lincet.

l'édel de cléron (Franche-Comté) Gently pasteurized cow's milk. This faux Vacherin comes banded with the traditional strip of aromatic bark. Very well-respected and delicious cheese for those months when Vacherin is not available!

époisses (Burgundy) AOC pasteurized cow's milk. This is one of the great cheeses of the world. In a wooden box, with washed rind. Berthaut is the sole AOC producer of Époisses. Smooth, reddish-brown rind; rich, huge flavor; delightfully smelly and barnyardy!!

explorateur (Île-de-France) Pasteurized cow's milk triple crème invented in the 1950s in honor of the first U.S. satellite, *Explorer 1.* Soft-ripened, cylindrical-shaped, with bloomy rind (Brie-like crust). Salty, mushroomy tang. Bone-colored pâte, very buttery, rich, smooth. Eat it with champagne!! Fat content 75 percent.

le fougerus (Île-de-France) A version of Coulommiers, a Brie-style cheese made by Robert Rouzaire (the man who brought you Pierre Robert). Its name comes from the fern leaf draped across the top. You may see versions of this cheese at other cheese shops, but the ones we serve are from *affineur* Jean d'Alos, so they are super-special!

fourme de rochefort-montagne (Auvergne) Raw cow's milk farmstead cheese. Semi-hard, with slightly bloomy natural rind. This cheese has been around for over 200 years and should be as famous as its fellow Auvergne cheeses (Cantal, Bleu d'Auvergne, Saint-Nectaire). Toward the end of the eighteenth century, this cheese was used as a method of paying rural taxes! It has a unique flavor, slightly of dried fruit, with a touch of acidity and a warm brioche taste.

fromage du curé affiné au muscadet (Nantais) Pasteurized cheese first made by the local curé or monk who was fleeing from the French Revolution. This was the first cheese made in this butter-producing region. It has a smooth, wet washed rind and soft, slightly elastic golden and supple pâte. This version is aged in muscadet.

le grain d'orge au calvados (Normandy) Made by Fromagerie Graindorge. Semi-soft cheese made from pasteurized cow's milk. Very similar to its cousin Livarot. Its rind is washed with Calvados and is not too pungent. However, the cheese will grow stronger with age. The flavor is delightfully fruity and milky, with a hint of mushrooms and apple. What ties it all together is a pronounced meaty flavor. Serve with hearty red wines, such as Burgundy, Côtes du Rhône.

gratte paille (Rouzaire) Pasteurized cow's milk. The name of Rouzaire's decadent double crème translates roughly as "scratching straw," though explanations for this differ. One is that the cheese sits on straw mats to dry and ripen. The more romantic version is that the cheese is named for the alleys of Meaux, which are so narrow that the straw from hay wagons would stick to the walls as they passed through. With a 70 percent butterfat content. It is smooth, rich, and soft. The flavor is buttery and ripe. It is produced in 12-ounce blocks about 3 inches tall and 5 inches across.

grès des vosges au kirschwasser (Alsace) Very exciting raw cow's milk cheese, popular with Munster lovers (also from this region). The rich soil of Alsace lends itself to glowing, juicy cherries—farmers make kirsch with it. This semi-soft cheese is first washed in light saltwater for 3 weeks, then aged another 3 weeks while being bathed in kirsch! Yum!

grise des volcans (Auvergne) Raw cow's milk cheese, semi-hard, with natural rind. Named for the natural volcanoes in the region. The pâte of this cheese has scattered eyes and a complex and surprising flavor somewhere between a ham-and-cheese sandwich and a lobster with lots of butter that spent a little too much time under the broiler—a.k.a., *it rocks.*

jean de brie (Île-de-France) Bloomy-rind pasteurized triple crème from the *fromagerie de brie*—but this cheese is not *a* brie, it is *from* Brie! Rich and buttery, but with a nice tang to balance it.

jean grogne (Seine-et-Marne) Pasteurized cow's milk, artisan cheese made by Robert Rouzaire. This triple crème has a subtle lactic flavor with a slight bittersweet aftertaste and a spash of fruitiness.

langres AOC artisanal pasteurized cow's milk cheese from the high-plains area surrounding the town of Langres in the Champagne region. Small drum-shaped soft cheese with washed red-orange rind—uncooked, unpressed. The color is produced by constant brushing with a brine made from annatto seeds. The cheese has a concave top called a *fontaine,* a kind of basin into which champagne or marc may be poured—this is characteristic of wine-producing regions. In order to create this *fontaine,* the cheese is only turned twice while draining. Rich, soft texture; huge flavor—spicy, intense, and wonderfully stinky! Some say it has a smoky-bacon-like aroma. As you can see, a lot of work goes into making this special cheese!

lingot dauphinois (Provence) Raw-milk bloomy-rind cheese by *affineuse* Chantal Plasse. A *lingot* is an ingot. This looks like a little paving stone. Milky and delicious—rare artisanal cheese.

livarot (Normandy) Pasteurized partially skimmed cow's milk. Washed rind wrapped with 5 pieces of raffia, and always in a wooden box. Contains 40 to 45 percent fat. Straw-colored interior; strong, beefy, nutty flavor.

maroilles (Picardie) AOC raw cow's milk cheese from northern France from *affineur* Pascal Beillevaire! Boxed square shape—it is especially rare to find a raw milk version of this cheese. Powerful flavored, can be smelly. This cheese is said to have been created by a monk in A.D. 962. The pâte is golden, soft, and oily. A sweet taste lingers in the mouth. Washed rind, uncooked, unpressed. For the Époisses and Munster fan.

mimolette (Nord-Pas de Calais) Pasteurized cow's milk cheese. Same method as for making the Dutch cheese Edam. Some say this cheese originated in Holland, but others maintain that it has always existed in France. Probably in the seventeenth century, when the French prime minister forbade the import of foreign goods, the French started making it themselves. Firm, pressed curd, organically dyed orange inside and out. Cool spherical shape, slightly flat on top and bottom. About 7 or 8 pounds. Mild flavor.

morbier (Montmorot) Semi-soft AOC raw cow's milk cheese from Franche-Comté, made in a round shape with bulging sides and a horizontal black layer through the middle. This cheese was originally made for personal consumption by cheesemakers in the region. Natural, rubbed rind and supple, sweet pâte. In the past, soot was sprinkled on the cheese to separate the milk from the morning and the milk from the evening milkings. It has the compelling and pungent flavor of nuts and fruits, with a fresh hay aroma. Ours is from *affineur* Jean d'Alos.

munster-géromé (Alsace and Lorraine) Raw cow's milk. One of the world's great cheeses. Until the AOC was granted in 1978, Munster was from Alsace and Géromé was from Lorraine. The AOC is for Munster-Géromé. The cheese is characterized by pungent smell and soft, smooth pâte with the consistency of melting chocolate. Huge, beefy, nutty flavor.

nenuphar (Vendée) Raw cow's milk cheese created by *affineur* Pascal Beillevaire. From the southern Vendée region, which is along the western coast. It is marshy land, and the cheese is named for a water lily that grows in the marshes. It is washed and then dipped in tarragon and parsley to cover completely, then matured in caves (by Beillevaire) until the pâte is soft and flexible. Juniper berries are delicately placed on top.

pavé d'auge père gautier (Normandy) Semi-soft washed-rind cow's milk cheese, similar to the famous Pont l'Évêque. Super rich, it takes more than 5 liters of milk to make one Pavé, so production is somewhat limited; this is why most Pavé d'Auge are almost exclusively destined for local markets or cheesemongers. At least 10 weeks of aging is necessary for the heart of this cheese to be perfect. In a carefully controlled climate, where humidity and temperature are key, surface mold ages the cheese before any rind is formed for one week. Then it is washed with salt brine and brushed regularly in the cave while aging. The rind is progressively covered with a fine, pale mold and takes on a grayish-rose tint with reddish striations. The cheese acquires a characteristic taste of hazelnut. It is rich and soft without being unctuous. A *pavé* is a paving stone, usually rather rough and square, that one finds throughout France, often in the town center or surrounding town churches.

pays de retz (Loire-Atlantique) Washed-rind raw cow's milk cheese from *affineur* Pascal Beillevaire. First created in 1880, in a small village on the banks of the Loire, to the southeast of Nantes, it continues to be made according to traditional methods, using only the freshly collected morning raw milk. It is produced in traditional copper *cuvés* or kettles, the production not exceeding 1,000 cheeses per day. The cheeses are washed with salted water and Muscadet wine during 4 to 8 weeks of aging, which gives them a bright, shiny, smooth rind, yellowish in color. The soft pâte is speckled with small eyes that are irregular in shape. Its nose is unmistakable and captivating.

le petit fuxéen des pyrénées (Pyrénées) Washed-rind disk of runny, smelly, amazing raw cow's milk cheese. Highly allocated from a small producer in the Pyrénées—same people who make Petit Fiancé. A gourmand's fantasy!

petit sapin (Franche-Comté) Pasteurized cow's milk cheese made by Fromagerie Perrin. A creamy cheese from the Jura region, modeled on the wonderful raw milk Vacherin Mont d'Or. Like the original, it is wrapped in bark and comes in its own wooden box. The flavor is rich, earthy, and buttery with notes of cacao and coffee and a texture of heavy cream.

pierre robert (Seine-et-Marne) Buttery and rich pasteurized cow's milk triple crème from the maker Rouzaire in Île-de-France. This is basically a longer-aged Brillat-Savarin with crème fraîche stirred in for a nice tangy finish.

pont l'évêque (Normandy) Soft raw cow's milk cheese. A very rich cheese with a strong, pungent aroma of a well-used cow barn! The flavor is creamy and full-bodied, especially if you choose to eat the rind. The interior is soft to semi-soft and supple, with a few small eyes and a uniform butter color. Traditionally served with a glass of hard Norman cider.

reblochon (Savoie) AOC raw cheese made on the eastern border with Switzerland. The name of this cheese is derived from the verb *reblocher,* which means "to pinch a cow's udder again," because this cheese is made from the thicker, richer second milking of specific breeds of cows (Abondance, Montbéliard, and Tarentaise). It has a velvety washed rind and a moist, smooth, supple, fatty pâte. It comes in 1-pound disks tucked between two paper-thin wafers of wood and then wrapped in paper. Contains 50 percent fat. Has a delicious sweet, nutty, almost beefy flavor. Steven Jenkins says, "a triumph of cheesemaking—its rind is like the velvet on a deer's antler, its flavor like filet mignon." Need I say more?

rocher nantais (Couëron) Farmstead semi-hard raw cheese made in the shape of a rock (*rocher*) from this region near Nantes ("Nantais" means "from Nantes"). It is pressed and washed to obtain a rough, almost cracked exterior. From *affineur* Pascal Beillevaire.

sablé du boulonnais (Nord-Pas-de-Calais, northern France) Semi-soft raw cow's milk cheese. They say this cheese is "pre-salted" since the milk is salty because the cows are raised near the sea. The rind is washed with beer and is moist and red. The pâte is elastic in texture. A little on the stinky side!

saint-andré (Aveyron) Pasteurized cow's milk triple crème. Extra creamy, with soft, fluffy texture. A little salty.

saint-félicien (Le Dauphiné) Small disk, pasteurized cow with subtly sour taste, very soft and creamy. Thin white moldy rind and melt-in-your-mouth texture. Try with a Sancerre or Pouilly-Fuissé. Similar to Saint-Marcellin, but softer and creamier. Le Dauphiné is the old name for a region between what is now Provence and the Rhône-Alpes.

saint-marcellin (Rhône-Alpes) Small disk of soft, rindless raw cow's milk cheese. Creamy interior, intensely rustic, nutty, yeasty, fruity flavor. Originally, this cheese from the mountains to the east of the Rhône Valley, in the south of France, was made with goat's milk. Contains 50 percent fat.

saint-nectaire (Auvergne) Raw cow, with natural rind. Henri de Sennecterre, a seventeenth-century marshal from the Auvergne region of France, used to serve this cheese at his own well-appointed table. Finally, there came a time to present it to Louis XIV at Versailles, and the Sun King, who adored it, christened it "Saint-Nectaire." In 1911, Jean Dischamp, who came from a farming family, assumed control of a cheese business that was reputed to be the origin of the genuine Saint-Nectaire. Today, 3 generations later, the Dischamp family is still making this historic cheese. With a slightly firm yet supple straw-yellow pâte, this AOC raw cow's milk cheese is pleasantly weighty on the tongue and chewy in the mouth. It is fruity and acidic, with a strong smell of the rye straw used in the ripening process, as well as dark humid cellar notes. Yum!

saint vernier (Jura Alps) Made by Perrin Vermot Fromagerie. This is a soft pasteurized cow's milk cheese made in the Franche-Comte region of France. During the aging process, it is washed with a local wine. It is very mild for a washed-rind cheese, having a buttery flavor and soft, oozing texture.

secret du couvent (Loire Valley) Raw cow. From *affineur* Pascal Beillevaire. The sisters of the Coudre Abbaye have called upon the Fromagerie Beillevaire to revive this excellent monastic washed-rind cheese. Made from warm raw milk collected from the neighboring farms closest to the abbey in the secular tradition of the sisters, this cheese is pleasant and fruity, with a compact and chewy pâte reminiscent of the Trappist classic, Saint-Paulin.

le somport (Pyrénées) Raw cow's milk cheese made in the same style as Ossau-Iraty. This large tomme of full-flavored cheese is unusual, in that most cheese from this region is made with sheep's milk.

soumaintrain (Burgundy) Moist raw-milk disk of soft double crème with creamy light pâte and medium-to-strong flavor. The method of aging is similar to that of Époisses and Langres. Lightly washed in brine.

timanoix (Morbihan) Semi-soft raw cow's milk cheese washed in walnut liqueur from Brittany. Pressed, uncooked cheese, aged 2 to 4 months in humid, cool caves. The recipe was actually created by Trappist nuns in the Dordogne, who shared their recipe with a group of monks from Morbihan. From *affineur* Pascal Beillevaire.

tome de chalosse (Aquitaine) Pasteurized cow. From the ladies at Cowgirl Creamery: "The Aquitaine region, where Tome de Chalosse is made, is known for its beautiful

Côte d'Argent, its superior oysters, and that most powerful and intelligent of twelfth-century women, Eleanor of Aquitaine, queen consort of 2 countries. The Aquitaine is also one of France's gastronomic centers, where one can find Armagnac brandy, foie gras, Sauternes, other Bordeaux wines, and sumptuous pots of cassoulet. This sticky, washed-rind cow's milk cheese is aged for 4 months, during which it develops a pungent semi-soft texture and a deep, nutty flavor." Aged by Jean d'Alos.

tome de couserans (Bethmale) Raw-milk tomme from Jean Faup. Cheesemakers have been making Couserans since 1904. Made with traditional rennet and aged on the premises, in the Ariège region of the Pyrénées. Covered with a thick beige crust, the semi-soft cheese is buttery and supple with well-developed eye structure. Earthy and mildly pungent in flavor. Ours, in January 2009, was finished by Jean d'Alos.

tomme de berger (Franche-Comté) Semi-hard raw cow's milk tomme from the same region as Morbier. Uncooked, pressed cheese. Aged at least 2 months in a moist cellar. Beautiful, flexible, fatty wheel with natural golden rind (a result of energetic brushings during the aging process). The pâte is elastic, with scattered eyes; it has the mellow, nutty flavor of the beautiful mountains of this region. From *affineur* Pascal Beillevaire.

tomme de boudanne Raw milk, special version of Tomme de Savoie. Creamy and intense, sticky on your teeth (in a good way, of course!).

tomme de savoie (Savoie) Made with raw cow's milk that is pressed and uncooked. The natural rind is grayish with splotches of yellow or red molds. The pâte is butterscotch in color, pierced with tiny holes. This cheese has an assertive aroma but sweet, delicate flavor, with fruity and sometimes grassy or nutty notes. From Pascal Beillevaire.

vacherin mont d'or (Franche-Comté) Raw cow's milk. AOC. This is one of the world's great cheeses. Franche-Comté is on the border with Switzerland, south of Alsace-Lorraine.

It is the coldest region of France. A seasonal cheese, made only in the autumn and winter, from the milk of cows fed cold-weather vegetation—dry grass, hay, and grain (most cheeses are made with spring or summer milk, which is considered the creamiest). The AOC rules specify that the milk must be produced in the mountains, at 2,297 feet or higher. Also, milk must be collected every day, and pasteurizing equipment is not even allowed on the premises of the dairy or cheesemaker! Each wheel of Vacherin is banded with a piece of resinous, aromatic spruce bark and then packed in a wooden box with a lid. The top rind is wavy and velvety. The texture is supple but oozy. Big fruity flavor—faintly raw, woodsy, nutty—with strong aroma. Another good champagne cheese . . . or a light red would be nice.

vendéen bichonne (Loire Valley) Raw cow. This cheese is aged by Pascal Beillevaire in an old railroad tunnel, no longer in service. The result is a fantastic, dense, ivory-colored pâte with a mineral and earthen flavor. The thick, rustic natural rind imparts many other subtle flavors of the *terroir* that pass pleasantly through this sturdy semi-firm tomme. This is a rare and exceptional example of a cow's milk cheese from the Loire.

vieux lille (Nord-Pas-de-Calaís) Here is the stinky cheese you have all been crying for! Raw cow's milk. Lille is a town in the north of France. Semi-soft, washed-rind Maroilles—soaked in brine to make it extra-salty! It is also known as Puant de Lille—*puant* means "stinky," and the stinkier it gets the more the locals love it! From *affineur* Pascal Beillevaire, *bien sur*!

GERMANY

alpkase spicherhalde (Sennalpe Spicherhalde) Made by the Vogel family. This is artisan, seasonal Alpine cheese-making at its best. The Vogel family move their Brown Swiss cows to the mountains each summer to make cheese and butter. They average about two 50-pound wheels per day. The raw cow's milk is at once floral, earthy, and buttery: a true embodiment of the Bavarian.

backsteiner (Gunzesreid) Made by Kaserei Gunzesreid. This raw cow's milk cheese is made by Bavaria's oldest cooperative. Locally, it is known as a brick of gold for its shape and orange washed rind. The cheese has a bit of acidity that cuts the rich, creamy texture, and the barnyardy flavor is balanced with a certain milky sweetness. Traditionally paired with dark bread and onions, but it adds an extraordinary experience to the best cheese plate. Dark beers would be a natural, but it would also work nicely with Riesling or a light Pinot Noir.

ITALY

asiago stravecchio (Veneto) Hard, pasteurized cow's milk cheese. Asiago was originally created a little before the seventeenth century using sheep's milk. Asiago has DO status and is semi-cooked and aged for 6 months. This special and rare Asiago Stravecchio is aged for at least a year—sweet flavor, with the taste of mountain grasses—a beloved cheese of Italy.

la beola (Piemonte) Raw cow. Unique cheese—large slab with a thick, natural mold rind. Irregular, very rustic shape that is very rare and unusual to see here in the U.S. From what I can gather, it is named for a type of stone that is mined in italy called *la beola*—it is reminiscent of a stone slab! Made by Caseificio La Giuncà (who also make Cappello del Mago). When it's young, its texture is reminiscent of a Taleggio; when more aged, like a toma. Very flavorful!

boschetto al tartufo (Tuscany) Pasteurized cow's milk cheese. Semi-soft, with shavings of black truffles in it.

bra duro (Bra, Piemonte) Although little known in the U.S.A., this pasteurized DOP cow's milk cheese has long been a staple of the Italian Alpine diet. Aged 5 to 6 months, it has a slightly piquant flavor with a lingering nutty finish. Especially great with red wines, such as a Montepulciano or Amarone.

brescianella alla aquavitae (Lombardy) Pasteurized Robiola made from whole cow's milk and aged 2 to 3 months. Moist rind, very soft melting center, full intense flavor. Covered with a coating of grape pommace (the raw materials for grappa), this pungent cheese takes on a fruity fullness and a pleasant bite.

brescianella stagionata (Lombardy) Pasteurized. A relative of Taleggio, this exceptional washed-rind, soft-ripened cow's milk cheese has a beautiful smooth, sweet pâte with wonderful rich flavors and a lingering grassy aftertaste. This cheese also pairs well with a spicy Alsatian white wine, or with Amarone.

caciocavallo silano (Basilicata) DOP pasteurized cow's milk cheese that is ripened for at least 15 days. It is semi-hard, and its rind contains small grooves left by the restraining cords; it has a beautiful seal burnished into the rind.

cappuccetto rosso (Piemonte) This cheese is produced at an altitude of 1,100 meters in the heart of Alta Valsesia National Park. Produced exclusively with raw cow's milk from 20 local farmers, each owning just a few cows, Cappuccetto Rosso is handmade according to an ancient recipe that uses natural fermentation. The noble molds that grow on each of theses cheeses are indicative of its exceptional quality and craftsmanship. Each piece spends 60 days aging, adorned by the bark of the red fir tree, which imparts the intriguing combination of intense, decisive flavors, with a subtle earthy finish. Seasonal.

castelrosso (Biella) Raw cow's milk. This style of cheese is perhaps one of the most ancient in all of Piemonte. Similar to Castelmagno (famous DOP cheese), this semi-firm cheese has a unique, almost flaky yet dense texture. Aged for about 3 months. The flavor of the cheese fills your mouth and lingers at the finish—relatively mild, slightly tart, nutty. Pressed curd with buff-colored natural rind.

cremosina (Piemonte) Bloomy-rind cow's milk cheese, mild and approachable. The cheese is aged in caves with high humidity, which allows the thin, edible *Penicillium camemberti* rind to bloom. During the short aging period, the cheese develops a supple texture, buttery flavor, and subtle depth.

estivo (Veneto) New pasteurized cow's milk cheese from Sergio, who also makes Condio, Sottocenere, and all the Ubriacos. Aged in hay, verbena, mint, and chamomile. Sergio is very inventive and for a while has been making different trial cheeses with hay and herbs to test the flavors. This one he got just right; it has an earthiness yet also fruitiness. The square shape makes it particularly unusual as well.

fontina val d'aosta (Piemonte) The orginal Fontina produced in the Italian Alps, a semi-soft unpasteurized cow's milk cheese aged about 3 months. Its label shows the "Consorzio Produttori Fontina," which guarantees its unparalleled quality. Fontina is a rich, buttery cheese that finishes like truffles—excellent for fondues and au-gratin dishes.

laciarin de la paja (Piemonte) A summer mountain cheese aged on freshly harvested hay. A traditional raw-processed cow's milk cheese. Summer temperatures and the hay's earthy aromas combine to impart a creamy pungency.

lagrein (Alto Adige) Pasteurized cow's milk. Made by a small cooperative near the Austrian border. Steeped in the local wine of the same name, along with garlic and black peppercorns. Has a rustic natural rind, which picks up a good amount of mold. You can't miss the garlicky perfume of the pâte, which also has a faint sausagey aroma. Great paired with the local speck.

lou bergier pichin (Piemonte) This 60-day-aged raw cow's milk toma is produced with thistle flower, which grows wild on the mountainside. Cheesemaker Mario Fiandino named it after his grandfather, the "man of the hut"— delicate aroma with a full-flavored creaminess.

montasio (Friuli) DOP pasteurized cow's milk cheese. Takes its name from the convent in Giulia Alps, where it was first produced during the 13th century. This Montasio is aged 60 to 90 days and is pale straw-yellow in color. Its characteristic flavor is mellow, with a full-flavored finish.

montegrappa (Veneto) Semi-hard pasteurized cow's milk cheese, produced for centuries at the base of a mountain named Grappa. It comes from the same region as Asiago but exhibits a different flavor—nutty, with a sweet finish, like cheddar. It is aged 8 months and is gold in color, with its name branded into the rind. It is not, despite the name, bathed in grappa!

muffato (Veneto) Pasteurized cow's milk cheese made by Sergio of Sottocenere fame. He ages the cheese in oak barrels with marjoram, verbena, chamomile, and mint, then pierces it like a Gorgonzola.

passito (Veneto) Pasteurized cow's milk cheese made by Sergio, of Sottocenere fame. For this cheese, he uses 1-year-old Asiago Vecchio and immerses it in Raboso wine must, which has been left on the vine longer to raise its residual sugar content. It soaks for 30 to 60 days. The flavor and aroma are fruity and intense.

piave vecchio (Veneto) Pasteurized cow's milk cheese. Produced with milk from the Bruna Alpina breed of cows, which are fed on fresh foliage from surrounding mountainous pastures. The rich, high-protein milk is particularly apt for cheesemaking and imparts the special sweetness so characteristic of the cheese. Small batches of cheese are made from cooked curd from 2 milkings, one of which is partially skimmed milk. Some say it's like a sharp cheddar, and others say like a smooth Parmesan. Named for the Piave River. Vecchio is the Piave that is over a year old. Staff loved it.

pio vecchio (Veneto) One-year-aged pasteurized cow's milk. Similar to Piave but with a more savory finish.

provolone mandarone val padana Pasteurized true provolone (not the bastardized, commercial stuff on a sub!) from Latteria ca' de' Stefani, in the Val Padana region of Italy. This cheese has a funny history. It was traditionally typical of southern Italy, but in the first half of the nineteenth century, some of the best of the Neapolitan cheesemakers moved north, giving new life to the northern regions' cheese world. Ironically, this cheese has now all but disappeared from the south. In fact, it became such a valued and cherished prize of the Val Padana region that in 1993 it was awarded DOP status. To make the traditional provolone, animal rennet is added to whole milk, creating curds that are then "spun"—the sticky, stringy mixture is molded into funny, traditional shapes, then salted and aged 7 months. Sharp, tangy flavor.

raschera (Cuneo Province, Piemonte) Natural-rind pasteurized cow's milk cheese with a smooth, sweet flavor. Generally aged for 50 to 60 days. Very little of this cheese makes its way out of Italy, so it's a real treat. Its name comes from a lake in the area.

robiola di bosco (Lombardy) Pasteurized small squares of washed-rind cow's milk cheese. From Val Taleggio, made in the same style as Taleggio. It is stinky but not as strong-tasting as its smell—silky, smooth, sexy texture! Do not confuse Robiola di Bosco with Robiola Bosina, which is a mixed-milk cheese (cow and sheep). Staff loved it.

robiola rustica (Lombardy) This raw cheese is washed, with yellow-ocher rind. A soft cheese without holes, it gets a sharp and lovely aroma.

rosso gratin (Piemonte) Pasteurized, small barrel-shaped cheeses from famed Caseificio Pier Luigi Rosso (see Rosso Maccagno). The name Gratin is typical for a long-aging cheese that is to be preserved and grated (Italian *rattare*). In reality, the texture is very delicate. Gratin is a semi-hard cheese, made from whole cow's milk, rennet, salt, and enzymes, with a natural, dark, and wrinkled rind with splotches of yellow molds. The pâte is white, compact, creamy toward the rind, and crumbly in the center. Flavor-wise, it has a touch of acidity, salt, and the round, rich taste of fresh cream. It smells of fresh pasture and mountain air. The wheels are aged in "fresh and humid" rooms on white pinewood boards for about 45 days.

rosso maccagno (Piemonte) Semi-soft raw cow's milk cheese from the Alpine valleys north of Biella. From famed Caseificio Pier Luigi Rosso. All cheeses produced by Caseificio Rosso are traditional Biellesi cheeses and are made with milk from the cattle breeds Pezzata Rossa (Red Dappled) and Bruno Alpina, selected rennet, and salt. Ripened, following the traditions, in underground cellars, on boards of silver fir. Although they are all soft cheeses, they differ in taste, because the milk, collected from different valleys, is obtained from cows eating different pastures. The different cheeses will have different levels of maturity, which will distinguish one cheese from another in its taste. Maccagno is smooth, creamy, and sweet, with small holes and grassy, nutty flavor.

sottocenere (Veneto) An exotic, semi-soft pasteurized cow's milk cheese aged in ashes to preserve it, as per Venetian farmers' tradition. These ash ingredients include nutmeg, cloves, coriander, cinnamon, licorice, and fennel, and the cheese itself has black truffles in it. Rind aromatized with truffle oil. Staff loved it.

taleggio (Lombardy) DOC soft, pasteurized cow's milk cheese with pressed curd and washed rind. Its flavor can range from mild to pungent, depending on its age. When it's young, its color is pale yellow and its texture semi-soft. It has 48 percent fat content. Thick square of stinky cheese. The smell is generally much stronger than the taste. Refined cheese with sexy, milky, soft mouthfeel. As it ages, it can become more nutty and meaty.

toma montanara alle erbe (Piemonte) Raw cow's milk tomme from artisanal producer Caseificio Pier Luigi Rosso (making cheese since 1894). Made with milk from a special breed of Piedmontese cattle called Pezzata Rossa (Red Dappled). The toma is well aged in underground caves, according to tradition, on silver-fir boards. Semi-hard white interior with widespread holes, flavored with coriander, fennel, and cumin seeds (the *erbe*, or herbs).

toma piemontese (Piemonte) Semi-soft pasteurized cow's milk cheese. Aged for a minimum of 90 days, it is creamy and full-flavored, with a smooth but lingering fin-

ish. It has a rustic natural rind that accrues mold—the yellow is the sign of a healthy cheese.

torta ambros (Lombardy) Pasteurized washed-rind large round wheel (9 pounds). This cheese is made by the favorite Taleggio producer of Michele at Forever Cheese. It is smooth, creamy, slightly earthy, and Brie-like. Rich flavor, and the taste of the sweet milk.

ubriaco alla birra rossa (Veneto) Raw cow's milk cheese, washed in artisanally made red beer.

ubriaco al fragolino (Veneto) Raw cow's milk, 12-pound wheel aged for 8 months in a local sweet wine called Fragolino. Smooth, sweet flavor with a lingering finish. Great aroma, too! Sergio also makes Condio and Sottocenere.

ubriaco del piave (Veneto) Pasteurized cow's milk cheese created by farmers in Piave, who preserved their cheese by immersing it in fermenting wine must during the grape harvest. Today the cheese is bathed for 40 hours in must consisting of Cabernet, Merlot, and Raboso grapes, to form a rough violet rind that still has remnants of grape seeds and leaves. It is sweet, with a fruity finish, and it has a fragrant aroma. *Ubriaco* means "drunk" in Italian.

ubriaco al prosecco (Veneto) Semi-cooked 4-to-5-month-old pasteurized cow's milk cheese, rubbed with Prosecco must, which gives it a scent of apple, pear, apricot, and rose. Has an aftertaste of almond. Eat this with Prosecco! From Sergio, the cheesemaker who produces Sottocenere and Condio.

ubriacone (Veneto) Raw cow's milk cheese bathed in a local wine must and then pierced like a Gorgonzola to let the aroma and flavor permeate the cheese. *Ubriacone* is an affectionate term for "great big drunk." The cheese is covered in grape leaves to cover the piercings so that mold won't grow in them.

vento d'estate (Veneto) Pasteurized cow's milk (possibly other milks mixed in, but they don't tell us). The name means "summer wind." It is a *barricato* cheese, meaning that it is aged in wine barrels. This one is covered in hay, which gives it a perfume of lilac, pear, and straw. Staff loved it.

THE NETHERLANDS

gouda pittig Very hard Gouda made from pasteurized cow's milk. *Pittig* translates to "full-bodied" in English, and it is an apt description of this tasty cheese. During its 4-year *affinage,* it develops a muted caramel color matched by a full, tangy flavor and slightly granular, Parmesan-like texture.

north hollander Pasteurized cow's milk Gouda, aged 4 years. This cheese is from the north of Holland, and the cows graze on pastures that were previously under the sea. This unique *terroir* imparts a special flavor to the cheese. Hard but not crumbly, some crystallization and crunchiness. Amazing butterscotch and caramel notes, with just a hint of salt. I have been tasting Goudas and Gouda-style cheeses for years, and they have never really done anything for me until *now*!!! This one is delicious!

wilde weide (Zwanburderpolder, Holland) Organic raw cow's milk. Traditional rennet, firm, aged 15 months. Jan and Roos van Schie have one of the only small-production farmstead cheeses made in Holland. Located in the south of Holland, on a lake island, the Schies' farm was established in the late eighteenth century. Wilde Weide, an organic Gouda whose name means "Wild Meadow," is made with milk from their mixed herd of Montbéliard and red Friesian cows that graze year-round. Made in a traditional Gouda custom, the curds are washed but are then pressed using a manual, hand-cranked press for at least 24 hours before being bathed in brine, salted, and put in the cave for ripening. The cheese is then aged for 15 months, resulting in a straw-colored wheel with a distinct and fine sandy texture that melts in your mouth, leaving aromas of hazelnut, butter, whey, and bourbon.

PORTUGAL

são jorge (Azores) DO raw cow's milk cheese. This group of Portuguese islands are 900 miles west of mainland Portugal. Lush, subtropical mountains rise steeply from the ocean, opening into Mediterranean forests and broad pastures filled with cows from which the Queijo de São Jorge (Saint George Cheese) is made. The combination of untreated milk and traditional aging methods gives it its unique and distinct flavor. Its hard rind protects the slightly crumbly, light-yellow cheese within. Cured, semi-hard cheese with small irregular holes throughout. This famous cheese is said to get its particular flavor from the unique *terroir* and climate conditions. Great barnyard flavor! Emigrants from Portugal have been making this cheese since the fifteenth century.

SPAIN

afuega'l pitu (Asturias) Very unusual raw cow's milk cheese. Absolutely artisanal, and one of the oldest cheeses from the region. A small, round cheese with crazy texture and bright-orange color. The name translates from Asturian dialect to "sets fire in your gullet," because of its dry texture and acidic nature. It is piquant but deliciously nutty, flavored with paprika. Beggar's-purse-shaped. The form is created by pressing the cheese in a cloth. It is aged 1½ months. Steve Jenkins, the cheesemonger, describes it as follows: "brilliant cheese, seemingly neolithic in its primitive and rustic appearance, intense flavor of black walnuts; amazing palate-coating mouthfeel; a little cheddar like in flavor with a long, spicy finish!"

aragonés (Aragón) Raw cow's milk, washed-rind cheese. There are not that many interesting cow's milk cheeses, but this one from the same producer as our beloved patacabra is one. Fruity, earthy, and delicious.

arzúa ulloa (Galicia) Pasteurized DO cheese from the north of Spain, one of the classic traditional cheeses of the region. Soft texture, with the taste of fresh milk. The cheese is semi-cured. Its rind is clean, smooth, waxy, and yellowish. The cheese itself is also yellowish, creamy, and without holes.

canal de ciercos (Peñamellera, Asturias) Soft-ripened traditional raw milk cheese of the region. Small disk. The name refers to "open space" or "cavern between the mountains." Buttery. This cheese is sometimes made with a mix of cow, sheep, and goat.

casin (central Asturias) Raw milk from a breed of cows called Casina. They use lactic fermentation in making the cheese, and before they put it in molds, the curds are unified, using special rollers that create a cheese that melts in your mouth. It is shaped like a tart and has an identifying mark indented into its top. Yellowish color and somewhat strong and slightly bitter but pleasant flavor.

castellot (Catalonia) This is a very special cheese from Michele at Forever Cheese. It is made by a man she calls "one of the most talented artisans I have met"—and that's saying a lot, because she spends her life meeting these people! Castellot is a raw milk cheese made in Catalonia in the style of a Piedmontese Toma Brusca, Castelrosso, and Castelmagno—rare, ancient semi-hard full-flavored cheeses. It takes cheesemaker Salvador Mauro 9 hours to make this labor-intensive cheese. He only makes 9 or 10 a year!!—so we are really lucky to have one!

la cueva llonin (Peñamellera, Asturias) Pasteurized cave-ripened cow's milk cheese. Bloomy rind and soft texture, like a Camembert. It has a pale-yellow interior and an aroma of dried herbs and mushrooms, a subtle, lingering finish. Named after one of the famous Paleolithic caves in the town of Llonin. Staff loved it!

mahón riserva DO thermalized (not pasteurized) cow's milk cheese from the island of Minorca (the farthermost of the Balaeric Islands, off the eastern Spanish coast). This cheese is the second-most-popular cheese in Spain (after Manchego). Aged 10 to 12 months. Deep-yellow color with numerous "eyes" and a characteristic fiery-orange rind. Sharp flavor with sweet, buttery finish.

challerhocker (Toggenburg) Cheesemaker Walter Rass says that producing Challerhocker is his passion. It's incredibly creamy, silky, and dense, with slight crystallization. Made by thermalization rather than pasteurization, it smells like peanuts, caramel, and roasted meat.

le charmand (Toggenburg) Washed-rind thermalized cow's milk cheese. Made by Walter Rass of Challerhocker fame. He also makes a washed-rind cheese called Forsterkase, which is crazy strong—Le Charmand is milder than Forsterkase but still stinky enough for the curd nerds!

heublumen (Toggenburg) Made by the Stadelmann family. This firm, rich cow's milk cheese is, uniquely, covered in hayflowers. Another wonderful mountain cheese from this producer, the flavors are complex, nutty, with an herbal, grassy character acquired from the coated rind.

krummenswiler (Toggenburg) Raw cow's milk cheese made by the Stadelmann family. Firm cheese; it has a dense, straw-colored pâte with a complex, nutty flavor. Similar in style to the better known Appenzeller, it has a much richer, sweeter flavor.

scharfe maxx (Schafthousen) In Switzerland, on the edge of Lake Constance, 3 master cheesemakers use thermalized cow's milk to create a firm and powerful cheese. Brine-and-herb-washed, aged 6 months, it is definitely sharp and occasionally barnyardy. The creaminess always remains, on account of the whole milk and touch of cream used.

selun bergkase (Toggenburg) Made by the Stadelmann family. A semi-soft, washed-rind cow's milk cheese in the tradition of Saint-Nectaire. It has a strong farmy aroma and a big, almost savory flavor. The whole wheel is beautiful when purchased intact, because it is decorated with hayflower to spell out the name "Selun." This cheese has a rich and creamy texture, with complex milky flavors, full of *terroir*.

le tonneau (western Switzerland) Raw-milk "barrel-shaped" (*tonneau* is "barrel" in French) wheel of semi-hard cheese with black wax coating. This cheese has the word "Switzerland" imprinted in its side (very patriotic!). It smells sort of like Gruyère, starts out milky and fruity, but finishes with a nice tang. Aged over 1 year.

U.S.A.

andante dairy (Petaluma, California) Artisan cheesemaker Soyoung Scanlan brings her background in science and classical music to her craft. She names her cheeses after musical terms. **nocturne** Pasteurized. Soft-ripened cheese made from cow's milk. Slightly hard when very young; moist and creamy at maturity. Soyoung says, "It has a pleasantly tart flavor with some sweetness. The color of this cheese reminds me of Whistler's painting *Nocturnes.* Its delicate flavor and slow cheesemaking process are reminiscent of the gentle movement of Chopin's piano nocturnes, which I like to play the most." **picolo** Pasteurized cow's milk. Soft-ripened triple-crème cheese. Slightly hard when very young, then moist and creamy. **variation no.1** Raw cow. Soyoung Scanlan's variation on an aged Gouda.

bittersweet plantation dairy (Gonzales, Louisiana) Started by chef John Folse, Bittersweet Plantation Dairy is one of the best-respected artisanal American cheesemakers. The dairy works to create products that represent the 7 nations that came together to create the Cajun and Creole heritage. The fleur-de-lis is, of course, the symbol of France. **fleur-de-lis** Bloomy-rind triple-cream cow's milk cheese; it won the gold medal at the World Cheese Awards. **fleur-de-teche** Bloomy-rind, French-style, pasteurized 80-percent-butterfat triple-cream cow's milk cheese. A line of vegetable ash weaves its way through the cheese.

black butte (Orland, California) Gouda-style farmstead cheese (they have 70 cows and are one of only 10 farmstead dairies in California) from a small family operation in northern Sacramento County. The Pedrozo family come from 3 generations of dairy farming. In 1998, Tim

Pedrozo decided to try cheesemaking—he took a cheesemaking course at UC—and now the whole family (including 2 kids) is involved. Their college-aged daughter even does the PR! They are very pro-slow-food—keeping the old traditions alive. The cheeses are 20 pounds and made with traditional Dutch forms. They won the silver medal for the Black Butte at the World Cheese Competition in England in 2000. Great milky flavor with cheddarlike tang. Black Butte is only made with spring milk. Mount Lassen, their other cheese, is the same way but with the rest of the year's milk.

blythedale camembert (Corinth, Vermont) Farmstead Camembert-style (duh!) lightly pasteurized cow's milk cheese from Blythedale Farm. Jersey milk, bloomy rind. Cheesemaker Karen Galayda loves her herd of 40 or so Jersey cows. She hand-ladles all her cheeses—her Brie and Camembert require a great deal of hands-on care and are considered the most difficult to make.

brindisi (Salem, Oregon) Raw Jersey cow's milk. Made by Rod Volbeda of Willamette Valley Cheese Company. Firm cheese inspired by the great Fontinas of Italy, this cheese has a warm, golden glow and a complex flavor. It is lightly salty with a shelf-aged hard rind that lands sharply on the palate and mellows immediately. The rugged gray rind contrasts nicely with the ivory-to-pale-yellow pâte. The texture is springy and delightful.

carmody reserve Raw cow's milk from bellwether farms in Petaluma, Sonoma County. The Callahan family spent time in Italy with cheesemakers, as well as studying cheesemaking at American universities. They are considered one of the premier American artisanal cheesemakers. The Carmody is a round, Italian-style table cheese—firm-textured, with deep, earthy flavor. The Reserve is made with raw milk and aged over 6 months.

colorouge (Fort Collins, Colorado) Made by MouCo Cheese Company. Soft-ripened cheese made from pasteurized cow's milk. Sports a warm orange rind shot with clouds of white, which comes about naturally during the "smearing" process. During the two-week aging process, each cheese is rubbed, or smeared, by hand, to encourage such a glowing tint and to develop flavor within the cheese. It has a wonderfully creamy texture, with buttery undertones and lingering creamy flavors, all complemented by a well-defined, assertive nutty character; as it ages, it becomes quite spicy and complex. Pairs well with a white or fruity red wine.

cowgirl creamery (Point Reyes Station, California) Peggy Smith, who founded Cowgirl Creamery, used to be my chef at Chez Panisse many years ago. She is an awesome cowgirl! **buckaroo** Buckaroo is made from organic pasteurized milk from Straus Family Creamery. A semi-firm, washed-rind cow's milk cheese, aged 60 days. The Buckaroo is slightly soft, rich, and buttery. With sweet notes at first followed by a slight savory tangy finish as well as subtle grassy notes, the cheese has a nice complexity. **inverness** Pasteurized cow's milk. Inverness is one of Cowgirl Creamery's newer offerings. The small cylindrical cheese has a surface-ripened rind with a tangy lactic curd and a dense, creamy mouthfeel. This cheese is made with whole organic milk from the Chileno Valley Jersey Dairy and traditional rennet, then aged for 3 weeks. **mt tam** Pasteurized triple crème from the Tomales Bay area, north of San Francisco. Made with organic milk from Straus Family Farms. The milk is very gently pasteurized (145 degrees for 15 minutes, rather than 165 degrees for 10 seconds), and then the small rounds are aged for 3 months. Contains over 70 percent fat! Buttery, white mushroom flavors with a clean, milky finish. Some taste of the grasses from pasture (seasonal) and hints of white truffle. Subtle, rich, full mouth flavor. **pierce point** Bloomy-rind pasteurized whole cow's milk cheese from Tomales Bay area (see above). This cheese is produced only in fall and winter, using Straus Family milk. It is washed in Moscato and then rolled in dried local herbs. Semi-firm yet creamy, complex but not overpowering. **red hawk** Pasteurized triple crème washed-rind full-flavored cheese from the Tomales Bay area. It is made in the French style, with milk from Straus Family Farms. The milk is very gently pasteurized (145 degrees for 15 minutes, rather than 165 degrees for 10 seconds), and then the small rounds are aged for 3 months. Won Best in Show at American Cheese Soci-

ety in 2003. **st pat** Pasteurized. St Pat is a seasonal cheese created to celebrate the beginning of spring. These rounds are made with whole organic milk and are wrapped with stinging-nettle leaves. After 3 weeks of aging, St Pat is mellow, soft, and full of flavor. According to the Cowgirls the nettle leaves impart a "smoky, artichoke flavor." **wagon wheel** Cowgirl Creamery's "everyday" cheese. Scanlan's 25-pound wheel is made with pasteurized cow's milk from neighboring Straus Family Creamery. Wagon Wheel was designed to be on hand for everyday cooking and snacking. Has a mild, sweet, milky flavor, similar to Asiago.

estero gold (Modesto, California) Raw cow's milk cheese made by Valley Ford Cheese Company. Their herd of Jersey cows has grown over the years to about 450. The goal was to produce a cheese that pays homage to the family's Swiss-Italian roots while showcasing their fantastic Jersey milk. The result was Estero Gold, a raw-milk, natural-rind wheel that most closely resembles Asiago. The name refers to the Estero Americano, which flows near the lush green hills of the farm. Made in 9-pound wheels and aged for 120 days. Rich, buttery flavor and smooth, firm texture. This cheese is delicious eaten with salami and some crusty bread.

fiscalini (Modesto, California) Fourth-generation dairy farmer John Fiscalini started making cheese 5 years ago and had great success with his Bandaged Cheddar. **bandaged cheddar** Raw cow's milk, 30-month-aged, 60-pound wheel wrapped in bandage in the British tradition. This cheese won Best Extra Mature Traditional Cheddar in the World at the 2007 World Cheese Awards. **san joaquin gold** Semi-hard raw cow's milk. John's second cheese got off to a rougher start. They tried to make a Fontina-style cheese but didn't have the right recipe or equipment—it was far off the mark and tasted nothing like Fontina. He was very upset and thought he had wasted 5,000 pounds of cheese, but it turned out people *loved* it! Then he had to figure out what he had done "wrong" so he could do it again! These 30-to-34-pound wheels of lightly cooked, pressed cheese are rubbed with oil and turned every day to equalize the distribution of moisture and fat throughout the cheese. Aged 14 months, it has a natural rind and butter-colored pâte. Smells of toasted nuts and brown butter! Firm and glistening, with pleasing acidity and salt; deep flavor with nice sweetness.

hook's 10 year cheddar (Mineral Point, Wisconsin) Pasteurized cow's milk cheddar made by Tony Hook. An incredible farmstead cheddar made by this accomplished Wisconsin cheesemaker. Its silky, melt-in-your-mouth consistency and incredibly complex flavors make it truly unique. The long aging has mellowed any sharpness and left deep nutty, almost caramel flavors.

hooligan (Colchester, Connecticut) Made by Elizabeth MacAlister of Cato Corner Farm. Semi-soft cheese made from raw cow's milk. This washed-rind cheese has a soft, creamy interior and a gorgeous orange rind. The wheels are bathed twice a week in brine to encourage the growth of pungent, surface-ripening bacteria during the minimum 60-day aging period that goes on in the farm's underground caves. Each wheel is made by hand; the milk comes from a herd of 40 Jersey and Brown Swiss cows, which are allowed to graze freely.

jasper hill farm (Greensboro, Vermont) Operated by Mateo and Andy Kehler. constant bliss Raw cow's milk cheese. Constant Bliss was originally based on a Chaource recipe, which was modified to suit the cheesemaker's production schedule and cheesemaking facility. The result is a cheese that hardly resembles a Chaource. It is a slow-ripened lactic curd made only with fresh—right out of the cow, uncooled—evening milk. harbison Pasteurized from Jasper Hill Farm. Harbison is a beautiful bloomy-rind cheese wrapped in bark cut from Jasper Hill Farm's woodlands. There is a sweetness in the pâte as well as herbal and woodsy flavors from the bark. moses sleeper Pasteurized cow's milk cheese. Traditional rennet, bloomy rind, aged 3 to 6 weeks. Per the Jasper Hill Web site, "Moses Sleeper was developed by Mateo Kehler. When it's young, the flavor is buttery, bright, and savory; when longer-aged, the paste is creamier and takes on the aroma and flavor of *Brassica* vegetables." winnimere A raw-milk, washed-rind cheese. Winnimere is washed with lambic-style beer that is brewed from Jasper Hill Farm's own wild yeast. This cheese

is available only from November to April. A strip of spruce bark cut from Jasper Hill's own trees is wrapped around the full-flavored, pleasantly aromatic cheese. Recalling the tradition of French Vacherin d'Abondance, the spruce strip permeates the cheese, giving it a gentle woodsy flavor.

meadow creek dairy (Galax, Virginia) This dairy is beautifully located in the Appalachian Mountains at an elevation of 2,800 feet, with pure water, bright and clean air, and rich, untainted soils. appalachian Farmstead raw Jersey milk cheese aged 60 days. Supple, straw-colored, mild, and buttery, with a hint of mushroom. grayson Washed-rind semi-soft raw cow's milk. Soft, finely textured cheese made with rich Jersey milk. Styled after Taleggio but not as stinky—rich and beefy, with nutty, sweet overtones. The taste reflects the diverse pastures and soils of Meadow Creek Dairy Farm, in the mountains of southwestern Virginia. mountaineer Raw cow's milk. This cheese was inspired by a trip the cheesemaker took to the Alpine region. They came back home to produce this dense, complex cheese in the style of a European mountain cheese that reflects the *terroir* of their own region. Aged for 6 months, giving it a concentrated toasted and nutty flavor with a hint of butterscotch, Mountaineer has a smooth supple texture and a natural brushed rind.

old world portuguese (Petaluma, California) Made by Spring Hill Farms. This Jersey cow's milk cheese is certified organic. The texture is semi-firm and masked in tiny holes. This domestic version of the Portuguese cheese São Jorge is washed in salt and extra-virgin olive oil.

oma (Waitsfield, Vermont) Brothers Sebastian and Dan von Trapp of the Von Trapp farmstead (yes, they are related to *those* von Trapps) released Oma, an amazing cheese from the Mad River Valley in Vermont. A washed-rind raw cow's milk cheese, Oma has a silky texture (soft and supple, but not runny), perhaps its most unique feature—earthy, barnyardy, and buttery. The raw milk provides a lot of complexity and deep flavor. *Oma* is German for "grandmother," and the cheese is named after Sebastian and Dan's *Oma,* Erica von Trapp, who started the family farm more than 55 years ago.

pennsylvania noble (Lancaster County, Pennsylvania) Raw organic milk from grass-fed cows at Green Valley Dairy. Made by Amish dairy farmers. Rich, yellow, tangy, vintage cheddar-style cheese. Even though it is aged only 7 months, it has character and rich flavor, with a smooth aftertaste. It is more creamy, soft, and smooth than many cheddars, because it's not exactly like cheddar: it does not have as salty a feeling, because the cheesemakers skip the brining part of the usual cheddar process.

sally jackson renata (Oroville, Washington) Raw aged cow's milk cheese from a single Brown Swiss cow (Sally's beloved Renata)! Very very rare, small production. I bought all of it! Reclusive cheesemaker Sally Jackson is best known for her Sheep's Milk Cheese, in chestnut leaves. She and her husband make small batches of handmade cheese at their farm in the Okanagan Highlands in Washington State. They are known in the cheesemaking world as eclectic folks who care for their animals as if they were their children—you read that how you want!

seastack (Port Townsend, Washington) Made by Mt. Townsend Creamery. From Aniata Cheese Company site: "Semi-soft cheese made from pasteurized cow's milk. This is a soft-ripened cheese with bloomy rind sprinkled with some vegetable ash. It is rich and flavorful, with pronounced mushroom and toasted-nut flavors. It has some meaty and salty notes that make it perfect to pair with more robust white wines like Viognier, or with reds, such as Pinot Noir or Syrah."

serena (Lindsay, California) Raw whole cow's milk cheese from Three Sisters Farmstead Cheese, at the foothills of the Sierra Nevada (near our friend James Birch at Flora Bella Farm). The cheese is made by the Hilarides family from their own herd of Jersey cows. It is pressed into 20-pound wheels, wrapped in cheesecloth, and aged 10 to 12 months. I love blogger Stephanie Lucianovic's quote about this rich, nutty, and brightly flavored cheese—"If classic Italian Parmigiano-Reggiano and tulip-sniffing Gouda were to marry, Serena would be their delicious progeny."

sprout creek farm (Dutchess County, New York) Sprout Creek Farm is a 200-acre working farm started by 3 teachers at a snotty girl's school in Connecticut (I can say that, I went to Marlborough!). The teachers felt the girls needed some grounding and to understand the bigger picture, so they started a small farm project at the school to make cheeses in the age-old European tradition. All the milk for their semi-hard cheeses comes from their own herd of grass-fed Guernsey and Jersey cows. **ouray** Farmstead, cheddarlike crumbly white-rind raw cheese with yellow interior. **toussaint** Farmstead, buttery, sharp, and complex semi-hard raw cheese. Dry, cheddarlike, tangy, full-flavored, super-nutty, and floral!

sweet grass dairy (Thomasville, Georgia) This 140-acre family farm in southern Georgia has been receiving much praise and many awards for their goat's and cow's milk cheeses. They focus on sustainable grass-based rotational farming systems. **georgia gouda** Aged raw-milk semi-soft 10-pound wheel with tart and tangy flavors and a smooth, sweet finish. **myrtlewood** Hard, raw cow's milk cheese with wax myrtle (a native plant that is like candy to the animals—they seek it out in the mountains and go crazy when they find it), balsamic vinegar, and pecans. Natural rind, inspired by French mountain cheeses. Bright-yellow color; dry, complex taste. **thomasville tomme** Aged raw-milk semi-hard large 10-pound wheel with mellow, buttery flavor.

tarentaise (North Pomfret, Vermont) From Thistle Hill Farm. Raw cow, traditional rennet, natural rind, firm. Made in the tradition of French Alpine cheeses, Tarentaise is made using imported French cultures, which gives the cheese a deep complexity. Tarentaise reflects the *terroir* of Thistle Hill Farm, and in the smooth, subtle nuttiness of the cheese you can detect its soil, climate, and flora. It is certified organic by the Northeast Organic Farmers Association. Took Second Place Ribbon, American Cheese Society competition in Burlington, Vermont, 2007.

tipsy cow (Orland, California) Raw cow's milk farmstead (one of only 9 or 10 in California), hard, small wheels soaked in red wine (hence the Tipsy!) from Sacramento County. See Black Butte, page 399, for more info on Pedrozo Farm.

uplands pleasant ridge (Dodgeville, Wisconsin) Raw cow's milk cheese, 9-pound wheel. Uplands Cheese Company were the first to get back to artisanal cheesemaking after Kraft and other industrial producers bought up most of the small dairies. This cheese is rich and bacony! On August 28, 2010, Pleasant Ridge Reserve won the American Cheese Society's annual competition, besting over 1,400 of the nation's finest cheeses to be crowned Best of Show. This is the third time they have earned this honor in the past 10 years, making this cheese the most decorated in the competition's history.

widmer's cheese cellars brick cheese (Dodge County, Wisconsin) Pasteurized cow's milk. "Brick cheese" is the oldest type of cheese to originate in the U.S.A. Often described as a cross between cheddar and Limburger. Swiss immigrant John Widmer settled 70 years ago in the cheesemaking area of Dodge County. This Wisconsin original is weighted down with bricks, then placed in a brine (salt solution) for 12 hours, then cured in the aging rooms, where the cheeses develop a nice orangeish rind. Traditionally served with pumpernickel bread, mustard, and pickled onions. Great with draft beer, dark beer, or apple cider. Earthy, sweet flavor, semi-soft texture, with a slightly bitter finish.

buffalo

casatica di bufala (Bergamo, Italy) Pasteurized. This soft-ripened cheese with a bloomy rind, traditional of Bergamo, highlights the characteristics of buffalo milk. It is creamy and smooth with a sweet flavor.

moringhello di bufala (Lombardy, Italy) Pasteurized buffalo milk. After it is made, Moringhello is placed in a hot part of the cheese plant for an entire evening, so that it reaches a level of acidity that makes the pâte slightly chalky yet particularly flavorful. This versatile cheese can be eaten

in many different ways—semi-soft, semi-firm, firm. The flavor is intense and slightly spicy.

oriol de montbrú (Catalonia, Spain) Pasteurized buffalo-milk cheese. This cheese was originally created by the son of two famous Spanish cheesemakers (Pere and Irma of Barcelona) named Oriol. Oriol bought a surplus of Italian buffalo from a neighbor and began developing his own buffalo-milk cheese. The cheese is sweet, creamy, and versatile. Aged 20 days, it is a small wheel with a slight covering of blue-gray mold.

quadrello di bufala (Lombardy, Italy) Pasteurized buffalo. Buffalo were originally brought to Italy in the seventh century, and references to cheese made from their milk appeared in the fourteenth century. Today, the cheese dairy Quattro Portoni makes over 25 different types of cheese from buffalo milk. Essentially a buffalo-milk Taleggio, the Quadrello has a soft, ivory-pink rind with a deliciously creamy pâte. The flavor is rich and slightly sweet.

blue

AUSTRALIA AND NEW ZEALAND

meredith blue (Victoria, Australia) Pasteurized sheep's milk cheese by Julie Cameron at Meredith Dairy. Roquefort-style, creamy, mild, aged 2 months.

roaring forties (Tasmania, Australia) Pasteurized cow's milk blue from King Island. Full-flavored, with a sweet, nutty character and good aftertaste, this cheese is a major crowd pleaser! Matured in wax to retain moisture and create a smooth, creamy texture. Won Best Cheese at New York's Fancy Food Show in 2000. King Island is considered to have some of the cleanest air and greenest grass in the world. "Roaring Forties" is the name of the wind that blows across the Southern Ocean. A Lucques and A.O.C. staff favorite.

tarago river shadows of blue (Gippsland, Victoria, Australia) A rich double-cream, blue-vein cow's milk cheese, with a mild taste and creamy texture. It is ideal for first-time blue eaters. The cheese is sold coated in wax. The wax assists in flavor development and in holding in the moisture during maturation. Tarago River Cheese Company is located in the dairying heartland just 1 hour from the center of Melbourne, next to the picturesque Tarago River. Since its inception in 1982, the company has sourced all its milk from its own herd of 400 Friesian cows.

tarago river strzelecki blue (Gippsland, Victoria, Australia) Pasteurized blue-veined goat's milk cheese. This cheese has a natural rind and is the grand champion of the Australian Cheese Awards. Rich yet tangy, with an amazing range of flavor.

whitestone windsor blue (Windsor, Central South Island, New Zealand) Pasteurized cow's milk cheese. Organic. Buttery and flavorful, but not too strong. It has won many national and international competitions.

BRITISH ISLES AND IRELAND

beenleigh blue (Devon, England) Pasteurized sheep's milk blue. Since the 1970s, Robin Congdon has been farming on the Sharpham Estate. This is one of only 3 sheep's milk blues made in Britain. Semi-soft, natural rind, vegetarian rennet. Neal's Yard Dairy.

blue stilton (Leicester, England) Made by Richard Rowlett and Billy Kevan of Clawson Dairy. Firm cheese made from pasteurized cow's milk. It has a dense texture with a pale-ivory pâte, grading to amber at the edges, and marbled with greenish-blue veins. The rind is dry and crusty, gray-brown in color, slightly wrinkled, and with powdery white patches. The flavor ranges from mild with a sharp edge when young, to rich and tangy when mature.

cashel blue (Tipperary, Ireland) Generations of the Grubb family have been millers and butter makers here. In the mid-1980s, Louis and Jane Grubb became the first

makers of Irish farm blue cheese. Aged about 6 months, the cheese is creamy and salty with a clean, blue tang. Made from pasteurized cow's milk, it is inoculated with *P. roqueforti* and uses vegetarian rennet. The 3-pound wheels are wrapped in gold foil and sold either as whole wheels or as individually foil-wrapped quarters.

colston bassett stilton (Nottingham, England) Pasteurized cow's milk blue. Stilton was first recognized as a type of cheese at the beginning of the eighteenth century. Oddly, Stilton was never actually made in Stilton, and even today, protected by a trademark, it can be made only in the 3 adjacent counties of Nottinghamshire, Derbyshire, and Leicestershire. *Penicillium roqueforti* is used to create the classic blue veining. Colston Bassett is a cooperative of local milk producers. Creamy, smooth, and intense.

crozier blue (Tipperary, Ireland) This new blue cheese is made by the Grubbs, who are also the makers of Ireland's most popular farmhouse blue cheese, Cashel Blue. The Grubbs are descendants of butter makers who were expelled from England in the seventeenth century. The cheeses are all handmade. The Crozier is made with sheep's milk (as is Roquefort). It is tangy, with a sharp, pronounced flavor that mellows with age, firm but moist. It won the 2011 bronze medal at the British Cheese Awards.

harbourne (Devon, England) Pasteurized goat's milk blue. Crumbly, firm-textured cheese with floral, subtle milk flavors enhanced by the blueing. Unusual to see an English goat, and even rarer a blue goat! Aged by our friends at Neal's Yard Dairy.

royal blue stilton (Wiltshire, England) Pasteurized cow's milk cheese, aged and almost orange in color with blue veins. Fairly strong, with great crystals! Made by Coombe Castle.

shropshire blue (Nottingham, England) Pasteurized cow's milk cheese made by Colston Bassett Dairy. Rich, creamy, strong-flavored blue, colored with annatto (it has a brilliant orange hue). *Penicillium roqueforti* is used for the veining. Similar in flavor to Stilton. This cheese was only first made in 1970! There is a long, involved story of a Scottish cheesemaker who trained in the making of Stilton in Nottinghamshire. He moved back to Scotland to make the cheese but ran into many problems. Eventually, the cheesemaking was taken over by another man, who moved the whole operation back to Nottinghamshire!

stichelton (Nottinghamshire, England) Raw cow. From Neal's Yard Dairy. Made with organic milk by Joe Schneider at Collingthwaite Farm. Stichelton is, according to Cowgirl Creamery, "fruity and appley, with underlying nutty toasty notes and a long lasting savouriness with a spicy element from the blue mold. The flavors expand and develop in the mouth and last long after swallowing. The texture is rich, soft, and creamy."

strathdon blue (Tain, Ross-shire, Scotland) Pasteurized cow's milk. Made by Ruaridh (pronounced "Rory") Stone at his brewery-turned-cheese-dairy by the sea. Milk is from a small cooperative of 6 farms. The flavor is milky and savory, and sometimes quite salty. Ruaridh is still experimenting with the recipe! From Neal's Yard Dairy.

FRANCE

bleu de gex (Franche-Comté) AOC raw-milk blue made exclusively from the milk of Montbéliards cows. Unlike most blues, which come in foil-wrapped cylinders, Bleu de Gex is produced in flat wheels with a natural rind. Although Bleu de Gex is now inoculated with *P. roqueforti*, originally it blued naturally. It derives its unique characteristics from the Alpine violets on which the cows graze. The cheese is marbled liberally with blue veining and weighs 12 to 14 pounds. It is from our hero *affineur* Jean d'Alos.

bleu de laqueuille (Auvergne) Pasteurized cow's milk blue. Antoine Roussel, from the village of Laqueuille, first made this cheese in 1850 with mold grown on rye bread! This cheese belongs to the same family as Fourme d'Ambert (natural rind, soft pâte with blue mold, uncooked, unpressed).

bleu de sassenage (Rhône-Alpes) Raw cow's milk blue from our new best friend *affineur* Pascal Beillevaire. It is a large, 12-pound wheel with natural rind. Semi-soft, slightly pressed, aged 2 to 3 months. A traditional mountain cheese similar to Bleu de Gex, it was first made by monks. It's chewy and sweet, with hints of bitterness at times.

bleu d'auvergne AOC pasteurized cow's milk, creamy blue from central France. Rich, with full flavor. Rindless salty exterior; white-to-beige-colored interior with liberal blue veining. Again *affineur* Jean d'Alos!

bleu des basques (Pyrénées) Made by Onetik. Firm cheese made from pasteurized sheep's milk. This blue cheese is aged for at least 3 months and is both creamy and slightly crumbly, with a rustic look and great flavor. It is rich and complex without being overly sharp or salty.

bleu des causses (Rouergue) AOC raw-milk blue from the Causses Mountains, above the region where Roquefort is from. Some call it a milder cow's milk version of Roquefort. Traditional rennet; creamy, soft, complex. Aged on oak shelves in limestone caves in the mountains! Try with a sweet white wine like Jurançon, Beaumes-de-Venise, or Sauternes. From our hero *affineur* Jean d'Alos. Bleu des Causses has existed for centuries. It is aged in numerous caves on the hard limestone plateaux called the "Causses." The milk is rich with the perfume of wild plants that grow on the plateau. Bleu des Causses is made using traditional methods. It is salted, brushed, and then pierced with long needles in order to facilitate oxygenation, which aids in the development of the *Penicillium* mold. It is rounder in flavor, less salty, finer in texture, and less rustic than its close cousin Bleu d'Auvergne, the more renowned of the 2 cheeses.

bleu de sévarac (Aveyron, Midi-Pyrénées) Raw sheep's milk blue. Semi-soft, with natural rind. Made exactly like Roquefort (same region), except it doesn't age in the prestigious cellars of the Combalou Caves (an AOC requirement for Roquefort). Creamy, tangy, and sublime. See what you think!

bleu de termignon (Haute-Savoie) Pascal Beillevaire selection. This is a very rare type of blue cheese, raw. Unlike other blue cheeses, in which the mold is inoculated into the milk, this cheese has natural mold introduced while the milk is held in a temperature-controlled room. It is made at a high altitude, and ripened in mountain caves. After ripening in the caves, it is stored in cold cellars until sale.

bleu du bocage (Vendée) Pasteurized goat's milk blue from the western edge of the Loire Valley, traditionally a butter-producing region rather than a cheese-producing one. This unique cheese is made with the same technique as Roquefort, but the seaming (of the blue veins) is like that of Bleu d'Auvergne. Selected by Pascal Beillevaire, who started as a raw-butter producer in Nantes (northern France), then expanded by starting to buy and age cheeses. He now has 5 shops in Gay Paris.

bleuet (Touraine) Made by Pascal Jacquin. Firm cheese made from goat's milk. This cheese is a most unusually shaped triangular log. It has a white, bloomy rind and generous blue veining. The texture is thick and smooth; the flavor is rich and often likened to a goat's milk Gouda, with a distinctive blue sharpness and tang, though it maintains a softer flavor than most blues.

fourme d'ambert (Auvergne) Raw cow. From *affineur* Jean d'Alos. This is one of the oldest cheeses in France. According to folklore, Fourme was being enjoyed by the Druids long before Julius Caesar rolled into Gaul. With its deep, dark flavor and smooth, creamy texture, this cheese has been known to convert even the staunchest blue-cheese resisters! This is an AOC cheese.

fourme de montbrison (Auvergne) Raw cow's milk cheese. Fourme de Montbrison is a cousin to Fourme d'Ambert. Both of the cheeses are members of the AOC family. Its pâte is creamy and firm. As with Roquefort, first blue mold is injected, and then air is introduced to allow it to develop its smooth flavors.

fourmette croix de chazelles (Auvergne) Farmstead raw cow's milk cheese made by the Vergnol brothers in the traditional way their great-grandfather did it in the early 1900s. Blue cheeses in the Auvergne date back to the Romans and are venerated in this region. In order to master this specialty, one of the Vergnol brothers had special training at Écoles Nationales d'Industrie Laitière in Aurillac and created this small Fourme, a cousin to Fourme d'Ambert. They patiently cultivate a specific culture strain, which is then added to curd every day, creating this small cheese. The flavor is assertive without being aggressive, tangy, and a tad nutty. The Jean d'Alos version is raw and coated with an inedible brown crust.

montbriac (Auvergne) This pasteurized cow's milk blue is creamy, rich, and unctuous. A 6-inch disk covered in ash.

persillé de chèvre du beaujolais (Rhône-Alpes). Pasteurized goat's milk blue from our *affineur* friend, Hervé Mons. A modern cheese from the Pierre Dorées, this blue cheese has a natural rind and beautiful white pâte. A certain goatiness contrasts nicely with the sharpness of the blue, and there is a lingering finish of mushrooms.

persillé du malzieu (Languedoc-Roussillon) This is a raw sheep's milk blue cheese in the style of the more famous Roquefort. It's made by a co-op that groups the milk of 36 Lacaune sheep dairies. The cheese is then aged for 3 months in natural caves. The result is a robust blue cheese with excellent balance between the milk and the sharpness of the blue. Selected by *affineur* Hervé Mons.

queso azul (Basque Country) Pasteurized. From the region along the border of northern Spain and southern France, this mountain blue cheese has a creamy texture and mild, slightly tangy taste. Made from the milk of indigenous sheep grazing on the high mountain pastures of the Spanish Pyrénées (although the cheese itself is made in France), and slowly aged in mountain caves for 3 months.

rocbleu (Auvergne) A soft, creamy blue cheese made with pasteurized cow's milk (Roquefort and blue cheese combined). It comes from the mountains but is not an old cheese. It was created a few years ago, for the pleasure of people who like blue cheese and sweet cow's milk. The rind is colored with vegetable ash.

roche montagne (Auvergne) Raw cow's milk blue. A medium-sized disk with natural rind, aged by Pascal Beillevaire. Not too much info out there on this one!

roquefort Roquefort's history can be traced back to the Romans. According to legend, a shepherd out with his flock near one of the Combalou Caves, was in a hurry to meet with his shepherdess girlfriend. In his haste, he accidentally dropped a piece of bread spread with sheep's milk curd in the cave. On his return to the cave several weeks later, he found his piece of bread, which was now covered in a white-and-blue paste. He tasted it and liked it— Roquefort cheese was invented. One of the oldest forms of cheese, it is also known as the "Cheese of Kings." Roquefort can be matured only in specially adapted cellars, built in the prehistoric caves around Mont Combalou, which lies close to the village of Roquefort. These cellars are ventilated by natural funnels, called *fleurines,* which maintain an ambient temperature of 7° to 8°C (about 44° to 46°F) and propagate the *Penicillium roqueforti,* a fungus, which covers the walls. In 1411, Charles VI gave the people of Roquefort (in the Aveyron region of southern France) the monopoly of ripening the cheese in their caves, as they had been doing for years. Clean, forceful flavor with strong salt but also sweetness from the milk. The texture of the pâte is moist and crumbly and melts on the tongue with a burst of flavor. Rich and spicy. **carles** (Aveyron) AOC raw sheep's milk cheese. Carles is one of the finest makers of Roquefort. **gabriel coulet** In 1872, Guillaume Coulet was building a wine cellar when he discovered a *fleurine* (the natural underground cave used for maturing Roquefort), so he decided to make Roquefort! For 100 years and 5 generations, the family has been handmaking their special cheese. This is my very favorite Roquefort! **jean d'alos** AOC raw sheep's milk cheese. This particular Roquefort is chosen by Jean d'Alos (amazing *affineur* from Bordeaux) as the best there is, and then aged carefully to perfection.

saint agur (Pyrénées) Pasteurized cow's milk. Medium-strong, very creamy blue cheese with elements of a triple crème. Another slightly slutty cheese that is a true crowd pleaser. An easy means to converting those wimpy types who think they don't like blue cheese, but still respected and adored by foodies, cheese heads, and curdnerds.

ITALY

blu del moncenisio (Piemonte) Raw cow's milk blue, aged in natural caves for 45 to 90 days, rich and pungent without being overpowering. Tastes a little of the sea. A pressed cylinder similar to Fourme d'Ambert.

blu di bufala (Lombardy) Pasteurized. Blu di Bufala is a semi-firm buffalo-milk blue from one of the most beautiful towns in Italy, Bergamo. It is rare to find an aged buffalo-milk cheese. This one is a distinctive, full-bodied blue. It has a balance of sweetness with a slight tang in its lingering finish. Bruno Gritti and his brother Alfio run the Quattro Portoni dairy. They began raising cattle in 1970, and then decided to raise water buffalo in 2001, as well as to run their company in a way that made minimal impact on the environment. In 2005, Bruno decided to make cheese, highlighting the particular qualities of buffalo milk. The company started producing cheese in 2006 and today makes over 25 different types.

blu di langa (Piemonte) Cow-goat-sheep. This eccentric and delicious creation from the Caseificio dell'Alta Langa represents the combination of northern-Italian cheesemaking with modern innovative flair. It has a tasty, edible natural rind that may be covered in a light-blue mold, depending on its age. The breakdown of the pâte directly beneath the rind is both sublime and unctuous, with a potent earthy flavor. Toward the center of the cheese, the pâte firms slightly and possesses a cool, milky flavor packed with patches of snappy and spicy blue mold.

erborinato (Lombardy) Pasteurized 90 percent sheep's and 10 percent cow's milk cheese. "*Erborinato*" means "parslied"—it's a term for naturally blue cheeses, not injected with bacteria to create bluing but inoculated by needling, which means they pierce the cheese with a sort of darning needle to let in the air and bacteria from the outside. Anyway, this cheese is barely blue at all—it has amazing deep flavor and is soft and creamy.

gorgonzola piccante (Piemonte) Pasteurized, buttery, cow's-milk cheese with soft green mold, made with milk from both morning and evening milkings, thus allowing for a creamier cheese. It is then aged in caves. This is Gorgonzola Piccante/Naturale, or Mountain Gorgonzola, as opposed to Gorgonzola Dolce, "sweet." It has a deeper color, more blue veins, a more pungent odor, and an intense, sharp flavor. This is not your average Gorgonzola!

long aged gorgonzola (Piemonte) Pasteurized cow's milk blue is aged 130 days instead of the 90 days for regular Gorgonzola Piccante. From Forever Cheese: "For this particular product, milk from the Alto Vergante region in Piemonte is used. This is a mountainous region between Lakes Maggiore and Orta. The cows are pasture-fed as opposed to eating feed. The Penicillium used produces a deeper blue than that of the Penicillium used for the regular Gorgonzola Piccante. This cheese is also more compact which allows it to be aged longer and develop a more intense flavor. More of a crumble to the paste."

ovin sardo (Sardinia) This pasteurized sheep's milk blue cheese is produced by a small dairy in the northwestern corner of an island with more sheep than people. Their by-hand production methods balance generations of skill and modern technology. The cheese has a soft yet solid texture. The taste hints of sheep and hay underlying the overwhelmingly rich, milky flavor. A stern blue balances everything perfectly. Pair with off-dry whites or a peaty Scotch.

strachitunt val taleggio Raw milk. This creamy, unctuous cheese crosses the texture of Taleggio with the appearance and flavor of Gorgonzola. It is from the Alpine area of Val Taleggio. The milk is collected twice a day. Combining the warm morning milk with the cool evening milk facilitates the growth of the mold (hence the blue veins). The 2 milks also create 2 different textures—one soft, one firmer. The bluing is completely natural—no *Penicillium* is added. This cheese is produced the old-fashioned way and aged 70 to 80 days. The acidification of the curd—coupled with piercing, which is done halfway through the aging process—favors the development of natural molds which characterize the aromatic flavor of the cheese. Strachitunt is round, with a natural light-brown rind. The interior is pale yellow with some bluing. It is aromatic, with a pleasant odor of brush and hazelnuts. The sweetness of the milk is balanced by a subtle tanginess and earthiness on the finish. A really rare and unusual cheese—made by a single family who produce only 100 rounds per year!

toma blu alle erbe (Treviso) This blue cheese is produced with whole cow's milk from one or more milkings that have been pasteurized. After a few months of traditional seasoning on wooden planks, the cheese goes into barrels, where it is garnished with aromatic herbs and spices. After a long period, the forms are extracted and left to stand for a while longer. Toma Blu won the gold medal at the Caseus Veneti in Verona, October 2004.

verdecapra (Lombardy) Pasteurized goat's milk blue from our favorite Taleggio producer, Ambrogio. VerdeCapra has a moisture level similar to that of Gorgonzola Dolce, making for a deliciously creamy texture. Pleasantly tangy, with a well-balanced flavor.

NETHERLANDS

delft blue (Delft) Pasteurized cow's milk cheese. This cheese comes from the village of Delft, just outside The Hague, which was actually home to the artist Vermeer. Delft Blue, also known as Blue de Graven, is rich and creamy with a buttery, mellow taste, and a clean finish. It has a nice underlying sweetness, and is not at all salty.

SPAIN

azul de asturias (Asturias) Pasteurized cow's milk marketed under the Peña Azul brand, is similar to Cabrales and Picon cheeses. Common traits include the cow's milk coming from the Asturias and Cantabria regions, which contain rich Spanish pastures. Similar blue aging process, but Azul de Asturias lacks the typical bacteria forming the brownish and strong-smelling rinds of Cabrales and Picon. Produced at a small factory in Oviedo province, from pasteurized unskimmed cow's milk. Aged 2 to 4 months with traditional maple leaves.

azul peñacorada (León) Pasteurized cow's milk. Named for the rocky, mountainous region of northern Spain from which it comes, this blue is creamy, buttery, and rich. A traditional mountain blue cheese, wrapped in maple leaves and aged between 2 and 4 months. The maple leaves provide an earthy suppleness, resulting in a cheese that is creamery, peppery, and tangy.

cabrales DO raw blue made with a mix of milks. Semi-firm, cave-aged for a minimum of 3 months, wrapped in maple leaves. Moist, crumbly, with rich, intense salty flavor.

estrella la peral (Asturias) Pasteurized Spanish blue from northern Spain that is not very blue but has intense, deep, rich, almost meaty flavor (kind of like a Munster). It is crumbly in the beginning and then becomes very creamy.

mitibleu (La Mancha) Raw sheep's milk cheese in the style of Roquefort. Creamy like Roquefort.

monje azul Raw-milk farmhouse blue cheese produced in Panes, one of the 4 towns of Asturias where blues are made. (The others are Cabrales, Valdeon, and Picos de Europa.) Wrapped in chestnut leaves, Monje is usually made with cow's milk, as are the others, because goat's and sheep's milk are extremely scarce, and available for only a short period in spring. Generally more aged than similar blues in the region, with slightly less bluing and a sharp, robust flavor. Before the DO was created for Cabrales, this used to be grouped under the Cabrales name. Really cool cheese.

valdeón (Asturias) Raw cow, goat, or pasteurized DO mixed-milk blue cheese from the north of Spain. This cheese (and Monje Azul) used to be called Cabrales until Cabrales got its own DO. Valdeón is, in my opinion, more delicious, creamy, and a little milder than Cabrales. It is wrapped in maple leaves.

SWITZERLAND

blaues wunder (Detligen, Bern) Semi-soft blue cheese made from thermalized cow's milk (U.S. FDA considers this still to be raw milk, whereas the European Union considers it pasteurized), made by Christoph Raz. This cheese is gray in color and has a thin, yet surprisingly sturdy bloomy rind that provides an excellent textural and aesthetic counterpoint to the pale bone–colored pâte. The aroma is loamy and woodsy, with a faint hint of autumn leaves. The flavor is mild and slightly sweet with the softest hint of "blue." The finish is pleasant and clean, and the "autumnal" feel of this cheese is carried through to the end, providing yet another level of interest to this striking and memorable cheese.

bayley hazen blue (Greensboro, Vermont) Farmstead raw cow's milk cheese in the shape of a Fourme d'Ambert (tall cylinder with natural rind) from Jasper Hill Farm. It is rubbed with sea salt—salty and slightly crumbly. They milk the cows three-quarters of the year and say that the season of the milking really affects the taste and texture of the cheese. Named after a military road used during the Revolutionary War.

big woods blue (Nerstrand, Minnesota) From Shepherd's Way Farms. Farmstead raw sheep's milk blue from Friesian and Lacaune ewes. Rich, creamy, flavorful, with balanced tang and saltiness and a long finish.

blythedale farm jersey blue (Corinth, Vermont) Farmstead raw cow's milk blue made in the style of Stilton at Blythedale Farm. A 5-pound natural wheel made from whole unprocessed milk (hand-ladled!) with minimal salt. Crumbly, but with a high enough butterfat content to assure a "melt in your mouth" quality.

ewe's blue (Old Chatham, New York) Pasteurized sheep's milk blue from Old Chatham Sheepherding Company in the Hudson Valley. Made in the style of Roquefort. Creamy texture with subtle blue notes.

harmony blue Triple-cream cow's milk blue cheese made by a co-op of 40 Amish dairy farmers from 3 communities in northern Iowa and southern Minnesota called Golden Ridge. The dairy producers milk their own herds by hand, cool the milk with groundwater, and sell the milk in 80-gallon stainless-steel cans (for religious reasons, they do not use technology or machinery in the process). Five years ago, they realized that no one wanted to buy the milk in such small quantities, so they had the idea to build a cheese factory—they got permission from the leaders of the Old Order Amish to open it, although they still cannot work the machinery themselves. They decided to make blue cheese because they felt that many of the great blue cheeses in the world are made from milk handled in a similar way. Any-way, Golden Ridge produces 3 cheeses: Schwarz und Weiss ("Black and White"), Harmony Blue (which has extra cream added), and Ultimate 50 (half cow, half goat). Harmony Blue is mellow and buttery with tangy blue overtones. It won first place in the American Cheese Society Awards in 2004.

great hill blue (Marion, Massachusetts) Raw non-homogenized cow's milk cheese, handmade. Remember, homogenization is when they agitate the milk to separate the fat. Full-flavored, smooth.

hook's cheese company (Mineral Point, Wisconsin) Hook's Cheese Company makes their blue from milk produced in southwestern Wisconsin—some on Amish farms in the area. The cheese is produced during the period of the year when the sheep are out grazing on the lush grasses that grow on the rolling hills. **hook's blue paradise** Made by Tony Hook. A truly beautiful, creamy blue! Made in the traditional way, from pasteurized cow's milk with the addition of cream to give it rich texture and a sweeter, milkier flavor that contrasts nicely with the sharpness of the blue. **little boy blue** Raw sheep's milk blue that won first place at the American Cheese Society competition in 2011, as well as third place in the World Cheese Championship in 2010. **tilston point** Semi-firm raw cow's milk blue. Tony also makes some great cheddars. With this cheese, he set out to make a Stilton-style blue inspired by the English who settled in and around Mineral Point. This cheese is an amazing blend of Old World tradition and New World artisanship. Rich, deep flavor accented by earthy overtones and dense but creamy texture. Tony uses only spring and summer milk, which gives the cheese a yellow color. We at A.O.C. are very impressed with this cheese!

mossend blue (South Albany, Vermont) Farmstead raw sheep's milk blue cheese from Bonnieview Farm. See page 381 for information on Bonnieview Farm. This creamy mild blue is named after the family farm back in Scotland!

point reyes blue (Point Reyes, California) Raw cow's milk cheese from about an hour north of San Francisco. Roquefort-style, slightly wet, white pâte. Tangy, delicate sharpness, great mouthfeel. Very different from our other blues. Less creamy than Roaring Forties.

rogue creamery (Central Point, Oregon) Cheese-maker Ignacio Vella is thought of as the godfather of American artisanal cheese. Rogue Creamery has been making artisanal cheeses since 1935. Today, it is run by David Gremmels and Cary Bryant, who continue to uphold the practices and principles of artisan cheesemaking as set out by the Vellas. caveman blue Caveman Blue is a rich, raw cow's milk complex blue, deliciously sweet and fruity, with slight vanilla tones and a texture of butter and crystals. It has nuances of beef and bacon and grass and hay, and is firm and lower in moisture, with a natural rind featuring extensive blue mold development. Aged 6 to 12 months. The brand Caveman Blue was used by the Rogue Gold Cheese Co. from the 1940s until the late 1990s with the tag line "aged in the domain of the cavemen." echo mountain Raw goat's and cow's milk blue from the Willamette Valley. This cheese won first place in blue mixed-milk categories at the American Cheese Society awards in 2007. Very small production. Earthier than most blues, creamy, rich, and well balanced, with a lovely salty tang. flora nelle Pasteurized cow's milk blue. Named for owners David Gremmels's and Cary Bryant's grandmothers, this is the creamery's latest innovation in American artisan blue cheeses. Unlike their bolder blues, such as Crater Lake or Caveman, this cheese possesses a lighter flavor, almost resembling tropical fruits, with the classic savory finish of any good handmade blue cheese. It is also perfect for those on special diets, because this blue cheese is "Independently Certified Gluten Free," as well as being made of "Organic and Food Alliance Certified" whole milk. Flora Nelle is sure to be the star of any after-dinner cheese selection, immediately capturing the eye with a dusty rind courtesy of a roll in vegetable ash. Much as with ash-coated goat cheeses, this helps to keep Flora Nelle moist and sliceable, as well as lowering the acidity of the finished cheese. oregon blue vein Raw cow's milk Roquefort-style cheese. Rogue Creamery has been making this Oregon classic since 1957. This cheese is mild, creamy, and flavorful. oregonzola Raw cow's milk. Oregonzola claims its Italian roots in its very name. Like Gorgonzola, this blue cheese manages to be sharp, fruity, and spicy at the same time. After being aged for 120 days in Rogue Creamery's caves, Oregonzola gets slightly creamy without becoming wet. rogue river blue Raw cow's milk Roquefort-style cheese from Rogue Creamery. These wheels are aged for up to a year in rooms constructed to simulate the ancient caves in Roquefort, France. This aging process imparts to the cheese naturally occurring molds that are part of the Rogue River Valley *terroir,* including hints of pine, wild berries, hazelnut, morels, and pears. Each wheel is wrapped in grape leaves harvested locally, which have been macerated in local pear brandy and tied with raffia. The leaves add complexity and preserve the moist, creamy texture. This cheese made history as the first American blue ever to win "best blue" at the World Cheese Awards.

shaft's blue (Roseville, California) Cow's milk blue from Napa Valley, aged for 1 year. Piquant flavor and creamy texture.

two face blue (Doty, Washington) Made by Willapa Hills Cheese. Semi-soft cheese made from raw, heat-treated sheep's and cow's milk. Moderate-to-intense blue flavor. This cheese is creamy, with some spots of green mold. The pâte is ivory in color and possesses some light-green and blue veins. It has a wonderfully rich, fudgy texture, with just a hint of saltiness and deep earthy, nutty flavors that contrast nicely with the sharpness of the blue.

This list is meant as a last resort or backup shopping plan. Depending on where you live you may be able to find all these ingredients locally—and if you can, please do! Shop at your local butcher shop and ask them for pork cheeks and duck legs. Seek out a retail "gourmet shop" that sells saba and other interesting condiments. You will probably find new and different items not mentioned here. But if the local route is not an option, fortunately these days most of the ingredients in this book are available online.

abbamele Zingerman's, www.zingermans.com; Manicaretti, www.manicaretti.com

apple balsamic vinegar Zingerman's, www.zingermans.com

beans, dried Zürsun Idaho Heirloom Beans, www.zursunbeans.com

beef Niman Ranch, www.nimanranch.com

capers I prefer salted ones from Pantelleria. Zingerman's, www.zingermans.com

cheese Artisanal Premium Cheese, www.artisanalcheese.com; Cowgirl Creamery, www.cowgirlcreamery.com; Murray's Cheese, www.murrayscheeese.com

chiles de árbol The Spice House, www.thespicehouse.com

dates duvalledates.com; Flying Disc Ranch, www.flyingranch.com

duck Liberty Ducks, www.libertyducks.com

duck fat Liberty Ducks, www.libertyducks.com

hazelnuts Trufflebert Farms, ph: 541-686-6186, trufflebert@aol.com

olives I love lucques (obviously), castelvetranos, nyons, arbiquina, bella de carignola, and niçoise; all available at Zingerman's, www.zingermans.com

pistachios Santa Barbara Pistachio Company, www.santabarbarapistachios.com (Once you try these you will be hooked.)

polenta bobsredmill.com

pomegranate molasses Try your local middle eastern market if available, or Zingerman's, www.zingermans.com

pork Niman Ranch, www.nimanranch.com

prosciutto, jamon, speck La Quercia, www.laquercia.us

saba Zingerman's, www.zingermans.com; Manicaretti, www.manicaretti.com

salt cod, casuelas, piquillo peppers, marcona almonds, quince paste, and other Spanish ingredients The Spanish Table, www.spanishtable.com; La Espanola, www.laespanolameats.com

salumi We love the sopressata, coppa, and cacciatorini from ALPS in Long Island City, alps.com

spices The Spice House, www.thespicehouse.com

tamarind paste A local ethnic market, or The Spice House, www.thespicehouse.com

torchio and other fun artisanally made dried pasta Zingerman's, www.zingermans.com

(Page references in *italic* refer to illustrations.)

SUZANNE GOIN was born and raised in southern California and graduated from Brown University. In 2006 she was the recipient of two awards from the James Beard Foundation (Best Chef California and *Sunday Suppers at Lucques* won Best Cookbook from a Professional Viewpoint), and she has received five nominations for Outstanding Chef of the Year. Goin is the chef and owner of Lucques, A.O.C., Tavern, and The Larder, all in Los Angeles, where she lives with her husband, David Lentz, and their three children.

CAROLINE STYNE was raised in Los Angeles and has been in partnership with Suzanne Goin since the opening of their first restaurant, Lucques, in 1998. She runs the business operations of their five restaurants, and has been twice nominated for Outstanding Restaurateur by the James Beard Foundation. Styne also serves as the wine director for their entire restaurant group and writes humorously about her life with wine in her blog, Styne on Wine. She is married to art dealer Michael Kohn, with whom she has two children.